# Disability and Mobile Citizenship
# in Postsocialist Ukraine

# Disability and Mobile Citizenship in Postsocialist Ukraine

SARAH D. PHILLIPS

INDIANA UNIVERSITY PRESS
*Bloomington and Indianapolis*

This book is a publication of

Indiana University Press
601 North Morton Street
Bloomington, Indiana 47404-3797 USA

www.iupress.indiana.edu

| Telephone orders | 800-842-6796 |
| Fax orders | 812-855-7931 |
| Orders by e-mail | iuporder@indiana.edu |

LIBRARY OF CONGRESS CATALOGING-IN-PUBLICATION DATA

Phillips, Sarah D.
   Disability and mobile citizenship in postsocialist Ukraine / Sarah D. Phillips.
      p.   cm.
   Includes bibliographical references and index.
   ISBN 978-0-253-35539-3 (cl : alk. paper) — ISBN 978-0-253-22247-3 (pb : alk. paper)   1.
People with disabilities—Ukraine.   I. Title.
   [DNLM: 1. Disabled Persons—Ukraine.   2. Health Knowledge, Attitudes, Practice—
Ukraine.   3. Health Services—Ukraine.   4. Human Rights—Ukraine.   5. Social Support—
Ukraine.   6. Spinal Cord Injuries—Ukraine.   HV 1559 P563d 2010]
   HV1559.U38P55 2010
   323.3—dc22                                                                 2010017542

1 2 3 4 5   16 15 14 13 12 11

*For Nina and Sabina*

*It's hard to be a human being, very hard,*
*but altogether possible.*
*And you don't have to stand*
*on your hind legs to do it.*
*Not at all. I believe that.*

—RUBEN GALLEGO, *White on Black*

# CONTENTS

ACKNOWLEDGMENTS    xi

LIST OF ABBREVIATIONS    xv

MAP    xviii


INTRODUCTION: Living Disability and Mobilizing Citizenship
in Postsocialism    1

1. A Parallel World    13

2. Out of History    43

3. Disability Rights and Disability Wrongs    97

4. Regeneration    139

5. Disability, Gender, and Sexuality in the Era of "Posts"    170

CONCLUSION    231


NOTES ON TERMINOLOGY AND METHODS    249

NOTES    257

BIBLIOGRAPHY    265

INDEX    283

## ACKNOWLEDGMENTS

It is a pleasure to be able to acknowledge the many colleagues, friends, and institutions that supported and contributed to my research and the making of this book. At the top of the list are all the research informants in Ukraine and Russia who generously shared with me their experiences and their time. Many of you welcomed me into your homes and your lives, for which I am humbly grateful. I have chosen to keep the identities of most of these persons confidential, but I am glad to acknowledge by name Oleg Poloziuk, Olha Alekseeva, Lev Indolev, Mykola Swarnyk, Oksana Kunanec-Swarnyk, Yaroslav Hrybalskyy, Ihor Rasiuk, Anna Kukuruza, and Denise Roza. For more than a decade Olga Filippova has been my constant companion in scholarship and friendship, a gentle critic and supportive *sestra. Spasibo, dorogaia!* In Ukraine I am also grateful to Yury Sayenko, Polina Alpatova, Masha Bakhtagozhina, Tanya Zub, and Natalka Yasko for their collegiality and support. Many thanks are due Anna Savenko, Galya Sagan, Svitlana Taratorina, Maya Garbolinskaya, and Liz Moussinova, who transcribed countless interviews for me.

For their thorough, generous readings of previous versions of this manuscript, I heartily thank Maria Bucur, Devva Kasnitz, Catherine Wanner, Erin Koch, and Maryna Bazylevych. The book has benefited enormously from your criticisms, insights, and suggestions (but all remaining errors and shortcomings are, of course, my own). Students in my medical anthropology seminar at Indiana University also contributed helpful feedback, especially Anna Batchellor, Rebeca Hernandez, Kaylan Huber, Carrie Lawrence, David Lewis, Casey Mace, Hallie Orgel, Elizabeth Pfeiffer, Mia Ranard, Abigail Rich, Devorah Shubowitz, and Kristiana Willsey. Rebecca Tolen, my editor at Indiana University Press, and Candace McNulty, my copyeditor, have both been wonderful to work with. I am particularly grateful to my husband, Sasha Savytskyy, for his engagement with this project and above all, his patience. I thank Yuriy Lazarenko and Yuri Solomko for permission to use their marvelous photos.

Without generous support from numerous institutions this project could not have come to fruition. Indiana University facilitated the research and writing by extending me a summer research grant (2003), a New Frontiers in the Arts and Humanities Exploration traveling Fellowship (2005), a summer stipend from the Office of the Vice President for Research (2006), and a College Arts and Humanities Institute Faculty Fellowship (2008). A Collaborative Humanities Fellowship from the National Endowment for the Humanities (administered by ACTR/ACCELS) allowed me to pursue research jointly with Oleg Poloziuk during 2005, and in 2006 I did further research with the support of an International Research and Exchanges Board (IREX/IARO) Short-Term Grant. A generous Postdoctoral Research Fellowship from the Social Science Research Council in 2008 offered me much-appreciated time to write unencumbered by other academic responsibilities.

I have been honored by invitations to present my works-in-progress at multiple venues; I always received beneficial feedback and critique, and all these conversations helped sharpen the arguments in this book. I would like to thank in particular the organizers and co-participants of the 2007 symposium on "Challenges, Choices and Context: Health Behaviors in Eastern Europe and Eurasia" at the University of Texas, Austin (especially Michele Rivkin-Fish and Cynthia Buckley); the 2008 symposium "Operationalizing Global Governance" at the Indiana University School of Law-Bloomington (esp. Hannah Buxbaum); the 2008 Health and Human Rights Lecture Series at the University of North Carolina at Chapel Hill School of Public Health (esp. Elizabeth King); the 2009 Liz Lerman Dance Exchange Residency with "Ferocious Beauty: Genome" at Indiana University (esp. Anya Peterson Royce); the 2009 Medical Anthropology Colloquium Series at the University of Kentucky (esp. Erin Koch); the 2009 symposium "Russia's Role in Human Mobility" at the University of Illinois at Urbana-Champaign (esp. John Randolph); and the 2009 Inaugural Congress of the Sociological Association of Ukraine (esp. Olga Filippova).

Portions of this book have appeared elsewhere, and I am grateful to the publishers for permission to use some of those materials:

Phillips, Sarah D. 2009. "'There Are No Invalids in the USSR!' A Missing Soviet Chapter in the New Disability History." *Disability Studies Quarterly* 29(3).

Phillips, Sarah D. 2010. "Disability, Sexuality, and Masculinity in Post-Soviet Ukraine." In *Sexuality and Disability Research: Sexual Politics, Identity, Access and Policy,* ed. Russell Shuttleworth and Teela Sanders. Leeds: The Disability Press.

Phillips, Sarah D. 2009. "Civil Society and Disability Rights in Post-Soviet Ukraine: NGOs and Prospects for Change." *Indiana Journal of Global Legal Studies* 16(1):275–291.

# ABBREVIATIONS

---

AR          Active rehabilitation
AZR         Association of Outdoor Advertising of Ukraine
BSM         British social model
CCDS        Canadian Centre on Disability Studies
CIDA        Canadian International Development Agency
DPI         Disabled Peoples' International
FRI         L'viv Oblast' Section of the Foundation for the Rehabilitation
            of Invalids
ILC         Independent Living Center
InvaSport   National Committee for Sports of Invalids of Ukraine
IPRI        Individual Program of Rehabilitation and Adaptation of the
            Invalid
KHOIU       Confederation of Civic Organizations of Invalids of Ukraine
LILRC       L'viv Independent Living and Resource Centre
MLSP        Ministry of Labor and Social Policy of Ukraine
MSEK        Medical-Social Expert Commission (entity responsible for
            assigning disability)
NADU        National Assembly of Disabled of Ukraine
NGO         Nongovernmental organization
PT          Physical therapy
RG          Rekryteringsgruppen for Active Rehabilitation
SoBez       Social protection office, local branch of MLSP
SOIU        Union of Organizations of Invalids of Ukraine
UAH         Ukrainian *hryvnia*, the Ukrainian currency
UNDP        United Nations Development Program
UTOG        Ukrainian Association of the Deaf
UTOS        Ukrainian Association of the Blind

| VIKO | All-Russian Production-Consumption Union of Invalids, also called the *Promkooperatsiia* |
| VOG | All-Russian Organization of the Deaf |
| VOI | All-Russian Organization of Invalids |
| VOS | All-Russian Association of the Blind |
| VTEK | Medical-Labor Expert Commission (Soviet era) |

# Disability and Mobile Citizenship in Postsocialist Ukraine

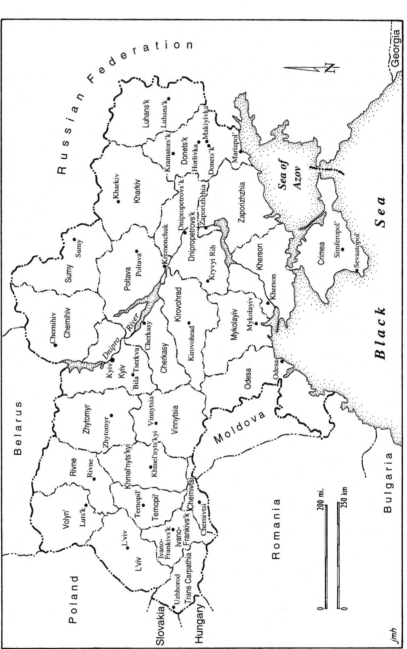

Map of Ukraine, showing oblasts and cities with populations over 200,000. *Created by John Hollingsworth.*

# Introduction: Living Disability and Mobilizing Citizenship in Postsocialism

On a warm spring day in 1999, eight friends in Kyiv, Ukraine, gathered at the home of a man named Dmitrii to drink tea and catch up on one another's news.[1] Dmitrii's small two-room apartment barely accommodated everyone, but the close quarters and mild inconvenience were nothing new for this group. And anyway, the space was relatively uncluttered, since Dmitrii had little in the way of furniture—he had just finished a capital spring cleaning and purged the apartment of the old wardrobes and shelves left behind by his mother, who had died the previous year. Dmitrii flung open the windows of his ground floor apartment, and the breeze gently rustled through the climbing roses he had planted just outside his bedroom years earlier.

Spring was in the air, and a sense of new beginning was palpable for the eight friends gathered there. As Dmitrii described to me several years later, they all yearned for change, and "we had the feeling we could reach out and grab it." Although the "group of eight," as Dmitrii jokingly called them, was all roughly the same age—in their early thirties to early forties— they embodied the diverse facets of ethnicity, language, and class identity characteristic of post-Soviet Ukrainian society. Ukraine, which declared its independence from the Soviet Union in 1991, is a mosaic of ethnically and linguistically diverse peoples. Oleg and Maria self-identified as ethnic Ukrainians, while most of the others claimed Russian or Russian-Ukrainian roots. Dmitrii called himself an Asian, having been born to a Russian father and a Kazakh mother. Both Ukrainian and Russian are widely spoken in Ukraine, and many other languages and language combinations are also familiar, including Polish, Romanian, Hungarian, and others. This particular group of friends was accustomed to speaking Russian with one another. Although Oleg preferred to speak Ukrainian, he switched to Russian seamlessly and willingly. Dmitrii described himself as working class; after finishing high school he had done manual labor such as welding and plumbing. Oleg, in contrast, possessed a law degree from the Taras Shevchenko National University of Kyiv, and worked off and on as a practicing lawyer. In terms of education, most of the others fell somewhere in between these two men.

Despite these differences, there was one identity marker that brought the group of eight together and offered a common experience—*invalidnist'* (literally, invalid-ness), or disability.[2] Everyone who gathered at Dmitrii's that day had experienced traumatic spinal cord injury as a result of diving accidents, car crashes, or on-the-job mishaps. As a result, they all used wheelchairs to get around. In a sense they had come to be identified and to self-identify on the basis of their spinal injuries and their resulting limited ambulation—colloquially these people and others like them were known as *spinal'niki*, persons with spinal injuries or diseases, and *vizochnyky*, wheelchair users (the word for wheelchair in Ukrainian is *vizochnyk*). The category of spinal'nik is usually associated with the spinally injured, but it also can include amputees and people with tuberculosis of the spine, spinal meningitis, hernias, spinal hemorrhaging, and rheumatoid arthritis. As spinal'niki Dmitrii, Oleg, and the others had gone through examinations administered by a government commission, which categorized them as group I invalids, or invalids of the most severe disability category. This meant that, in the state's eyes, the group of eight and hundreds of thousands of others in Ukraine were considered "incapable of working," and "requiring constant care" from others. They were granted lifetime invalidnist', defined in Ukrainian legislation based on their "loss of health" and "extent of bodily defects."

In the Soviet Union, although some individual invalids, veterans of World War II in particular, were held up as examples of the state's benevolent rehabilitation and social inclusion of the disabled, millions more lived in isolation, effectively hidden away in private homes or public institutions. Before Ukrainian independence in 1991, for instance, Oleg, who was a pre-adolescent when he experienced a spinal injury in 1981, ventured out of the apartment where he lived with his parents only a few times a year. And then, it was usually for medical appointments. Oleg was rather exceptional in that he obtained a university education and even a law degree. Dmitrii described the limitations placed on the opportunities for the disabled to study, work, and participate as full-fledged members of society in the Soviet Union: "Being an invalid meant having a 'pass' and a license to do nothing. No one thought us capable of contributing to society."

*[handwritten margin notes: "injury as an identity", "few examples obscure many", "lation to", "response/resp", "biases", "and be of that, they can't be in society?"]*

In present-day Ukraine it is estimated that around 2.64 million persons are classified as invalids—nearly 5.8 percent of the total population of approximately 45.7 million—but adequate statistics on the disabled population have not been gathered (Ministry of Labor and Social Policy [MLSP] 2008:28). Those deemed invalids receive attendant state-provided benefits such as pensions, subsidies, and other entitlements. Of these, 278,195 are assigned to group I, the category to which most persons with spinal injuries and others who are significantly mobility disabled would be assigned (MLSP 2008:27). Disability in Ukraine today is governed by legislation and policies that are hybrids consisting both of Soviet-era classifications and definitions, and post-Soviet reforms promising the disabled increased access to education, employment, and basic civil rights. Some of these promises are being delivered, albeit in a piecemeal fashion.

For example, in the early 1990s, with Ukrainian independence and the political and socioeconomic transformations it engendered, the Soviet-era secret directive that forbade group I invalids from enrolling in higher education was rescinded (Rasiuk 2002a:24). Having until then received individual instruction at home, Oleg began to study law through correspondence courses. He possessed a firm grasp of English, having learned it by watching instructional television programs during his years of seclusion at home. This proved advantageous, and upon graduating from the law faculty Oleg began to work as a lawyer for several of the international development organizations that set up shop in Ukraine and other states of the former Soviet Union beginning in the 1990s. He also did legal consultations for his local housing commission. As seen in Oleg's story, international connections, particularly partnerships formed between Ukrainian disability rights organizations and disability advocacy groups from abroad, have played a crucial role in helping carve out opportunities for disabled persons in post-Soviet Ukraine. Indeed, transnational disability advocacy initiatives and the social lives such initiatives take on when they hit the ground in Ukraine are central to the story of living disability after socialism.

Others in the group of eight experienced similar life changes to Oleg's. Instead of being "all holed up between our own four walls," as many informants described their Soviet-era lives to me, they became invested in a variety of activities. Everyone in the group of eight had taken part in active rehabilitation camps introduced by the Swedish advocacy group Rekryteringsgruppen for Active Rehabilitation (RG), whose representatives began visiting Ukraine, Belarus, and Poland in the 1990s. Thanks to the camps, these wheelchair users developed the self-confidence and skills necessary to venture out in public in spite of the disabling built environment, which takes little account of the needs of the disabled. Most had become involved in some type of community organizing or business enterprise, some of which were related to disability issues, physical rehabilitation in particular. Dmitrii worked for a doctor who had opened a private rehabilitation clinic for people with spinal injuries. Maria was an office assistant for an international nongovernmental organization (NGO).

As Oleg, Dmitrii, Maria, and the others became more mobile citizens, and I use "mobile" here to describe both enhanced physical and social mobility, they had access to more information about the politics of disability at home and abroad. They became part of new social networks that stretched across the city, the country, and beyond. As they met activists from abroad, and in some cases traveled abroad themselves, they came to know that disabled people—and spinally injured persons in particular—tended to live very different lives in Sweden, Canada, the Netherlands, New Zealand, and elsewhere: many drove cars and vans, had full-time jobs, and held positions of authority in their communities. In other words, although problems remained, they learned that spinally injured persons abroad were for all intents and purposes social participants who lived fulfilling lives. The group of eight shared a conviction that life for the disabled in Ukraine could—and must—improve. Their vision of this new life was rooted in two fundamental principles. First, the state must play a committed role in supporting disabled citizens, providing improved economic support, rehabilitative services, and opportunities for education and employment. Second, members of the disability community themselves must be empowered to steer decision-making at multiple levels, including individual/personal and social/political planes.

On that spring day in 1999, the friends committed their collective vision to paper. Maria wrote out the text. When Dmitrii handed me the handwritten document six years later, he smiled and referred to it as "The Invalids' Manifesto." The manifesto read:[3]

Our slogan: "Open society for all," including each one of us.

Our main goal: contributing to the full and genuine integration of invalids in society (and not ju through physical, psychological, and social rehabilitation). We believe that no one understands better the needs of spinal'niki than spinal'niki themselves, or how to solve their problems. We are prepared, relying on our own experience and strength, and utilizing the foremost methods of Ukrainian and foreign schools of rehabilitation—and with the support of civic and state structures—to take the most active of roles in developing (preparing?) the following plans for a comprehensive long-term program of integration of invalids into society.

The program should consist of three main interconnected component parts: the most crucial and primary one is psychological rehabilitation, which will include ~~re~~ special training of medical and social workers, as well as ~~state~~ civil servants who have direct contact with invalids, and also those persons who surround [the invalid] ~~who fell into trag~~ most closely, who experience a difficult psychological state ~~afterward~~.

Physical rehabilitation is also a key component—methods of physical rehabilitation used in Ukrainian medicine today are outdated and in need of reform. Early, intensive interventions are required, and the goal of physical rehabilitation should be to prepare the invalid for as active and healthy a life as possible.

Finally, social rehabilitation of the invalid is a collective responsibility. Everyone should have access to comprehensive information, starting with the invalid himself, and all the way up to government structures. The invalid must be prepared to act in accordance with the received information. The state, including social organizations, must also be prepared to act in accordance with the received information, as well as in accordance with the wishes, needs, and demands of invalids. Social organizations should function as a link in a chain—a mediator— between society and the state (medical conferences, social conferences, organizers, implementers).

The primary goal is the all-around development [of the person].

There is a group of young, energetic, committed people who are ready today to work on the future. These people have impairments of the skeletal-muscular apparatus, resulting from serious spinal traumas. Included are:

Oleksandr—director of the firm Reliable Repairs

Sergei—head of the physical rehabilitation division of Chance Center, engineer at the factory Luks

Dmitrii—instructor in rehabilitation unit for persons after spinal trauma

Maria—secretary at Global Fund of Trust

Petro—instructor at Stimul, the mini-rehabilitation center for spinally injured persons

Ruslan—businessman

Vsevolod—notary public for the state

Oleg—lawyer and consultant, housing commission

The manifesto is a good example of how marginalized citizens such as the disabled seek to redefine themselves in relation to the state and to other citizens to claim their collective and individual rights. In Ukraine, this is spurred by intense sociopolitical and economic change brought about by processes of globalization and neoliberal reform. The neoliberal project as it has unfolded in postsocialist Eastern Europe has led to the shrinking of social safety nets and the privatization of responsibilities previously allocated to the state or to work and other collectives, as citizens are cut loose from much state support to fend for themselves. Anthropologists and others studying postsocialist societies have expressed concern about the negative effects that the introduction of a neoliberal market system has had for many people in countries such as Ukraine, Russia, and Poland (Dunn 2004, Phillips 2008, Rivkin-Fish 2005), especially for more vulnerable segments of the population—certain groups of women, workers, and others. Scholars have pointed out that when social problems become individualized, as often happens with neoliberalization, the effects for already marginalized persons can be devastating. Indeed, all these processes are evident in the lives of the disabled, who are being encouraged to rely less on state support and forge their own strategies for survival.

In effect, in their manifesto the group of eight proposed a new social contract, one shaped by their experiences of living disability in the Soviet Union and their reading of the new Ukrainian state's shifting priorities and changing responsibilities to its citizens. Such redefinitions of citizen-state relations are not unique to the postsocialist world, though they may be more pronounced there due to the relatively recent introduction of market capitalism. The uneven and sluggish nature of the associated neoliberal economic and social reforms, which mean a scaling back of government and deflated social programs, gives such attempts at redefinition a certain urgency. The worldwide economic crisis that began in 2008 adds yet another layer to these citizen-state negotiations, as some of the shortcomings of neoliberal policy have been laid bare and states across the globe scramble to repair broken economies. The disabled population in Ukraine, located as they are on society's margins, has much to teach us about the struggles of different disempowered population groups for recognition and redistribution (Fraser 1997) in the face of general economic and social uncertainty.

Such struggles often contain contradictions, and the case of the disabled in Ukraine offers some vivid examples. For instance, as part of neoliberal economic reforms, the system of social welfare in Ukraine and other postsocialist states is being scaled back, and state-based support for categories of citizens previously deemed vulnerable is gradually receding.

The can-do language of the free market economy, a language that emphasizes personal initiative and responsibility, individualism, and the entrepreneurial spirit, animates this process. Ironically, however, due to barriers in education and employment, very few opportunities exist for those
from whom the state is withdrawing its support to actually become self-
sufficient citizens. Thus, disabled persons who want to hold onto their
disability benefits, which are crucial to their very economic and physical
survival, must perform a balancing act.

On the one hand, many follow the Soviet-era model of emphasizing
bodily infirmity or one's physical lack to argue for "biological citizenship,"
or claims for "a form of social welfare based on medical, scientific, and
legal criteria that both acknowledge biological injury and compensate for
it" (Petryna 2002:6). At the same time however, it is increasingly necessary
to couch one's claims for state benefits in the proactive, self-reliant terms
of neoliberal democracy: "I need the state's support to give me an equal
chance with healthy people to become economically self-sufficient," or
"Since I cannot navigate the inaccessible built environment in my wheelchair the state should fulfill its promise to provide me with a car, which
would allow me to secure employment and contribute to the country's
economy." Many informants articulated versions of these hybrid claims
to me, alternatively emphasizing as the basis for their deserved belonging
as citizens of Ukraine either their physical limitations, or their potential
social and economic contributions. These claims reflect the savvy ways
that people learn to redefine and reposition themselves vis-à-vis the state
in response to policy shifts. Such negotiations will only accelerate as a
result of the global financial crisis of the early twenty-first century.

Related to this point, just as it has become important to alternatively
emphasize or de-emphasize one's bodily impairment to claim belonging as
a citizen, disabled persons also find themselves variously privileging other
aspects of their identity, including gender, occupation, or sphere of interest, or fulfillment of a particular social role (e.g. mother, activist, political
actor, athlete). In this their experiences are good examples of intersectionality, or how aspects of one's identity such as age, gender, sexuality, race, social
class, and disability are assembled in particular contexts. Depending on the
situation, one or several of these identity vectors may take precedence or
recede backstage, playing a more or less formative role in shaping a person's
self-perception and contouring how others see them. In contexts where a
given characteristic is highly stigmatized, as is disability in Ukraine, people
may employ a strategic intersectionality—one may intentionally downplay
invalidnist' while emphasizing other characteristics. On the other hand, a

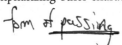

disabled person may consciously put his or her invalidnist' front and center precisely in order to perform disability in a rather unexpected way with the goal of challenging negative social stereotypes.

Both of these practices—alternatively centering and de-centering one's "loss of health" or "extent of bodily defects" to claim official status as a citizen and assert one's rights to requisite benefits and entitlements; and variously playing up or playing down invalidnist' as a more or less central aspect of personal and social identity—are indicative of the creative strategies being used by people on the margins to assert claims to full citizenship, strategies I refer to as *mobile citizenship*. The concept of mobile citizenship is particularly rich for exploring intersections and intertwinings of disability and mobility in a variety of contexts. The disabled in postsocialist Ukraine are very much looking to become the kind of "mobile, flexible, self-enterprising subject" that increasingly defines the standard of what it means to be a citizen in a world of global capitalism (Ong 2006:500). But how is such mobility achieved in the absence of adequate rehabilitation therapy, an accessible built environment, or adaptive technology? Does one have to be physically mobile to be a mobile, flexible, self-enterprising subject, or can social and economic mobility be enacted rather via the internet, the World Wide Web, and other means of digital communication? If one achieves a certain state of mobility, whether physical, social, or virtual, is one then no longer disabled? These are matters of import beyond the case of postsocialist states, and even beyond the question of disability *per se.*

My choice to focus on mobility disability and the experiences of people with limited physical mobility has multiple origins. Primary is my interest in unraveling an apparent contradiction: there are ways in which people who are not very mobile, or who at least are thought to be immobile, can nevertheless become mobile citizens. Also, I became connected to the mobility-disabled community through my activist friend Zoia Pavlova, who was a key informant for my previous project on women social activists in Ukraine. It was through Zoia and her son Sasha, himself spinally injured, that I met Dmitrii, Oleg, and many others, who in turn connected me with their own personal and organizational networks. Beyond my relatively easy access to the community, my choice also grew from the fact that within the Ukrainian disability rights movement, the spinal'nik community is one of the most visible and politically plugged in, thanks in some part to the work of Valery Sushkevych, a key political figure who is a polio survivor. The mobility disabled have been at the forefront of advocacy initiatives involving international organizations and foreign activists,

FIGURE 0.1. In 2005 when Oleg Poloziuk requested a new wheelchair from the Ministry of Labor and Social Policy, he was offered a museum-ready model of the kind used by Vladimir Lenin after his injury in World War I.

which also makes the group a good one to study in order to track transnational dynamics of rights advocacy.

As an ethnographer, I believe in the power of stories and personal narratives to humanize the big questions, and I draw on stories told to me by my informants and friends in Ukraine to ponder these theoretical and practical issues of disability, mobility, and citizenship. My primary strategy has been to forge long engagements (Plath 1980) with diverse persons in my population of study, who have granted me the privilege of following their lives and joining them in an ongoing dialogue over time. I have been privileged to record the personal histories of diverse individuals, people such as Dmitrii and Oleg, who agreed to enter into a long-term, sometimes painful dialogue with me about the politics of life itself (Rose 2006) in a struggling post-Soviet state. I have sought to reflect on their experiences in the historical, political, economic, and institutional contexts in which they are situated and shaped, to the extent that one person's experience can be translated and rendered by another (Strathern 1996). I have come to interpret these stories as narratives of mobile citizenship, and it is these stories that form the heart of this book.

The group of eight did not go on to form their own organization or political coalition; they did not, in the end, engage in a tight-knit, collective pursuit of an "open society for all" as intimated in the Invalids' Manifesto. Today, Oleg, Dmitrii, Maria, and the others still interact and participate in many of the same disability-related events, conferences, and sports competitions. But overall they live out their lives according to different credos. They have divergent ideas about who they have been, who they are, and who they want to be. As people designated as invalids they share much in common, and they are all subject to a system that would evaluate, monitor, penalize, and reward them according to the extent of their invalidnist'. Yet, the group of eight—even though they all fall into the category of persons known as spinal'niki or vizochnyky—are remarkable in their diversity. Indeed, in the pages to follow we shall meet a number of people who just happen to be mobility disabled, but for whom being disabled has become a central anchor for personal and social identity: Sasha, a self-described computer geek; Dmitrii, an athlete and activist; Viktoria, a cosmetics distributor; Anton, a yachting enthusiast; Nadia, a social worker and young mother, and many others. If in these people's stories the reader recognizes a valuable shared humanity, I will have achieved one of my major goals for this book.

### Outline of Chapters

In chapter 1, I offer a life history of Sasha Pavlov to introduce pivotal aspects of living disability after socialism. The reader will follow Sasha, a young man with a spinal injury, through his experience of trauma, rehabilitation, and emerging disability identity. Sasha's story provides a doorway to key issues to be explored throughout the book: medicine; disability and stigma; dynamics of family and social networks; structures of education, employment, and rehabilitation; and personal and collective strategies for empowerment, including NGOs. Comparative data from the United States situate these discussions in a broader context.

In chapter 2, I present a historical overview of disability rights issues in the context of state socialism in the former Soviet Union, especially the Russian and Ukrainian Soviet Socialist Republics. The Soviet state's governmentality of disability, and the little-known history of Soviet-era disability rights movements, produced important legacies that shape disability policy and discourses, rights movements, and experiences of disability in the region today. By focusing on Soviet approaches to housing, education, rehabilitation, and work vis-à-vis the disabled, and documenting the varied responses of disability communities, I encourage readers to reconsider some assumptions about the evolution of disability rights outside the West. I interweave discussions of Soviet-era state policy with descriptions of people's personal experiences to emphasize the ways that disabled people in the former Soviet Union have been active agents—if not organized advocates—across the twentieth century. In this chapter I tie discussions of disability history to the recent emergence of disability studies and new physical rehabilitation paradigms in the region. I track recent shifts away from claims to biological citizenship and outline further the import of strategies of mobile citizenship for disability rights empowerment in Ukraine today.

The focus of chapter 3 is the institutional structures and relationships through which disability politics and activists' personal identities are formed. I pay particular attention to the social life of NGOs and the nuanced politics of disability rights movements in Ukraine as I present ethnographic and historical examples. I profile several key rights activists in the Ukrainian disability movement, track some of the transnational networks that have facilitated advocacy movements, and examine the potentials and limitations of various approaches to collective rights organizing. Several detailed ethnographic cases provide examples of key empowerment strategies employed by disability rights activists and their NGOs.

In chapter 4 I examine the variety of symbolic and discursive aspects of disability that structure the treatment of disabled people in Ukraine, and the mobility disabled in particular. I focus on representations of disability in advertising, public service announcements, the popular press, and contemporary Ukrainian visual arts, among others. Of particular interest are how media and other popular representations of disability reflect and shape public opinion, and the effects of such representations for the life experiences of disabled persons. In light of these hegemonic, largely negative commentaries, how do the disabled then "perform" disability? Ethnographic examples provide insights into this question.

In chapter 5 I apply a gender analysis to disability experience by focusing on the life experiences of disabled men and women. I seek to understand how having a disability affects men's and women's ability to enact gender in contemporary Ukraine, and further, how disability and gender intersect to inform their citizenship struggles. I consider how the stigmatization and marginalization that disabled women and men face might contribute to the creation of alternative gender identities. A focus on men and masculinity, and in particular on how disability interferes with men's performance of hegemonic gender roles, provides added texture to discussions of gender and citizenship. These areas—disability narratives, community organizing, public discourse, and others—resurface in the final chapter, the conclusion, where I argue for kinship terrain as a fertile space for expanding notions of family and interdependence to advance the rights agenda in Ukraine.

# 1. A Parallel World

*Fate capriciously hangs up*
*the mirrors*
   *ha-ha*
*My life is a fun house.*
   *ha-ha*
*I cry and laugh,*
*Dance and sob,*
*I spread around smiles and just then . . .*
   *fall asleep . . .*
*from boredom.*
    *The clocks tick . . .*
*The world goes up in a flash of light . . .*
*My world of mirrors.*

          —POEM BY ZOIA

## Becoming Broken

Sasha Pavlov has only vague recollections of the accident that he says divided his life into pre- and post-trauma at the age of 16. Sasha's mother, Zoia, an engineer and nature enthusiast, always sought ways for Sasha to escape the burdensome heat of Kyiv (Ukraine's capital city of approximately 2.7 million) during the summer. This year—1991—she'd sent him to spend a month with his grandmother, who lived in a mid-size town on the banks of the mighty Dnipro River, downstream from the capital city. Sasha was a strong swimmer and had spent much of the summer in the water with friends. Sasha does not remember that final, "unlucky" dive,

the one that "broke" him, but he does recall briefly regaining consciousness underwater. In that moment, he says, he realized he "couldn't feel
himself," neither his arms nor his legs.

Press articles about Sasha and the accident report that his friends
dragged him from the water, but Sasha and Zoia tell a different story. In
fact, says Sasha, he doesn't quite know how he made it to shore, because he
was diving and swimming out of sight of the others. But he does remember having a peculiar vision, like a dream: a figure, "like a whitish fish,
or an angel," was swimming in the water, beckoning for Sasha to follow.
Somehow Sasha managed to accompany the figure to shore, an improb-
able feat that Zoia aptly calls "our miracle." Sasha briefly regained consciousness in the ambulance; he recalls a woman's voice, a nurse, pleading
with him: "Don't sleep, don't sleep."

On average, 2,066 people receive spinal cord injuries in Ukraine annually, and the incidence increases by 91 injuries each year.[1] It is estimated that
32,000 people in Ukraine are living with a spinal cord injury, or around
.07 percent of the entire population.[2] For comparison, in the United
States around .08 percent of the population are living with a spinal injury
(259,000 persons), and around 12,000 new injuries occur each year.[3] As in
the United States and other Western countries, in Ukraine major causes
of spinal cord injury are vehicular accidents, falls, and sports-related traumas, but no disaggregated statistics by cause of injury are available. The
spinally injured persons I met in Ukraine and Russia commonly refer to
their injuries as events of "breaking" (*zlamatysia*). In recounting their
experiences or arranging a personal life timeline for instance, one might
say, "I was broken (*zlamavsia*) in 1997," and they might divide their life into
before and after becoming broken.

Diving accidents like Sasha's often involve injury to one or more of the
cervical vertebrae, the seven vertebrae at the top of the spinal column.
When an injury to the spinal cord occurs, information flow to the rest
of the body from the point of injury down is interrupted. Depending on
whether the injury is complete or incomplete, the person will experience
either a total (complete) or partial (incomplete) loss of function and sen-
sation below the affected vertebrae. (A complete injury does not necessarily mean the spinal cord has been severed.) When the injury occurs in
the cervical region, legs, arms, respiratory function, and all other organ
systems may be affected.

When a person experiences a spinal cord injury, his or her chances for
survival, the eventual extent of injury, and prospects for restoring function can hinge upon the skill and speed with which immediate medical

care is offered. In Ukraine, the average person knows little about spinal trauma or the importance of stabilizing the vertebrae to avoid further injury. Although medical personnel may possess this basic knowledge, most ambulances are not equipped with long spine boards (backboards). Because spinally injured persons are frequently handled improperly immediately post-trauma—the spine is not immobilized, for example— outcomes may be compromised. Additionally, individuals with spinal injuries are often transported long distances in rickety ambulances over roads pockmarked with potholes and other hazards.

Zoia was at home in Kyiv when she received news of Sasha's accident, and she frantically made her way to the train station to catch the first train going in her son's direction. Born in 1945, Zoia had grown up in a Siberian town to which her grandfather, an engineer with noble roots and an independent spirit, had been exiled before she was born. Zoia had known hardship—in Siberia she had been forced to live in boarding schools she hated, and the harsh climate had compromised her health. More recently she had separated from Sasha's father, Ivan, who had become increasingly quarrelsome and verbally and physically abusive. And now, Sasha.

Whenever Zoia recalls those first days after Sasha "became broken" she always tells the story of her bargain with the Madonna. Zoia hates to cry, especially in front of other people, but each time she recounted the bargain to me—five or six times, at least—her eyes filled with tears. Zoia had been raised in an atheistic household, and prior to Sasha's accident religion held no special meaning for her. But when she learned of Sasha's trauma she felt a strong need to pray. As Zoia waited impatiently for the train that would take her south, she ran to the banks of the Dnipro river, the same body of water responsible for her son's unlucky dive hundreds of miles downstream. At the river, and later on the train, says Zoia, she implored God and the Madonna to keep her son alive. In return, she promised that both she and Sasha would devote themselves completely to helping other people.

Sasha considers himself fortunate, all things considered. Doctors at the local hospital where he was initially taken arranged to have him transported by medical airlift to a nearby city hospital with better facilities and more expertise treating spinal injuries. Doctors at the city hospital informed Zoia, who by now had arrived from Kyiv on the train, that Sasha had a break in the cervical region of the spine, with damage to the spinal cord. They offered to perform surgery, but Zoia decided to have him transported to Kyiv's Neurosurgical Institute, which happened to be just a few blocks from the family's apartment. At the time of Sasha's accident in 1991, the Soviet Union and the Soviet medical system were both still in place. Ukraine seceded from the Soviet Union and claimed its independence in August of that year, but changes in the system of health care developed only slowly, and not very successfully.

The Soviet Union offered its citizens health care that was nominally free and accessible to all citizens, a system that prioritized workers' health and succeeded in improving public health up to the 1970s, when epidemiological indicators began to fall. The system was a centralized, hierarchical one with health care planned and administered by the Ministry of Health. The Soviet health care system has been criticized on many fronts, among them limited patient freedoms, lack of technological innovation, inadequate financing resulting in significant unofficial out-of-pocket expenses for patients, and others. This is the system that Sasha entered into as a spinal patient in the early 1990s. This state-run system is still in place in Ukraine, though reforms are slowly making themselves felt and a parallel system of privatized medicine continues to grow.

In the West, after a spinal injury it is customary to use immediate drug therapy such as corticosteroids, which reduces cell damage and may decrease paralysis. No such measures are taken in Ukraine, but surgical interventions for spinal cord injury are relatively well developed. My friend Oleg believes this is in part because medical personnel in the Ukrainian system are rarely concerned with medical malpractice. They perform more surgeries than their Western counterparts, and exploratory surgeries are not rare. As Oleg said, "Tests are not done with fancy equipment, but with scalpels." The development of Soviet neurosurgery was closely tied to military medicine, in particular the treatment of gunshot and open wounds to the nervous system acquired in battle (Konovalov, Yartsev, and Likhterman 1997). This constrained scope, compounded by restrictions placed on Soviet neurosurgeons' contact with their colleagues abroad, placed limits on advancements in spinal surgery. Indeed, with the exception of a few model facilities such as the Burdenko Neurosurgery Institute in Moscow—the largest neurosurgery institute in the world— neurosurgeons and medical professionals almost across the board in the former Soviet Union must make due with a severely limited technological base. Today, the quite well qualified and talented physicians, surgeons, and support personnel who staff the resource-deprived state hospitals must do their best to serve spinal patients in far-from-ideal conditions.

An operation to relieve the pressure on Sasha's spine was performed in Kyiv five days post-trauma, well after the 24-hour window considered optimal in the West for surgical interventions after spinal injury. Despite regrets that Sasha's surgery was so delayed, Zoia and Sasha are glad they entrusted his operation to a seasoned surgeon in the capital. But even in this relatively elite institution, conditions in the spinal ward were difficult. Sasha was one of six spinal patients housed in a single room, with no curtain dividers between patients. No private bathrooms were available; in fact, there were only two bathrooms on the entire floor. The institute faced the same problems common to all state health care facilities at the time—problems that continue today: inadequate financing and a poor technological base. This resulted in reliance on labor-intensive methods (needles and other materials being sterilized and reused rather than disposed of, and an absence of equipment for speedy diagnostic procedures, for example), which contributed to a shortage of skilled support staff such as aides, orderlies, and maintenance staff. In this context, as is still customary in Ukraine, relatives provided much patient care, and they slept in the room along with patients, either in chairs, in a spare hospital bed, or on the floor. Relatives brought in most of the patients' food since the hospital fare consisted mostly of thin soup and plain oatmeal. On most days Sasha's mood matched the glum surroundings—Zoia says he stared at the ceiling, refusing to talk, and she thought he had lost the will to live.

Sasha's post-operative condition was extremely precarious. The year before, one of Sasha's schoolmates had died unexpectedly, and Sasha had asked Zoia to have him baptized. Zoia was not against the idea, but they had kept putting the baptism off, which Zoia now regretted. Zoia quickly arranged a baptism ceremony at a Russian Orthodox church in Kyiv, even though Sasha could not be moved from the hospital. Zoia became fixated on the lit beeswax candle she held throughout the ceremony—she was convinced that Sasha would die if she let the small flame go out. By the time she rushed back to the hospital room, she says, Sasha's condition had begun to improve.

Sasha was fortunate to have the support of a family friend who had already experienced a similar spinal trauma. In 1986 Zoia had taken Sasha and his older brother on vacation in the Caucasus, where they made many friends who were interested in tourism, hiking, and mountain climbing. When they returned to Kyiv, Zoia and the boys joined a hiking club. A few years later one of their friends from the club, Vanya, had a spinal injury while mountain climbing. After Sasha's accident, Zoia notified Vanya, and his support and advice proved invaluable, as Sasha recalled during a conversation in 2005:

By the time I had my accident, Vanya had been a spinal'nik for several years, and Mama called him immediately. When he came to the hospital he brought pillows for preventing pressure sores and a notebook where he'd written down all kinds of instructions for her—how to turn me to prevent bedsores and such like that. It really helped a lot, to have it first hand. And he talked to me about things, about what it would be like for me now, and with his support I took the news okay.

It's different for a lot of other people. Medicine here is very conservative, and for some reason doctors insist on giving people false hope—they don't tell them the truth. The doctor will say, "Everything's fine, take these pills, and we'll give you some shots; don't worry, you're getting better! See, you can move your toe now! You'll go home soon and in a month or so things will have improved."

So people go for years thinking they will walk again. But when they visit the sanatorium [treatment center] for the first time, and see hundreds of people in wheelchairs, the realization hits them and they go into shock. It was different with me. I knew I had a serious spinal cord injury and I figured, "Well, a wheelchair it is, then." I was prepared for it.

Sasha felt lucky to have someone like Vanya confront him with an honest assessment of his condition. Many individuals are not so lucky after spinal injury. When I interviewed him in 2006, Russian journalist and disability rights activist Lev Indolev described the ambulocentric nature of the Soviet medical culture in the following terms:

Earlier there was a tendency . . . in relation to spinal injury . . . to get the person back on his feet at all costs, to get him walking again, no matter what, so he could walk around the room himself, move around, and get to his Zaporozhets [a small automobile provided to the mobility disabled in the Soviet Union] by himself. . . .

There are many reasons for this ambulocentrism. In the Soviet Union, and to a considerable extent in Ukraine and Russia today, the lack of adaptive technology and the absence of accessible built spaces, wheelchair ramps, and other accommodations makes it extremely difficult for the mobility disabled to access public space and in some cases even carry out daily living tasks. On the other hand, the dominant medical culture of getting spinally injured persons "back on their feet" has provided little incentive or opportunity for the development of these technological and architectural interventions.

In Ukraine, 76 percent of spinally injured persons do not survive longer than one year post-trauma (Poloziuk 2005b). This contrasts markedly

with the United States, where 85 percent of people who survive the first
24 hours after a spinal trauma are still alive ten years later.[4] It is generally
agreed that the high death rate after spinal injury in Ukraine is attribut-
able to several key factors. First, although there are some excellent neurol-
ogists, neurosurgeons, and orthopedists in the country—particularly in
large cities such as Kyiv—their services are not readily available to many
persons with spinal injuries, particularly those living far from the cities.
They are often left in the care of physicians who have not been trained to
deal with spinal injuries. Also, there is no coordinated or widespread system of rehabilitation through physical therapy. The Soviet rehabilitation
system focused primarily on returning the injured person to work, not on
his or her physical rehabilitation. In this context, most medical personnel
are not well versed in the philosophies and techniques of physical therapy common to Western countries like the United States and Canada: the
development of a long-term plan of care in negotiation with the person
and his or her family or other support persons, the need for patient-re-
lated instruction and counseling, and so on. People in Ukraine are thus far
unaccustomed to seeking medical advice via resources such as the internet, although this trend appears to be growing.

revolving—
door
medicine.

Given these gaps, the importance of meticulous self-care is not stressed
to spinally injured persons by medical caregivers in Ukraine, and until
very recently literature on the subject was virtually nonexistent.[5] Pressure
sores (bedsores) are a major cause of mortality—sustained pressure causes
injury to the skin and underlying tissue, which begins to die due to lack
of oxygen and nutrients. Preventing these and other problems requires
extraordinary vigilance, and the overburdened, understaffed, and under-
financed Ukrainian health care system is inadequate to provide the care
most spinal patients need. Basic equipment such as catheters and urine
bags are not always available; neither are more specialized prophylactics
such as Varihesive gel, a preparation commonly used in Western countries for preventative and early treatment of pressure sores. Pressure sores
can develop into deep ulcerations reaching all the way to the bone. Such
wounds are often fatal, and only one hospital in Ukraine—the Donets'k
Regional Hospital for Restorative Treatment—is equipped to treat them,
usually with last-resort radical surgeries and amputations. Persons with
spinal injury and their families are also poorly informed about the dangers of bladder and kidney infections, and renal failure and related complications are another frequent cause of death after spinal injury.[6]

In these conditions, Sasha's survival was never assured, but he did have
several things going for him. After his surgery Zoia took over most of

Sasha's care in the hospital. Under Vanya's tutelage and upon countless consultations with other experienced spinal'niki and with doctors, Zoia learned to bathe and feed Sasha, shift his position to prevent pressure areas, constantly check his skin for signs of breakdown, insert and remove a catheter, drain urine bags, massage Sasha's muscles, and perform countless other tasks. An engineer who was working on her kandidat degree (a higher degree that falls between a master's and a PhD), Zoia took an extended leave and eventually quit her job to care for Sasha.

Fortunately the family had adequate means at their disposal to finance Sasha's first several months of intensive medical care, since he was covered by the obligatory medical insurance offered by the Soviet government to all schoolchildren. After his accident Sasha and his family received 15,000 rubles in insurance money.[7] Although nominally all medical care in the Soviet Union was free, and officially this is still the case in many Ukrainian clinics and hospitals, by 1991 the health care system had begun to crumble and people often were obliged to pay significant sums for medical services. The insurance payout was enough to cover Sasha's medical care during the critical first six months post-trauma. The major expenses included his operation; various medicines, vitamins, and hygienic materials; and miscellaneous expenses incurred during his lengthy hospital stay. The money also took care of the family's necessities such as food. In addition, Sasha received a monthly group I disability pension, and his mother also received a very small pension as his primary caregiver.

Sasha says he hates to think about what it would be like to be "broken" in Ukraine today, when the system of medical insurance he enjoyed has dissolved, the health care system is in further disarray, and costs—especially for acute care—have gone through the roof by Ukrainian standards. In 2006 post-trauma care after spinal injury cost between 200 and 300 UAH (the *hryvnia*, the Ukrainian currency) a day ($45–$65). This totals around $10,000 over 180 days, which, according to most of my informants, is the average hospital stay for spinally injured persons in Ukraine.[8] When the average GDP per capita (PPP US$) is $6,914,[9] serious traumas like spinal injury can deal a devastating economic blow to families. The Ukrainian government's public expenditures on health are relatively low, just 8.8 percent of total government expenditure in 2006.[10] To pay for initial medical expenses, the injured person and his or her family members often are obliged to pool all available resources; they may have to borrow money from relatives and friends, and sell personal belongings such as cars and furniture. Some find themselves seeking sponsors who can help pay for the costs of care. Sponsors might include local entrepreneurs, candidates for political office, or foreigners. NGOs and other support networks may offer resources, and businesspersons may be willing to donate money or tangibles (medicines, equipment), even though the Ukrainian tax system does not reward charitable donations with tax breaks.

As with Zoia, a family member usually is obliged to leave work to become a full-time caregiver, at least in the initial months, which causes additional financial hardship. In Ukraine and other postsocialist countries, caring for others—children, the elderly, the ill, the temporarily or long-term disabled—is considered women's work. Therefore, in the overwhelming majority of cases, it is women who are obliged to make the major sacrifices necessary to cope with the challenges of disability in the family. In contexts of economic crisis and lack of adequate state support for medical and rehabilitative care and social services, this is a daunting responsibility. These gendered expectations, particularly the assumption that women are less vital to the Ukrainian workforce and therefore more expendable as salaried workers, point to the widespread gender inequalities that characterize the labor market. Although more women than men have a tertiary (higher) education—75 percent of Ukrainians with higher degrees are women—women's salaries on the whole constitute just 59 percent of men's. In 2007 the estimated earned annual income for men (PPP US$) was $8,854, but for women it was just $5,249.[11] Zoia had enjoyed her engineering career very much. Over time she did develop a wide portfolio of other interests, and she later thrived in community organizing, but I always sensed that she harbored regrets about abandoning her profession.

All these pressures impact family life. Unable to rely on the state financially or for adequate health and social services, individuals and their families must cobble together their own support systems and survival strategies. Sometimes the stress proves too much and families fall apart; it is common for women to be left alone with a disabled child, for example. Sasha's parents formulated a rational, if not always comfortable, solution: although Zoia and Sasha's father Ivan were separated, after Sasha's accident they decided to, as Zoia described, "work together as a family." Ivan, who had been living with another woman and her children, moved back into the apartment he had shared with Zoia and Sasha before the separation. He contributed his earnings to the family budget and helped Zoia care for Sasha, but he spent most of his time at home alone in his own room.

## "On Immediate Measures for Creating Favorable Conditions of Living for Persons with Limited Physical Capabilities"

After nearly six months in the hospital, Sasha returned home to the family's three-room apartment on the top floor—the ninth—of a concrete apartment complex. Situated at the crest of a steep hill, the building affords residents plenty of cardiovascular exercise and also an impressive view of the city of Kyiv. The edifice was constructed according to the standardized plans of most apartment buildings in the Soviet Union, so the building entrances all include two short sets of stairs leading to an elevator landing. Ivan took it upon himself to fashion makeshift wheelchair ramps out of metal rails that he drilled into the concrete steps. Some of the building's other residents complained that the rails were unsightly and a hazard for others, but Zoia ignored their grumblings with characteristic aplomb. Sasha needed a way to get in and out of the building, and until a better solution could be found, the temporary rails would stay. They were still there in 2006, my most recent visit to the Pavlovs' apartment.

Sasha and his father have their own separate rooms, but Zoia sleeps in the apartment's one common room on a pull-out couch with a lumpy mattress and rumpled woolen covers. The apartment, it seems, never keeps a comfortable temperature. The family has a south-facing unit, so the sun streams through the windows in summer, making the apartment unbearably hot. The concrete walls are extremely cold in winter and early spring, and the strong seasonal winds seem to whip right through the apartment. The first time I visited the Pavlovs in February 1999 Zoia invited me to have tea in the living room, where she and I perched together on the couch. Even though I was sitting a good ten feet from the closed windows, I could still feel the intermittent wind gusts blowing across my face.

In the hospital Sasha had gradually begun to use a wheelchair, varying his position from bed to chair throughout the day to avoid pressure sores. He did hope his condition would improve, and he followed a rigorous self-styled program of exercises to help restore function to his hands, arms, and shoulders, but he was accustomed to the idea that he would not walk. His friends from school, where he had finished the ninth grade, came to see him, but he soon grew tired of these visits: "They acted like they'd come to a funeral," he offered. The only friends Sasha really enjoyed were the alpinists, people of all ages from the hiking club he and Zoia had joined nearly six years earlier. Instead of trying to encourage Sasha with platitudes, the climbers brought interesting books, told funny stories and jokes, and entertained one another with games. Periodically they took up a collection to help the Pavlovs financially, and they brought bags of groceries for the family whenever they visited. Sasha could relax around the climbers and be himself; he did not have to worry about attracting unwanted attention, stares, and displays of pity as an "invalid."

Outside the apartment, however, it was another story. The disabled are stigmatized in postsocialist states such as Ukraine, the legacy of a state ideology that devalued difference and often denied the existence of the disabled population. Physical disability challenged the ideal of the fit, uniform, and capable body of the New Soviet Man, thus threatening to disrupt the hegemonic body cultures of socialist states (Brownell 1995). As Ethel Dunn has noted, in the Soviet Union, "talking about the disabled or showing pictures of them was as taboo as talking about train wrecks or natural disasters" (2000:153). Indeed, during the 1980 Olympic games in Moscow, a Western journalist inquired whether the Soviet Union would participate in the first paralympic games, scheduled to take place in Great Britain later that year. The reply from a Soviet representative was swift, firm, and puzzling: "There are no invalids in the USSR!" (Fefelov 1986). This apparatchik's denial of the very existence of disabled citizens encapsulated the politics of exclusion and social distancing that characterized disability policy under state socialism. In this context visibly disabled persons were hidden from the public, isolated in their homes, and thus made seemingly invisible (Dunn and Dunn 1989). This official position colored the perceptions of ordinary citizens toward the disabled. One man who became a spinal'nik described his attitudes toward disabled persons prior to his spinal injury: "I was eating breakfast, looking out the window. I saw a girl down below, and something struck me. She probably had cerebral palsy. I found myself thinking—cynically, and now, I realize, stupidly—Why do people like that live near us? Why can't they all be rounded up, all those old, weak ones who can barely walk. Let them live separately, far away, to keep them out of sight." Additionally, it is often assumed that the disabled are at fault for their injuries or physical shortcomings; this is particularly the case for the spinally injured. Such attitudes in turn affect the self-perception of disabled persons. One woman in her mid-fifties who had polio as a child and walks with a cane told me that until she was a teenager she "did not realize there were other invalids in the world," because, she said, "I never saw anyone like me on the street." Her words highlight the psychologically demoralizing aspects of both standing out and standing outside, and having to deal with the practical lack of care at literally every step.

In this context disabled persons, especially those who look "different" and move differently, must weather the pitying, curious, and sometimes downright hateful stares of others. The extremely inaccessible built environment is also a major hindrance, and the creation of a built environment accessible to all citizens is a major goal of many who are involved in the Ukrainian disability rights movement. Mobility disabled persons in particular face many difficulties due to the lack of accessible housing, public spaces and buildings, and limited accessible public transport. Many live in so-called *khrushchovki,* five-story apartment buildings without elevators built as temporary housing after World War II that were never replaced or improved. Some wheelchair users and others who have trouble getting around have managed to install makeshift ramps; others, men especially, have grown accustomed to going up and down stairs in their wheelchairs. Many must rely on family members, friends, or passers-by to assist with overcoming architectural barriers. For all these reasons, during Soviet times many wheelchair users rarely left their places of residence, and this is still true for many. In fact, serious legislative attempts were not made to address problems of accessibility until 2005, when on June 1 President Yushchenko signed Decree No. 900, On Immediate Measures for Creating Favorable Conditions of Living for Persons with Limited Physical Capabilities, a document that outlines steps to be taken to provide for equal access to "objects of social infrastructure" to the disabled population.[12]

Sixteen-year-old Sasha was embarrassed to leave the apartment during daylight hours, so Zoia went out with him after dark instead. He did not like being stared at, and part of the problem was a technical one. As a disability entitlement, the Soviet state—and later the Ukrainian state—provided wheelchair users with chairs based on a model made by the German company Meyra. The model most commonly available in the Soviet Union, the KIS, was a large, unwieldy standard wheelchair, a one-size fits all (or, to quote Zoia, a one-size fits no one) model suited for short-term use. The KIS was so wide that it usually did not fit through the doorways of the average Soviet-made apartment, which were all built to uniform dimensions. Wheelchair users often were thus unable to spontaneously move from one room to another in their own apartments. Furthermore, wheelchairs for children, small adults, larger than average adults, and others with supposedly nonstandard bodily dimensions were not available. Sasha recalls that using the KIS was like riding in a tank, and he got jostled around with his hips banging against the armrests. Oleg, who was injured in 1983 at the age of ten, for many years used a wheelchair that his engineer-father constructed out of spare parts and bicycle wheels.

Reluctant to go outside, Sasha developed an indoor routine of exercise, rest, and study during the day. He no longer attended high school but a teacher came several times a week to tutor him and check his lessons. During most evenings he went around the neighborhood to get some fresh air under cover of dark.

Having been physically active before his injury—he loved hiking, and had also done martial arts—Sasha was eager to get back in the best physical shape possible. There were few formal resources for him to do so. Physical rehabilitation was not well developed in the Soviet Union; when the disabled were offered rehabilitation services, most often they were focused on vocational rehabilitation, the maintenance of the labor force being the priority of the socialist workers' state. The culture of denial and nondisclosure surrounding spinal injury also played a role. Spinally injured persons frequently were sent home from hospital "to await improvements" after surgery with little or no physical rehabilitation. During the last decade several private residential rehabilitation centers for people with spinal injuries have opened in the country, but these programs are prohibitively expensive at around $200 a day. These centers offer access to modern exercise equipment and consultation and treatment with a range of specialists. In Kyiv I visited two private rehabilitation centers, one of which occupied a ward in a central hospital right alongside a state-run spinal ward. The two wards—public and private—competed for patients, with a number of spinally injured persons declaring a preference for the state facility, which though also operating on a fee-for-service basis provided comparable care at more affordable prices. The other private center I visited several times was located on the edge of Kyiv, sited in a group of buildings surrounded by green spaces and conveniently located to several shops. It was valued for the range of exercise equipment available, the accessible facilities, and the positive attitudes of the local residents and shopkeepers with whom clients would come in contact.

Such facilities did not exist at the time of Sasha's injury, and by the time they became available, he could not afford their services. Left to his own devices, Sasha was compelled to cobble together his own regimen of physical rehabilitation. His father helped set up some exercise equipment in Sasha's room, and Sasha also continued to use the exercise facilities of the Neurosurgical Institute where he had been treated.

Like many of his "brothers and sisters in misfortune," as Zoia refers to people with spinal injuries, Sasha made do without the benefit of a so-called IPRI, or Individual Program of Rehabilitation and Adaptation of the Invalid, a program approved by the Ministry of Health in 1992.[13] In theory, an IPRI is an individualized support mechanism for the disabled that would detail the social services to which one is entitled, and require the requisite state, business, and civic institutions to provide such services (Poloziuk 2004). However, the development and implementation of this policy has been wracked with problems, and such an individual rehabilitation plan was not available for Sasha at the time of his injury.

Without a formal IPRI, Sasha for two years made do with his own cobbled-together program of physical exercise. When asked to talk about pivotal moments in his life, Sasha always mentions the camp for active rehabilitation (AR) that he was invited to attend in 1993 in the Western Ukrainian city of L'viv. AR for wheelchair users is a program developed by the Swedish advocacy group Rekryteringsgruppen for Active Rehabilitation (RG). Zoia summed up the importance of the AR program for improving the lives of the disabled in Ukraine when she said, simply: "Sasha is convinced that the Swedes saved his life."

The expansion of AR into Eastern Europe was largely the initiative of Katarzyna Trok, a neuroscientist and Polish émigré to Sweden who has a long-time affiliation with RG. Seeking to extend the benefits of AR to wheelchair users in Poland, Trok and her colleagues organized the first AR camps there in 1988. From there RG expanded its international program to other Eastern European countries by sponsoring an AR camp in 1990 in Saki, Ukraine, the site of a large sanatorium for persons with spinal injuries and others who are mobility disabled; in Moscow, Russia, in 1991; and in L'viv, Ukraine, in 1992.

Yaroslav Hrybalskyy, a wheelchair user and rights activist from L'viv who attended the 1991 Moscow AR camp, was instrumental in bringing AR to Ukraine. With the support of Katarzyna Trok and RG in the initial years, and later under the direction of Ukrainians who had become AR instructors, camps were organized in several Ukrainian cities, including L'viv, Kyiv, Rivne, Poltava, and Mykolaiv. AR was also introduced in Belarus and Lithuania.

AR camps, which are still held in Ukraine on a somewhat limited basis, are intended primarily for persons with "fresh" spinal cord injuries, a population perceived to be in greatest need of physical and psychological rehabilitation and the long-term empowerment that learning to navigate barriers can provide. AR is introduced to small groups of wheelchair users during an intense, highly structured, seven- to ten-day closed camp. Nonparticipants, including family members, friends, and representatives of the press, are referred to as "outsiders" (Ukr. *storonni*) and may visit the camps only on the final day. At these camps, wheelchair users are exposed to a firm philosophy of individual independence, and they receive training in wheelchair sports and negotiating architectural barriers (navigating steps, doorjambs, and curbs, for example) and how to independently carry out activities of daily living (e.g., dressing, eating, and transferring from bed or chair to wheelchair). Psychological rehabilitation is also central to the AR method. Participants glean information on self-care, relationships, self-image, and sexuality by watching videos, listening to instructors, and talking with one another. Instructors are wheelchair users themselves who are qualified to conduct the training camps according to the specific parameters set by RG. Instructors have been through training courses that prepare them to serve as comprehensive resource-persons for the camp participants. Instructors should be prepared to give advice on anatomy and medical care, dealing with representatives of the state bureaucracy, choosing a wheelchair, making modifications to living spaces, planning one's future (education, employment), addressing social problems, sexual relations after spinal injury, and many other topics. One of RG's slogans is, "You have learned, now teach someone else."[14]

AR cannot take place in the absence of lightweight, maneuverable "active" wheelchairs of the type that were unavailable to Sasha and other wheelchair users in the early 1990s. When organizing the initial AR camps in Ukraine, the Swedes provided participants with used active wheelchairs from Sweden, which participants were allowed to keep. The active wheelchair that Sasha was given by the Swedes changed his life. It was worth over a thousand dollars, a sum he never could have afforded to spend on a wheelchair at the time. Mastering the techniques of AR allowed him to negotiate architectural barriers more independently and with more confidence, and to become more mobile. No longer so ashamed of his wheelchair, Sasha liked to get out and experience the city as part of his daily routine, and these outings began to replace his previous nighttime excursions:

I started going out into the courtyard of our apartment building, and I also liked to go to the banks of the Dnipro and just watch the activities on and around the river. I used the streets, and when I got to the tram I'd ask a couple of strong-looking guys to lift me in and out, and then I'd take the tram wherever I wanted to. I might go to the animal market to see the dogs and cats, or to Khreshchatyk [the main thoroughfare that runs through the city's downtown]. . . . I didn't really have anything else to do and I needed some diversions, so I tried to keep myself busy. I went to the Neurosurgical Institute practically every day to talk to the new spinal'niki, to answer their questions and teach them some skills.

Sasha also got involved in wheelchair sports and started participating in marathons. During the mid-1990s he won several Ukrainian wheelchair marathon championships; he also competed internationally in Russia. Wheelchair sports were well developed in the Soviet Union and the successor states, even in the absence of quality wheelchairs appropriate for use in athletics. As many of my informants explained, getting involved in some kind of sport was one of the only modes of physical rehabilitation available for many people with spinal injuries and other disabled persons. Wheelchair sports were an avenue for disabled persons to establish their social worth as citizens by engaging in a pursuit highly valued in Soviet society—the training of one's body in a spirit of working on the self and engaging in healthy competition. Also, forming sports clubs and organizing athletic competitions allowed the disabled to form collectives that were presumably apolitical and thus did not come under official suspicion as potentially subversive. For wheelchair users like Sasha, this was a valuable way to build up physical strength after injury, challenge oneself by setting and achieving personal goals, and become part of a collective on the basis of common interests and experiences.

## Out of Work in the Former Workers' State

Sasha and Zoia say they were focused on making the best of a bad situation. Sasha finished high school through tutoring at home, which is still common for many young disabled people in Ukraine and other post-Soviet countries. In the mid-1990s, the idea of inclusive education was just making its way into discussions of education reform (Raver 2006, 2007; Raver and Kolchenko 2007). Sasha was lucky to have a tutor who really cared about his learning and held him to high standards. Oleg's tutor was different, and more typical, he says: "She went through the motions, but I could tell she was thinking, 'Why does he need to know this? What can he possibly achieve in life as an invalid?'"

Sasha did not even consider enrolling in a technical college or a university. He was not the academic type, he says, and anyway, back then it was almost unheard of for disabled persons to pursue a higher education. Prior to Ukrainian independence in 1991, a secret directive commonly excluded the disabled population from attending universities (Rasiuk 2002a). Disabled individuals who did want to further their education beyond the secondary level usually were obliged to study in specialized vocational or technical schools. Many of these were residential institutions to which the disabled were segregated. Only after Ukrainian independence was Oleg able to pursue a law degree at the National Taras Shevchenko University of Kyiv. Still, Oleg completed most of his coursework from home through correspondence courses and visited the university only for exams and special lectures.

About a year and a half after Sasha's accident the Pavlovs began to find themselves in financial trouble. Ivan's job as a low-level engineer did not pay enough to support the entire family, and Zoia started to regret her decision to quit her job. By 1992–1993 she only received a nominal caregiver's pension from the state—less than $2 a month, a sum she did not even bother to go collect. Sasha's group I disability pension was only slightly larger, just around $10 a month. If she had known, says Zoia, about the existence of AR, and the benefits it would bring Sasha, she would not have given up her career. Perhaps she would have cut back to part-time, or just taken a temporary leave. But now it was too late, and Zoia needed a plan. The family's economic crisis came to a breaking point in 1993, when hyperinflation caused prices in Ukraine to rise 100-fold.

In 1994, about three years after Sasha's injury, Zoia accepted an invitation to be interviewed, with Sasha, for a national radio program. They talked about their experiences, described the family's situation, and thanked the friends and colleagues who had supported them. In the broadcast Zoia went on at length about the AR camp Sasha had attended—she praised the Swedes and described the colossal difference Sasha's active wheelchair had made in his life. At the end of the program, the announcer gave out the family's phone number and asked listeners to help the family if they could.

Zoia was unprepared for the avalanche of phone calls and assistance the family received. To her surprise, people transferred money to the family's bank account, dropped off food and clothing, and offered words of encouragement over the telephone. In my research experience the overwhelming goodwill and material support the Pavlovs received from strangers is not representative. Zoia remembers Sasha's reaction: he was loath to accept charity and asked Zoia, "Aren't you ashamed to do this?" Zoia was firm in her reply; she told Sasha that accepting the donations meant the family now had a responsibility: "Later, when we are able, we'll be obliged to pass along this help to others many-fold."

Around that time, quite by chance, Sasha was hired at the institute where his mother had worked before, and where his father still worked. This was an opportunity for Sasha to learn valuable skills, earn money, and become part of new social networks, as he described to me during a conversation in 2005:

Mama and I were going past the institute one day and we decided to stop in so she could talk to some of her former co-workers. The building was accessible so I went in too. We visited one of the laboratories and decided to ask if we could type something up—an advertisement or something, I don't remember now. It was the first time I had seen a computer! But I had a typewriter at home and I more or less knew the keyboard.

So I sat there typing, and the director walked in. He remembered Mama, and we all started talking. He liked me, I guess, and he asked me if I wanted to work there. Really, he just needed to employ an invalid, to fill the quota [of disabled workers required by law at each firm]. But he was a good person and I worked there for two years, actually. I started by just typing things up, and little by little I began to learn my way around the computer.

There were a couple of programmers who taught me a bit about operating systems, utilities, the structure of a computer, how to take it apart and put it back together, how to set up a processor, add components, and all of that. It was also really good training for me to work in a collective. They treated me absolutely normally. They made no exceptions for me—if the workday went until 11:00 PM sometimes, I worked right on with everyone else.

The institute was close to our house—I just had to go down the hill a couple blocks and I was there. I couldn't enter through the front door, because there were twenty or so steps. So I'd push the buzzer on the gate at the back where the freight trucks came through, and the guard would let me in. I'd go through the back door and ride the elevator up to the laboratory. It was really convenient and I consider myself very lucky in that regard.

Indeed, Sasha was lucky, as the opportunity to hold a formal, paying job eludes most disabled persons Ukraine, particularly group I invalids, and especially those such as Sasha with visible disabilities who have trouble getting around. In 2002 official statistics indicated that the disabled constituted just 1.6 percent of the entire workforce in Ukraine, and only 14.5 percent of the disabled population was employed (Derzhavna Dopovid 2002:96).[15] By 2007 the situation had improved somewhat, and 22 percent of the disabled were employed (MLSP 2008:137).

In 2001, attempts to usher disabled workers into the workforce were made through a change to the 1991 Law on the Basis of Social Protection of Invalids (No. 2606–III).[16] Via a quota system modeled on legislation in France, Germany, and Poland (Derzhavna Dopovid 2002:99), the law requires that each employer hire a certain percentage of disabled workers. For a workforce of greater than 25, at least 4 percent of workers must have disability status. In an organization with 100 workers, for example, at least four must have disability status. Small firms that hire only 15 to 25 workers are required to reserve one job for a disabled worker. According to the statute's Article 20, employers who are unwilling to comply with this law must pay a fine equivalent to the estimated average annual salary of the firm's other workers into the Ukrainian Fund for the Social Protection of Invalids. The law requires that monies from such fines are then channeled back into programs for social, vocational, physical culture/sport, and professional rehabilitation for Ukraine's disabled population (Derzhavna Dopovid 2002:99).

Although some businesses in Ukraine comply with the equal employment legislation, others are reluctant to hire disabled workers, citing fear of absenteeism and expectations that such employees will be unable to carry out work responsibilities. Additionally, many employers are unwilling to make accommodations for disabled workers, who may require architectural renovations and special chairs and equipment to access the workplace and perform their jobs. Employers who decline to hire disabled workers have two options: they may pay the requisite fine or they may fake the hiring of disabled workers, an arrangement that saves costs. My informants commonly referred to this latter practice as the hiring of "dead souls." The dead souls practice entails officially hiring the worker but paying a reduced salary; the worker is usually paid half the official salary for work he or she never does. This complimentary salary was around $50 a month in 2006. Such hollow or duplicitous (non)compliance with the law is, of course, also a legacy of Soviet times. Recent years have seen a steady increase in the amount in fines paid to the Fund for the Social Protection of Invalids (MLSP 2008:86), but there still are several loopholes in Article 20 that allow firms to avoid paying the requisite fines, including provisions that excuse firms that do not make profits from paying the fines (Baranova-Mokhort 2005).

Almost every person in my study was involved in the workbook arrangement, commonly described as "having my workbook lie at [name of firm or company]." My informants have been fictitiously employed at places such as the Kyiv Zoo, a city newspaper, and the Nestle Company. In reality, most people with group I disability status survive on a small pension and earnings from these fake work arrangements while cobbling together other sources of informal income and support. This is what Sasha has done since the director who hired him died and Sasha was let go from the institute after two years of working there. He gets odd jobs thanks to his computer skills—he designs websites, helps people install and fix programs, and so on. But now, much of Sasha's workday is devoted to Lotus, the NGO for active rehabilitation of spinally injured persons that he and Zoia founded in 1996.

## Organizing Empowerment

*Are states of being so important?*
*Are they all we live for?*
*What do we live for?*
*And what are light and dark,*
*Sorrow and joy?*
*We talk about this, and that . . .*
*Our words are nothing but fuss.*
*Words can't express thoughts*
*Words can't convey feelings.*
     —POEM BY ZOIA

The first time I met the Pavlovs in their home in 1999, I spent most of the visit talking to Zoia in the living room. Upon learning of my interest in disability issues, a friend, Andrii, offered to introduce me to a young man in a wheelchair who visited his church from time to time. And so here I was, having tea with Zoia while Sasha and Andrii absconded to Sasha's room to talk computers.

I could tell right away that Zoia was a character. She talked practically nonstop, switching topics freely and frequently, waving her hands in the air for emphasis. Points of conversation included hiking in the Caucasus, the price of meat at the market, descriptions of Zoia's student days, the merits of poetry, the upcoming Parliamentary elections, the famous but fictional Siberian healer Anastasia, and many topics in between. Despite her verbosity, Zoia continually stated that she valued actions and deeds over words. By way of illustration she related a recent experience that seemed to encapsulate this philosophy:

Recently a couple of missionaries knocked on our door and wanted to talk to us about God. I guess they were Baptists, you know, evangelicals, who have started proselytizing intensively in the last few years. I would have let them in—I have nothing against them, and in fact we have some good friends in the building who are evangelicals—but I was really busy. I'm not exaggerating: I was dealing with Sasha's toilet, and I had on rubber gloves, and believe me, it just was not a good time for visitors. I told them as much.

They started getting rude; they said, "You have to make time to talk about God, and about your salvation, and that of your son, especially if he's an invalid." I said, "You know what, you stand there and talk about God, but here, let me give you some gloves and you can come help me. That's what I really need from you—some help, not just talk about God and my salvation." They turned around and left. You see what I mean? If someone is not willing to get involved, to do the dirty work, all the words in the world are of no use.

Unlike the squeamish visitors she had sent on their way, Zoia was doing the dirty work in her capacity as co-director, with Sasha, of Lotus, a civic (*hromads'ka*) organization they ran out of their home. Zoia conceded that Lotus was born out of a sense of both obligation and need. On the one hand, she and Sasha felt indebted to those people like Vanya who had been such a resource for them after the accident. Having weathered Sasha's traumatic injury and emerged in pretty good shape, Zoia and Sasha wanted to help others in turn. They knew from experience how important and difficult it was to track down the information and resources necessary for survival after a spinal injury. Having amassed a certain amount of expertise and knowledge, Zoia and Sasha sought ways to assist others.

Zoia also suffered from guilt. In addition to the copious offers of assistance they had received thanks to the radio interview, Zoia and Sasha also got many inquiries about active wheelchairs. Many callers wanted to know where they, too, could get one. Zoia said, "I began to feel really guilty about how we'd gone on and on about the active wheelchair over the radio. I realized it wasn't fair to talk about all the merits of the chair, to talk about having one, if we couldn't help other people get one, too. It was really frustrating that our country was so behind in wheelchair design and production." In founding Lotus, Zoia and Sasha decided to make the production and distribution of active wheelchairs in the country one of their main priorities.

All the same, Zoia admits that Lotus initially emerged as a survival strategy for their family. She unabashedly confesses that, "Lotus helped me save my son, and parallel to that I helped others like him." Originally, one of the organization's main functions was to procure humanitarian aid in the form of medicines and medical supplies, clothing, food, and other tangibles for distribution to spinally injured persons. A portion of this aid went to Sasha and the Pavlov family. In 1999, when Sasha's group I disability pension was just 37 UAH ($8), and Zoia's pension as his caregiver was only 4.60 UAH ($1), Zoia referred to Sasha's two high-quality active wheelchairs as "our earnings."

Following the principles of AR promoted by the Swedish activists they had met, the Pavlovs envisioned Lotus as a source of information, resources, and social support to facilitate the "effective social integration of wheelchair users on the basis of their active rehabilitation," as stated in the organization's promotional materials. The Pavlovs also drew on the idea of the exemplary model, which is central to RG's empowerment philosophy. Exemplary models (role models) are people who are disabled themselves and use wheelchairs, who act as "living proof of how far you can get toward an active and meaningful life if you train" (Rekryteringsgruppen 2002:3). Similarly, the Pavlovs envisioned AR as a method by which spinally injured persons can "learn to conduct an active way of life and instruct other wheelchair users to do the same," as noted in their organization's brochures. They recruited spinally injured persons to volunteer as first contact people to visit persons with recent spinal injuries in the hospital to offer support and advice, a model also borrowed from the Swedes. A network of spinal'niki developed around Lotus, and the organization helped plant disability support organizations in other Ukrainian cities and towns. Zoia and Sasha got commitments from several steady sponsors, including one local disabled entrepreneur and a prominent Ukrainian manufacturing company.

When I began getting to know the Pavlovs in the late 1990s, Lotus had become a vibrant organization that kept Zoia, Sasha, and Ivan very busy. Along with providing social, material, and informational support to the newly injured, the Pavlovs' primary focus was to collaborate with local manufacturers to facilitate the design and production of active wheelchairs for wheelchair users in the country. Zoia and Sasha were also committed to ensuring the widespread availability of active wheelchairs for all who could use them, as a guaranteed disability entitlement. This meant frequent meetings and negotiations with representatives of the state, a slow, frustrating process mired in bureaucratic red tape.

At the same time, Zoia seemed to envision Lotus as a catchall organization with a plethora of different goals and foci. She shared with me a mind-boggling assortment of grant proposals that she and Sasha had submitted to develop the following: a wheelchair design and repair workshop, with ten employees; a video production company; a rehabilitative art studio for disabled children; a center providing computer literacy courses for the disabled; a comprehensive information and resource center on disability issues; and a consultation service for patients in spinal wards in Kyiv and their families.[17] Unfortunately, most of these proposals were unsuccessful and funding was not received. Additionally, they sought financial support from private sponsors and from the state to allow them to carry out their own AR camps. Zoia often discussed other projects she had in mind, including introducing comprehensive programs of AR for disabled children into Ukraine's orphanages, developing art therapy curricula for disabled children and adults, and sponsoring a regular television show on disability issues. It was clear to me that Zoia and Sasha had many exciting ideas, but they possessed neither the time nor the resources to pursue them. As I came to know many different social organizers in and outside the disability community, I was to learn that Lotus was plagued by problems common to many grassroots initiatives in postsocialist contexts: inter-NGO competition for information, funding, and networks; frequent agenda changes produced by the need to follow the grant money; and charges of cronyism and corruption.

## Active Worlds

After living in Kyiv for two years during 1998–1999, I returned to Ukraine for several shorter research trips in 2002, 2003, 2005, 2006, and 2009. During most trips I spent considerable time with Zoia and Sasha, who had become my good friends. Lotus continued to function, but the Pavlovs' vision for the organization had grown more modest. They had not received substantial financial support from any of the international development organizations offering grant assistance to Ukrainian NGOs, and another activist surmised that Zoia and Sasha might have refused to guarantee grant administrators the customary 10 percent kickback expected of successful grantees.[18]

The Pavlovs had persisted in their quest to jumpstart the production of active wheelchairs in the country, with positive results. After much bureaucratic wrangling, in the early 2000s the activists convinced representatives of the Ministry of Labor and Social Policy (MLSP), one of the bodies responsible for administering disability benefits, to agree that those who needed them could receive an active wheelchair from the state at no cost as part of their disability benefits. With this agreement, the activists persuaded representatives of the Kyiv factory Artem, known for its production of vacuum cleaners, to start intensive domestic production of active wheelchairs. It was important for Zoia that several experienced wheelchair users who had either gone through AR camps or had become AR instructors themselves work together with the Artem factory's engineers on the wheelchair design. That the stated needs and knowledge of stakeholders was central to the process was a departure from standard disability policy in Soviet and post-Soviet Ukraine where, as my friend Oleg summed it up, "We are tired of bureaucrats who know nothing about our lives as invalids making decisions for us. Who better than invalids themselves knows what we need?" (see also Charlton 1998).

Initially, the chair was available only to those who could pay for it. In October 1996 the Artem chair cost 650 UAH, or $367, far beyond the means of most wheelchair users living on a group I disability pension (P'iatilietov and Hrybalskyy 1996). Today, qualifying wheelchair users in Ukraine are entitled to two new active wheelchairs every four years, which represents a milestone in disability policy.[19] Unfortunately this benefit is not always enforced, and the cadres in the MLSP, the main entity responsible for filling requests for active wheelchairs, sometimes are ignorant (or feign ignorance) about people's rights.

In the 1990s and early 2000s active wheelchairs began to be produced by factories in four major cities: Kyiv, L'viv, Kirovohrad, and Zaporizhzhia. Zoia conceded that the agreement with the ministry came with a price: in order to keep costs down for the state ($200 per active wheelchair), compromises were made on the chair's design. Ideally, each active wheelchair would be manufactured to the specifications required by the individual user. Instead, the Ukrainian chairs were produced with a gradation of standard widths, so they were not maximally individualized. Nonetheless, Zoia considered the project a victory. In 2003 she offered, "We made the first, hardest steps in the right direction. It will be up to the next generation of activists to perfect the system of wheelchair politics." She was encouraged by her successful cooperation with state cadres, and told me, "It seems that finally the state is starting to meet us [NGOs] halfway."

Unfortunately, the indigenous production of active wheelchairs that Zoia, Sasha, and a few other activists had cultivated fell apart in the late 2000s when the contract to produce wheelchairs for Ukraine's disabled population was denied the Ukrainian-based factories. Instead, it went to a Chinese manufacturer who could make active wheelchairs more cheaply (around $215 per chair versus the $440 proposed by local manufacturers). Today, Ukrainian wheelchair users complain that these chairs are poorly made and start falling apart within two weeks to a month of regular use. In this situation, many wheelchair users, young people in particular, instead seek to scrape together the $1,000 needed to buy a used chair of Swedish or other European/North American design (such chairs are sent to Ukraine as humanitarian aid and become available for purchase on the "underground" market).

By 2005 Zoia, now fifty-seven years old, did not have the physical stamina to pursue the kind of fast-paced activism she was used to. During an outing, Zoia was helping Sasha navigate the escalator in the Kyiv subway, only two stations of which feature elevators for passenger use. He fell on top of her, and her arm was broken severely in three places. Zoia experienced other problems with her health, which she attributed to the harsh Siberian climate in which she had grown up: cardiovascular problems, osteoarthritis, and problems with her teeth. She still commanded respect among disability rights activists as an initiator of the rights movement, but many activists believed that Zoia's time had passed. They intimated to me that she should leave the struggle to the younger generation.

Life also changed for Sasha, who began to leave the family's apartment less frequently. He no longer took part in wheelchair sports; an injury to his tailbone had left him unable to assume a racing position. I assumed Sasha had been injured while training or racing, but he explained that no, he had fallen from his wheelchair trying to navigate the stairs in the entrance to his still-inaccessible apartment building when a disgruntled neighbor had temporarily removed the makeshift ramp. By 2005 a mutual friend described Sasha as "living in a virtual reality" via his computer. Sasha sometimes went to select disability rights events, and he left the apartment for daily exercise, but his social network appeared to have shrunk. Sasha told me he had "grown weary of socializing with invalids," and said he rarely visited the Neurosurgical Institute's spinal ward to mentor newly injured people. When they were dealing with an especially difficult case the nurses would call on Zoia and Sasha for assistance, but otherwise Sasha kept his distance.

In 2005 I asked Sasha to describe for me his typical day:

Sasha: I wake up around 7:30 and get on the internet, while it's morning and the telephone calls haven't started yet. I'll check the weather, read the news, get my mail, and check out the forums. Plus, I'm an administrator in the site Active Worlds, it's like a virtual world where you can enter and interact as a virtual person.[20]

Sarah: What's the main goal?

Sasha: Just interaction (Rus. *obshchenie*), that's it.

Sarah: Do you make friends with those people?

> Sasha: We interact on the site mostly, and sometimes on the telephone, or in internet chats. There are people from all over Russia—most of them left to live in Israel, America, Australia, or Germany.
>
> Sarah: Then what do you do?
>
> Sasha: Then I have some tea and go back to sleep until 11:00 AM or so. That's when I work, and the phone calls start coming in, until 9:00 or 10:00 in the evening. After that I take a nap for an hour or so and wake up again around midnight. I spend a couple more hours on the internet, and then I go back to sleep. That's it. I eat when I have time, but usually I just have tea. In the evenings I might go outside, to the shop on the corner, for example. In winter I sit at home mostly, since we live on a hill and in inclement weather it's impossible to go anywhere in the chair. So I might just go out in the courtyard and sit for a half hour and then go back home.

Sasha described his role in Lotus as the "main *komp'iutershchik*" (computer geek) and characterized his work as primarily informational in nature. He managed Lotus's accounting, organized the NGO's library of print and video materials, managed e-mail correspondence, and designed and maintained the organization's website. Officially this was unpaid work that Sasha carried out on a volunteer basis, since Lotus was registered as a nonprofit civic organization.

In 2006 Sasha's group I disability pension was a little over 300 UAH a month, around $60. He received additional income through the common workbook arrangement; as a registered employee of a firm in Kyiv he probably received around $50 a month. Sasha took on additional jobs in web design for small businesses, artists, and others in need of their own website. I did not feel comfortable asking directly, but other NGO activists suggested that the Pavlovs had other, more nefarious, sources of income. Supposedly they made money by selling items received from abroad as humanitarian aid such as wheelchairs and tire tubes. Ivan did wheelchair repair on a fee-for-service basis, another source of income for the family. In this way the Pavlovs eked out a modestly comfortable existence, "saving themselves while helping others," as Zoia had said so many years before.

Having achieved her most important goal—facilitating the production and distribution of active wheelchairs—Zoia continued to pursue the theme of active rehabilitation. She sought sponsors to help Lotus organize AR camps like the one Sasha had attended more than a decade before. Her persistence in the AR arena sometimes generated tension between Zoia and other activists in the wheelchair-user community, and I heard about these conflicts from both sides. Younger activists, many of them leaders of their own NGOs, complained that Zoia should be happy with what she had achieved and should leave AR to them. Zoia countered that she had nurtured the younger generation of activists ("they all came through me, through Lotus") and they were being ungrateful. Furthermore, she said, "I would be happy to leave the rest to them, if they'd actually step up to the plate and do the work." Despite these fraught relations, Zoia continued to work closely with many other NGO activists and their organizations in Ukraine. Lotus had contacts in Russia, but Zoia and Sasha did not envision any joint projects with Russian activists or organizations. Their most valued international networks were with disability rights groups in the West—Sweden, the Netherlands, the United States, and Canada.

And what of the ambitious plans to found a resource center, a video production company, and a repair workshop? Each of these projects was at least partially realized, but the results were modest in the absence of adequate financing and human capital. In 2005 and 2006 Lotus had only four regular employees: Sasha, Zoia, and Ivan, plus a man named Leonid, also a wheelchair user, who provided his services as a driver on an as-needed basis.

Overall, a substantial gap exists between Zoia and Sasha's organizational vision and the actual, on-the-ground realities of Lotus. Although Lotus is officially called a rehabilitation center, the organization has always been run out of the Pavlovs' three-room, ninth-floor apartment. The wheelchair workshop is located in Ivan's room, and he is the workshop's only employee. Lotus has produced several videos, but they are of amateur quality and have not been widely shown or distributed. The NGO also advertises an informational resource center that includes a video library of around 65 films and television shows on disability issues and a collection of books and articles on disability topics, particularly those relevant to spinal injury. Zoia and Sasha also put together a printed compilation of informational materials for people with spinal injuries that they distribute free of charge to anyone who requests it. There are complete sets of the main disability-related newspapers in Ukraine and Russia going back to the late 1980s; Zoia and Sasha allow visitors to peruse the newspapers and make copies of articles they would like to keep. An important element of the organization's informational arm is Lotus's website. The site includes electronic versions of newspaper and journal articles on contemporary disability issues, self-help medical literature, a database of Ukrainian legislation pertinent to disability, a photo archive, a forum, and a guest book.

## Stalling Out?

Although there is no typical experience of trauma, rehabilitation, and disability identity in Ukraine or anywhere else, Sasha's personal history does provide a window to key aspects of disability experience in Ukraine and other post-Soviet states. The stories of his injury, the subsequent medical care provided him, and his struggles to pursue physical rehabilitation provide a grim picture of the state of health care and social services in Ukraine. Sasha's experiences after spinal cord injury illustrate the continued importance of social networks and word of mouth for accessing adequate information and resources for surviving crises like traumatic injury. Based on their own experiences, Sasha and Zoia have devoted much of their time and energy to providing the spinally injured population with crucial self-care literature and encouraging seasoned spinally injured persons to share their own accumulated know-how with novice spinal'niki. They have tried to fill the yawning gap between the culture of denial and nondisclosure regarding spinal injury and disability that pervades the medical system, and the real-life reality and medical needs of the spinally injured population. This signals the need for major reforms in the Ukrainian system of health care, rehabilitation, and social services.

Sasha's story also brings into focus the major institutional barriers to inclusion of disabled persons in contemporary Ukrainian society. Despite far-reaching legislation to guarantee equal rights to education and employment, the disabled struggle mightily to access opportunities for study and work. This leaves many economically vulnerable, since the state disability pension is inadequate even for basic survival. It was not until 2008 that disability pensions were indexed to the officially calculated minimum standard of living for persons considered unable to work, as previously many disability pensions fell well below that level (MLSP 2008:49). In 2009, disability pensions were low, an average of only 740 UAH ($88) a month for those like Sasha in group I.

Like Sasha, many of the disabled are compelled to rely on family and friends, enter into demeaning fake hiring arrangements, and seek out unofficial ways to earn money. One such strategy is to found an NGO as a means to, in Zoia's words, "save oneself while helping others." Zoia often described Sasha's existence—and by extension her own—as "a parallel world." By this she meant that as an invalid, someone deemed unworthy and even expendable because of his compromised physical state, Sasha was cast into social isolation, the world of the broken and abandoned. But he was not alone there, because this parallel world was the social space he shared with other disabled persons—Vanya, Oleg, Dmitrii and others who understood and shared his experiences. As another friend, Anton, said, "Zoia is right when she refers to 'the parallel world.' It's true that there are two worlds here, the world of the healthy, and the world of invalids, and the two practically never intersect." Social stigma and historical cultural attitudes have much to do with this segregation, but architectural barriers are a significant contributing factor as well.

Lack of accessibility places limits on people's opportunities to pursue an education at all levels, from primary school through higher education, and constrains employment possibilities and opportunities to pursue social, cultural, athletic, and recreational activities. In these conditions, methods of active rehabilitation can have transformative effects. AR helped Sasha become more mobile and more self-confident—it motivated him to engage in competitive sports and be a more mobile citizen of his city. But as long as architectural barriers remain, AR is a welcome yet only partial and temporary strategy to empower individual wheelchair users. Without far-reaching and permanent infrastructural and institutional changes, the benefits of AR will likely remain localized, individualized, and somewhat privatized. Indeed, Sasha began spending the majority of his time indoors, in front of his computer, which became the main medium for his work and social lives. One might see this as a negative development, as a retreat into a virtual reality. On the other hand, if we concede that virtual worlds are practically just as real as the "real" world (Boellstorff 2008), Sasha's life in Active Worlds becomes not an escape, but a creative way for him to transgress the boundaries of the "parallel world." Given the inaccessibly built reality, perhaps roaming cyberspace allows Sasha the opportunity to pursue a more mobile citizenship. Is it a coincidence that Sasha turned from "active" rehabilitation to "Active" Worlds, or are the two domains in fact related?

The little history of Sasha's and Zoia's NGO, Lotus, likewise illustrates some key characteristics of civic organizing in post-Soviet Ukraine. Lotus arose from its founders' personal crises and need for material resources. The Pavlovs launched Lotus as a survival strategy; in the face of economic hardship and inadequate state support for the disabled, the NGO became for them an alternative form of employment. This is typical for civic organizations in post-Soviet states, particularly mutual-aid associations that are formed around a specific group of marginalized citizens and their needs (Phillips 2008).

Lotus and its ups and downs are also indicative of the challenges that NGO organizers in the region often face. On the one hand Zoia and Sasha were well connected in the NGO sphere; their organizational network was vast. They helped plant disability advocacy groups in numerous Ukrainian towns and cities, and they cooperated with many other activists and groups to design and implement projects. At the same time, Lotus and the Pavlovs had fraught, competitive relations with some other activists and groups. Some of these conflicts were rooted in personality differences, but others were structural. NGOs in the disability rights arena found themselves jockeying for support from the same sources—international development agencies, foreign activists, the Ukrainian state, and well-placed bureaucrats. Some local activists believed this engendered a sense of healthy competition, but it clearly was detrimental to inter-group cooperation.

In this situation of spotty and unpredictable support for their NGO, Zoia and Sasha felt compelled to diversify Lotus's functions and seek funding from multiple and varied sources. They strove to remain mission focused, and all their proposed projects offered much-needed support for spinally injured persons. However, there was a sense in which Lotus was spread too thin across an array of undertakings.

Finally, Zoia's experiences point to the generation gap that increasingly characterizes civic organizing in the Ukrainian disability rights sphere. Zoia and others of her generation are often referred to as the old guard of social activists—those who came of age in the Soviet Union and were at the forefront of rights struggles during the early years of Ukrainian independence. Overall, younger people appear less interested in civic organizing and the collective pursuit of social justice for disadvantaged groups such as the disabled. This is a characteristic of the disability rights movement in the United States as well, a development often attributed to changes such as school mainstreaming and shorter rehabilitation stays for the current generation of disabled youth. If in the United States this shortage of new cadres in community and rights movement leadership has sparked many youth programs, the situation in Ukraine is rather different. Younger members of the Ukrainian disability community are more likely to pursue individual strategies for empowerment. By comparing the life narratives and strategies of disabled people from the Soviet generation and the post-Soviet generation, I have come to the conclusion that the neoliberal paradigm of citizenship, which places individual initiative and achievement at the center of being a citizen, has been successful in changing the self-perceptions of people in postsocialist Ukraine, especially the younger generation. For this reason, it appears that the disability rights movement on the whole is in danger of stalling out at the grassroots even as it enters a new phase at the level of the state.

# 2. Out of History

The history of disability experience and state disability policy in the Russian Empire and the Soviet Union has been little researched, and in many respects disabled persons living under these regimes remain an "unknown population" (Poloziuk 2005b). Until very recently historical sources were largely unavailable to Western scholars, and in the Soviet Union questions of disability were not considered an appropriate subject for ideologically correct scholarship. In this chapter, I seek to fill these gaps by bringing the former Soviet Union—particularly Russia and Ukraine—into the worldwide "new disability history" (Longmore and Umansky 2001) through historical and ethnographic explorations of disability experience, policy, and rights movements in the Russian Empire and the former USSR. I rely on the available Russian, Ukrainian, and English-language published sources, as well as my own ethnographic data, particularly life history interviews. In line with my primary research interests, particular emphasis is placed on issues related to mobility disability.

I begin with a discussion of disability in the pre-Soviet Russian Empire (circa 1700–1917), where relatively few efforts were made by state authorities to regulate or support the lives of the disabled. I then turn to Soviet-era disability policy, which I characterize as a functional model of disability. Areas of particular concern include the system of institutionalization, the special education system, and Soviet approaches to rehabilitation and work placement. I then examine key moments and figures in the struggle for disability rights in the Soviet Union.

This historical material offers an important backdrop for understanding the barriers to social inclusion and full citizenship rights that disabled persons living in former socialist states continue to face. Although improvements in disability rights have been made in post-Soviet Ukraine and Russia, there are important legacies of the socialist era that have shaped current disability policy, official and popular discourse about disability and disability rights, and the strategies that advocacy groups develop and are able to pursue. Considerable reform has been achieved in disability rights legislation, but many Soviet-era structures, institutions, and practices are still in place either de facto or de jure.

These historical legacies become evident as I unfold the story of living disability in contemporary Ukraine in the latter part of the chapter. At the same time, transnational engagements to promote disability rights in Ukraine since the early 1990s have produced important strategies for reforming rehabilitation medicine, revamping social services, and building a more accessible built environment. Disability studies as an applied academic discipline is also developing in the country, a phenomenon I also explore.

## Disability in the Pre-Soviet Era

Little is known about the lives of disabled persons during pre-modern (pre-eighteenth century) and modern history in the territory that encompassed what is today Ukraine and Russia, since historians and ethnologists have not systematically studied this question. We do know that in traditional Ukrainian and Russian cultures the physically and developmentally disabled were not socially isolated. Traditional life was village-based and centered on the Orthodox Church (Vovk 1995:122) and disabled persons presumably were integrated into their communities. They worked alongside others to the extent possible, for example making baskets and fishing nets, sewing, and embroidering (Bondarenko 2005, personal communication). None of the most thorough and respected historical accounts of Ukrainian traditional culture and folklore (Naulko 1993, Voropai 1993, Vovk 1995) mention the disabled. This indicates either a broad disregard for questions of disability in the Ukrainian ethnographic tradition, or is evidence of the social integration of disabled persons in their local communities.

Literature on the premodern period refers to wandering minstrels, who often were blind, and "strolling beggars," many of whom may have been disabled, who solicited charity in and around Orthodox Churches and monasteries. Such persons were often referred to in Russian as ubogi, a term that translates literally as "of God," iurodivye—"God's fools" or "holy fools," and proroki, or "prophets." Because of their close association with churches and religious moral culture, apparently these wanderers often were respected and revered. However, persons thought to be mentally ill were also treated in a dualistic fashion—some manifestations of mental illness were valued, while others were feared (Brown 1989:15–16). Rasputin, favored advisor to the last royal family of the Russian Empire, was considered a holy fool. There is a possibility that the descriptions that have come down in the scant literature for this period are rather romanticized, but the relative absence of negative portraits is also quite striking. Sociologist Liia Iangulova (2001) argues that our contemporary interpretations of iurodivye are inevitably influenced by modern psychiatry, resulting in a tendency to medicalize their behavior and mistakenly insert it into established psychiatric categories. She makes the convincing case that holy fooling was as much a social practice as it was a manifestation of mental illness.

Beginning in the eighteenth century, the main caring subjects for the disabled were families, the elites, and the church, but the tsarist state played an increasingly important role. In the early 1700s, under Tsar Peter I (Peter the Great, r. 1682–1725), for instance, the state began to take a more forceful role in identifying and regulating the lives of the disabled. As part of his efforts to regularize and make compulsory the service obligations of the Russian nobility, Peter required all gentry-persons suspected to be mentally disabled (called *duraki*, Russian for "fools" or "idiots," a term with more negative connotations than ubogi and iurodivye), to appear before the senate for certification. This certification allowed individuals to be exempted from state service, and it also limited their property rights and forbade them from marrying (Brown 1989:17). Peter made unsuccessful attempts to exclude the church from responsibility for caring for persons thought to be mentally ill—in 1723 he decreed that such individuals no longer be sent to monasteries, and several secular institutions were organized in Saint Petersburg—but these efforts were abandoned by Peter's successors. Iangulova (2001:197) notes that Peter's reforms were accompanied by the "development of scientific and policing practices (for example isolation and statistical data collection) [which] facilitated the registration, surveillance, comparison and analysis" of categories of persons such as iurodivye, making a unified, official narrative possible, one that was counter to that previously based in Christianity.

One might expect that this heightened regulation would lead to the creation of institutions to manage such populations, and this is precisely what happened. In 1775 Catherine II (Catherine the Great, r. 1762–1796) established regional Departments of Public Welfare as part of her reforms of local government. As in many Western societies, this was the "era of madhouses," (called *doma dlia umalishennykh* in the Russian Empire, or "homes for the mad/lunatic"), and these departments were responsible for building asylums to accommodate the "insane," institutions modeled on German asylums of the time. Julie Brown (1989:19) notes that through the next century the asylums were viewed with dread and suspicion, and for the most part the mentally disabled were supported and cared for by their families.

The position of the disabled in pre-Soviet society changed further during the nineteenth century with urbanization and industrialization in the Russian Empire. Community support structures for the disabled eroded as increasingly more people settled in cities. Despite Peter's earlier reforms, support for disabled persons and others who were socially disadvantaged (the elderly, orphans, the destitute) still rested with the Orthodox Church, which provided homes for the disabled in monasteries. Also, the elites of society—especially the royal family and intellectuals—cared for the disabled in a tradition of patronage and secular philanthropy known as *metsenatstvo* (Rus.). The first school for deaf children, the Murzkina school, was founded in 1807 in Pavlovsk with the personal funds of the Empress Maria Fedorovna; in 1809 the school was moved to Saint Petersburg (see Burch 2000). A school for blind children soon followed. Philanthropists supported various schools, hospitals, and other institutions by donating money and services such as free medical consultations and pedagogical assistance.

The latter half of the nineteenth century and the early twentieth century saw a huge increase in institutions for the mentally ill and disabled in the Russian Empire; between 1860 and 1912 the number of asylums nearly quadrupled to include 160 such institutions housing 42,489 persons (Brown 1989:26). Most of those institutionalized were of peasant origin, and it has been suggested that this reflects the erosion of social support structures of peasant families during this post-emancipation period, and also the peasantry's continuing economic hardships (Brown 1989:29–30). The establishment of the psychiatric profession in the 1860s, which increasingly held sway over diagnosis, treatment, and institutionalization, also accounted for the marked growth of the asylum population. Overall, the prerevolutionary development of policies and attitudes toward disabled persons was similar to changes in Western countries: increasing state-based interventions, growing networks of institutions to house and treat individuals, medicalization, and the validation of "expert" knowledge (Brown 1989:33).

Much of what little is known about the life stories of persons considered to be mentally disabled in the nineteenth century Russian Empire was reported by Ivan Pryzhov (1827–1885), a member of the radical intelligentsia who documented the lives of "social misfits" in Moscow in the mid-1800s. Pryzhov was an independent scholar, having been dismissed from Moscow University in 1850. The life of Moscow's impoverished and marginalized citizens was not considered a worthy topic of study, and Pryzhov, who was a minor civil servant, was unable to make a living with his writing. He published mainly in newspapers, and for his manuscript *26 Moscow Prophets, God's Fools, and Fools, and Other Works on Russian History and Ethnography* (1996) he did not even receive an honorarium. The impoverished and disillusioned Pryzhov, who joined the secret revolutionary anarchist group Narodnaia Rasprava (People's Reprisal), was involved in the murder of the student Ivanov, an incident that was later fictionalized by Fyodor Dostoyevsky in his book *The Possessed.* Pryzhov was sentenced to 12 years hard labor and eternal exile in Siberia, where he died in 1885 (Lur'e 1996).

Ahead of his time methodologically, in his research Pryzhov used methods of cultural anthropology to conduct a social history of the poor. In addition to perusing existing writings on the topic, he gathered stories, did interviews, and conducted participant observation in taverns, markets, churches, and asylums. Pryzhov focused his studies on two specific categories of people—"prophets and holy fools," and "hysterics" (Rus. *klikushi*), women believed to be possessed by the devil or evil forces who had the capacity to bring (or "call," from the verb *klikat'*) misfortune upon others. Pryzhov's writings are lively and witty, but he takes a decidedly utilitarian view of holy fooling (Rus. *iurodstvo*) as a calculated way for the marginalized to make a living. This conclusion is underscored by Pryzhov's frequent use of the verb "to holy fool" (Rus. *iurodstvovat'*), which frames the solicitation of alms and playing the fool as a profession. Indeed, Pryzhov's *Nishchie na Sviatoi Rusi* (The Destitute in Holy Russia), originally published in 1862, was intended as an exposé of what he considered the deceitful nature of most begging; he sought to deter his fellow Muscovites from offering the casual dole (Lindenmeyr 1996:137). However, the level of detail provided by Pryzhov as to the personal histories of the holy fools and their participation in social life gives a general sense of social attitudes toward difference and disability in the Russian Empire.

In Pryzhov's work a common theme is the continued association of the iurodivye with the Orthodox Church. This relationship was formalized in some instances, as in the case of Danilushka Kolomenskyi (Danila from Kolomna), who was mentored by the leadership of his local church from an early age (Pryzhov 1996:45–48). In turn, Danila contributed his earnings from begging to the church for projects such as building bell towers and painting icons. Pryzhov (1996:48–49) describes women iurodivye who wore garb approximating that of nuns and priests (black bell-shaped robes with a sash, and black scarves or caps), and who were paid by many Muscovite families for their prayers and participation in weddings, funerals, and other religious services. Like these women, many of the iurodivye were only unofficially and rather ambiguously tied to the Orthodox Church—church officials often did not recognize them as religious or holy figures, and the iurodivye frequently engaged in practices such as "telling" (predicting the future) and curing that were not sanctioned by the church. There were notable exceptions, however, and today the Russian Orthodox Church recognizes 36 iurodivye saints, or "fools for Christ." Perhaps the most well known of these is St. Vasilii Blazhennyi, who lived in the sixteenth century, and for whom the famous St. Basil's Cathedral in Moscow is named. Overall, prior to the seventeenth century iurodivye were more closely associated with and recognized by the church, but the church began to distance itself from them for theological and political reasons (Iangulova 2001:195–196).

Overall, Pryzhov's descriptions of iurodivye in Moscow paint a picture of these individuals as part of the social fabric, even local celebrities in some cases, who at a minimum were tolerated by fellow Muscovites. Most of the iurodivye profiled by Pryzhov had come to Moscow from small cities and towns in the Russian provinces, and they continued to travel throughout their lives. Traveling was not necessarily a solitary undertaking. For example, in the late 1850s or early 1860s (no date is given), Pryzhov himself participated in a pilgrimage from Moscow to Kyiv, organized and financed by a nun named Mother Matrena Makarevna. The goal of the pilgrimage is not clear, but Pryzhov reports somewhat cynically that, "for the sake of a livelier trip," Makarevna took with her "an entire group of various iurodivye and strange men and women (Rus. *stranniki* and *strannitsy*), people from the poorhouse (Rus. *bogadelki*) and beggars (Rus. *prizhivalki*)." According to Pryzhov, Makarevna began with an entourage of 100, but by the time she reached Kyiv 300 persons accompanied her. The pilgrims were not allowed into Kyiv proper, and instead set up camp in a forest outside the city limits. Pryzhov does not detail further what happened to Makarevna and her companions, but he does indicate that the group collected donations from bystanders during their journey from Moscow to Kyiv.

In Moscow, according to Pryzhov, persons of means, usually merchants, often housed the iurodivye. The iurodivye lived in basements and kitchens and were looked after by the owners' servants. The iurodivye were closely associated with markets, where they solicited alms. Market traders believed that donating to the iurodivye brought them good luck in business, and those iurodivye who were believed to possess powers to predict the future and heal afflictions were particularly venerated. The most colorful example of this homage is found in Pryzhov's description of Ivan Iakovlevich, a famous "prophet" who moved to Moscow after living in the forests outside Smolensk, where he had gained a reputation for predicting the future. In Moscow he was placed in Preobrazhenskoe hospital-asylum, where he lived until he died. According to Pryzhov the prophet lived in squalid conditions, but this did not deter a constant stream of visitors from near and far, many of them nobility, who paid him for his "seeing" and healing services. Ivan Iakovlevich performed services of prediction via written correspondence with some clients, and some of these exchanges are recorded in Pryzhov's book (1996:36–39). In Pryzhov's description, Ivan Iakovlevich's wake and funeral were attended by huge crowds, and some mourners gathered up his personal effects and even "sand" and "liquids" from his very coffin as valuable relics, which were subsequently sold for ever-increasing sums (1996:41–42).

Like Pryzhov's, most of the scant studies of issues related to disability in the eighteenth to early twentieth century Russian Empire focus on holy fools and other wanderers (blind minstrels, for example), but little is known about the lives of physically disabled persons or those sensory disabled people other than the blind. Contributing to this lacuna is the fact that, outside asylums, the military, and a few special schools for the disabled, there was no real consistent and formalized structure for defining and assessing disability; disability was not part of public discourse, and we have few traces of disability experience, social attitudes toward disabled persons, or institutional interventions. All this changed when the Bolsheviks came to power.

## Disability and Governmentality in the Early Soviet Period

If ubogi and iurodivye were labels most commonly used to denote persons thought to be mentally disabled, during the nineteenth century the term "invalid" emerged to describe the physically disabled. In the tsarist period, invalid was used primarily in reference to the military and soldiers, and it did not necessarily carry the negative connotation of one who is "less" or, literally, "in-valid" (Hartblay 2006:49–50). Indeed, in his comprehensive dictionary of Russian compiled in the 1800s, Vladimir Dal defined "invalid" as "one who served, revered warrior; unable to serve because of wounds or physical damage—worn out one."[1]

However, with the Bolshevik Revolution and the establishment of the Soviet state and a formal system of classification and administration of disability, the meaning of "invalid" changed to designate those Soviet citizens who had lost the capacity to work. The definition of disability, or *invalidnost'* (Rus.), as loss of labor capacity was a cornerstone of disability policy in the workers' state of the Soviet Union (Madison 1989), where citizens were required to engage in paid labor as a "socially useful activity."[2] The citizen's social utility was measured in terms of potential role in production, and level of disability was assessed according to a scale of labor potential. Therefore, the Soviet state's approach to disability was not really the medicalized, individual, tragic model found in the United States, Great Britain, and elsewhere that was so criticized by disability rights advocates beginning in the 1960s. Rather, the Soviet state employed a functional model of disability, based on a person's perceived "usefulness for society."

The emphasis on labor capacity as the primary criterion for applying the label of invalid to Soviet citizens was reflected in some of the first legal discussions to appear on the heels of the Bolshevik Revolution in 1917. November 1917, for example, saw the publication of a legal directive about the inclusion of all types of loss of work capacity in the state program of social insurance. (There was a pre-Soviet precedent here, since the first attempt to address the concerns of workers facing disability was initiated in the Russian Empire in 1903 with the passage of a law introducing workplace insurance for those injured on the job (Iarskaia-Smirnova and Romanov, eds., 2002:322)). The Statute on Social Protection of Workers, which guaranteed state assistance to those unable to support themselves due to loss of labor capacity, followed in October 1918.

Early Soviet disability policy was formulated in a context of numerous armed conflicts—World War I and the Russian Civil War both produced significant numbers of disabled veterans—which led to a "hypertrophy" of legislation relating to "war invalids" (Shek 2005:380). Indeed, until the mid-1920s only the war injured could be classified as invalids. Ol'ga Shilova (2005:106–107) notes that, when the fledgling Soviet state extended support to disabled Red Army veterans of the Russian Civil War (1918–1921), emphasis was placed on "restoring" veterans' lost labor capacity in order to return them to the workforce. They were offered housing and vocational training in shelters, schools, workshops, and "homes for invalids."

Beginning as early as 1918 the Bolshevik government sorted invalids into two broad categories: those who could work or who possessed the potential to return to the labor force eventually; and those "total invalids" who could not (Shilova 2005:107–108). This focus was solidified further in 1921 when invalids' homes were reorganized and designed to accommodate citizens based not primarily on cause or type of disability, but according to their level of work capacity (Shilova 2005:114). Institutions to house the disabled included three main types: those for persons who had total loss of labor capacity and required constant care (these institutions had a medically focused mandate); those for invalids who had lost most labor capacity but could be trained to do light, irregular work "for themselves and for the institution"; and institutions for "supplementary social support" (Rus. *dopolnitel'nogo sotsial'nogo obespecheniia*) for those whose partial loss of labor capacity left them unable to make an independent living. Residents of the latter type of institution were required to work in specialized workshops and factories. Tellingly, a fourth type of invalids' home was developed: "exemplary institutions" (Rus. *pokazatel'nye uchrezhdenii*), exceptional facilities that presumably were used to showcase best practices (Shilova 2005:114).

In 1932 a disability classification was introduced that divided invalids *[kind of one-size-fits-all]* into three groups based primarily on a calculation of degree of ability to work. These categories are still used to designate disability status in present-day Ukraine and Russia. Group I includes those considered unable to work and deemed to require constant nursing care; group II includes those not perceived to require constant nursing care who have lost some capability to work but may work in special conditions; people in group III are considered the partially disabled who have lost some work capability but may engage in part-time or casual work (Madison 1989:171–172).

Whereas before 1932 doctors conducting examinations of those seeking disability status were required to assess level of disability and the amount of labor capacity the candidate had lost, the new regulations required doctors to determine the candidate's *remaining* labor capacity (Fieseler 2006). *[even this language treats it like a precious resource]* If in 1941 work was conceded as a "right" for disabled persons, subsequent regulations posited work as a "duty" and, later, a "compulsory measure" (Fieseler 2006). In this context, being deemed unable to work (Rus. *nerabotosposobnyi*, Ukr. *nepratsezdatnyi*) had negative consequences and conferred on the individual a standard set of presumed negative qualities: social (exiles), psychological (loners fixated on their personal misfortune), work-related (low-qualified workers of limited skill and intellect), and economic (dependents, pensioners). Indeed, the *Comprehensive*

*[aren't these all self-fulfilling prophecies?]*

*Ukrainian-English Dictionary* defines *nepratsezdatnist'* as "disablement, disability, incapacity to work" (Popov and Balla 2005:327).

In a system that is still in place in present-day Russia and Ukraine, in the Soviet Union those categorized as invalids and their dependents were offered several types of material support: pensions for those no longer working due to disability, pensions for survivors of deceased invalids, pension supplements for dependents of unable-to-work individuals, and a range of entitlements such as reduced utility expenses and rent, free or discounted public transportation, and the free provision of technical equipment (e.g., wheelchairs, crutches, hearing aids, specialized vehicles). Pensions were designed to compensate for wages lost, rather than for the physical or mental harm sustained. In general, disability pensions were calculated based on one's disability group, reason for the disability, work history at the onset of disability, and former salary.

*[margin note: slapping a dollar on as a band-aid]*

## "Suffering Victors"

The post–World War II period is important for understanding Soviet approaches to assessing, regulating, and compensating for disability, because it was during this time that many of the state's disability policies were formulated and refined. During the late 1920s and 1930s, two main groups constituted the bulk of the population considered invalids: the elderly, and disabled veterans of World War I and the Russian Civil War. With the huge numbers of war wounded during World War II (1941–1945, called the Great Patriotic War in the former Soviet Union), the ranks of invalids in the Soviet Union grew rapidly.

Under Stalin, the Soviet state's approach to dealing with citizens disabled during the war was guided by two main ideas. First, it was thought imperative to provide adequate support to war invalids, in part to placate them and prevent them from rebelling against the government, as had disabled veterans of the war of 1812. Indeed, the World War II–wounded returning from the front sometimes were called "neo-Decembrists," in reference to the Decembrist uprising of 1826 (Tchueva 2008:96). At the same time, however, in Stalin's trend of silencing or denying any negative aspects of the war, images of war invalids were excluded from the official interpretations of the war experience and representations of postwar life. The war wounded—many of them amputees in wheelchairs, who colloquially were called "samovars" (Lev Gudkov [2005:4] explains that they seemed like "human stumps on little wheels")—were a grim and "superfluous" reminder to the populace of the inhumane traumas of war. As Gudkov

*[margin notes: of ; purity! ; does NY advertise its homeless population?]*

writes, "The invalids in the postwar period . . . were left to the mercy of fate, people were ashamed of them, turned away from them, hid them with an unpleasant feeling of guilt and a sense of the ugliness of life—everything was done to keep them out of the official [festive] picture of peace-time life." These dynamics are important because they show how the war wounded, especially when labeled as disillusioned "neo-Decembrists," were somehow excluded from the widespread sense of Soviet citizenship that the war otherwise engendered as a huge (Soviet) nationalist project.

This dual approach to addressing disability—the provision of state support for the material needs of the disabled, but within a culture of stigma and social isolation—was to characterize Soviet disability policy throughout most of the twentieth century. Because the problem of war invalids was a taboo subject, official statistics were scant, and the existing Soviet-era statistics are highly questionable. As a result, we do not know how many disabled war veterans were living in the Soviet Union after the war. Beate Fieseler (2006:46–47) provides a conservative estimate of nearly 2.6 million, or 7.46 percent of the Soviet Army's 34.5 million, but she concedes that the true number of disabled veterans must have been significantly higher, since Soviet authorities were reluctant to grant invalid status to wounded soldiers.

In the early 1940s, with disabled veterans already returning from the front, a series of resolutions were passed providing benefits to war invalids. The earliest of these concentrated on specialized vocational training, job placement, education, and housing. Disabled veterans were trained as clerks, accountants, photographers, beekeepers, cobblers, carpenters, and cheesemakers, and were taught skills such as basketmaking and watch repair. Although the Soviet state advertised these efforts as evidence of its beneficence toward wounded veterans, immediately after the war only a fraction of war invalids could take advantage of this training. In Saratov oblast' in 1945, for example, there were more than 30,000 World War II invalids registered. Of these, only around 1,500 received vocational training (Tchueva 2008:105).

The state's priority was not so much to physically rehabilitate the war disabled *per se* as to facilitate as robust a workforce as possible during the traumatic war and postwar periods. Within the Soviet ideology of modernization and industrialization, all citizens, including the disabled, were viewed as a potential labor resource. In this context, many war veterans who were significantly disabled nevertheless were denied disability status and thus required to work, or were assigned to group III, the category of least severity. As Mark Edele (2008:82) notes, "One of the basic functions of the labour-medical boards (VTEK) in the postwar years was to classify as many invalids as possible as 'third group' because the incentives to go back to work were highest there." As a result, less than 2 percent of non-officer war invalids in Russia received group I status, while 68 percent were assigned to group III and thus considered work-ready (Edele 2008:82). This is despite the fact that retraining efforts were unsatisfactory and technical interventions underdeveloped (Fieseler 2006:48–49).

In step with the state's emphasis on labor capacity as the essence of disability policy, during World War II institutions for the war disabled were divided into two main types: work institutions (Rus. *trudovye internaty*), and hospital-type institutions (Rus. *internaty bol'nichnogo tipa;* Shilova 2005:123). The work institutions were nominally set up as work cooperatives for disabled veterans, most of them group III invalids. Yet although these veterans were supposed to have privileged access to employment there, by the end of the 1940s they still made up only 26 percent of all workers in such work institutions (Edele 2008:88). Conditions there were deplorable, and usually no special accommodations were made for the needs of disabled workers. Not surprisingly, "invalids fled these establishments in great numbers," with departures reaching between 60 and 80 percent in some cases (Edele 2008:89). Conditions in hospital-type institutions were no better.

Beate Fieseler's (2006:51–52) research has shown that disabled veterans' mobilization into the labor force frequently came at the expense of their previous professional and social status, since invalids inevitably were assigned low-skilled and poorly paid work. A coordinated effort was made to channel the war disabled into production work, and disabled workers were monitored and assessed for improvements in health and signs that they were "adapting" to the new work conditions. Thus, notes Fieseler (2006:47), "the participation in productive work was considered not merely an effective remedy, but a main tool of rehabilitation."

Tchueva (2008:106) further interprets this push to reintegrate disabled workers into the labor force as a reflection of the important mediating and surveillance functions the workplace played in the Soviet Union:

> Work, and more precisely, the Soviet enterprise, was the primary agent of social politics in the USSR, being a key channel of distribution and a powerful means of control. As a result, for the state, unemployment represented an undesirable complication in procedures of control of the citizen, and for the citizen it meant lack of access to channels of distribution of resources.

Tchueva's analysis adds to our understanding of the Soviet functional approach: not only did the state emphasize vocational training and employment of the disabled in order to maintain a strong workforce; the policy was enacted to save resources and maintain social control. After all, labor in specialized schools and workshops was the primary channel through which disabled citizens received the Soviet socialist ideological indoctrination (Shek 2005:391).

Another cornerstone of Soviet disability policy that solidified during the war period was the provision of disability pensions. In 1944 a resolution was passed providing pensions to disabled veterans of all ranks (Tchueva 2008:97). Disability pensions and other entitlements for veterans were differentiated along three planes: one's salary before being mobilized, military rank, and disability group (degree of disability). This support was chronically inadequate—the pensions paid to group I invalids were not enough to live on, and those in groups II and III received even less—and being an invalid quickly became synonymous with impoverishment. Disheveled war veterans soliciting alms and seeking to sell their own meager possessions at train stations, markets, and street corners were common after the war, visible if unwelcome evidence that disabled veterans were deprived, "suffering victors" (Fieseler 2005).

The war wounded also were offered early retirement, expedited access to housing and health trips, specialized medical care, and other benefits (Madison 1989:185–188). Veterans' hospitals were established, but, particularly in the early postwar years, the number of beds was inadequate and conditions were sub-par (Tchueva 2008:104–105). Furthermore, medical services offered to disabled veterans primarily focused on the provision of prosthetic limbs and wheelchairs, which were antiquated in design and in short supply (Fieseler 2006:54; Tchueva 2008:104). Fieseler (2006:57) describes the Soviet state's approach as "the singling out of a few invalids who, styled as heroes of both war and labour, were the recipients of exemplary care and support."

The Soviet approach privileged the physical manifestations of disability—and the use of techno-medical interventions to address them—over considerations of the psychological trauma of war. In her study of literature in the late-war and immediate postwar Soviet Union (1944–1946), Anna Krylova (2001:316) notes that "[c]ircumscribed within the limits of a physiological paradigm, the [Communist] Party press presented the war legacy as readily remedied by means of reconstructive surgery and high-quality false limbs." Likewise rooted in material explanations for psychological disorders, Soviet psychiatry also located war-related mental trauma

in the sufferer's body and sought physiological bases for veterans' psychological problems. In this context, Soviet writers were assigned the role of
"healers of wounded souls" of the war disabled. Writers such as Aleksei
Tolstoi, Wanda Wasilewskaia, and Nikolai Pogodin produced newspaper
articles, novels, plays, and poetry that constituted what Krylova (2001:321)
calls a "Soviet healing literature."[3]

It is important to bear in mind that in the Soviet ideology stories of
pain, suffering, and disability had to be presented exclusively in the framework of dialectical materialism. Discursively there was simply no room
for dealing with issues of disability, difference, or any type of "abnormal-
ity," and chronic conditions could not be publicly integrated into a larger
normative whole. Thus, the communist ideology could publicly (in representation and policy) account for disability only through a narrative of
"overcoming." In this context the entire Soviet population was rendered
complicit in hiding these problems. This is the history that makes possible contemporary negative public narratives about disability and the
disabled.

In the postwar Soviet press and literature, those invalids who were able
to "overcome" the traumas of war and "rise above" their physical disabilities were glorified as heroes, while the voices of others disabled by war
were not represented (Krylova 2001:316). Examples include the canoniza-
tion in fiction of war heroes such as the fictional Colonel Voropaev (the
semi-autobiographical creation of Petr Pavlenko [1950]) and the real-life
combat pilot Aleksei Mares'ev who appears in Boris Polevoi's 1946 novel *A
Story about A Real Man*, both of whom were amputees (Dunham 1989:152–
153). The wounded but persevering soldier also figured in postwar film as
a "sign of the times, symbolizing the consequences of war, the devastation
with which [citizens] must continue to endure, and which [they] must
overcome" (Romanov and Iarskaia-Smirnova, forthcoming).

In this heroic genre of film and literature the prewar cult of exceptional
invalids was revived. One example is the resurrection of the story of Pavka
Korchagin, the protagonist of Nikolai Ostrovskii's semi-autobiographical novel *How the Steel Was Tempered* (1932), a work that literary and
film scholar Lilya Kaganovsky (2008:11) calls "*the* model socialist realist
text." Korchagin, who "ends his life in bed, blind and paralyzed" (Krylova
2001:316) was invoked by the newspaper *Pravda* as an example for the
country's invalids of how to overcome war trauma. In her book *How the
Soviet Man Was Unmade* (2008:3–5), Kaganovsky points out that, ironically, although in early Soviet and high Stalinist culture the iconic or ideal
man embodied "the figure of virile, undamaged masculinity," nevertheless

"socialist realist novels and films of that [Stalinist] period surprisingly often rely on the figure of the wounded or mutilated male body to represent the New Soviet Man." Kaganovsky argues that the damaged male body was fetishized as a model of exemplary masculinity; in the "Stalinist fantasy of masculinity" the model New Soviet Man is turned into a heroic invalid. Korchagin, a young soldier who sustains one bodily injury after another, Kaganovsky argues (2008:23–25), radically embodies "the 'bodily obligation' of the New Soviet Man" and "bodily sacrifice for the Soviet cause." Korchagin was the model Soviet subject, since he literally risks life and limb and incurs repeated physical traumas to work for the Party.

Indeed, Korchagin's gradual bodily dismemberment parallels his rise through the bureaucratic ranks, as each wound he sustains earns him a new, higher position (Kaganovsky 2008:22). Kaganovsky points out that much of Korchagin's story is structured by the logic of observation and surveillance; institutions of the state predominate the networks in which he is embedded (pp. 28–29). Korchagin internalizes the state's watchful eye to become a disciplined subject. Faced with an inability to fight, he contemplates suicide but in the end decides not to end his own life. Writes Ostrovskii, as Pavka: "Learn how to go on living when life becomes unbearable. Make it useful" (p. 33). Pavka does so by writing a novel based on his life, as did his very creator, Nikolai Ostrovskii. The themes of surveillance and self-discipline are key to the text's socialist realist message.

Here we should underscore the male-centric nature of Soviet disability discourse, a bias that grew out of the postwar context of a proliferation of disabled veterans—who were predominantly men—but was also tied to the Soviet national project. In literature and film, whatever role the disabled, in-valid body played, whether itself as a symbol of exemplary masculinity or as a foil for the supremacy of the "real Soviet man," it was always a male body under scrutiny. As Iarskaia-Smirnova and Romanov (2009) note: "Not until *perestroika* [Gorbachev's program of "restructuring"] did children and women with disabilities even appear on the screen. They simply did not fit into the frame of the Soviet political-aesthetic project with its characteristic heroism of war and work."

Even if, as Kaganovsky argues, the male invalid with his damaged body was fetishized as representative of Stalinist masculinity, and a few disabled war heroes were glorified in Soviet literature, the press, and state propaganda, the vast majority of war invalids were isolated and left to "heal" in private spaces such as the home, or institutions. Indeed, Kaganovsky (2008:173) concludes that the glorification of maimed invalids was primarily in the realm of rhetoric and fantasy, and "Stalinist ideology was never able to tolerate for very long the presence of actual invalids on the streets of its major cities." In a context where one's usefulness and productivity were key for inclusion as *bona fide* citizens, she writes, "The challenge of the maimed or 'non-able-bodied' individuals in Soviet society was to prove their ongoing usefulness to the Soviet state, while the consequences of disenfranchisement ranged from the everyday—restriction or denial of housing, taking away of ration cards, loss of medical care and access to education—to the severe: deportation, arrest, and forced labor" (p. 174).

This phenomenon is indicative of another important characteristic of Soviet disability policy just after World War II: the state continually shifted the burden of supporting disabled persons to local government structures and social support networks, including the *kolkhoz* (collective farm) and the family (Tchueva 2008:103), women in particular. Edele (2008:98) found that group I disabled war veterans' "social standing depended largely on the income of the other family members, as they could only contribute an insufficient pension." Indeed, Krylova (2001:325) describes how, as revealed in the postwar Soviet literature, the private sphere was demarcated as the "healing place" for the war wounded, with women (usually wives and mothers) assigned the role of "social therapists of traumatized male souls."

This was problematic, since not all disabled veterans enjoyed family support structures, and the drastic hardships of the postwar period necessitated multiple interventions. Fieseler (2006) notes that, for a time, the tsarist-period tradition of philanthropy was revived in Soviet cities and towns, where citizens were called upon to give charitable donations in support of the needy, many of them war invalids. But, more often than not, this supposed "volunteerism" was initiated not at the grassroots, but through local Communist Party structures, the Komsomol (Communist Youth Organization), and the trade unions, and was therefore a deeply duplicitous practice. Group III disabled veterans fared somewhat better, since they often could combine their small disability pension with paid work; however, the latter tended to be unofficial and also illegal (Edele 2008:99).

There was an even more disturbing side to Soviet policy vis-à-vis disabled veterans, whose continuing need for more support was unwelcome evidence of the Soviet state's inability or unwillingness to adequately provide for all citizens' needs. During the late 1940s and 1950s disabled veterans were dispersed from Moscow and other large cities for forced resettlement in remote areas. In Soviet discourse the "social parasite" or *tuneiadets* (Rus.) was one who refused to do socially useful labor and lived off the work of others. According to Fieseler (2006:51), kolkhoz supervisors in rural areas, in order to shed inefficient disabled workers, sometimes turned them in as parasites; such workers were then deported, presumably to labor camps. Penal camps were established in the Soviet Union for disabled prisoners and disabled veterans of the Russian Civil War and the two world wars. The most infamous of these is the Spasskaia labor colony near Karaganda, Kazakhstan, to which 15,000 disabled prisoners were sent in the late 1940s and early 1950s (Solzhenitsyn 1985). Similarly, disabled World War II veterans were secretly exiled from Leningrad (now Saint Petersburg) and Leningrad oblast' to the Valaam archipelago, in the Republic of Karelia (Russian Federation). Valaam and the fate of those veterans are still shrouded in mystery (Fefelov 1986:51–57).

## "All Invalids are Not Created Equal": Disability and Differentiation

An important characteristic of Soviet approaches to disability classification and compensation was the principle of differentiation. Disability benefits for various categories of invalids—whether based on age at onset of disability, cause of disability, extent of disability, or other criteria—were measured and allocated according to different scales.[4] As discussed above, within disability groupings/categories such as disabled veterans, pensions were differentiated according to certain criteria such as pre-disability salary, military rank, and so on. Similarly, members of some disability categories—in particular persons disabled by war and those disabled on the job—were entitled to more privileges than others. These categories also were accorded a privileged place in official discourse. In official post–World War II propaganda, for example, the issue of disability figured only as related to disabled veterans and persons disabled on the job, who were singled out and praised for their service to the country (Shek 2005:382). Of course, as we have seen, the state's stance was more than hypocritical, since the real assistance offered to most disabled veterans was wholly inadequate and only begrudgingly granted.

According to the Soviet functional approach, which privileged work capacity as the primary criterion for citizenship, some disabled persons were deemed less "useful" for society (disabled children, and the intellectually and mentally disabled, for example), and thus were offered fewer entitlements (Iarskaia-Smirnova and Romanov, eds., 2002:203). In fact, the Soviet state's reliance on work capacity as the sole criterion of disability status meant that congenitally disabled children were excluded from the ranks of invalids and the concomitant benefits and entitlements (Shek 2005:386). Not until 1967 was all-Union legislation adopted providing benefits to disabled children, and the term "child-invalids" (Rus. *deti-invalidy*) emerged only in 1979 after the United Nations declared that year the International Year of the Child.

The Soviet functional approach resulted in a hierarchical ranking of invalids, a situation colorfully described by Lev Indolev, a journalist and key figure in the Russian disability rights movement. Although Indolev (2001:147) was writing about post-Soviet Russia, the roots of the differentiation he describes lie in the Soviet period:

> All invalids are not created equal (Rus. *invalid—invalidu rozn'*). . . . At the head of the line stand the all-important invalids of World War II. Behind them we find other invalids of military conflict who have similar entitlements, starting with participants in squelching anticommunist protests in Hungary and Czechoslovakia, and ending with those wounded in Afghanistan and Chechnya. Further back [in the line] are invalids of military service, the Ministry of Internal Affairs, the KGB and other "forces." Then invalids of the workplace and those injured "at the hands of others" get their turn. Those accident victims (Rus. *bytoviki*) who are themselves at fault come in last, along with the congenitally disabled, who have no one at all to blame.

This ranking of disability categories caused friction between members of different disability groups, who found unfair the privileging of some groups and some types of disabilities over others. This official categorization produced a pronounced demarcation between disability groups, and persons who were differently disabled (e.g., the blind, deaf, and mobility disabled) did not for the most part develop a shared disability consciousness across the disability spectrum. (This phenomenon is found in other countries as well, including the United States.) This lack of common identity was compounded by the competition that the state's strategy of differentiation engendered between groups and individuals. Categories such as disabled veterans were entitled to "extras" such as a specialized car free or at discount; the right to purchase furniture, carpets, televisions and other scarce goods without waiting in line; and numerous subsidies for telephone and rent. It is true that with time the status of war invalids as deserving of special entitlements was solidified in legislation, up through the 1970s (Edele 2008:87). Even so, these privileges were not always delivered, and even these special categories of the disabled generally remained severely impoverished. By no means did the promises of considerable benefits and entitlements for disabled people on paper mean that these promises necessarily were fulfilled.

The Soviet state choked off or carefully regulated potential outlets of collective consciousness and protest. For instance, for a time after World War II small cafés and bars known colloquially as Blue Danubes served as gathering places and points of information exchange for war veterans, including the war disabled, but these establishments were shut down by state authorities in 1948 (Fieseler 2006). The state may also have deployed the aforementioned strategies of differentiation as a way to foment competition and resentment between groups, to prevent collective consciousness and collective action against the state.

*[handwritten marginal note: prevents from forming organized grp]*

Indeed, in her study of the claims or complaints (Rus. *zhaloby*) that disabled war veterans in Saratov (RSFSR) sent to newspapers and local authorities, Ekaterina Tchueva (2008:100–101) notes that such claims were very individualized. The complaints were rooted in the claimants' own life experiences and perceived needs, rather than in a sense of group identity and collective rights of war invalids. Tchueva argues that the "individualization" of claims, which continued until the period of thaw under Khrushchev (beginning in the mid-1950s), indicates that the state successfully preempted the development of a disability consciousness among disabled World War II veterans, a conclusion that could readily be extended to other disability groups in the Soviet Union. At the same time, a key function of the state's strategy of differentiation and classification was the very grouping of persons who were similarly disabled in order to provide them with specific services, including housing.

## Separate and Unequal: Institutionalization and Education

In the Soviet Union, it was common for disabled citizens to be placed in specialized residence institutions called *doma-internaty,* or "home-internaty," and the internat system is still firmly in place in the region.[5] Historically there have been four main types of internaty: those for the elderly and disabled; for the disabled only; for "veterans of work" with especially long and revered work histories; and for persons diagnosed with psychoneurological problems. Additionally, internaty for disabled children serve such children until age 16–18, at which time usually they are transferred to internaty for adults. The number of disabled people living in institutions constantly grew: from 22,000 in 1926 to 60,000 in 1940 and 158,000 by the end of the 1960s (Iarskaia-Smirnova and Romanov 2009). In 1979, there were 1,500 internaty for the elderly and disabled in the Soviet Union, and a network of internaty stretched across the vast territory of the USSR. According to the available Soviet statistics, in 1979 internaty accommodated 360,000 persons, but it is not known how many residents were elderly, disabled, or both (Madison 1989:180). The stated goals of the internaty are as follows: material and practical support of residents and the provision of good, "home-like" living conditions; organized care for residents, including medical care; and measures to ensure their social and vocational rehabilitation (Iarskaia-Smirnova and Romanov, eds., 2002:325). In general, internaty are total institutions, functioning as "medico-social institutions intended for permanent residence of the elderly and disabled who require constant practical and medical assistance" (ibid.).

Although alternative strategies for organizing rehabilitation and delivering needed services were explored in the Soviet Union, the home-internat model became the standard. As detailed above, internaty for disabled veterans and the elderly were established beginning in the 1920s and continued throughout the post–World War II years. In the context of the Cold War, in the late 1950s and 1960s the system of internaty to house disabled children and adults grew exponentially. Ol'ga Shek (2005:383) attributes this push for institutionalization to two main factors: a perceived need to enhance the perception of the Soviet state as a beneficent force that provided for the basic needs of all its citizens; and the desire to remove from view those elements that could blemish the carefully constructed picture of the Soviet Union as a "healthy nation" free from social problems. Similar cleansing was done in the United States starting in the 1860s via unsightly beggar ordinances in major cities, the so-called "ugly laws" (Schweik 2009).

Care in internaty was framed as a right accorded to vulnerable citizens by the generous Soviet state, and the collective care of disabled persons in institutions designed especially for that purpose was considered optimal for their quality of life. At the same time, placement in internaty could also be a punitive measure. For example, the elderly or disabled who came under suspicion of the Soviet administration for "disrupting social norms" (e.g., begging or "wandering about" without permanent residence) were often forcibly placed in internaty (Iarskaia-Smirnova and Romanov, eds., 2002:325). Anne White (1999:32) correlates Soviet internaty with prisons and labor camps. She writes: "Homes were regarded by many administrators as closed institutions, with frequent searches and confiscations of property, and residents' letters to one another compared the regime to that of a prison." White also notes that at least one internat was sited in a former labor camp.

Stephen Dunn and Ethel Dunn (1989:209) observed that medical treat-  *encourages*
ment services often were hard to access for persons who refused to be per-  *removal from*
manently institutionalized. Clearly, the state strongly controlled institu-  *public sphere*
tionalizing procedures, but families also played a role. Families of disabled
persons, and parents of disabled children in particular, were forcefully
urged by medical personnel, social workers, and other representatives of
the state to place such persons in institutions, where specialized services
for them were concentrated. Lacking reasonable alternatives and having
no community-based services to draw on, families often had little choice.

*Special Education*

The Soviet system of institutionalization of the disabled was closely
linked to the philosophy and practice of special education. If the education of disabled children was the purview of social elites in the nineteenth-
century Russian Empire, approaches to special education began to change
in the early 1900s, when specialized medico-pedagogical approaches to
educating exceptional children emerged from the work of intellectuals
such as V. P. Kashchenko, I. V. Maliarevskii, A. S. Griboedov, and G. I.
Rossolimo. Special education during this period was based on the philosophy of curative pedagogy (Rus. *lechebnaia pedagogika*), which received
much inspiration from the specifically medicalized form of special education (Heilpädagogik) developed in the later half of the nineteenth century in Germany (McCagg 1989:46–49). However, Iarskaia-Smirnova and
Romanov (eds., 2002:370) argue that the curative pedagogy of Kashchenko
and his colleagues privileged social and behavioral aspects of development over the medicalized interventions and diagnoses that dominated
the German variant.

After the Bolshevik Revolution and the founding of the Soviet Union,
where private and religious-based philanthropy were, with a few exceptions during wartime and other crises, forbidden, special education
became the purview of the state. Although an outline for special education was developed in 1914, the infrastructure for developing this system
was put in place only in the 1930s (Iarskaia-Smirnova and Romanov, eds.,
2002:369). It was not until the 1960s that adequate state financing was provided for residential school-internaty for disabled children, which until
then had been in the hands of largely uninterested local administrations.
The Soviet system of general education was highly standardized via curricula that did not take into account the needs of exceptional children,
whose instruction was undertaken separately from other children.

Special education was formulated according to the science of defectology, which included elements of disciplines such as pedagogy, psychology, and medicine. Defectology is based on the influential work of L. S. Vygotsky and his concept of the "deficient child" (Iarskaia-Smirnova and Romanov 2007:91), but Vygotsky's ideas, which privileged an integrated and comprehensive approach to physiological, psychological, and social aspects of children's education, were reduced in Soviet defectology to the medical and psychological. Therefore, the more humanistic and holistic "curative pedagogy" of earlier years was replaced by the medicalized defectology, a system notable for the high degree of differentiation, categorization, and stratification. As Kate Thomson (2002:35) describes, "Categorization of children was rooted in an essentially clinical and pathological understanding of the nature of learning difficulties." This reductionism "facilitated the medicalization of special education discourse, turning it into a pedagogy for defective, anomalous, sick children in need of correction" (Iarskaia-Smirnova and Romanov, eds., 2002:371).

As noted by Andrew Sutton (1988), who evaluated the Soviet system of special education rather positively during the late 1980s, in the Soviet Union special schools were provided for the deaf, the hard-of-hearing, the blind, those with visual problems, and the mobility disabled, as well as children with scoliosis, heart conditions and rheumatism, a range of cognitive disabilities, and others. Sutton notes that "the system provides clear limits for what is possible in curricular terms" and that some categories of children who in the West would be offered special education programs (the severely mentally disabled, children with multiple disabilities, children with severe problems of movement or continence, and children with diagnoses such as autism) were considered uneducable and therefore were excluded from the Soviet special education system (1988:78–79).[6] As Sutton (1988:79) writes:

> Thus the social role of the Minpros [Ministry of Education] special-education system is not to provide education for all, however handicapped, adapted to the needs of the individual child, however deviant or limited. Rather it is to provide a common training, education and socialization to everyone in the younger generation who could conceivably benefit, leaving the residuum to be catered for elsewhere.

This "elsewhere" might be an institution where only basic, practical instruction was offered, or, more rarely, the child could be left in the care of the family without any state-provided special education.

## School-Internaty

The state—and particularly representatives of the medical establish-ment—put intense pressure on parents of disabled children to place them in internaty, most of which offered residential special education pro-grams. During interviews with parents of disabled children in post-Soviet Ukraine, I was frequently told of their struggles to resist institutionaliza-tion of their children during and after the Soviet period. In the absence of available resources to assist parents in caring for their children in the home setting, many parents indeed were compelled to place these chil-dren in internaty, and some did evaluate the system as beneficial. Those who refused often were criticized, since the choice to raise an exceptional child in the home was seen by many medical professionals, social workers, and the general public as irresponsible and unwise. As Mykola Swarnyk (2005:1), a founder of the parents' movement in Ukraine whose son has cerebral palsy, explains: "We all had rights on paper, but the [Soviet] state, where everyone was happy and was joyfully building communism, did not foresee special needs. Therefore, for these [disabled] children they built internaty outside of towns, which many consider a perfectly normal, rational way to deal with the problem of disability." [*removal from social space*]

The conditions in internaty for disabled children varied dramatically, and persons who lived in Soviet internaty report some positive assess-ments of their experience but also voice pointed critiques. There were some exemplary internaty with exceptional staff whose achievements in educating disabled young people were truly remarkable, given the limi-tations of the Soviet model. One such institution was the Tsiurupyns'kyi school-internat in Khersons'ka oblast of the Ukrainian SSR. Ihor Rasiuk, a man with cerebral palsy who lived at Tsiurupyns'kyi beginning in the mid-1970s, provides valuable firsthand accounts of life there (Rasiuk 2002a, 2002b).

The Tsiurupyns'kyi school-internat was founded in 1968, and it housed 200 children with group I disability status. As was typical, the internat was built "in the middle of a desert, far from human eyes," but within ten years the staff and students had turned the grounds into a green space (Rasiuk 2002a:24). Rasiuk praises the dedication of the teaching staff and notes that Tsiurupyns'kyi was unique for the emphasis placed on really educating dis-abled children, rather than "treating" or "healing" them. Despite a high student-teacher ratio (each group of 20 to 25 students worked with just two teachers), a surprisingly high number of Tsiurupyns'kyi's students enrolled in institutions of higher education—around 60 percent in the 1980s. This is remarkable given that in the USSR apparently there was a secret directive of the Ministry of Education that blocked significantly disabled persons (i.e., members of group I) from higher education (ibid.). Rasiuk himself undertook undergraduate and postgraduate study in Ukrainian literature at the National Taras Shevchenko University of Kyiv.

Despite these achievements, which may represent local initiatives that improve on the general institutionalized internat system, Rasiuk is frank about the internat's shortcomings, especially its remote location, which isolated the students and precluded their interaction with "the rest of the world." He writes, "In those [Soviet] times the state tried to hide invalids. When children were taken beyond the confines of the [internat] gates, people wrote angry letters to the director" (Rasiuk 2002b:23). Aware of this problem, the teachers invited guests to visit the internat, took the children on field trips, and sought other ways to facilitate their social interaction.

Nevertheless, Rasiuk concludes, the social isolation of disabled children, even in excellent institutions such as the Tsiurupyns'kyi school-internat, was not the ideal solution. In general, parents rarely visited their children in internaty, and for many students family relations became strained or severed. This made it unlikely that children in internaty would ever leave the system. Rasiuk offers, "Understand me, I am against internaty for invalids (it is a type of reservation); I would prefer that invalids study and live among other people. But today's reality is such that society is not ready to accept invalids, so for now we still need school-internaty" (Rasiuk 2002a:26).

In Rasiuk's writings, his relatively positive assessment of the Tsiurupyns'kyi school-internat diverges markedly from his experiences at the "home-internat for the elderly and disabled" to which he was transferred at the age of 18. In his autobiographical story "Zalyshytysia liudynoiu" (Ukr. "Remaining human"), Rasiuk (2002c) details his first few days at an institution on the edge of Kyiv. Referring to himself as "Iunak," or "the Youth," Rasiuk describes how he was moved to the internat after being refused entrance into a regular school. Upon arrival he was not welcomed by staff, who immediately ushered him into "quarantine," a "room with tiled walls, like a morgue . . . a horrific room devoid of hope" (Rasiuk 2002c:25). Rasiuk goes on to describe the overcrowded, chaotic conditions of the internat, where the elderly and disabled slept in corridors, and sounds of screaming and "barking" emanated from the rooms. Residents lived two to four to a room, with just two aides (Ukr. *sanitarky*) per 32 residents. This was a place, he concludes, not for "living," but for "existing" (Rasiuk 2002c:26).

Ruben Gallego articulates a similarly critical judgment of Soviet inter-naty in his remarkable semi-autobiographical book, *White on Black* (2006).[7] Gallego, who was born with cerebral palsy and grew up in vari-ous internaty in the Russian SSR beginning in the late 1960s, describes the inhuman treatment he and other residents endured—squalid con-ditions, inadequate food, and indifferent attendants. These accounts are barely softened by his memories of warm holidays, and some kind, car-ing attendants, many of them religious "believers" (probably evangelicals). Like Rasiuk, Gallego emphasizes the dramatic contrast between many school-internaty for children and the dreaded "old folks' homes," where "everyone who couldn't walk ended up . . . not for any particular reason, just because" (2006:120).

The assessments of Soviet internaty that Rasiuk and Gallego provide underline shortcomings in the Soviet system of institutionalization—the quality of internaty varied widely, and appropriate provisions were not made for long-term care and housing of disabled youth and young adults who had been educated and brought up in school-internaty. Fur-thermore, the behemoth internat system, which was dependent on the ever-strapped state budget, has proven unable to withstand the economic crises that rocked the former Soviet Union in the 1990s. Tragically, during 1995–1996, 38 children died of hunger and cold at the very "exemplary" Tsiurupyns'kyi school-internat under discussion (Rasiuk 2002b:24). If, as Rasiuk indicates, Tsiurupyns'kyi was a model school-internat, the fate of many other such institutions has undoubtedly been even worse.

Overall, then, the internat system produced mixed effects. In the con-text of the Soviet system of social policy, medicine, and housing, for some the internat arrangement was preferable to the main alternative—life in a family but with few or no community or state resources to draw on. In internaty, disabled citizens were provided with at least basic material and social protection, albeit on the state's terms (Shek 2005:393). Still, residents of Soviet internaty were made to feel guilty for surviving at the expense of the state, and were taught to be grateful for the state's care. When Gal-lego asked one attendant, for example, why he should study if as an invalid he was presumed to be without a future, she replied, "You have to study because you're being fed for free" (Gallego 2006:35).

Former internat residents speak about some of the advantages of living in "invalids' collectives" where a nascent disability culture could flourish, within measure. And it is important to note that the Soviet-era disability rights activism that emerged beginning in the 1960s came out of internaty (see Indolev 1998). This is evidence that, despite their many shortcomings, the internaty had a beneficial if unintended side effect: the close proximity of people with similar experiences, concerns, and grievances allowed a disability rights consciousness to foment. At the same time, however, the tight state control on internaty meant that the rights movements were also squelched there, because the state could easily move people from internat to internat to disrupt social networks (see the case of Gennadii Gus'kov, below). In the end, the social isolation of disabled persons allowed other members of Soviet society to forget about them and "facilitated the production of their second-class citizenship" (Shek 2005:375).

### Education, (Dis)Continued . . .

In the Soviet Union, disabled individuals who sought to further their education beyond the secondary level were compelled either to study in specialized (sometimes residential) vocational or technical schools, or to enroll in training courses designed especially for the disabled. Presumably, the rationale behind this restriction was that persons with severe disabilities would be unlikely to secure work requiring an advanced degree—manual, unskilled labor was deemed more "appropriate" for the disabled—and thus should be prevented from draining resources from the state-funded system of university education. On the surface this seems a paradoxical case of limiting the physically disabled to work that might be more difficult for them to master than, say, intellectual endeavors. However, if one examines the likely biodeterministic assumptions at the base of this practice and policy—that a disabled body must hide or harbor a lesser mind—its disturbing logic becomes clearer.

Obviously, this discriminatory system placed disabled citizens at a disadvantage socially and economically, creating a permanent underclass of invalids. As one informant reflected back on the 1970s and 1980s: "There were very few intellectuals among invalids. We did a survey, and no one on our list was doing intellectual work—they were all blue-collar workers, without any meaningful education." Through great effort and social support, some individuals were able to obtain a higher education at university, but such cases were rare. As Oleg described: "On the basis of personal experience I can say that only the psychological, material, and physical support of my family members allowed me to receive an education in the law faculty of the National Taras Shevchenko University of Kyiv, where the law building has four floors without an elevator" (Poloziuk 2005b:9). Others, I learned in personal interviews, skirted the *de facto* ban on higher education by arranging to have their disability status "reduced" to group

II or III. This made it easier to enter university studies, but with reduced disability benefits, which caused increased financial hardship.

## Rehabilitation and Work

During the years of the New Economic Policy (NEP) (1921–1929), when some restrictions on private enterprise were relaxed, some of the disabled formed several large collectives as a grassroots strategy for economic empowerment. The most well-known, powerful, and long-lasting of these were the All-Russian Association of the Blind (VOS), the All-Russian Organization of the Deaf (VOG), and the All-Russian Production-Consumption Union of Invalids (VIKO, also called the Promkooperatsiia), founded in 1925, 1926, and 1921, respectively. The practice of housing and educating disabled populations in internaty and special schools facilitated this process. Through these societies, which had analogues in other Soviet republics, the labor of disabled persons was consolidated in segregated work collectives called artels or RabFaks (Rus. "work faculties"), which functioned as "enclosed factory-educational facilities" where people who were blind, deaf, or otherwise disabled received training and worked (Burch 2000:396). Promoted as an oasis to protect the disabled from cruelty and prejudice, the artel functioned as a sort of closed mini-city with its own infrastructure, enterprises, and culture. In the VIKO cooperatives, workers produced clothing and other goods and provided services such as shoe repair, hair styling, photography services, and others. By the end of the 1950s, in the Soviet Union there were nearly 220,000 persons working in over 4,000 artels for disabled persons (Indolev 1998:22–26).

Typically, the state administration directed its economic and administrative support to organizations such as artels and did not contribute resources to more open and integrative mechanisms of vocational rehabilitation and employment. Although state enterprises were by law required to reserve 2 percent of work places for disabled workers, the quota was not enforced. VOS and VOG were regulated by the Ministry of Social Services, and thus were subject to Party control. Likewise, VIKO came gradually but increasingly under the authority of the Russian Soviet of Ministers during 1956–1960 as various industrial ministries appropriated the VIKO enterprises, and the organization was eventually liquidated. The reasons for the takeover are still unclear, but it occurred during a time of centralization of economic institutions and the nationalization of organizations of labor, rest, and education. Anne White (1999:45) also notes, "It was claimed that the [VIKO] enterprises were economically inefficient and that the state could deal with all disabled people's problems." It is possible that VIKO was perceived as a threat on several fronts: disabled workers were empowering themselves economically, independent from the state; work cooperatives could contribute to collective consciousness and protest; and the VIKO enterprises put disabled persons in contact with the "healthy" population. In any case, in the Soviet Union after 1960 only the VOS and VOG had large artels.

Although the segregation of disabled workers from the rest of the workforce was a problematic strategy to address unemployment, the benefits should not be overlooked. In a context where integrated employment was considered impossible, and later (1968, see below) was even forbidden, artels provided the disabled the opportunity to make a living and take part in a peer collective. Susan Burch (2000) has detailed the relative advantages the VOG imparted, for example, to deaf and hard-of-hearing Russians. Thanks to the VOG, which enjoyed the approval of Party functionaries, deaf people were able to nurture a deaf culture and improve the social standing of the disabled as highly productive workers.

Disabled people other than the deaf or the blind enjoyed only limited work opportunities after 1960. Manual, unskilled labor was the norm, and sometimes disabled persons were trained for unskilled piecework at home. As one of my informants in Ukraine noted: "Usually, if [the disabled] worked at all, they worked at home, making handicrafts (Ukr. *kustarna robota*), for example. I worked for many years at home myself, making nets and belts. I knew only a few people—one in Georgia, and a couple of guys in Dnipropetrovs'k—who were also wheelchair users and worked regular jobs, outside the home."

Disabled persons who lived in institutions may have been trained and provided with work, depending on the profile of the institution and the individual's disability group. In some cases, a patronage-like relationship existed between internaty for the elderly and disabled and various state enterprises. Soviet work collectives, required by the Law on State Enterprises to contribute to solving social problems, often participated in building internaty; they also provided these institutions with assistance in the form of tangible materials and financing. In turn, residents of internaty were provided "opportunities" and special conditions in which to work for the enterprises. Work for residents of internaty, however, often was sporadic, and at times coercive. In her analysis of written correspondence between internat residents from the 1960s to the 1980s, White (1999:37) reports that "[d]irectors seem sometimes to have regarded residents as slave labour . . . and tried 'come what may to squeeze the last drops of their capacity to labour out of disabled people.'"

If until 1968 internat residents were allowed to pursue work opportunities outside the institution, this right was rescinded that year, a decision apparently made on the basis of "administrative convenience" (White 1999:37). Paradoxically, although vocational retraining and employment for the disabled was a cornerstone of official Soviet discourse, in reality the majority of disabled persons were unemployed, particularly those in groups I and II. By 1988, only about 30 percent of the disabled were employed. Most of the employed were group III invalids, and only approximately one in 35 group I invalids had jobs (White 1999:35).

## Rumblings of Dissent: Soviet-Era Rights Movements

After the state appropriated the artels in the late 1950s, some individuals and nascent groups began to protest Soviet policies toward the disabled. As Lev Indolev told me, "There were a few groups, rather informal, self-made groups, for the most part led by a group of enthusiasts, or even one activist working alone. To varying degrees they were either loyal to the authorities, or aligned themselves with the dissident movements." These activists tended to be mobility-disabled persons who had grown up in state institutions.

Throughout the 1960s, and more vigorously in the 1970s, these individuals agitated for greater rights for the disabled, particularly in the areas of education, housing, and work. Some activists sought to forward their agendas within the framework of the state's focus on labor issues. Gennadii Gus'kov, for example, was a polio survivor who sought in the 1960s and 1970s to found an All-Union Invalids' Society. Working from the internat where he resided in Voronezh (Russian SSR), Gus'kov established a workshop where, he hoped, physically disabled citizens could earn a living for themselves and improve their material and cultural situation. Initially, Gus'kov had some success working with state authorities, but after he began to associate with notorious dissidents, he was put under constant surveillance and was forcibly moved from internat to internat as the state sought to curb his influence (Indolev 1998, White 1999).

Although much of the dissident activity took place in Moscow and other cities in the RSFSR, rumblings of dissatisfaction were audible in other areas of the Soviet Union. Two of the most important sanatoriums for the mobility disabled in the Soviet Union were located in the Ukrainian SSR—in Saki (the Crimea) and Slavinsk (Donets'k oblast')—and these

were major sites of networking and exchange of information and ideas
between persons taking advantage of health trips provided by the Soviet
state. Rights activist Yaroslav Hrybalskyy recalled the following incident
in Saki:

> The dissident movement played a role in disability issues as well. I
> remember an incident from the 1970s—I went to the Crimea regularly,
> to Saki, which was practically the only city where you could get around
> freely in a wheelchair, so Saki was like an entire city of invalids. Just
> then the government was discussing the new Brezhnev Constitution,
> and suddenly all the [wheelchair] ramps (Ukr. and Rus. *pandusy*) were
> removed. We gathered at the sanatorium and wrote a letter to General
> Secretary Leonid Brezhnev: "Dear Leonid Il'ich, please make an excep-
> tion in this city, where many invalids visit," and so on. . . . And later,
> everyone who signed the letter was hounded by the KGB. They ques-
> tioned us, did searches, asked who the initiator was.
> So I'll tell you, in the fight for disability rights, for human rights,
> there were no political motives, no one was seeking a political coup,
> they just wanted favorable conditions—for example so invalids could
> visit some small city in the Soviet Union [like Saki]. But it was inter-
> preted as some kind of insubordination, and those who brought up
> these issues were treated like dissidents. So extreme measures were
> taken against them—they were shut up in special internaty so their pro-
> tests would go no further.

Concerted attempts to mobilize the disabled to political action were
promptly squelched. Iurii Kiselev, for example, founded in 1978 the Action
Group to Defend the Rights of the Disabled in the USSR (Raymond 1989;
White 1999). The group produced a samizdat publication called the Information Bulletin that criticized Soviet disability policy, provided readers
with needed information, and related personal accounts of abuse. Kiselev
was committed to working in opposition to the Soviet state and allied
himself with prominent dissidents such as Andrei Sakharov and members
of the Moscow Helsinki Group, a risky strategy that caused other activists
to distance themselves from him. However, he did have some allies, and
the Action Group announced itself to the world by appealing to several
foreign governments and advocacy organizations.

The group's leadership was hounded by the KGB, especially Valerii
Fefelov and his wife Ol'ga Zaitseva. Associating with the Action Group's
leaders subjected others to similar surveillance. One of my interviewees in

FIGURE 2.1. Anonymous participants in Soviet-era disability rights initiatives. *Photo courtesy of Valentyna.*

Kyiv, Valentyna, remembered meeting Fefelov in the 1970s when he traveled to the Ukrainian Soviet Republic. Authorities learned of their meeting, Valentyna's apartment was searched, and she was warned by KGB agents to cut off all ties with Fefelov and his colleagues. She did so, and carefully hid evidence of their meeting, including several photographs Fefelov had given her of fellow disability rights activists. After being harassed continuously for their activities and threatened with arrest and trial, Fefelov and Zaitseva fled the Soviet Union for West Germany in 1982. With their departure, the Action Group's activities all but ground to a halt.

In this context, some would-be activists sought to improve their lives in ways that state authorities would not perceive as threatening. One such avenue was disability sports. Developing disability sports was in line with the socialist state's focus on "physical culture" and the perceived benefits of athletics for health and discipline among the citizenry (Brownell 1995, Riordan 1977). Athletics was just one component of physical culture, which Soviet doctrine conceptualized as "the sum total of social achievements connected with man's physical development and education. . . . [It is] part of the overall culture of society and represents all measures taken to make people healthy and to improve their physical abilities" (Riordan 1977:4). Historian Tricia Starks (2009:191) notes that the rhetoric of physical culture was one of "redemption through physical exertion" and that physical activity was valued for imparting character and strengthening the will. As an aspect of physical culture, athletics was viewed not as a pursuit merely for fun and leisure, but as an inherently valuable activity, valued as enriching the individual, who in turn enriched society; a strong and healthy work-force could be honed through sports and the broader physical culture, which therefore benefited production (Riordan 1980:41). Thus, engaging in a sport was not just fun and games; it was a contribution to society.

In this light it should not be surprising that disabled persons would pur-sue athletics, and that the Soviet state would support disability sports—or at least not interfere too much with its development—as a socially useful endeavor. It allowed the disabled to counter negative stereotypes of invalids as degenerates, beggars, and social parasites. The philosophy of physical culture identified athletics as an activity for rebuilding and restoring, goals of obvious relevance to the disabled. Disability sports allowed disabled per-sons to "work on themselves" in officially and socially sanctioned ways.

Sports clubs in the Soviet Union for the disabled did not appear until the early 1980s. Some of the first clubs were Ortsport (Orthosport) in Len-ingrad (now Saint Petersburg), and Invasport in Tallinn. Many other orga-nizations for the disabled that coalesced in the 1980s also centered around athletics, as one of the only politically acceptable bases on which to offi-cially register a civic organization with state authorities (Indolev 1998:97). In the waning days of the Soviet Union in 1991, athletics was at the heart of an important event that successfully drew public attention to the rights and needs of the disabled population—the so-called super-marathon, the first of several to take place in the former Soviet Union. On May 12, 1991, eight wheelchair-using athletes set off from Moscow's Pushkin Square on a grueling trip of 1,400 kilometers. (The sole woman participant was Ukrai-nian Svetlana Trifonova.) Over the course of several months they traveled, in their wheelchairs, from Moscow to Kyiv, and from Kyiv to Kryvyi Rih, in the south of (then) Soviet Ukraine. Local media outlets covered the super-marathon extensively, and as one participant, Oleksandr Sukhan from Mukachevo, Ukraine, said, the group attracted crowds of onlookers who came out to "see for themselves that it was possible, to verify that we were doing it ourselves."

Other organizations that were tolerated beginning in the 1970s included several networking-oriented groups. Examples are organizations founded in the Russian SSR such as Prometheus (Prometei) and Korchaginets, whose major goals were to facilitate written correspondence between dis-abled individuals, many of whom lived in isolation; to publish informa-tional materials (bulletins, journals); and to put pressure on the state to provide support for specific disabled persons in need. Some of these groups had branches throughout the Soviet republics, and thus they engendered

FIGURE 2.2. Activist Olha Alekseeva interviewing Oleksandr Sukhan at a conference in Lʹviv, 2003.

a sense of common experience among members. However, the organizations did not raise controversial issues or stand in opposition to the state's disability policy, and publications and even content of personal letters were self-censored and void of potentially objectionable political content.

Gusʹkov, Kiselev, and other disability rights activists had launched their activities with the goal of founding a united All-Russian Organization of Invalids (VOI) similar to those that had long existed for certain categories of disabled—the deaf and the blind. This goal was realized only in 1988, made possible by Gorbachev's policies of reform. By autumn 1991, around one quarter of all people registered as disabled in Russia had joined the VOI, which had 1,100,000 members (White 1999:13). Two parallel but contradictory processes shaped the VOI's formation. On the one hand, the movement came from the grassroots, as the disabled created their own organizations and formulated goals for action and revising legislation. On the other hand, it also was a top-down affair, since the Cabinet of Ministers of the Russian SSR coordinated the actual formation of the VOI, and the group's leadership included Party functionaries. In its early years the main achievements of the VOI were the adoption of far-reaching disability-related legislation, which provided for improved social protection and increases in pensions, and the return of more than 300 enterprises from the state to work collectives of disabled people.

This overview of disability policies and experiences in the Soviet Union has revealed several important trends that shaped the lives of disabled people in Soviet Russia and Ukraine and other Soviet republics. The state's two-pronged policy of care and control was applied unevenly across space and time, and produced myriad contradictions. The disabled sometimes suffered from too little state attention and intervention; they also "benefited" from too much. Soviet disability policy was characterized by harsh realities that produced constraints on people's lives and denied many Soviet citizens a common humanity. Yet in light of the numerous challenges that market reforms and the collapse and revamping of social policy pose for disabled persons in the former Soviet Union today, it may be conceded that the former system provided some relative benefits. Despite the many injustices, the Soviet state did provide some disabled persons and groups with the basic necessities for life, albeit in exchange for political complacency. *i mean that some familiar*

At the same time, the many disconnects between state rhetoric and state action are striking. I have considered here numerous examples of how Soviet official discourse and policy regarding disability often held little relation to on-the-ground, lived realities. This gap is indicative of the Soviet culture of *pokazukha*, or "window-dressing." In the case of disability policy, representatives of the state made many declarations, trotted out a few exemplary institutions, and groomed a handful of heroes and other shining examples of the state's beneficence toward invalids. But the high rates of institutionalization, the relative lack of education and employment opportunities, and the low economic status of most disabled persons—problems that only came to light after Gorbachev's policies of *glasnost'* (openness) and *perestroika* (restructuring)—speak volumes about the state's inability or unwillingness to ensure equal rights to the disabled.

The Soviet state's continuous emphasis on work capacity as the key disability criterion, and on labor as a primary mechanism of rehabilitation and empowerment, is particularly interesting because of the numerous paradoxes involved. In the early post–World War II years, with millions of Soviet casualties, returning disabled persons to the workforce was seen as necessary for the Soviet state's huge push to modernize and industrialize. This often was accomplished coercively, by withholding recognition of individuals' disability status and refusing adequate social support (Edele 2008). When, however, through groups such as the VIKO, the disabled sought to affirm and assert their labor potential, such initiatives were squelched. Equally contradictory, although official state proclamations touted the benefits and necessity of labor for disabled citizens, at no point did the state take adequate measures to empower the disabled to compete with other workers. Education was withheld, vocational training was often lackluster, and quotas for hiring disabled workers in state enterprises were not enforced.

All this is evidence of how, in the Soviet system, the needs, rights, and potential avenues of empowerment for disabled persons were defined exclusively in the state's terms. The state defined what social contributions disabled citizens would be allowed to make, set the parameters of education and work possibilities for this population, and closely regulated the development of disability consciousness. The extent to which disabled people were kept unaware of developments in the worldwide disability movement and of human rights struggles in other countries is conspicuous, but it is not out of line with Soviet citizens' general lack of information about human rights. In the Soviet Union, disabled persons were considered subjects to be cared for and controlled, not active agents or stakeholders. Even grassroots self-help initiatives that likely would have benefited the state economically and administratively—the organization of work collectives, for example—eventually were curtailed by the state. Overall, Soviet disability policy was a rigid system quite incapable of adapting to changing circumstances. The effects have been long lasting, and continue to reverberate today in very real terms in the former Soviet Union.

Even so, throughout the twentieth century the disabled—to the extent that it was possible in the confines of the Soviet state—challenged the system and chinked away at injustices. Throughout the 1960s and 1970s in particular, small steps paved the way for the establishment of a VOI and thousands of smaller disability rights organizations once restrictions were relaxed during perestroika beginning in the mid-1980s. However, because they had been so insulated, it was not until the late 1980s and early 1990s that disability rights activists in the former Soviet Union were able to tap into international advocacy networks and rights movements. In very substantial and traceable ways, institutional structures, narratives and attitudes, and other legacies of the past continue to shape disability policies and experiences in the region today.

## Social-izing Disability in the Postsocialist State

Socialist-era legacies are not the only influencing factors on how disability is evaluated, lived, and governed in contemporary Ukraine. Having been involved in disability communities since the late 1990s, I have been struck by the extent to which activists, political actors, and other

FIGURE 2.3. Mykola Swarnyk (left) and Yaroslav Hrybalskyy (right) conducting an accessibility assessment. *Photo courtesy of the Canadian Centre on Disability Studies.*

stakeholders increasingly draw on international approaches to understanding and addressing issues of disability. Disability studies as an academic discipline has not really developed in the country, although a disability studies course is taught at L'viv Polytechnic University in the Faculty of Social Work. The course was developed as part of the Reforming Social Services Canada-Ukraine Project (1999–2003) funded by the Canadian International Development Agency (CIDA) and implemented by the University of Manitoba Faculty of Social Work, L'viv Polytechnic University, the Canadian Centre on Disability Studies (CCDS), and several NGOs in L'viv including the Independent Living Resource Center, an NGO consortium directed by Yaroslav Hrybalskyy (Khomenko 2003).

The course Disability Issues in Social Work was developed and is taught by Mykola Swarnyk. The aims of the course are to provide future social workers with an understanding of social attitudes toward disability in historical context and in the Ukrainian cultural environment; legal bases of social protections of the disabled in Ukraine and relevant aspects of state policy; issues of living with a disability from the perspective of the individual, the family, and society; goals and aims of social and rehabilitation services; methods of analyzing, planning and delivering services to disabled individuals; theory and practice of integrated and nondiscriminatory approaches to service delivery in the spheres of education, health care, employment, and others; and principles of consumer-directed approaches, self-help models, and partnership-based models of services. Specific topics covered include these, among others: worldwide approaches to/models of disability (biomedical, functional, environmental, rights-based, etc.); institution-based versus inclusive education of disabled children; ethical codes of social work; principles of universal design; and the independent living concept.

These foci—in particular the attention given to principles of independent living, inclusion, and partnership—evidence the strong influence of the CCDS and its late founder and Executive Director Henry Enns (1943–2002) on conceptualizing disability and strategizing empowerment for L'viv-based activists and scholars. Enns helped develop the first Independent Living Centres (ILC) in Canada, played an instrumental role in the founding of Disabled Peoples' International (DPI),[8] and was the

FIGURE 2.4. Mykola Swarnyk, head of the L'viv commission on accessibility, points out that the entrance to a newly built bank does not conform to accessibility standards.

instrumental force in the establishment of the CCDS, a national organization based in Winnipeg that takes an integrative approach to advancing disability rights through research, education, awareness, and international development. The CCDS is "guided by the philosophies of independent living and community living, emphasizing human rights, self-determination, interdependence, equality, a cross-disability focus, and full and valued participation of all citizens in the community."[9]

The integrated approach to empowerment promoted by the CCDS has been very influential for disability rights activists in L'viv, who draw upon the concepts of self-help, consumer-driven approaches, and independent living, perspectives clearly influenced by IL concepts developed in Canada and the United States. One result of the Disability component of the CCDS-CIDA Reforming Social Services Canada-Ukraine Project was the creation of the L'viv Independent Living Resource Centre (LILRC), an organization run by Yaroslav Hrybalskyy alongside another group he heads, the L'viv Oblast' Section of the Ukrainian Foundation for the Rehabilitation of Invalids (FRI). The LILRC has been a hub for networking and dissemination of diverse information on disability-related issues and empowerment strategies.

The Resource Centre has promoted IL concepts by translating fundamental literature on the topic, and through the LILRC Yaroslav has championed the Swedish-developed strategies of active rehabilitation, which are closely linked to principles of independent living. A wheelchair-repair workshop is based out of his organizations, and Yaroslav is a major figure in the movement for accessible architecture in Ukraine, all of which dovetails with the IL focus on economic empowerment of the disabled and the removal of barriers. As further evidence of the influence of IL perspectives in the country, in 2002 a redacted version of Gerben DeJong's (1979) influential article "Independent Living: From Social Movement to Analytic Paradigm" appeared in Ukrainian translation in the journal *Liubomyra*, a gender and disability-focused journal previously published by activist Liubomyra Boichyshyn.

IL movements have an eventful history in the United States, the U.K., and Canada (Thomas 2007:114–117), but I do not have space to recount that history here. What interests me more are the ways that Ukrainian disability rights activists understand concepts of independent living in their own contexts, and how IL principles are being applied in Ukraine. IL movements began in the United States in the 1970s, most notably in Berkeley, California, and Champaign-Urbana, Illinois; Canadian IL movements began in the early 1980s. In both countries IL Centers became the cornerstone of the IL approach—the disabled were able to access an array of support services (transportation, training in IL skills, housing referrals, and many others) that facilitated inclusion and allowed disabled persons to live independently in their communities. Key IL principles are self-determination, self-help, peer support, empowerment, community inclusion, cross-disability inclusion, risk-taking, and integration.[10] Fundamental to IL is the idea that disabled persons themselves must set the activism and reform agendas and must be empowered to shape disability policy.

All these principles are in evidence in the L'viv-based movement. IL Centers *per se* have not been developed, and, as its name implies, the center started by Hrybalskyy with CCDS support operates more as a resource center than a formal Canadian or U.S.-style IL Center. Yet these activists have taken the general IL principles of inclusion, community-based support, and economic empowerment and used them to drive local disability rights efforts. Mykola Swarnyk and Oksana Kunanec-Swarnyk were instrumental in the development of a day center for disabled children in L'viv, particularly those with cerebral palsy. The day center, Dzherelo, provides many educational and enrichment opportunities for children and allows families to care for them at home instead of having them institutionalized. A new CCDS-CIDA project is underway to promote inclusive education for disabled children in regular schools (see below). Workshops such as Yaroslav Hrybalskyy's provide employment for disabled adults. Both Mykola and Yaroslav now serve in local government, and have thus operationalized the principle of stakeholders as policy-shapers that is fundamental to IL concepts. Because of the historical and continued lack of community support mechanisms for the disabled, community-based services such as those fundamental to IL initiatives in the United States and Canada are conspicuously absent in Ukraine. In this context, Mykola Swarnyk and his colleagues have developed a family-centered approach that seems to be working well. In his capacity as a leader of the organization Nadiya for disabled children and their families, Mykola has implemented many projects to facilitate IL for disabled children via empowerment of families through various kinds of psychological, physical, and material support.

Social models of disability, in particular the British social model (BSM), have not been as visibly influential in Ukrainian rights movements as have IL approaches. This is not to say that none of the social model tenets resonate with activists in Ukraine, but rarely have these approaches been taken up and articulated as such. It is not my goal to provide a comprehensive discussion of social models of disability, which have been vigorously debated by studies scholars for the past decade. Rather I wish to highlight the few instances of direct appeal to the BSM and other social models of disability that I have run across in Ukraine, and focus the discussion on how the "social" figures into local Ukrainian approaches to understanding disability and advocating for disability rights.

The BSM originated primarily not in scholarly circles, but rather in the trenches of disability rights activism in the 1960s and 1970s. The social approach of the BSM grew out of materialist and Marxist perspectives that located the roots of disability in the economic exclusion and social oppression of people with impairments. The BSM has been generative of a distinction between impairment, defined as "the functional limitation with the individual caused by physical, mental, or sensory impairment" and disability, which is socially produced (Barnes 1991:2). Generally stated, the BSM holds that disability is not caused by impairment, but rather by the restrictions placed on people with impairments. The BSM is often contrasted with the medical model, which is criticized for medicalizing disability as a problem of the individual, and turning it into a tragedy rather than a social issue.

The BSM has been very influential for disability studies scholars and activists, particularly in the U.K. But the BSM recently has come in for serious criticism on many fronts (Corker and Shakespeare, eds., 2002; Shakespeare 2006). The impairment/disability distinction is questioned by many who assert that for a myriad of analytical and political reasons impairment must be brought back into the discussion about disability (Thomas and Corker 2002, Tremain 2002). Indeed, Devva Kasnitz has identified "developing a more nuanced theory of impairment-disability" as one project at the cutting edge of disability studies (2008:29). The strong materialist approach of the BSM, and its reliance on binary oppositions that may break down under scrutiny, are increasingly evaluated as inadequate for addressing the complexities of disability politics and experience in diverse cultural and sociopolitical contexts. And as explored by Tom Shakespeare (2006:9–28) the BSM is not the only social game in town; in fact, he identifies a "family of socio-contextual approaches to disability." These include, among others, the minority group model of U.S. disability rights activists, which argues that discrimination must be addressed through civil rights legislation to ensure individual rights, and the Nordic relational model, which frames disability as situational, as a continuum rather than a dichotomy (i.e., disability as relative), and as "a mismatch between the individual and the environment" (Tøssebro 2004).

Engagements with theoretical understandings of disability in Ukraine are still quite new and are limited mostly to those rights activists who have traveled abroad, interacted with foreign disability scholars and rights activists, and familiarized themselves with debates over disability politics in other countries. I would not say there is an identifiable Ukrainian social model of disability, but the "social" does figure prominently in many discussions about disability empowerment. Commitments commonly espoused by my informants include the following: strategies to address disability issues must be social in nature and should involve the disabled themselves as partners, the integrity of the individual must be respected, and he or she must be given an "equal starting point" with other citizens—meeting these conditions can facilitate independent living for disabled persons. Themes of cooperation and partnership between the (disabled) individual and society are stressed, and disability sometimes is interpreted as a kind of "cultural variation" ideally seen as unproblematic in a pluralistic society (Poloziuk 2005a). Overall, concepts of IL as they have developed in the United States and Canada—and which, it must be noted, are also decidedly social in nature, as they focus on supports and partnerships—have been more influential in the Ukrainian context than have BSM-based ideas rooted in the impairment-disability distinction and focusing on the material bases of disability. The BSM may not fully resonate with people in postsocialist countries like Ukraine for an obvious yet important reason: after 70 years of Soviet rule (around 50 years in Western Ukraine, which was annexed during World War II) and a state-imposed functional approach to disability policy that centered around issues of work and labor capacity, with noticeable negative effects, many are understandably wary of ways of conceptualizing disability that are rooted in materialism and Marxist thought.

The integrated approach, promoted by the CCDS and further developed by Ukrainian activists, is important to return to here. In his disability studies course, Mykola Swarnyk teaches future social workers to consider the disabled person in social context. Examples of issues to be considered include material/economic contexts, unemployment, and dynamics related to culture, communication, health, lifestyle, and other factors. In his teaching and activist work, Mykola advocates a holistic disability approach, one that looks at the whole person and considers his or her needs and possibilities in light of the person's "strong sides," "inner resources," and talents. Key principles of this approach include integration, self-determination, independence and interdependence, and strategies that are family-centered, society-based, and rooted in partnership (e.g., between the individual, society, and various advocates). This philosophy, which privileges the integrity of the individual without discounting important contextual factors, resonates in the postsocialist milieu where, as Oksana Kunanec-Swarnyk (2005) has said: "[People long suffered under] Soviet concepts that disregarded individual needs, completely repressed individuality, and leveled [the populace]."

## Back to the Future: What Was Biological Citizenship, and What Comes Next?

And what of the Ukrainian state's disability policy? Have similar changes characterized official understandings of disability and strategies to support disabled citizens? A shift in the official narrative has occurred, to be sure. To what extent this shift marks a real change in the state's stance, or signals actual policy reform, is a question that requires further consideration. As we have seen, in the socialist workers' state, a person's social worth was measured in terms of a narrow definition of the individual's contributions to society, based largely on the contribution of his or her paid/productive labor. Labor capacity was in this context firmly rooted in physical bodies, themselves examined and controlled by the centralized state administration via a "categorization of bodies as more or less useful with greater or lesser prospects of survival" (Petryna 2002:13). Those who possessed bodies deemed incapable of working received "compensation" in the form of (paltry) pensions, services, and entitlements. Little was expected of many disabled persons, who were in effect plucked from the social fabric and offered minimal economic support in exchange for complacency and social estrangement. As this kind of biopower, or control over life (Foucault 2008), was deployed by the state, invalids were made, and many so designated came to see themselves as particular kinds of citizen-subjects.

In contemporary Ukraine disability continues to be defined and governed by a biobureaucracy, or institutionalized biologically informed methods for "making sense of and responding to existence, otherness, and misfortune" (Kohrman 2005:7). In what is a socialist legacy of nearly impenetrable bureaucratic stonewalling, no less than five government ministries and state funds are responsible for coordinating disability policy. Communication between these entities is not at all smooth or transparent; as Oleg complained, "The right hand never knows what the left hand is doing." Some policies are contradictory between the ministries, which sometimes duplicate services or collectively fail to provide guaranteed services.

The Soviet-era body responsible for evaluating disability status and assigning benefits was the Medical-Labor Expert Commission (VTEK), which defined disability based on loss of labor capacity (Kikkas 2001:113, Madison 1989). In 1991 VTEK was renamed MSEK, or the Medical-Social Expert Commission. This name change did little to actually introduce a "social" approach to disability that would define disability beyond the individual, defective body to take into account social factors. As Oleg Poloziuk (2005b) notes, the shift marks a redefinition of disability from loss of work capacity to a measurement of loss of health, a formulation still within the Soviet state's functional approach to conceptualizing disability. Indeed, Article 2 of the Law of Ukraine No. 872–XII On the Basis of Social Protection of Invalids of Ukraine (from March 21, 1991) defines an invalid as "a person with persistent disorder of bodily function, caused by illness, the result of a trauma, or birth defects, which result in limited life activities (*zhyttiediial'nist'*) and in the necessity for social assistance and protection."[11]

The MSEK structure in independent Ukraine very much conforms to the Soviet model of disability verification and management. It includes 428 MSEKs, which between them employ 1,626 physicians and other medical experts (MLSP 2008:42). For the person seeking disability status, becoming entangled in the biobureaucracy is inevitable. My informants told bureaucratic horror stories (Herzfeld 1992:4) of being volleyed between MSEK, the Ministry of Health, the Ministry of Labor and Social Policy, the Ministry of Education and Science, the Ministry for Family, Youth, and Sports, local branches of these Ministries, clinics and hospitals, social workers, and others. Being evaluated by MSEK alone is a process requiring the person who seeks invalid status to compile and present no less than 16 documents (Ipatov et al. 2005). Many of those granted disability status still must undergo extensive physical examinations on a regular basis—every six months to a year. Being given disability status "for life" commits one to a constant conversation with the state and a lifetime of biobureaucratic involvement.

But due to shifts in state policy, especially nascent welfare and pension reform, the nature of this relationship may be changing. Since March 1991 when the aforementioned Law on the Basis of Social Protection of Invalids of Ukraine was adopted, no fewer than 63 laws, 13 bylaws, 31 decrees, 81 resolutions, and 26 directives related in one way or another to governance of disability have been passed. This legislation pertains to broad areas such as health care, housing, physical and professional rehabilitation, athletics, recreation, collective organizing, and others. Much of it includes elements of social insurance, pensions, and entitlements, and ongoing social welfare reform has major implications for the lives of the disabled.

As in the Soviet Union, in Ukraine today persons who have received disability status are assigned a monthly pension and are entitled to a range of benefits. These benefits, though extensive on paper, are usually inadequate for the individual's survival. At the beginning of 2008, the average monthly pension for a group I invalid, the category to which most spinally injured persons and other wheelchair users are assigned, was 740 UAH (US$148) (MLSP 2008:48). For comparison, the minimum monthly wage in January 2008 was set at 515 UAH, or $103. The monthly living costs were 592 UAH, or $118 (Arzinger and Partners Ukraine 2008). The dismal group I pension puts recipients in an extremely precarious position, especially those who have little material support from family or friends.

In the current climate of economic crisis and inflation, social welfare restructuring and the rearrangement of entitlements as part of neoliberalization of the economy are major concerns for many who have historically been the beneficiaries of a broad range of entitlements such as pensions, subsidies, and material goods: the disabled, large families, single parents, the elderly, and others. Some initiatives for welfare reform have focused specifically on revamping support for the disabled. The extensive system of disability compensation is recognized as a huge drain on the Ukrainian economy, especially disability benefits connected to the 1986 Chernobyl nuclear catastrophe (Petryna 2002). The current pension system with respect to disability is criticized by state cadres and some disabled people themselves for a number of perceived shortcomings: pensions are based on minimum living standards, the system is highly abused and people "faking" disability or who are only slightly disabled drain the fund of resources for those who really need them, and the pension system creates dependence among citizens who could otherwise be self-sufficient.

Even if reforms on paper do not always signal actual, immediate change in how disability is governed, tracking the language of reform is important for understanding the narrative shifts driving policy change and imminent structural changes as well. Government support of the disabled has in the last several years been articulated as "targeted assistance"—technical support focused on rehabilitation, job placement, and inculcating self-sufficiency in individuals.[12] Reforms in disability policy have been stymied by the chronic instability of the Ukrainian government since 2004, but many already have felt the effects of scaled back privileges as the market is restructured and made leaner and fitter. Legislation adopted in 2005 proposes a reassessment of the status of all citizens who receive disability pensions; the reevaluation is to focus especially on citizens' capacity to work. Unlike current regulations, the new rules would prohibit some categories of the disabled from working and receiving a disability pension simultaneously. An attendant differentiation of pensions was also planned. In 2004 over 30,000 people were assigned a "lower" disability category than they previously had, which meant a reduction in state-provided benefits and support. An additional 15,000 were moved from the group considered "unable to work" to those considered work-ready (Marunych et al. 2004:22), a shift that also involved a dramatic loss of benefits. Representatives of the state administration framed this development as evidence of the success of vocational rehabilitation programs, a questionable conclusion given the poor state of most programs for physical and vocational rehabilitation and a serious lack of financing for such programs.

Further narrative shifts in state policy become apparent when we compare two official reports on "the state/condition of invalids" (*stanovyshche invalidiv*), the first published in 2002 (Derzhavna Dopovid 2002) and the second in 2008 (MLSP 2008). Both reports were prepared by the National Assembly of Disabled of Ukraine (NADU), a coalition of disability advocacy organizations, in cooperation with various ministries and other governmental and nongovernmental organizations. Since the reports were prepared at the request of the president and the Cabinet of Ministers, we may assume that they reflect the state's official position in terms of framing the issues and strategizing state policy. This position is articulated in direct terms in each report's introductory section.

The 2002 report emphasizes the "needs of invalids" (*potreby invalidiv*) as the essential basis for formulating social policy: "the basis for further development of social policy toward invalids must be the necessary and steadfast accounting of the needs of invalids in all spheres of life" (Derzhavna Dopovid 2002:6–7). These needs are described as the "basic element of planning work and policy on different problems of invalidity." An apparent corrective appears in the 2008 report, which implicitly criticizes the needs-based approach, now negatively characterized as a "social defense" or social protection approach: "[We] must move from the social protection of invalids to the genuine securing of their rights" (MLSP 2008:8). In a marked change from the 2002 report, the 2008 document declares, "State policy toward invalids has the [following] goals: first, to guarantee their rights to maximum participation in the economic and social life of society, especially stimulating their employment and participation in the labor market; and second, to provide a guaranteed income, so people with disabilities are not deprived of the possibility to live decently" (MLSP 2008:5). The report faults current legislation for "conceptualizing disability as a social problem, [and] not guaranteeing the removal of barriers constraining their basic rights—to work, education, rehabilitation" and others (pp. 7–8). Indeed, this rights-based approach is front and center in the report's introduction, which makes frequent reference to international declarations and conventions vis-à-vis disability rights, in particular the 2006 UN Convention on the Rights of Persons with Disabilities, which Ukraine signed in September 2008. (The United States signed it only in July 2009.)

Although the 2008 report makes specific reference to the "social model," the understandings of "social" used throughout the document are inconsistent and contradictory. As noted above, the report takes issue with the state's (previous) "social" approach; here it is presumably the Soviet-era system of entitlements and material compensation that is being rejected. Another reference to disability as a "social phenomenon" is made, but the meaning conveyed is that disability is a universal phenomenon "that no society can avoid" (MLSP 2008:5). Further on it is stated that, "Ukraine is making a consistent political transition from a medical [model] to a social model of disability" (MLSP 2008:18). This shift is described as working to "unravel the complex problems of disability" and create "cardinal changes in disabled people's economic and social lives in society" by addressing their health status and their educational and professional opportunities, and by promoting the status of disabled persons as full-fledged citizens. Here the social approach to disability is closer to that of the BSM, which rejects medicalization of disability and identifies disabling barriers that prevent people from full social participation. Thus, the official narrative has yet to work out what is meant by employing a "social model" or a social approach to disability policy, and whether such a social approach is in fact desirable.

These threads—discussions of rights, the social model, and many of the specifics of social policy reform—are lost in the rest of the document, which focuses on statistical data and details the provision of pensions, entitlements, and services. Tellingly, other than in discussions of international conventions such as the UN Declaration, reference to invalids' "rights" appears most frequently in two contexts, both of them reminiscent of the Soviet state's policy of care and control: the right to a pension, and the right to work. These are crucial rights, of course, but placing primary focus on them (and passively denying the right to work in any case) positions the disabled as dependent, as users of the system instead of full-fledged, contributing citizens.

The numerous references made to international guidelines and standards in the 2008 report mark a shift in focus of state priorities, at least at the declarative level. Such discussions were muted in the 2002 report, but the 2008 document is explicit about the importance of signing and adhering to international conventions such as the UN Declaration, especially as discussions in Ukraine continue about strategies for joining the European Union. This focus on the need for "harmonization of indigenous legislation with international standards" (MLSP 2008:6) accounts in large part for the rights language that guides the introduction to the 2008 report. It is part of the language and technologies of modernization that further animate this official narrative; the report promotes standardization, decentralization, the "establishment of control," and "systematic approaches to rehabilitation." We learn that "an informational base in the form of a centralized database on problems of disability is being developed" (MLSP 2008:7). All this focus on quantifying, data collection, and standardizing makes one pause: are we witnessing the (re)-emergence of practices of surveillance and control described by Michel Foucault (1963, 1977) as disciplinary mechanisms to manage certain populations (in this case the disabled)? Can these "reforms" right the wrongs created by the Soviet policies of care and control?

In this context of stop-and-go reform, many of my informants, who have seen the relative value of their disability pensions and other entitlements fall steadily in the face of inflation and economic crisis, are waiting for the other shoe to drop. Previously subjects of a biopolitical regime that, at least in theory, assigned disability and concomitant benefits according to uniform criteria (Petryna 2002:115–148), people designated as invalids find themselves increasingly subject to processes of differentiation (*dyferentsiatsiia*). At this juncture, as processes of reassessment and differentiation pick up speed, the disabled must simultaneously invest themselves in forming a relationship with the state (as biological citizens), yet also reach *beyond* the state as it transforms and parts of it collapse, or threaten to.

Thus, on the one hand, in conditions of economic uncertainty and shifting state support, staking citizenship claims through one's damaged biology becomes a survival strategy, and identity as an invalid is one many people are compelled to invest themselves in (Petryna 2002). People are obliged to operationalize biological citizenship to claim sociopolitical belonging, since, as stressed by Foucault and others, it is biopower and the management of bodies through which contemporary regimes of authority (i.e., the state) operate. Here we witness "the reconstitution of citizenship as an unequal social bargain with the state, not for political rights and opportunities, but for the most elementary conditions of physical survival" (Rivkin-Fish 2003:503). This unequal social bargain comes with a price: membership in the so-called parallel world of the disabled confers upon one an identity fundamentally rooted in stigma and the subtraction of worth. Becoming identified—and self-identifying—as disabled can accrue one much-needed social and economic benefits but still is not, on the whole, a desirable state. And, in the era of neoliberal reform, where individual initiative, self-sufficiency, and privatization are stressed, being dependent on the state and on other people (as invalids are assumed to be in Ukrainian legislation and the public imagination) makes one far from the ideal or full-fledged citizen.

On the other hand, however, the disabled in postsocialist states increasingly are mobilizing strategies to establish both a social and a political sense of belonging *in addition to* and *beyond* the fact of being disabled. These negotiations become increasingly important as plans and procedures for social welfare reform unfold as part of the neoliberalization of the Ukrainian economy. As citizens jockey for the state's attention and care, the disabled must persuasively assert that they are not "taking the food out of other people's mouths." They have to convince the state and fellow citizens that they do not "want too much." These were the kinds of phrases some of my informants used to describe how they thought the nondisabled perceived them. As members of a marked category, the disabled are burdened with justifying themselves as *bona fide* citizens both worthy of investment and possessing the potential to make contributions to society. They find themselves in the awkward position of needing simultaneously to emphasize their disabled status to secure recognition and support from the state, and to de-accentuate it in the face of the increasing valorization of independence and individual responsibility that accompanies neoliberal reform. This process involves making new bargains with representatives and institutions of the state, and also carving out new spaces of belonging for heretofore marginalized populations such as the disabled. As illustrated in the example of the Invalids' Manifesto penned by a group of friends in 1999, without letting the state off the hook, and all the while emphasizing the important role significant social others such as families, community organizations, civil servants, and social workers play in the "integration of invalids in society," disabled persons in Ukraine are struggling to stake citizenship claims in their own terms, to take ownership of how disability is defined, valued, and governed. This is a huge task enacted in multiple planes and contexts, and entails the suturing together (and, at times, collision) of diverse visions of what it means to be a full, deserving, and active citizen in a postsocialist, neoliberalizing state.

In seeking to broaden the repertoire of values of citizenship, the disabled in Ukraine reveal themselves to be "mobile" citizens in every sense of the word. The sources of such reworked engagements are multiple, and they emerge at the intersection of the national and social (legal frameworks, attitudes, history), the international (international standards and declarations, transnational advocacy movements), and the person (self-perception, agency). Transformative factors include interactions with disability rights advocates from abroad who have visited Ukraine regularly since the early 1990s; prominent among them are scholar-activists from the CCDS described above, and representatives of the Swedish advocacy group Rekryteringsgruppen for Active Rehabilitation (RG). Ukrainians have traveled abroad for disability sports competitions, conferences, and workshops, to learn from foreign counterparts and share their own experiences and empowerment strategies. The internet is an important mediator for some who can virtually rove the globe for resources, information, and support.

These engagements have opened possibilities for new articulations of citizenship rooted in changing perceptions of economics and the market, the politics of representation, human rights, and notions of gender and sexuality, among others. The disabled in Ukraine have begun to assert themselves in terms commonly used in disability rights discourse in the West—disability as social oppression (e.g., the BSM), disability as "everyone's problem" (universal models of disability), and the language of equal rights (minority group and civil rights approaches)—and authors of post-Soviet disability legislation in Ukraine have drawn on their knowledge of legal structures governing disability in other countries, including the Netherlands, Sweden, Canada, and the United States. This is not to say that these conceptualizations have been appropriated wholesale by Ukrainians and seamlessly applied to address their concerns. Rather, there are many dialogues going on at once, and the disability rights arena is crackling with competing interests, commitments, and notions of how disability and citizenship should and do intersect.

These debates are being negotiated and reworked both in dialogue with and independent of state discourses and official regulations. Still, mobile citizenship is difficult to operationalize in the absence of a willing state and in the face of negative public opinion and ignorance. For this reason, although the individual self, personal initiative, and independence are critical components of citizenship claims among my informants, they also find themselves in a constant conversation with the state. These conversations take on multiple dimensions, including the symbolic and discursive (models and meanings of disability, the respective roles of the individual and society) and the very material (calculations of social worth and economic "compensation," the politics of the spatial environment). Thus, the people I have come to know in Ukraine live their lives between competing, often contradictory, visions of what it means to simultaneously live disability and be a citizen in contemporary Ukrainian society.

## Living Disability in Today's Ukraine

How have the on-the-ground, day-to-day realities of life changed for disabled persons since the Soviet days of state-run internaty, segregated residential educational institutions, and minimal attention to physical and vocational rehabilitation? The institutionalization of disabled persons is still very much a reality. In total there are 321 so-called home-internaty (permanent residential institutions) in Ukraine, 83 of which house the elderly and disabled and 56 of which are for children age 18 and under (MLSP 2008:69). Since statistics are not disaggregated according to residents' age and disability status, it is impossible to know the percentage of internat residents who are elderly, disabled, or both. As of 2004 a total of 56,455 persons lived in internaty; of these an estimated 38,000 were disabled (MLSP 2008:69). Among the 8,853 children who reside in Ukrainian internaty, we know that around 7,000 are disabled children four to 18 years old, and 4,000 are children who have been orphaned or abandoned, or whose guardians have lost guardianship privileges (MLSP 2008:70). (Some children in these latter categories must also be disabled.)

Parents' groups and other disability rights organizations in Ukraine seek to develop alternatives to the institutionalization of disabled children. Activists have drawn attention to the poor conditions in which many institutionalized children live, and at an international conference in 2005 Mykola Swarnyk described how children's rights are curtailed in internaty:

> Our organization investigated the restrictions of internat residents' rights and found that there are violations of privacy and that restrictions are placed on choice of food and access to varied activities. In some cases children and adolescents are not allowed to have anything of their own, and sometimes they do not even have their own clothes. That is, they are dressed in whatever way the personnel see fit. These may seem like minor violations, but together they deny the children their individuality (*zneosobliuiut'*), and prevent them from exercising control over their own lives. (Swarnyk 2005)

Since the education of disabled children takes place primarily in school-in-ternaty in Ukraine, developing educational alternatives is a major compo-nent of deinstitutionalization. Anna Kukuruza, a psychologist in Kharkiv, founded the first early intervention center in Ukraine in 2000. The cen-ter offers various educational and therapeutic programs for developmen-tally disabled children six years old and under and their families. When I interviewed Kukuruza in 2006, she described how she and her colleagues developed an early intervention philosophy and practice that were influ-enced by models they became familiar with during travels to the United States, Canada, Hungary, and Germany. However, Kukuruza stressed that the Kharkiv Early Intervention Center is committed to serving children and families in their local realities, and the program combines different components that seem most effective and realistic. Parents are expected to play a major role in the early intervention process, and they are highly involved in the center's work. As a member of several NGO coalitions, the center also engages in lobbying activities to reform legislation protecting the rights of disabled children.

Another important educational initiative is a five-year CCDS project that began in 2008, titled Inclusive Education for Children with Disabili-ties in Ukraine. Funded by CIDA, the project involves several Ukrainian partners, including NADU.[13] Additionally, alternative forms of housing and service delivery have expanded in recent years. For instance, in lieu of the large, centralized internaty that may house hundreds of residents, an alternate institutional form is expanding in the form of smaller, more intimate institutions, many of them intended for temporary stays only. Today 323 such institutions now exist; they provide 8,345 beds and serve an average of 15,000 persons each year (MLSP 2008:70).

Another development is the establishment of territorial centers (Ter-Centers) designed to provide services to the disabled and elderly while allowing members of these populations to live outside residential insti-tutions. Ironically, the early Soviet state experimented with the TerCen-ter model but abandoned it in favor of the internat system soon after World War II (Iarskaia-Smirnova and Romanov, eds., 2002:202–204). At the beginning of 2008 there were 744 territorial centers in Ukraine pro-viding services to nearly two million people, including 500,000 disabled persons (MLSP 2008:71). The TerCenter model is not a panacea, and the system suffers from a lack of state financing. But the kind of integrated service delivery offered through TerCenters offers many advantages over the internat model, and it helps remedy some of the bureaucratic stone-walling and miscommunication that currently plagues social services for the disabled ("Analysis of the social service needs of the residents of Khar'kov" 2006).

The increased personalization of services in the TerCenter model is likewise reflected in ongoing reforms in state approaches to rehabilitation. In 1992 the Ministry of Health approved the development of the IPRI, the Individual Program of Rehabilitation and Adaptation of the Invalid. In theory, each person assigned to a disability group is entitled to an IPRI developed by MSEK. The IPRI is officially described as "identifying a complex of optimal types, forms, scopes, and timeframes of rehabilitative measures with determinations of their sequence and place of implementation" (MLSP 2008:43). A mechanism for funding the IPRI program was not approved until 2003, and the initiative still has not been fully launched because of gaps in funding. The program is financed through local branches of the Ukrainian Fund for the Social Protection of Invalids (FSPI), but the fund itself is poorly funded. Thus it has been impossible for the fund to carry through on its multi-vectored mandate to implement the IPRI program, facilitate the creation of jobs for the disabled, provide credit to businesses run by disability-focused NGOs, and others (Poloziuk 2002).

The IPRI was conceptualized as an approach to rehabilitation that would not only focus on medical and technical problems of the disabled, as did the Soviet model, but would also integrate economic and social concerns (Poloziuk 2004). The IPRI is supposed to tailor services to the needs of each person, in line with ongoing efforts to streamline and personalize services. Ironically, however, a 2006 legislative change resulted in the partial standardization of the IPRI; the Standard State Program of Rehabilitation now serves as a template of services and resources to which one is entitled, depending on age, sex, health status, and other factors (MLSP 2008:43).[14] As part of the "new form," the medical commission (MSEK) is required to include a recommendation regarding the disabled person's work capabilities in the individual's IPRI. Not all MSEKs take this requirement seriously, which puts disabled would-be workers at a great disadvantage.

In their study of the everyday lives of disabled persons in Kharkiv, sociologists Polina Alpatova and Tetiana Zub found that the IPRIs offered to their informants by MSEK were hardly rehabilitation programs at all, much less the individualized, socially and economically contextualized plans touted in official reports:

> Upon evaluation by the [MSEK] commission a person with special needs is supposed to receive an individual rehabilitation plan that describes the conditions in which she may be employed. Usually,

however, in place of an individual plan the invalid is handed documentation of their unemployability, which in most cases seriously compromises their chances for employment. (Alpatova and Zub 2006)

A promising development in conceptualizing and operationalizing rehabilitation in Ukraine is the introduction of physical therapy (PT) paradigms. A group of Ukrainian activists and educators from L'viv were introduced to physical therapy techniques when they became involved in AR camps. The development of the PT profession in Ukraine also has been spurred by Western-trained physical therapists like Oksana Kunanec-Swarnyk, who was born in Canada to Ukrainian-Canadian parents and began visiting Ukraine in 1993. Oksana eventually moved to Ukraine permanently and now lives in L'viv. With the assistance of consultants from the University of Manitoba who traveled to Ukraine to lecture on physical therapy and also recruited Ukrainian students to study in Winnipeg, a department of physical rehabilitation was founded at the University of Physical Culture in L'viv in the early 1990s. "Physical rehabilitation specialist" has been officially recognized as a profession in Ukraine since 1998, and today there are more than 30 programs at Ukrainian institutes and universities preparing specialists in physical rehabilitation. Graduates of the new PT programs have formed a Ukrainian Association of Specialists of Physical Rehabilitation, which currently has 120 members. Although some of these new specialists have found employment in private health care facilities, integrating Western-style physical therapy into existing medical paradigms in traditional, state-run institutions has been a huge challenge. This is ironic given that one of the officially stated difficulties of successfully implementing the IPRI program is a dearth of rehabilitation specialists among MSEK cadres (MLSP 2008:43). The Ukrainian Association of Specialists of Physical Rehabilitation seeks admission to the World Confederation for Physical Therapy (WCPT) in 2011, a status that hopefully would lend more legitimacy to the profession locally and help facilitate the integration of physical therapists into positions in the official health care structures.

PT in Ukraine is described as integrated rehabilitation, a model that takes into account the needs and wishes of disabled individuals themselves and their families and caregivers, as well as the knowledge and skills of rehabilitation specialists (Kunanec-Swarnyk 2005). The focus of rehabilitation is the individual and his or her concrete needs, but proponents of physical therapy recognize the importance of social conditions and social infrastructure, including state institutions and NGOs, in the rehabilitation process. Indeed, PT specialists lament that without appropriate infrastructures to support disabled individuals, they go through rehabilitation programs only to become "rehabilitated islands" without access to appropriate resources or social support (Kunanec-Swarnyk 2005). Clearly, the goals of physical therapy closely approximate those stated in the IPRI legislation, and more needs to be done to integrate the work of these newly trained, socially aware physical rehabilitation specialists into state service delivery.

Improving employment opportunities for the disabled remains a major challenge in Ukraine, where the idea that an "invalid" can actually work, and should be offered equal access to employment with the non-disabled, is difficult for many to accept. Along with maintaining work-place quotas to reserve jobs for disabled persons—a policy easily side-stepped and clearly not effective—the Ukrainian government has sought to expand retraining and job placement services for the disabled. Legislation adopted in 2006 and 2007 finally allowed disabled persons to register with state unemployment agencies (earlier the disabled were prohibited from registering on the state unemployment rolls). However, this is only possible for those whose IPRIs explicitly state that they have adequate capacity to work, and under what conditions. Those on the rolls who actively seek work may now get official status as unemployed persons and receive unemployment benefits. This in turn provides disabled job seekers with access to services such as career consultations and opportunities for job training (MLSP 2008:137–138). As a result, the number of disabled persons registering with state unemployment agencies increased threefold between 2003 and 2007. However, just 1.4 percent of those registering were in disability group I (MLSP 2008:138). The number of disabled persons who found work through state unemployment agencies more than doubled between 2003 and 2007, but it is highly likely that many of these hirings replicate the fictitious, "dead souls" employment model. When disabled persons are offered employment, oftentimes it is for relatively unqualified, low-paid work. This is the case even when job seekers possess good educational qualifications and higher degrees. Employers fear taking responsibility for disabled workers, and perceive them as stereotypically helpless and incapable. State-provided training programs for the disabled are developing, but the specialties offered are for jobs with low-level qualifications such as barber, woodworker, tailor, cook, bartender, cashier, secretary, shoe repair worker, and typist (MLSP 2008:139). So, despite some improvements, much work is still to be done at all levels—the state, civic organizations, the sphere of public opinion and public education, and others—to ensure that the disabled in Ukraine have opportunities to enact a more mobile citizenship.

# 3. Disability Rights and Disability Wrongs

*I would say that the disability rights movement (invalidnyi rukh) began in the USSR under Gorbachev, in 1988 or '89, when democratic processes were introduced and it became possible to form civic organizations. . . . And here in Ukraine, the movement likewise started in L'viv in 1989. The disability rights movement originated from athletics. . . . I personally got involved because I wanted an active lifestyle. I started participating in the sports competitions (spartakiady). . . . In 1990 I went to Moscow for an international auto race for people with disabilities. And that's where for the first time I met people from Germany, Czechoslovakia, and other countries, and from them I learned that in those states invalids live a completely different life. They are able to live an active life, because they have an accessible environment. It turned out that a worldwide movement for the rights of invalids had existed for ten years, and in the Soviet Union we hadn't heard anything and knew nothing about it. This was all new information for me. Later in 1991 I was invited to my first active rehabilitation [AR] camp. It was still the USSR. That's when I first met Rekryteringsgruppen [RG] from Sweden, and that's when my active role in this movement started. . . . Really, my goal was not to form an organization; I felt the need to invite RG to Ukraine so they could show lots of our [wheelchair users] how to live an active life. And to do this we needed some kind of legal entity—an organization. And that's how in 1991 in L'viv we founded the NGO that is still called Foundation for the Rehabilitation of Invalids. And I was elected head of the organization . . . .*

—YAROSLAV HRYBALSKYY, RIGHTS ACTIVIST AND PEOPLE'S
DEPUTY OF L'VIV REGIONAL PARLIAMENT, L'VIV, UKRAINE

*It's true that the Swedes gave a push toward the development of active wheelchairs. There was a wheelchair user [in Russia], Dmitrii Seniukov. . . . He was an artist and sold his wares in Russia, and Ukraine—back then it was still the Soviet Union. Somehow he decided to go to Sweden, and there he learned about the [active rehabilitation] movement, got to know that rehabilitation group [RG] and as a result he organized the production of active wheelchairs and training camps for active living. It developed parallel in Russia and Ukraine, simultaneously and in the exact same way. He [Seniukov] was probably first, because he showed up in his [active] wheelchair in [the sanatorium at] Saki, which was in Ukraine—this was after Ukrainian independence. And there he met a group from L'viv, who also got involved.*

—LEV INDOLEV, JOURNALIST AND ACTIVIST, MOSCOW, RUSSIA

*I kept getting frustrated because in a wheelchair I could not access a lot of places in our town. And I really started working on these [accessibility] issues after our trip to Canada. <u>Accessibility is really advanced in Canada</u>—wherever a healthy person can go, anyone using a wheelchair can, too. So I started approaching the business owners in our town about the lack of accessibility. . . . I brought photographs from Canada of accessible architecture to show them. I told them: "See, this exists over there" (Ot v krayinakh ie). . . . In Canada . . . why do I always mention Canada? Because it's a good example. They don't have [separate] homes for invalids, or toilets for invalids, or shops for invalids—everything is just for people (tam dlia liudei vse). For example, I was there for two weeks, and I could go into any place I wanted. I could use the same toilet as other people—there was just a stall that was a bit wider with a few modifications. I go in, I come out, and I don't feel like I'm a peculiar person (osoblyva liudyna). . . .*

*In 1999 I happened upon an active rehabilitation camp that Hrybalskyy was hosting in L'viv. And after those ten days I came back home with a completely different outlook on disability (nepovnospravnist') and everything else. The camps give you a really huge jolt (poshtovkh). After the camp you just can't stand to sit at home. Then Hrybalskyy started the five-year Ukrainian-Canadian [CCDS-CIDA] seminar project, and we were invited to participate. Before that I hadn't realized what we could—and should—do in our town. We learned that in the training [seminars].*

*Then in 2000 I was invited to another seminar on disability in Kyiv, sponsored by the UN. We started going to several seminars, with themes*

*like working with NGOs, working with the [state] administration, work-*
*ing with architects. We started compiling a lot of information, and a*
*strong information base is really important. So that's how, bit-by-bit, we*
*got started.*

—VASYL', ENTREPRENEUR AND ACTIVIST, L'VIV OBLAST'

Before the contentious 2004 Presidential elections, which sparked the
popular movement that became known as the Orange Revolution, most
people in Ukraine never gave much thought to the disabled population's
political participation, or the myriad discriminatory practices that mar-
ginalize the disabled on a daily basis, and many still do not. But as the
two presidential candidates wrangled over votes in the close election and
accused one another of election fraud, irregularities and violations concerning the access of the sick and the disabled to the ballot box came to the
fore. Early media coverage raised the issue when several persons—mostly
elderly people with heart problems and other health issues—reportedly
died when they ventured to polling stations to cast their votes (Koval'skaia
2004). It is difficult to know whether these reports were true, since media
accounts of the tumultuous elections often were heavily biased toward one
or the other contender, but the coverage did draw public attention to the
blatant violation of voting rights for certain populations, including the
disabled.

Media accounts revealed that inadequate provisions had been taken to
make polling stations accessible for the disabled, in particular the mobility disabled and the blind. Also, the accommodations that were made—
including the right of group I invalids to have a ballot brought to them
so they could vote from home, the hospital, or wherever they happened
to be—may have been abused by unscrupulous election workers who
exploited these provisions as a way to falsify ballots. The disabled became
pawns in the election frenzy as these special measures were hastily and
selectively modified, with the candidates accusing each other of "withholding the right to vote from the disabled." The situation was not resolved
to anyone's satisfaction, but the word was out: disabled people had been
disenfranchised during the presidential election.

Unfortunately, the situation appeared to improve little during the Parliamentary elections in 2006, when attention was again drawn to the inaccessibility of polling stations and the bungling of voting lists of group I
invalids entitled to vote from home. According to one media account, MP
and disability rights activist Valery Sushkevych said: "In one voting station in L'viv there are steps in front of the entrance, 13 more steps inside,

and—most amazing—there are two steps directly in front of the ballot box, one of which is nearly 30 centimeters high. How can you even talk about equal access to voting rights for invalids?" (Ponomar'ova and Melekhin 2006).

For some, these frustrations marked a broader political marginalization of the disabled population. Although a good number of my informants actively supported Viktor Yushchenko and his Our Ukraine party during the Orange Revolution, few wheelchair users participated in protests on Independence Square (which drew hundreds of thousands), citing the dangers of being in a large crowd in a wheelchair. Others reported feeling alienated from the euphoria of the "revolution." Dmitrii believed that money and resources spent to fortify protestors could have been better used to take care of vulnerable populations. During a 2005 interview he told me:

> When the "revolution" happened, I was so angry. . . . [I was] in the emergency room, and then in the hospital. And when I saw that hospital, those medicines that patients had to buy themselves . . . I saw what they were feeding them, that offal fit only for pigs. It was a nightmare. And out there everyone was walking around with orange ribbons. They were taking [the protesters] food, money, clothing. [And in the hospital] I saw two . . . not exactly homeless people, but elderly people who starved to death.

Dmitrii felt marginalized by this "democratic" revolution—the jubilation on the streets, he thought, contrasted sharply with the dismal situation in state hospitals where citizens' formal rights to free, quality health care were blatantly violated.

What sort of political life, then, characterizes the "parallel world" of the disabled? Ukraine has a multiparty system, with more than 170 parties registered with the Ministry of Justice as of mid-2009. Of registered political parties, only two are organized specifically around disability issues, both of them very small and not well known. The Ukrainian Party for Justice–Union of Veterans, Invalids, Chernobyl Victims, and Veterans of the Soviet-Afghan War (UPS-SVIChA) has only 166 members and one branch; the Party for Rehabilitation of the Chronically Ill of Ukraine has 5,744 members and 21 branches (Girman 2006:14). Questions of disability rights are not an explicit platform of concern for any of Ukraine's large political parties and coalitions, and in public discourse, discussions of disability rights or disability awareness are for the most part achingly absent. When I tell colleagues and friends in Ukraine who are not involved with disability communities that I am conducting research on the disability

*there is no war*
*in ba sing se*

FIGURE 3.1. Former Prime Minister Yulia Tymoshenko with MP Valery Sushkevych, 2008. *Photo by Aleksandr Prokopenko, courtesy of UNIAN.*

rights movement, I am often told in an authoritative tone that, "there is
no such movement." Most people in Ukraine are unfamiliar with even the
most basic terminology required to speak about disability issues, including words such as "ramp" (*pandus*) and "autism" (*autizm*). (Even some of
my disabled activist friends mispronounced *pandus* as *pantus*.) Ukrainian
athletes have had incredible success at recent paralympic games, in Athens
and Beijing in particular, but the Ukrainian media and the general public
usually takes little notice.

Despite a lack of party-level representation, the disabled population is
relatively politically active as members of an officially recognized "sociopolitical group" whose orientation is primarily "nonconfrontational" (Girman
2006:11). This political activism rarely involves disabled individuals seeking
positions of political power, but rather is rooted in "appealing to officials for
the defense of their rights and satisfaction of their needs; and cooperation
and collaboration with official structures" (Girman 2006:4). Research has
shown that in general the disabled population in Ukraine tends toward a
left-leaning political orientation, meaning the disabled tend to favor strong
government social programs, and are skeptical of economic reforms introducing a free market. There is geographical variation however, as disabled

persons in Western Ukraine, like the majority of Western Ukrainians, tend to favor free market reforms (Girman 2006:11–12).

High-level political action on disability rights is mediated primarily by one powerful coalition of disability advocacy NGOs, the National Assembly of Disabled of Ukraine (NADU, also commonly called the Assembly), a "civic-political partnership" whose membership includes 64 NGOs from all over the country. The Assembly's role as an intermediary between the state and civic organizations has led some to aptly characterize it as a "proto-[political] party" (Girman 2006). NADU was founded in 2003 by Valery Sushkevych, Ukraine's most visible disabled politician and broker of disability politics. Sushkevych, who uses a wheelchair after surviving childhood polio, was the first disabled person elected to the Verkhovna Rada (National Parliament) in independent Ukraine. His parliamentary victory in 1998 was a landmark event in Ukrainian disability history, but stories Sushkevych tells about his experiences as a newly minted MP illustrate the social stigma he nevertheless has confronted as a visibly disabled person, despite his powerful political status. When I interviewed him in 2005 Sushkevych related the following:

> I was elected to the Parliament of Ukraine and I got my ID and badge and went to the Parliament hall for the first time. I approached the doors . . . the Parliament is heavily guarded. . . . I approached the guard and showed my ID, just like all the other MPs. The guard looked at it, then looked at me in my wheelchair and said: "I have to call my superior before I can admit you." I was in shock. The mentality of that guard was a perfect reflection of our society's mentality: he couldn't fathom that, today, a person in a wheelchair with serious impairments could actually be a member of parliament . . . all he saw was an "invalid." . . . It was analogous to one time when I was near the produce market, alone in my wheelchair, and a woman came up to me, took out three hryvnias and said, "Take it, sonny." Those are two identical episodes. The social perception is that [an invalid] is second-class; he's a person whose rights must be circumscribed. . . .

In this context, where the common perception is that the disabled do not belong in "big politics," advocacy initiatives nevertheless have been able to grow, especially in the nongovernmental or civic sphere. Since the early 1990s, a range of organizations have emerged to raise public awareness about disability rights, provide services, conduct lobbying efforts, and take advantage of funding opportunities provided by international development organizations and the Ukrainian state. Sushkevych calls the period of the early to mid-1990s the "euphoristic" stage of early post-socialism, during which there was a "burst" (Rus. *vspyshka*) of enthusiasm and activity as disabled persons clamored collectively to secure their rights. Thousands of new community organizations were founded in the NGO boom of the early 1990s, and by 1996 14.6 percent of civic organizations were devoted to problems of veterans and the disabled (Sydorenko 2001:54).

Today, of the nearly 18,000 civic and charitable organizations in Ukraine around 900 focus their activities on disability issues, or 5 percent of such organizations. There are at least 38 registered NGO coalitions addressing questions of disability (Derzhavna Dopovid 2002:122). Charities, support groups, and organizations focusing on sports, the arts, entrepreneurship, and other endeavors offer opportunities for disabled persons to receive support and become part of new social networks. In many cases, these interactions have offered disabled individuals opportunities for self-realization and new ways of perceiving themselves as engaged citizens.

Disability rights advocates in Ukraine and Russia have benefited from contact with advocacy groups from countries such as the United States, Canada, the Netherlands, Sweden, Germany, and New Zealand, among others. Contemporary rights groups in Ukraine pursue diverse agendas, including providing material and social support to disabled persons, advancing disability sports, improving the accessibility of the built environment, and facilitating increased independent living opportunities, multidimensional rehabilitation, inclusive education, and job training and employment. However, my research has identified notable tensions between the small-scale successes that groups working in specific communities have achieved and the big politics of disability rights at the national level.

Rights initiatives vis-à-vis disability are shaped by several forces: the historical legacies of Soviet disability policy and disability experiences; the influence of transnational advocacy initiatives; the distinctive and complicated negotiations of civic organizing and elite politics in a postsocialist state; and unique sociocultural elements. The latter actively contribute to the challenges and successes of the Ukrainian disability movement but are not necessarily constructed only through institutions and policymaking. I want to focus on a few key moments and figures in the disability rights movement in order to assess the development of disability politics at different levels, including the local, national, and international. I am particularly interested in the visions for claiming equal citizenship that are reflected in—and that have emerged from—specific strategies for disability advocacy. What advocacy strategies have proven most effective for producing mobile citizens who can successfully claim their rights to belong? Before pursuing this question, I shall provide a brief overview of the challenges common to all would-be NGO organizers in postsocialist Ukraine, and then focus more specifically on the case of disability advocacy initiatives.

## Barriers to Postsocialist NGO Organizing

Although some challenges that NGO actors face in Ukraine are particular to postsocialist states, many will be familiar to NGO activists in other world regions.[1] Some of the major challenges that confront those seeking to carry out social activism through NGOs in Ukraine today include the following: bureaucratic red tape, inhibitive tax laws and laws governing humanitarian aid, financial vulnerability, interorganizational competition, and negative social perceptions. Although NGOs in Ukraine have not been subject to the same kind of scrutiny and pressure that NGOs in Russia have faced in recent years (Blitt 2008), the legal environment in Ukraine still is not conducive to the development of a vibrant NGO sphere. NGOs enjoy few tax benefits, and there is little incentive for businesses or individuals to make charitable donations. Those tax benefits that NGOs do enjoy put activists at risk of being enticed into unlawful activity: since NGOs can receive shipments of humanitarian aid duty-free, for example, many of my informants were approached by business representatives who asked them to illegally import consumer goods for them under the guise of humanitarian aid.

Financing and economic viability are a perpetual challenge for NGOs, which as nonprofits are limited in their means of generating capital. International donor organizations have been active in Ukraine and other postsocialist states during the past two decades, but such support appears to be waning. Organizations and corporations such as the Eurasia Foundation, Counterpart International, Inc., and Phillip Morris, among others, have supported disability advocacy NGOs through grants. The most visible and powerful all-Ukrainian organizations, many of them large NGO coalitions, receive considerable funding from the Ukrainian state through the State Budget for Civic Organizations of Invalids. In 2007, total payouts from this budget totaled over 40 million UAH, nearly $8 million (MLSP 2008:198–199). These organizations' reliance on state financing raises questions about the ability of the large all-Ukrainian coalitions to represent the interests of their constituents, rather than those of the state.

Some NGO leaders have successfully forged relationships with representatives of local governments and businesses, who act as steady sponsors. For several years during the late 1990s and early 2000s, organizations in Kyiv benefited from the Turbota (Care) program of then-mayor Oleksandr Omelchenko, which provided eligible organizations with financial support on a competitive basis. According to my sources in the disability rights movement, Kyiv's current mayor, Leonid Chernovets'kyi, is less supportive of disability advocacy issues, and of public initiatives to empower marginalized groups of citizens in general. In a country where charitable giving is not an established cultural or political practice for individuals, small businesses, or corporations, and foreign sources of funding are not constant, NGO activists must creatively seek ways to survive economically. The groups in my study have pursued diverse strategies, including social contracting; pursuing avenues to encourage state institutions to adopt the NGO's programs at the state level, thus taking pressure off the NGO for providing certain services; conducting independent fundraisers; and establishing social enterprises (NGOs with a business wing) to provide NGOs with a reliable source of funding (Phillips 2005).

In this context, the NGO sphere is highly competitive and NGO actors often are distrustful of one another. Groups with similar agendas and interests compete for resources, and information about sponsors, legislation, and project opportunities is at a premium. Furthermore, local government officials and businesspeople are often wary of NGOs, which they perceive as encroaching on their territory and their interests. NGO activists complain that they are compelled to contribute a great deal of time and energy to negotiate conflicts with other civic groups and with local bureaucrats.

NGO activists also face perceptual challenges, as societal perceptions of NGOs tend to be quite negative. There is a popular belief, sometimes not completely unfounded, that NGOs are more about unscrupulous individuals trying to acquire material benefits for themselves than actually seeking social change. One activist said that most of his disabled acquaintances distance themselves from NGOs even though they could stand to benefit from membership in advocacy groups. These perceptions have prevented some young people from taking part in disability rights NGOs, and for the most part NGO activists tend to be middle-aged and older representatives of the last Soviet generation. The long-term effects of this generational gap remain unclear, but my interviewees, many of whom were considered members of the "old guard" of disability rights activism and were in their forties and fifties, frequently lamented that there were no prospective members of the younger generation to take their place in the movement.

Despite these complications NGOs represent a widespread empowerment strategy for the disabled in post-Soviet Ukraine. There is a broad range of organizations, including generalized community-based organizations that unite people in a town or small city with different kinds of disabilities, disability-specific groups, mutual-aid associations for disabled persons and their families to secure assistance and pool their resources, and large countrywide NGO coalitions comprised of many small and large groups. Some organizing efforts have met with considerable success, while others have had only limited positive effects. The reasons are complex and have much to do with structural factors as mentioned above, but interpersonal relations and cultural factors are also important. Anthropological approaches, which combine attention to context and structural factors with an emphasis on day-to-day realities and experiences, are well suited to capture all these nuances. Starting on the ground with one rights organization and its founder, for instance, can end up taking us in many different directions, as disability rights activists and their advocacy strategies literally travel the globe. Following these movements and the changes occurring in their wake reveals a dynamic picture of disabled people's active pursuit of a more mobile citizenship in Ukraine today.

## From Sweden to George Washington Street: Transnational Connections and Local Realities

I first met Yaroslav Hrybalskyy during summer 2002. A resident of L'viv, where he is head of several advocacy organizations, Yaroslav was in Kyiv for a meeting with fellow activists from Ukraine and abroad. I volunteered as a translator for the meeting, which meant I could not really participate in the conversations myself or conduct my own interviews. Over the next few years, during which I returned to Ukraine several times for research, I met Yaroslav numerous times in Kyiv and L'viv but was unable to conduct a formal interview. In October 2006 I finally interviewed him during a research trip to L'viv.

Yaroslav invited me to his office on George Washington Street where, he joked, as an American I should feel right at home. We had an amiable conversation, and Yaroslav was an engaging and thoughtful interlocutor, but it was clear to me that he did not enjoy talking about himself. Earlier I had seen a Ukrainian television special about spinal'niki that had featured

Yaroslav and his initiatives (Myloserdia 2003); I found it interesting that most of Yaroslav's personal details—the story of his spinal trauma, his background in music and education, the details of his marriage and his close relationship with his daughter—are narrated not by Yaroslav himself, but by his sister and his wife. Through them we learn that Yaroslav received a spinal cord injury in 1971 when, as an eighteen-year-old teachers' college student doing obligatory work on a Soviet collective farm, he fell from a tree. He met his wife, a nurse, at a sanatorium for the disabled. Yaroslav's own dialogue in the video centers on disability politics, especially strategies for improving social infrastructure, the built environment, and societal attitudes. Likewise, during our interview Yaroslav steered the conversation toward the big picture of disability rights issues.

Accordingly, our conversation started on a general note. We began to discuss the major foci of the mobility disability rights movement in Ukraine today: the improvement of medical services; the formulation of a comprehensive system of post-trauma rehabilitation; the provision of suitable wheelchairs and other equipment; the deinstitutionalization of disabled children; the guarantee of equal access to quality education; equal employment; and the development of accessible transportation options, public spaces, and buildings. When I asked Yaroslav to talk about the history of the disability rights movement in Ukraine, he prefaced his remarks with the warning, "We each have our own history, and my perspectives are influenced by my own version of that history." Although he acknowledged that Gorbachev's policies had opened up spaces for community organizing, Yaroslav was careful not to over-romanticize the late 1980s as a time when the grassroots truly flourished. Rather, he emphasized that the Communist Party itself, in what Yaroslav called a Party "directive," actually organized the first "civic organizations of invalids." Accordingly, said Yaroslav, Party functionaries—many of whom had only peripheral connections to matters of disability—headed most of these early organizations. He voiced a clear division between the top-down, state-sponsored organizations and those founded by activists such as himself, representatives of a more bottom-up movement.

Yaroslav founded his own organization, the L'viv Oblast' Section of the Foundation for the Rehabilitation of Invalids (FRI), in 1991. One of the first disability advocacy NGOs to take up wide-scale empowerment initiatives, especially for the mobility disabled, FRI has had many different yet complementary foci and projects over the years. As described by Yaroslav in the interview excerpt above, FRI has promoted IL and active rehabilitation (AR) for wheelchair users using the methodology promoted by the Swedish RG group. One of Yaroslav's primary concerns is how to improve accessibility of the built environment in L'viv and in the country more generally; a related focus is the development of the AR methodology in Ukraine. Indeed, Yaroslav has become perhaps Ukraine's most vigorous proponent of the AR philosophy, and his personal motto is "There are no barriers!"[2]

As an activist situated at the intersection of local worlds, histories, and lived realities in Ukraine, all of which are additionally layered with transnational initiatives and the processes of globalization that drive them, Yaroslav and his experiences organizing empowerment can shed light on a host of important institutional and interpersonal dynamics. The story of AR in particular illustrates how within the contemporary Ukrainian disability rights movement, homegrown disability rights narratives and strategies intersect with and bump up against those introduced by representatives of disability rights organizations from other countries. The "social life" of AR is thus an excellent case study for exploring the effects of globalization on postsocialist social politics and institution building, and the important ways in which local histories and ways of knowing and (inter)acting still matter.

In contexts of major social and economic transformations, what happens when local understandings and strategies for empowerment meet up with more globalizing ones? What new possibilities for change do such intersections produce, and, alternatively, where do we find disconnects that thwart cooperation and the translation of ideas and tactics (Wedel 1998)? Importantly, what do these collisions reveal about Ukrainian experiences of organizing empowerment that might otherwise be obscured? And in practical terms, how successful have been the efforts of transnational advocacy groups to help disabled persons in Ukraine empower themselves, and how might such strategies be improved? All of these questions are important for tracking how mobile citizenship is produced in a globalizing world—to what extent is transnational advocacy effective for producing citizens who can be more at home in their own social and political milieu?

In the introduction to their volume *Disability in Local and Global Worlds,* Benedicte Ingstad and Susan Reynolds Whyte (2007) emphasize the insights that anthropological perspectives can lend to understanding local-level processes in today's era of transnational rights advocacy and international standards for regulating disability rights. The authors stress the importance of context when exploring local and global intersections in disability experience and governmentality, and they state further:

It is our argument that the energizing potential of human-rights declarations, progressive policies, and national statements of intent toward
disabled citizens has to be measured in the context of local worlds.
For that is where people are acting to make things work, and where
the potentials may (or may not) be effected and effective as they were
intended to be. (Ingstad and Whyte 2007:24)

In privileging the perspective of the local in these discussions of transnational advocacy, I want to emphasize that the local is anything but static.
This becomes clear when one considers the diverse little histories of disability rights groups, and the multiple perspectives on disability, rights,
and empowerment one finds at various nodes in the movement. Also, as
others have noted (Sassen 2000; Thayer 2001), it is tempting yet often a
mistake to view the local as a site of stoppages or an end point where globalizing discourses are received and ingested whole. Rather, we should
better recognize the local as a space of negotiation and dialogue, where
the global is variously played out. Such variation is illustrated in the social
life of one transnational advocacy initiative that has traveled from Sweden
via Russia to various Ukrainian cities and towns, before being institutionalized and fitfully, and only partially, fixed in place.

The initiative I have in mind is the active rehabilitation (AR) empowerment strategy introduced to Ukraine and other postsocialist countries
from Sweden. AR has had very real, positive impacts for wheelchair users in
Ukraine. Many of my informants cited "my first AR camp" as a major turning point in their lives, an experience that set them on the path to a more
fulfilling life. This was a narrative repeated over and over in personal interviews. I learned that despite attempts to standardize and regulate AR in the
Ukrainian context, there are interesting "grey zones" (Dunn 2005) where AR
narratives and practices have been taken up and reworked by local actors.
Within contexts quite specific to postsocialist states such as Ukraine, AR
has boiled over from discrete training camps—the form in which the program was introduced by Swedish activists—to inform the empowerment
strategies of disabled persons more broadly in a range of local settings. And
the rather standardized AR program has been tinkered with and sometimes
surreptitiously taken up and modified. Such engagements are important for
shedding light on how people variously interact with standardized forms, a
subject of ever-increasing relevance in today's world of standardization and
formalizing practices (Lampland and Star 2009).

The case of AR is also an example of the ways in which global processes
can become constituted inside the national (Sassen 2007), producing far-

reaching and ambiguous effects. Using ethnography to track the social life of AR and its multiple instantiations in Ukraine allows us to sketch out an example of Ukrainian disability rights advocacy at the intersection of the local, the national, and the global that may be instructive for other investigations of transnational advocacy endeavors in Eastern Europe and beyond. Key guides in this ethnographic endeavor have been Yaroslav Hrybalskyy, Oleg Poloziuk, Zoia, Sasha, and several other Ukrainian friends and informants, as well as two Swedish representatives of Rekryteringsgruppen.

### A Circle of People's Diplomacy: Active Rehabilitation

As previously noted, AR was introduced in Eastern Europe in the early 1990s via camps organized in Russia, Ukraine, Belarus, and other former socialist countries by the Swedish organization Rekryteringsgruppen for Active Rehabilitation (RG). With the resolute help of neuroscientist Katarzyna Trok, a Polish émigré to Sweden, AR moved around Eastern Europe in what Yaroslav calls a "circle of people's diplomacy, thanks to which thousands of people are living different and better lives." In the beginning, AR camps in Ukraine were carried out with logistical and financial support from RG and other foreign sponsors. The camps were intended primarily for persons who, in the local parlance, had new or "fresh" (*svizhyi*) spinal cord injuries, a population perceived to be in greatest need of AR. Representatives from RG ran the initial camps, and were also responsible for training Ukrainian wheelchair users as instructors. Today, Ukrainian instructors conduct AR camps themselves.

From the start RG's representatives made it clear that all instructors were to run AR camps without deviating from the structured and very specific RG guidelines. Since the camp is an intensive, closed event provided free of charge to wheelchair users, participants, instructors, and assistants/volunteers must be accommodated and fed for at least a week, and they must be provided with suitable equipment, especially lightweight wheelchairs. The Swedes were concerned that the effectiveness of the intensive program (which, after all, lasted just seven to ten days) would be compromised if modified, and they also stressed safety concerns. According to a number of my informants, RG appointed several Ukrainian individuals as monitors to ensure that all camps purporting to represent the RG active rehabilitation techniques adhere to the strict requirements.

Having fulfilled its stated mission to introduce AR and train a cadre of Ukrainian instructors, RG is no longer very active on the ground in Ukraine.

I was told that today the Swedes do not provide financing for the camps carried out in Ukraine, only technical advice. Running an AR camp is expensive by Ukrainian standards—according to one of my informants, in 2008 the cost for a seven- to ten-day AR camp was approximately $16,000. This is a large sum for NGOs to accumulate for a single event. Often instructors are not paid, but rather lead the camps on a volunteer basis. The standardization of AR camps has caused some difficulties for small, economically strapped NGOs to finance camps that satisfy the exacting standards set by RG. As a result, AR camps are held relatively infrequently, most camps are small, and participants are hand picked. In 2006 one of my sources estimated that of the approximately 2,600 persons who receive spinal injuries annually in Ukraine, no more than several hundred were invited to the camps. This number appears to be shrinking each year.

Writing about EU expansion, Elizabeth Dunn (2005:176–177) describes how, in conditions of postsocialism, standards in Eastern Europe are expected to function as "what Latour calls 'immutable mobiles': objects transferred from one community of practice to another, which have profoundly transformative effects without being transformed themselves." Representatives of RG whom I met in Kyiv presented AR as precisely such an immutable mobile. In 2002, I volunteered as a translator for discussions between Oskar and Maria (pseudonyms), who had come from Sweden, and about 15 Ukrainian wheelchair users. During the meeting, Oskar described AR as a "simple model" that uses no expensive equipment, and he framed AR as a "universal" model that does not need to be adapted to local contexts. He expressed a belief that rehabilitation programs should be standardized across the country, and he emphasized the need for a "uniform model, so things won't fall apart." He told his Ukrainian counterparts that if activists in different cities throughout Ukraine took up the same uniform and standardized rehabilitation programs, they would be taken more seriously by the international community and by local government authorities. Further, Oskar predicted that having the same program in different locations would encourage a healthy competition between advocacy NGOs.

In insisting on the immutability of their AR program, the Swedes proposed that it should "work" quite the same in Ukraine and other Eastern European countries as it had in Sweden, if it were adopted wholesale and unaltered. And indeed, everyone I met who had attended AR camps said it was an extremely empowering, life-changing experience. It is certainly not my intention here to disparage RG or the camps, which have helped provide many mobility disabled persons in post-Soviet countries a new lease on life. But the standardization of AR and the social life of this empowerment strategy in the Ukrainian context may provide important clues as to the potential limitations of transnational advocacy efforts that assume a universal experience where it does not exist.

AR as an instrument of standards is on a dramatically smaller scale than those such as the highly standardized protocol for treating tuberculosis through Directly Observed Treatment, Short-Course (DOTS), promoted by the World Health Organization (WHO), and Codex Alimentarius, the World Trade Organization's (WTO) global standards of food safety and hygiene. Whereas the movement of DOTS (Koch 2007) and Codex (Dunn 2008) in different geographical and sociopolitical contexts has been investigated by anthropologists to uncover how standards foster claims about power and who can control knowledge, AR sheds light on some additional aspects of standards and standardization in an increasingly interconnected world. First, the social life of AR in Ukraine lets us examine the ways that individuals interact with standard forms. What innovations if any are developed, and what can we learn from them? Second, AR points also to the problematic issue of translating metrics of success in varying sociocultural and political environments. Does AR appear to have "worked" in Ukraine? According to whom, and by what criteria?

For years anthropologists studying the international development industry have critiqued development programs that are uncritically transplanted from place to place and fail to take into account local realities (Escobar 1994, Ferguson 1994). Development organizations themselves have engaged in self-critique, and a recent trend is to focus on empowering persons from the grassroots and pay a good deal of attention to local contexts (Gardner and Lewis 1996, Lewis and Wallace 2000). It may therefore be surprising that RG would insist on strict adherence to the Swedish-developed program and eschew local innovations in the AR regimen. But we must remember that RG is not a development organization implementing large-scale programs. It is, to the contrary, a rather small advocacy group seeking to share powerful strategies for overcoming physical and psychological barriers with wheelchair users in places like Ukraine, where lack of accessible architecture significantly limits people's opportunities to socialize, study, work, and carry out the mundane tasks of everyday life. In the Swedes' eyes, seeking to ensure the continuity of the AR program as it traveled to Ukraine is the responsible thing to do.

The Swedes' insistence on the standardization of AR and their attempts to enforce it have produced a range of effects, some of them unexpected, many of them positive. First, AR as developed by the Swedes is possible only with lightweight, active wheelchairs. Such wheelchairs did not exist in the Soviet Union, and in the early days of the AR camps the RG representatives traveling to Ukraine to conduct camps brought used active wheelchairs from Sweden for participants to use and keep. This created local demand, and in the late 1990s and early 2000s several factories in Ukraine began domestic production of active wheelchairs. In the years since, these factories have discontinued production, but legislation now guarantees wheelchair users two new wheelchairs every four years, and even though this law is not always enforced, it represents a significant step forward.[3] In many ways, these positive developments are a result of the AR camps.

Second, in channeling AR through a few well-placed individuals, the Swedes—though they could not have predicted this at the time—actually ensured that AR programs could over time be incorporated into the state program for addressing disability concerns. Almost all AR camps in Ukraine today are implemented and financed by the disability sports program Invasport (the National Committee for Sports of Invalids of Ukraine). Cash-strapped individual NGOs no longer hold AR camps. Indeed, the last NGO-sponsored AR camp I heard about was in the Transcarpathian region in Western Ukraine (Zakarpattia) during fall 2006, and a hurricane disrupted it. This seemed an omen of trouble to come.

Through Invasport, AR camps are offered from May to October at the National Ukraina Center, a multimillion-dollar sports complex that MP Valery Sushkevych initiated in the early 2000s near the Crimean city of

FIGURE 3.2. National Ukraina Center, Evpatoria, 2005.

Evpatoria. The Ukraina Center was built primarily as a training facility for the Ukrainian paralympic team; when I visited the complex during summer 2005 I met members of the paralympic fencing team. It is a multiuse facility that seems to span Sushkevych's many activities as a key political player in disability issues. To my knowledge it is the only fully wheelchair accessible hotel, sports facility, and beach in the entire former Soviet Union. The Ukraina Center is a well-appointed setting by any standards, and the chance to spend ten days at a top-notch sports and vacation facility on the Black Sea, one that is fully wheelchair accessible, is a wonderful, once-in-a-lifetime opportunity for many participants of the AR camps.

The implications of the Invasport's quasi-takeover of AR are still unclear. On the one hand, there is a real possibility that AR could become a standard component of the system of social protection for the disabled and thus be offered to every wheelchair user as a part of his or her individualized program of rehabilitation (IPRI). In this scenario, perhaps standardization and strict control of AR actually have been the best means through which to institutionalize the strategy into a far-reaching national program and insure that, as Oskar put it, "things don't fall apart."

On the other hand, Invasport, which is closely tied to Sushkevych and NADU, is a potentially problematic broker for programs like AR. First, it is unclear what criteria are used when inviting camp participants; space is limited and personal connections undoubtedly play a role. Also, it has become clear that AR camps in Ukraine (which, to repeat, are held at a paralympic training center) are used as a first step to selecting and training elite paralympic athletes. Although the form and content of the camps themselves have remained consistent with RG's guidelines, the uses to which the camps are now put are quite different. Although all AR participants undoubtedly benefit from the camps, it appears they also have become a site of differentiation of spinal'niki between the "regular" wheelchair users and those with athletic (paralympic) promise.

Sushkevych's multiple leadership roles add further complexity. Not only is he the founder and head of NADU, he is also an MP; the head of the Ukrainian National Paralympic Committee; the head of Invasport; and the head of the State Committee for Pensioners', Veterans', and Invalids' Affairs. Some of my interviewees questioned Suchkevych's motives in his different positions. Why spend millions of dollars of government money on a world-class facility that would benefit only a tiny fraction of disabled Ukrainians? As one friend put it, "With the resources that went into the Ukraina Center, they could have built adequate rehabilitation facilities in all of the country's

[26] regions and all the major cities." From this perspective, it could appear that the Ukrainian AR program has been co-opted by a conglomerate of elite quasi-governmental institutions and sequestered in a lovely yet, for most disabled persons, distant and out of reach setting. Unfortunately, only two or three AR camps are held annually at the Ukraina Center, with probably fewer than 50 participants all year.

Other aspects of AR's social life reveal further complications. As Oskar (the Swedish RG representative) predicted, Ukrainian NGOs serving the mobility disabled have scrambled to organize their own AR camps, and this has indeed produced competition among various NGOs and among some activists. Whether or not this is the healthy competition that Oskar advocated is a matter for debate. Zoia and Sasha, for example, who founded their organization Lotus on principles of AR, were continuously discouraged from organizing AR camps by another activist (not Yaroslav) who framed AR as his exclusive territory. Did the standardization and streamlining of AR and the competition this engendered cause local NGOs to drop the ball while quasi-state institutions took over the program and channeled AR camp participants according to their own interests?

Although standards and the stories about them (Lampland and Star 2009) have drawn the analytical attention of social scientists in recent years, most research on standardization examines the development of various standards and metrics and uncovers the often obscure origins and history of standards, which have become so ubiquitous to modern life that most of us barely notice them. We do not know much, however, about how people made subject to standards interpret, follow, subvert, or innovate with standards, and why. As Elizabeth Dunn (2005) explored in her study of the application of EU standards to the Polish meat processing industry, in postsocialist contexts standardization across borders has great potential to produce inequalities between categories of people on the ground and often generates a "grey zone" where people take up strategies to circumvent standards and conduct their business in ways that suit their particular circumstances. So in Ukraine one would expect to find local innovations on the standardized AR program, and I indeed found several instances of such local modifications.

In 2006, for example, I was invited to attend a weeklong rehabilitation day camp sponsored by a small NGO in the eastern Ukrainian city of Kharkiv. The camp was designed to involve the city's wheelchair users in a variety of activities to allow them to develop social networks, master wheelchair-use techniques, and learn daily living skills such as supermarket shopping. There are approximately 900 persons who use wheelchairs in Kharkiv (Alpatova and Zub 2006), around 30 of whom attended the camp. A friend of mine, Pasha, who had attended an AR camp but was not certified as an AR instructor, led the wheelchair techniques lessons. The conditions of the camp were certainly not those specified by RG. Pasha used some components of the AR program but was compelled to improvise and develop new exercises, since some participants did not have active wheelchairs, some had very weak arms, others were fearful of trying to go over barriers such as curbs and bumps, and the volunteers enlisted to assist in the course had not been trained to support wheelchair users learning AR techniques. Also, participants went home at the end of the day rather than spending the entire week in a closed, intensive environment. When I discussed the event with Pasha I initially called it a camp (Rus. *lager'*), but he corrected me and insisted that he and the other organizers were carrying out "courses," not a camp, since the event was not officially approved as AR. Although he enjoyed teaching the course and believed some participants benefited a great deal, Pasha had some concerns for participants' safety. Pasha commented that he was "not supposed to be teaching this course," and said he hoped that others in the wheelchair user community would not get wind of his activities. However, he also challenged the appropriateness of applying AR as a standardized system of training and rehabilitation. Pasha voiced his frustration in the following narrative:

You can't just treat everyone alike and lump them together. One person is stronger, one will be weaker. Somebody has a stronger psyche; someone else's is weaker. It's not right [to apply one standard]. If we develop an approach but it does not conform to the standard canon, then *a priori* it must be discounted. That's not right. After all, the idea is to show someone a new path, new possibilities, and he will take it from there. How I show him [that new path] is of secondary importance. It doesn't matter whether it's by using a "pure" (Rus. *chistaia*) methodology that is accepted here, and in Poland, and wherever else the Swedes have been, or if it is something we've thought up ourselves, based on our own conditions (Rus. *usloviia*). I think that is a normal, perfectly acceptable approach.

This example shows how NGOs and activists have engaged in a type of self-surveillance vis-à-vis AR, but at the same time, this has not prevented the development of local innovations, limited though they may be. The camp—however small and improvised—allowed some of Kharkiv's disabled residents to become more mobile citizens in a physical and social sense. According to the camp's organizers, one participant, a woman in her late twenties, left the apartment where she lives with her parents for the first time in twelve years in order to attend the camp. Such local innovations are important as testing grounds for the disabled to cultivate various new strategies for achieving different kinds of mobility and citizenship.

Similarly, AR has allowed wheelchair users to take the skills acquired in the camps—in particular, increased facility in maneuvering the chair—and apply them to new contexts. One such innovation is the development of wheelchair sport dance in Ukraine, a form of ballroom dancing that is popular internationally. Wheelchair sport dance involves different combinations of dancers—sometimes two wheelchair users are partnered together, or a wheelchair user may partner with a nondisabled dancer. Several wheelchair sport dance clubs and teams have emerged throughout the country, and the dancers I have interviewed all point to AR as a major motivating factor. Wheelchair dance is quite different from AR—it is about grace and precision of movement rather than overcoming structural barriers—and wheelchair sport dance represents the perpetuation of AR strategies for increased physical mobility and self-confidence in ways not constricted by the standardization paradigm. It is thus an example of local actors successfully adapting AR in ways that square with their on-the-ground realities and interests.

At the same time, the real effects of an emphasis on standardization in programs like AR should not be overlooked. If the ultimate goal of AR is to give disabled Ukrainians the tools to empower themselves in their own contexts, then the reluctance of gatekeepers to encourage or even recognize possibilities for local innovations seems contradictory to that goal. In the case of the Swedish-promoted AR, this inflexibility accounted for at least one missed opportunity, an obvious one I was able to track during various meetings and conversations with Swedish activists and their Ukrainian counterparts. This missed opportunity involves an issue of great importance to Ukrainians after spinal injury—medical care.

During the 2002 meeting where I participated as a translator, RG representative Oskar discussed with the Ukrainian activists the concept and role of the exemplary model, or first contact person. The first contact person is an individual who has experienced a spinal injury himself or herself who visits newly injured persons in the hospital to serve as a resource and positive role model for living with a spinal injury. The Ukrainians, some of whom were undergoing physical rehabilitation at a center in Kyiv where the meeting was held, repeatedly asked Oskar about the exemplary model's potential role as a resource for information and advice on questions of medical care and interventions. In the context of a system of medicine that is very resource poor, understaffed, and low-tech, mortality rates for spinally injured persons are high, and proper immediate and long-term medical care is extremely important. However, Oskar refused to engage on this point, repeatedly stating that the RG model restricts first contact people from offering medical advice: "That is the realm of the medical professionals, not the exemplary model—they are not qualified to offer advice on medical treatment." This was contrary to the Ukrainians' experience, as a discussion I had later with several participants revealed. As one young man said, "It's just a different situation in Ukraine. We can't depend on the physicians, or the nurses, to know much about spinal injury, and to give us proper treatment. Anyone here will tell you that the people most knowledgeable about treating spinal injury are the spinal'niki themselves. If we had not relied on other spinal'niki for medical advice, half of us wouldn't even be here now." This lack of trust in the medical system was revealed in a survey of 100 disabled citizens of Kharkiv, only 17 percent of whom professed trust in medical personnel. It is striking that nearly the same percentage—16 percent—said they trusted the church.[4] Considering that eastern Ukraine was for 70 years subject to the official Soviet policy of atheism, this is no compliment to members of the medical profession. The RG representatives dismissed this situation-specific form of knowledge that contradicted the Swedish model, and an opportunity to adapt the program to local conditions was lost.

This is a limitation of transnational initiatives that is widely recognized by Ukrainian disability rights activists. As Zoia and Sasha wrote in one of their grant applications for Lotus: "Unfortunately, methods proposed by foreign sources do not take into account the specifics of our country and are not always appropriate in our contexts. The need to develop our own methods and systems of learning on the basis of native experience is extremely pressing." Could Ukrainian experience and knowledge be better integrated into AR's "circle of people's diplomacy?"

AR, of course, is more than just a technical program to teach people how to maneuver their bodies and their wheelchairs. Rather, AR is a discourse and praxis about helping develop the "physical and mental ability to take care of oneself, in daily life," as stated on the RG website.[5] During our interview Yaroslav described the benefits of AR in the postsocialist context as follows: "Active rehabilitation is more than something physical—it is moral and mental. In the USSR, invalids waited for things to come to them. AR lets you feel that you are a person too, that you don't have to depend on special entitlements." AR seeks to empower the individual wheelchair user by promoting initiative, self-confidence, and self-reliance, and "helps people become less reliant on the state," as Yaroslav put it. As such, AR dovetails with the general trends of privatization and individualization that characterize much of postsocialist life during the shift to market economies and the promotion of neoliberal ideologies and cultural logics (Dunn 2005, Phillips 2008, Rivkin-Fish 2005).

Not surprisingly then, AR philosophies have bubbled over into other spheres of disability advocacy, and activists readily extend the ideals of AR beyond the training camps. For example, some refer to AR to criticize the passivity they believe the Soviet state inculcated in disabled citizens. For these activists, AR allows the disabled to work on themselves to become as self-sufficient as possible in the postsocialist context—here personal independence is stressed as a goal. In other contexts, AR is valued because it allows wheelchair users to literally break through barriers that limit their life possibilities. Here the will and ability to become socially integrated and to have the pluck to present oneself in a hostile, barrier-ridden environment are applauded. AR, it seems, has interfaced in powerful ways with conversations about personal drive and responsibility in this postsocialist society. Activists have stretched the AR philosophy from the uniform and standardized training camps to inform the empowerment strategies of wheelchair users in a variety of ways.

The social life of AR in Ukraine shows how interventions that are seemingly straightforward, clear-cut, and universally applicable are often anything but. Given how this program now sits uneasily between the local(s) and the national, the fate of AR and its future potential as an empowerment strategy for wheelchair users is still unclear. If the scales tip one way and a solid government program coalesces around AR, each and every wheelchair user may have access to this powerful rehabilitation program. If the scales tip the other way, however, "true" AR will be reserved for a select few, those handpicked by elite representatives of the disability rights community. These two extreme possible outcomes underscore the importance of the state/national in determining what the end effects of globalization will be. At the same time, the strategies of those without access to the standardized, sanctioned AR camps to nevertheless patch together local innovations and bring AR in bits and pieces to their own communities speaks to the unexpected and varied ways in which the global becomes instantiated in local worlds. These uncertainties are what make AR a fertile site for enacting mobile citizenship, one that Ukrainians continue to tap.

AR also illustrates how international advocacy interventions can have a domino effect of sorts, as the process of implementing AR strategies has opened some avenues for further empowerment strategies. Yaroslav, for example, told me that there has been some difficulty in promoting AR in Ukraine due to the compromised physical state of many wheelchair users, who have not had access to advanced techniques of physical rehabilitation. Yaroslav and his colleagues in L'viv thus identified a need for trained rehabilitation therapists, and found willing, dedicated partners in Canada who have helped foster the development of a completely new profession in Ukraine, that of physical therapy based on Canadian models.

## Serious Politics in the Parallel World: Disability NGOs and Coalition Building

Having examined some of the complex dynamics of organizing empowerment at the nexus of the transnational, the national, and the local, I now turn to a discussion of disability rights initiatives in the world of "big politics" in Ukraine. Clearly, liaisons with foreign or international advocacy groups and donor organizations have been important for the development of agendas for Ukrainian disability rights NGOs. It is also important to consider more local dynamics of organizational life, and the prospects for local coalition building in particular.

It is generally recognized that coalition building is important for the success of social movements, especially for the purposes of directed collective action and lobbying. This is certainly true in Ukraine, where representatives of state institutions, as a matter of expediency, prefer to work with coalitions rather than with individual organizations. In fact, some bureaucrats insist on it; as one activist involved in Chernobyl-related advocacy told me, "We were compelled to form a coalition of a whole bunch of different Chernobyl NGOs. Otherwise we could not get members of the administration to meet with us and consider our proposals." Therefore, in many cases coalition building in Ukraine is not an organic process but one born of necessity. This situation can foment conflict within already fragile coalitions, which easily become fragmented.

This is not to say that coalitions of disability-related organizations do not exist. By July 2008, 66 all-Ukrainian (national) and international organizations for the disabled were registered with the Ministry of Justice (MLSP 2008:191). Only a few of them, however, are very visible. Many of these groups unite only people with certain types of disabilities—the blind, the deaf, veterans, Chernobyl victims—rather than representing the common interests of disability communities in a broad-based agenda.

In the case of disability rights, effective coalition building has been stymied in part by historical legacies, especially the control the Soviet state wielded over definitions and categorizations of disability, and the concomitant symbolic and physical segregation of people with different types of disabilities. Some of the largest and most visible coalitions of disability-related NGOs, such as the Union of Organizations of Invalids of Ukraine (SOIU), UTOS, and UTOG, are heirs of Soviet-era organizations. (The Soviet predecessor to the SOIU was founded in 1988, and the Soviet-era VOS and VOG were established in the Ukrainian SSR in 1933.) These groups were modeled on the top-down Party system model of the Soviet state and have unwieldy, rather ossified structures. They are characterized by institutional memories and procedures of operation ill equipped to address present-day issues of importance beyond the rather narrow agenda of retaining existing benefits for the disabled. SOIU has grown into a gargantuan umbrella organization uniting a total of 1,374 associations (25 oblast' or regional, 77 city, 313 raion or county-based, and 959 local) representing nearly one million people (MLSP 2008:192).

One promising example of successful coalition building among disability advocacy NGOs comes out of the parents' movement. The parents' movement around disability issues has developed in Ukraine over the last decade and a half and has been particularly strong in L'viv and in Kyiv, but activists from smaller cities and towns have played important roles as well. Key activists in the parents' movement include partners Mykola Swarnyk and Oksana Kunanec-Swarnyk. Mykola founded the NGO Nadiya (Hope) for disabled children and their parents in the early 1990s, and both Swarnyks were instrumental in starting the Dzherelo (Wellspring) rehabilitation center in L'viv (see Farrell 1999). Other key activists in the parents' movement include Maria Shchybryk, founder of the center Shkola Zhyttia (School of Life) for children with autism, and Raisa Kravchenko, who founded a charitable organization to support intellectually disabled children in Kyiv, also called Dzherelo. What these activists all have in common is the experience of parenting disabled children.

In 2003, these organizations and more than 20 other civic organizations of parents of disabled children formed a Coalition for Defense of the Rights of Invalids and Persons with Intellectual Disabilities (hereafter the Coalition) under the aegis of the Kyiv Dzherelo organization. An important factor in this process was that the member organizations agreed on the issue of "intellectual disability," broadly conceptualized, as the uniting concern of the Coalition. Member NGOs include those focusing on the needs of children with Down syndrome, autism, and others. Mykola Swarnyk (2005) describes the Coalition and its success in the following terms:

The unique characteristic of the Coalition is the fact that each organization retains its organizational independence, name, and sphere of
action. All collective actions are based in principles of voluntary coordination; participation in training leader-activists; organizing events;
collective lobbying of the Verkhovna Rada, the Cabinet of Ministers,
the Ministry of Labor and Social Policy, and other organs of power and
administration. . . . A system of services for persons with intellectual
disabilities has been formulated, including quality standards, as well
as an ethical code and many propositions for laws and legislative acts.
. . . Overall rights protection is one of the key priorities of the parents'
organizations.

The Coalition now includes more than 60 organizations from all over
Ukraine, and it has brought greater visibility to the parents' movement
and to the problems and unmet needs of disabled children, all the while
advancing these children's interests through lobbying and legislative proposals. As discussed below, Mykola is now a member of the L'viv city government, which means he is well placed to advance the Coalition's interests in that city. What makes the Coalition unique for Ukraine, and is the
likely key to its success, is the democratic nature of leadership and the
fact that the Coalition grew organically over time in response to commonly held perceptions about problems faced by disabled children and
their families, and how best to address them.

Other disability-related NGO coalitions are more centralized, with
decision-making power located at the top. This description aptly characterizes the most visible coalition of disability rights NGOs in Ukraine
today—the National Assembly of Disabled of Ukraine (NADU), the coalition formed under the leadership of Valery Sushkevych in 2001. Sushkevych, who became a champion swimmer, began his formal organizing
activities in the late 1980s. He focused his early social activism on disability sports, founding a club for physical culture and sports called Optimist
in his home city, Dnipropetrovs'k, in the 1980s. Sushkevych soon began
addressing questions beyond athletics, and gradually focused more on
social issues such as legislative and pension reform, social integration of
the disabled, and others. He was one of the founders of Dnipropetrovs'k's
first city-wide Organization of Invalids; in 1990 he helped found the first
all-Ukrainian Union of Organizations of Invalids (SOIU), where he also
took on a leadership role until 1994.

Parallel to these advocacy activities Sushkevych developed a notable
political career. Among my informants and other friends and acquaintances

who know of Sushkevych, he is universally respected for his incredible energy and drive, and his capacity to "get things done" and "produce results." Elected as a parliamentary representative from Dnipropetrovs'k in 1991, several years later Sushkevych was elected to the Verkhovna Rada. As described above, he has held many important administrative posts, all of which center directly on disability-related affairs.

As founder and head of NADU, Sushkevych's stated primary goals are to advance the constitutional rights and legal interests of disabled citizens and disability rights NGOs in the Ukrainian Parliament, the Cabinet of Ministers, and other organs of legislative power (Derzhavna Dopovid 2002:125). Thanks to Sushkevych's position in the state administration as an MP and head of several parliamentary committees, NADU has been instrumental in bringing disability issues to the fore, especially in terms of drafting legislation and lobbying efforts. NADU has successfully secured parliamentary hearings on disability issues and has commissioned several important state reports on the situation of the disabled in Ukraine (Derzhavna Dopovid 2002, MLSP 2008)—much needed and overdue official assessments of the state of education, medicine, employment and other important areas as they concern the disabled population. Sushkevych and NADU have been instrumental in the successful adoption of presidential decrees (such as Presidential Decree No. 900 on accessibility)[6] and other official documents to push enforcement of existing equal rights legislation.

Elsewhere I have used NADU as an example of successful coalition building at the national level (Phillips 2008:161), but the organization is not a panacea. It is true that having an energetic and committed individual like Sushkevych at the helm has streamlined change at the official level, and such change, arguably, has occurred incredibly quickly. In some ways, however, NADU represents the problem of elite capture of disability issues at the level of what Ukrainians often call "serious politics." In the "parallel world" of the disabled, Sushkevych has an immense amount of power, a fact not universally appreciated, and questions arise about possible conflicts of interest between Sushkevych's multiple political roles. Whereas some international observers have interpreted Suchkevych's dual role as head of NADU and head of the Parliamentary Committee on Pensioners', Veterans' and Invalids' Affairs as evidence that "there is close coordination between the different organizations" (Virtanen 2008:59), some local critics evaluate the situation more negatively as a kind of power grab.

Thus, the expediency of having power over the disability rights agenda so highly consolidated has come at a price. Some would-be advocates for disability rights, among them accomplished athletes, have become estranged

⸱ from political and social engagement due to conflicts with Sushkevych. His powerful role as a gatekeeper with one foot in government and another in the nongovernmental (or quasi-governmental) sphere makes him a central broker of agendas, networks, bureaucratic pathways, and most important, finances. Some find it ironic that the emerging agenda of disability rights, purportedly part of the "civilizing" and democratizing process in postsocialist Ukraine, should be mediated in such an arguably undemocratic fashion.

Nevertheless, streamlining the disability rights agenda through one consolidated organization has some distinct advantages. Although improvements are still needed, especially in enforcement, rights legislation—much of which is initiated by NADU—has been passed fairly quickly and effectively. Foreign governments, advocacy groups, and others find it efficient to work with one well-represented organization like NADU, which has brokered a plethora of international partnerships and programs.[7]

Coalitions seeking to rival NADU have not gained a real foothold. In 2004, the Confederation of Civic Organizations of Invalids of Ukraine (KHOIU) was formed under the leadership of entrepreneur Oleksii Zhuravko as an alternative to NADU. Some activists predicted that this would produce healthy competition. In 2006 one activist who is involved in neither NADU nor KHOIU described the confederation as a "turtle organization, a shell, with no substance." According to this source, who attended the founding meeting of KHOIU, rather than acting out of a real conviction about disability issues, the initiators of the group seized the lucrative opportunity to revive a previously existing all-Ukrainian organization that had become defunct ten years earlier. Reportedly, KHOIU was hastily assembled and welcomed "any and every NGO that wanted to join." KHOIU has some dedicated and hard-working proponents but overall, it would be hard to characterize KHOIU as a healthy competitor or credible complement to the more powerful NADU.

Recognizing the importance of effective coalition building for advancing important social issues such as disability rights, international development organizations such as Counterpart International, Inc., the Soros Foundation, and others have offered support in this area. These interventions have had mixed effects. On one hand, training sessions, workshops, and conferences—the bread and butter of much development aid in the region at present—provide valuable opportunities for community organizers with similar interests and agendas to network and form friendly working relationships that can lead to more formal cooperation. On the other hand, competition for grant money and other forms of assistance and recognition from donor organizations in some cases has caused local

groups to split further apart rather than form coalitions and undertake ~~downside of external support~~
joint projects. This has also been documented in the case of the Ukrainian
women's movement by Alexandra Hrycak (2006).

Given these formidable institutional challenges, how can persons and
collectives interested in advocating for disability rights issues best pro-
ceed? The strategies that some NGO activists have employed at the local
level provide some insight. My research has shown that, although the work
of coalitions such as NADU is important—particularly in terms of lobbying and legislative reform at high levels of government—other important
loci of change are small groups working for transformations in their own
communities, where stakeholders themselves are playing increasingly
powerful roles in disability rights advocacy.

Together, the following ethnographic examples reveal strategies NGO
activists are pursuing to more successfully promote a disability rights
agenda. The first example illustrates strategies of personalization in local
disability advocacy initiatives. To enhance employment opportunities for
the members of her disability advocacy organization, an activist named
Iryna forged a partnership between representatives of NGOs, the state,
and business, and simultaneously pursued a strategy of personification of
disability issues. Likewise, working as individuals to argue for improvements in accessibility, in the second example Vasyl' and Tanya personalized disability for state and business actors by confronting them as "real,
live" disabled people.

The development of accessibility campaigns in L'viv in the third ethnographic example further attests to the important contributions that
backing from abroad (in this case, from Canadian disability rights advocates) has made to implement a rights agenda in Ukraine. It likewise supports the argument that one of the best ways to move the disability rights
agenda forward and to solidify enforcement of protective legislation is to
field members of the movement for political office.

## We Began a Dialogue

Despite legislation to facilitate equal access to employment, a very low
percentage of the disabled in Ukraine are employed, and as most of the
disabled receive only small disability pensions, they have been hit especially hard by the economic crises that rocked Ukraine during the past
two decades. In an already tight labor market, they possess extremely limited opportunities for employment. A major barrier is the state's contradictory approach to disability and labor. Official reports emphasize that

today disability is assigned based not just on one's loss of work capacity, but "taking into account a complex calculation of state of health and level of limitations in life functions (*zhyttiediial'nist'*) (limitations in self-care, movement, communication, orientation, learning, control of one's behavior)" (MLSP 2008:42). Even so, disability groupings are still defined and categorized more or less as they were in the Soviet Union; loss of work capacity is a major criterion for getting invalid status, and the extent of this loss is noted in one's documents. This becomes a barrier to finding a job; as one person put it: "It's written in the certificate—'requires constant nursing care,' which really complicates getting hired" (Alpatova and Zub 2006:11). And although the IPRI and subsequent programs were designed to facilitate maximum rehabilitation, including professional rehabilitation, in reality the system currently works against the disabled in the labor market. Whereas an individual's IPRI plan is supposed to include a discussion of the conditions under which he or she can work, more often than not the disabled person is simply categorized as unable to work, a label that effectively shuts off opportunities for employment (ibid.). In this context some people who qualify for a disability classification and the attendant benefits decline them in the hopes of remaining employable.

In recognition of the problems disabled individuals face finding work, the state has patched together a partial safety net involving the state unemployment service, which functions as a register for job-seekers. According to legislative changes in 2006 and 2007, disabled persons enrolled with the service are automatically classified as unemployed and, if they have worked full- or part-time during the previous 12 months, are entitled to unemployment benefits. As persons designated as unemployed, such persons gain access to a range of other state services such as legal consultations, job training, and others. This resulted in a 300 percent increase in numbers of disabled citizens registering with the state unemployment service between 2003 and 2007 (from 7,041 to 22,155; MLSP 2008:138). However, in 2007 only a small proportion were members of disability group I—just 1.4 percent, as compared to 22.4 percent from group II and 76.2 percent from group III (MLSP 2008:139).

There is a widespread perception that people who are visually or hearing impaired have an advantage when it comes to employment, since the UTOS and UTOG historically have provided many of the blind and deaf with work through their associated factory enterprises. Although a few factories still exist, many have closed, since the products made are not competitive in the globalizing market, and managers have had little incentive to innovate. People who do find work in the factories are paid

very little, often no more than $20 a month (Petrov 2006). Also, the kind
of manual labor required in the factories, which produce such items as
brooms and matches, does not provide workers with transferable skills.
There are well-run workshops in the cities of L'viv and Rivne that provide
employment for disabled persons, but outside isolated initiatives like these
no viable widespread, state-supported programs for retraining, placement,
and enforcement of labor laws have been developed in Ukraine.

A few state-run centers for job training and retraining are operating, and
five such centers are under the Labor Ministry. They are described as "specialized educational-training facilities of the internat type, designed for professional, medical, physical and social rehabilitation, and for young people
between the ages of 15 to 35 in invalid groups I-III whose health permits
them to study and work at the selected professions, to obtain a working profession and specialty" (MLSP 2008:107–108). The selected professions are
mostly those one would acquire at one of Ukraine's professional-technical
(ProfTech) schools: typist, plumber, technician, secretary, cook, and so on.
In 2001 a new all-Ukrainian Center for Professional Rehabilitation of Invalids was opened near Kyiv (in Liutezh), with space for 136 persons. Disabled
individuals may submit through their local SoBez ("social protection" office,
as local divisions of the MLSP are commonly called) a request to enroll at
Liutezh for vocational training. This center is located in the suburbs and is
not easily accessible—it is basically a semiresidential center off the beaten
path, also prompting an association with old-style internaty. Zoia, for
instance, calls this center and others like it "reservations for invalids."

Savvy businesspersons also have been able to capitalize on this population's vulnerable situation in the labor market by hiring disabled workers en masse in factory production, an arrangement that is reminiscent of
the artels of disabled workers. But instead of controlling the artels themselves, the disabled are mere employees in these factories, which is redo-
lent of the disenfranchisement of disabled workers when the Soviet state
appropriated their artels in the 1950s. For example, in 2007 a friend in
Kharkiv, a university professor, asked her students to conduct a research
project on a local institution of their choice. One student interested in
labor issues decided to visit a local factory: the factory had widely advertised its impressive record of employing disabled workers. Upon further
investigation the student was surprised to learn that all the workers were
deaf. The work environment was intolerably and dangerously loud for
hearing workers, so instead of making investments to comply with safety
codes the management simply hired deaf workers as an expedient solution. In a similar case, one businessman, himself disabled, even told me of

his plans to create an "Invamistechko" (Ukr.), or Invalid-City, with a number of factories, workers' dormitories, cafeterias, and shops. He proudly predicted that his workers would never have to leave the Invamistechko—they would have everything they needed right there. He couched these plans in exclusively positive terms, but his motives were clearly monetary and centered on harnessing the labor of a rather captive labor force.

Recognizing these disturbing trends of unemployment and exploitation, some NGOs have successfully focused their efforts on providing job training and job placement for the disabled, especially the Alisa Society for the Disabled in Kyiv. Under the leadership of Svitlana Mishchenko, since 1997 this NGO has established six social enterprises (Alter 2002:22–30, Phillips 2005) that provide jobs to disabled individuals, including an office supply store, a café, a trading company, an architecture firm, an advertising agency, and a sports facility. The Alisa Society also serves as an employment agency, and in 2001 the organization provided job training and job placement services to more than 700 disabled persons. (It is not out of the question that some of these involved false hiring of disabled workers at a token salary, but I do not possess this information.) Disabled persons who have sought to use the services of regular employment agencies in Ukraine report discrimination from all sides: the agencies are reluctant to even propose disabled individuals as candidates to employers, for fear of losing clients' business (Petrov 2006).

In this context, where employers are reluctant to hire disabled workers, equal employment laws are not enforced, and individuals' state disability benefits are not enough to live on, what strategies are being pursued by disability rights activists regarding unemployment? Iryna, the head of an NGO in a small city in central Ukraine, set up a partnership with the local unemployment office to facilitate referrals for the members of her organization. Iryna soon learned that employers regularly contacted the unemployment office to recruit disabled workers specifically (to fulfill the state quotas for disabled employees), but the vacancies offered were exclusively for janitors or for people to do heavy lifting and other manual tasks. This was not work that many of her organization's members were able to do. Iryna realized that more needed to be done to link up employers with job seekers directly, and to dispel negative stereotypes among employers about the disabled and their supposed "limited intellectual potential." During an interview in 2002 she described the solution she pursued—a job fair:

> We had a job fair—we invited directors of firms and enterprises, and disabled people. . . . We let them know that among invalids there are

many qualified people. People become disabled at different times in their lives—not necessarily in childhood. People have some educational background. They were really surprised that we have people who can do computer work. And several people were hired right on the spot at the job fair because we began a dialogue. We tried to understand one another and it worked.

Iryna worked through her NGO to address a lack of dialogue among organs of the state (the unemployment office), those of the market (the employers), and disabled individuals. She also formulated a strategy to educate local employers about the potential of her NGO members as workers, and to disrupt erroneous perceptions of the disabled as people who could only perform manual work such as heavy lifting and janitorial work.

To carry out her approach, Iryna pursued a strategy of personification to advance disability awareness, a tactic used by many other activists I met. Historically the vast majority of people in Ukraine have had only limited or no contact with the disabled; this unfamiliarity has allowed fear and negative attitudes to proliferate. Or, they may form derogatory stereotypes about all disabled persons based on one or two negative encounters (Petrov 2006). In this context of unfavorable public opinion, NGO activists frequently take it upon themselves to, as one friend put it, "personify for others a real, live invalid."

## Let's Get Personal

"Starting a dialogue" by personifying disability and fostering new social networks has proven effective for advancing disability rights and changing social attitudes at local levels. Some informants described how they had used personification strategies to persuade store personnel to install wheelchair ramps and accessible toilets. Often this entailed asking the person to "imagine yourself in my position," or actually inviting the person to occupy one's wheelchair. One-on-one confrontations with business owners can be effective, as Vasyl', an activist from a small town in L'viv oblast', explained:

Let me tell you how I persuaded the owner of our town's restaurant to install a wheelchair ramp (pandus). I went right up to him, to that Petro Ivanovych, and said, "You need to put in a ramp." He just laughed. He said, "What for? Right, as if invalids have money to frequent a restaurant." I replied: "Some do, some don't. And anyway, what if there's a wedding, or somebody's birthday party, and they invite me? It's not very nice to have people staring at you, watching how others haul you up the stairs; when everyone is looking at you, it's really uncomfortable." I said, "Go ahead, try it, sit in the wheelchair and let them haul you around like a sack of potatoes." Right away he said, "Okay, okay, fine, give us the specs, and we'll do it." So now we've got the ramp and no one ever asks, "What for?" anymore.

The examples of Iryna and Vasyl' show how despite their precarious position as socially, economically, and politically marginalized persons, some disabled persons have been able to work within the ongoing neoliberalizing trends of individualization and privatization of social problems by taking up a strategy of personification. By asserting their worth as full-fledged persons and demanding rights on a par with other citizens, these individuals, and by extension, the other disabled people they represent as NGO activists, are forging personal relationships with important power brokers—representatives of state institutions such as the unemployment bureau, and local businesspeople—to advance their individual and collective interests. These strategies are interesting because they are hybrid socialist-postsocialist tactics, showing how citizens today are "building new worlds on the ruins of old" (Szmagalska-Follis 2008:331). On the one hand, they hearken to the Soviet-era strategies of using connections (Rus. *blat*) to get things done (Ledeneva 1998). At the same time, however, these new practices of personification are more individually assertive than blat practices, which involved such complex transactions as A knows/owes B, and B knows/owes C, so A asks C to arrange or acquire X. Personification, by contrast, is more of a one-on-one, person-to-person confrontation. Personification is also more politically inflected—Iryna and Vasyl' are not seeking help in acquiring scarce goods or jumping the line for services, as was facilitated by Soviet-era blat negotiations. They are asking for recognition as human beings of worth deserving of the same opportunities to work and socialize as others. Personification becomes a productive strategy for negotiating contradictions of neoliberalization—especially the paradoxes specific to the parallel world of the disabled—and thus for enacting mobile citizenship.

This is important for understanding how the disabled are staking new kinds of citizenship claims in postsocialist Ukraine. Here, Iryna and Vasyl' are not rooting their demands in biological citizenship (though they certainly may do so in other situations): they are not basing their arguments in their biologically based status as invalids deserving of certain kinds of recognition, support, or services. Iryna, for example, argued for the worth of her constituents not *because of* their disability, but in many ways *in spite of* it. She strove to personify her NGO's members not as invalids, but as unique individuals with a range of personal histories, training, educational qualifications, and talents. She emphasized what each one might contribute, not what each one deserved as an invalid.

The argument could be made that Vasyl', in asking that a wheelchair ramp be installed at his town's lone restaurant, in fact did draw on biological citizenship claims when he emphasized his bodily difference, and his incapacity to navigate stairs as a wheelchair user. Yet his intention was not really to prove himself worthy of investment—a hallmark of biological citizenship. To the contrary, by asserting himself as a potential customer-consumer, Vasyl' inserted himself into the market language of the new market economy. He became a new kind of citizen, as he demanded recognition as a full-fledged participant in the market society, one not (just) worthy of investment, but one possessing the potential to participate in spheres of social and economic life previously denied the disabled.

Tanya, a woman from a small town near Donets'k, in eastern Ukraine, produced a similar story to Vasyl's during a 2005 interview. When Tanya described how she and her family were finally granted a ground-floor apartment by her town's administration, it became clear that she had simultaneously wielded hybrid strategies of personification and Soviet-era approaches to "getting things done" through personal networks. Tanya and her husband, both wheelchair users, lived with Tanya's son and mother-in-law in a fifth-floor apartment in a building with no elevator. Having learned the technique at AR camps, Tanya and her husband could descend the stairs themselves in their wheelchairs, but in order to return to the fifth floor they were forced to wait—hours, sometimes, and often in inclement weather—until willing passers-by from the street could be convinced to carry both of them up five flights of stairs. Reflecting the changing face of benefits distribution in the country from universal or blanket entitlements to targeted assistance, Tanya relied on a strategy of personification in her request for a ground-floor apartment. This is how she described the process of acquiring a new flat:

> I met with the mayor and proposed a simple plan. I told him about our situation and said, "Ivan Aleksandrovich, why don't you come over, get in my wheelchair and try to get down the stairs by yourself from the fifth floor? If you can, I will wait for ten years, for 15, as long as you tell me to." He gave me the apartment without a word. . . . Within a week or two after he gave the order we were in the new apartment.

Rather than focus on what the state owed her as a disabled citizen by couching her request in the language of entitlement, when laying claim to a ground-floor apartment, Tanya relied instead on a narrative of individualization and personification. This strategy worked well within the current neoliberal climate, and it also revealed Tanya to be a savvy reader of the changing system. She articulated her claims on the state by addressing an individual—her town's mayor—who had considerable power and resources at his disposal to disperse targeted benefits to people like Tanya. This was an effective strategy in an environment where benefits are being scaled back and the rules of the game are constantly changing. To wit, as part of neoliberalization, the socialist-era entitlement discourse, which acknowledged broad categories of citizens as uniformly deserving of state-provided benefits (group I invalids, large families, single mothers) is giving way to new narratives of need and deservedness based on an individual's unique "case" and the person's demonstration that they are worthy of investment. Recognizing this, Tanya personalized her "case" for the mayor. Of course, Tanya's strategy is strikingly reminiscent of the Soviet-era practice of using personal connections to get things done and acquire certain goods and services. She creatively combined her access to personages such as the mayor with strategies of personification to become a more mobile citizen in every sense of the word.

Such personalizing strategies were effective, said informants, because "they finally understood us." Thus, even as neoliberal reforms pull the rug out from programs of social support, NGO rights activists such as Iryna, Vasyl', Tanya, and others find ways to turn some of the key facets of the postsocialist neoliberalization of the Ukrainian political economy into resources for staking claims to a fuller and more diverse citizenship: consumerism, "beginning a dialogue" (the exchange of ideas being central to democratization), the assertion of individuals as "cases," arguments for the individual's potential to contribute, and the personification of what could otherwise be considered social and infrastructural problems (e.g., lack of accessible architectural design). Although these approaches may not prove immediately effective for realizing broad societal changes in employment, accessibility, housing, and other issues, they are increasingly taken up by individual actors and by NGO leaders, and find resonance in Ukraine's current political and economic climate.

## Accessibility and Local Representation

Although the State Building Committee has since 1992 been prohibited from approving any plans for construction of new buildings that are not accessible, inaccessible buildings are approved routinely. On the initiative of NADU, on June 1, 2005, President Yushchenko signed Decree No. 900, On Immediate Measures for Creating Favorable Conditions of Living for Persons with Limited Physical Capabilities. The decree calls for the speedy provision of accessible public transport (including train cars and school buses), parking spaces, government buildings, dormitories, underground walkways, and so on. It challenges various state committees to implement European Union standards for guaranteeing the disabled equal access to public spaces. Unfortunately, laws on accessible architecture continue to be poorly enforced, and although some limited progress has been made (an accessibility commission now exists in Kyiv, for instance) for the most part the built environment remains inaccessible to many disabled people.

Projects on accessibility have been supported in Ukraine by a range of international partners, including the government of the Netherlands and the CCDS. Yaroslav has been an especially active proponent of accessibility issues, and he is the coordinator for accessibility concerns for NADU. In this capacity, Yaroslav has played a key role in drafting legislation—he was an author of Presidential Decree No. 900—and coordinating seminars and conferences on accessibility. In 2006, he was elected as a representative (*deputat*) in the L'viv regional government and in this position has been able to advance accessibility issues even further in the L'viv region. Under Yaroslav's watch, a small fleet of accessible trolley buses has been integrated into the L'viv city public transport system, and accessibility-related building codes finally are being enforced in L'viv.

In these areas, Yaroslav has cooperated with his colleague Mykola Swarnyk, who was elected as a representative to the L'viv city government in 2006. One of Mykola's priorities is to ensure enforcement of accessibility laws. He has said that because he is a well-known member of the disability rights movement and has a disabled son, builders, businesspeople, and city officials know that he will not simply "look the other way" from building violations as others have done, and they know he will not accept bribes to approve construction that violates accessibility regulations. Mykola developed a system he hopes will encourage builders to conform to accessibility codes: violators of the codes will be required to pay fines into an "accessibility fund." The fund will then be used to make public buildings like government offices and schools accessible.

As respected grassroots community activists with one foot in disability advocacy NGOs and one foot in government, Yaroslav and Mykola are well placed to foster reform and cultivate a culture of enforcing the existing legislation on disability issues. For the advancement of disability rights in contemporary Ukraine it is critical that those with a vested interest in ensuring such rights ( i.e., members of disability communities and their family members and other close advocates) occupy positions of decision-making in government. This kind of indigenous representation is especially lacking at the levels of city and local government in Ukraine (Girman 2006:13–14). At present, cadres in the various ministries that govern disability affairs tend to be ill informed about disability issues at home and abroad. Members of the disability rights movement have much to contribute to social service and policy reform, and rights activists must play a part in "big politics" to advance their agendas in effective ways. For all these reasons, disability advocacy NGOs should prioritize fielding their own candidates for political office. Developing a culture of inclusion and interdependence, and promoting the idea that it is members of the disability community who are best equipped to coordinate social policy, are key strategies to achieving this goal. Ushering more members of the disability rights movement into local and national government is an important way to pursue the overall rights agenda, foster effective enforcement mechanisms, and give voice to diverse contingents of the movement. Also, the participation of a range of voices from the disability rights movement in local, regional, and national government may prevent the over-consolidation of power at any single node.

## Living Disability in the New Moral Economy

There are some similarities between disability rights struggles in post-Soviet Ukraine and in countries such as the United States. In both places people have struggled against a culture of institutionalization and social stigma, sought to rectify economic inequalities, and fought for the enforcement of rights legislation. But taking a historical perspective reveals that the legacies of state socialism affected disability experiences and rights struggles in particular ways. Specifically, the managed quality of Ukrainian civil society has been a major determining factor in the development of disability rights consciousness and activism. With the fall of the Soviet Union many state assets were quickly appropriated by individuals and groups that had been well placed within the socialist system. The same was true of key political issues, among them disability. This has resulted in a certain elite capture of disability rights issues, a situation that threatens to limit the strides that small, localized advocacy groups are able to achieve.

Writing about postsocialist Romania, Mihaela Miroiu (2004) describes what she calls "no cost, room service feminism." Room service feminism is a situation where states have adopted ready-made policies to protect women's rights offered to them by international bodies such as the European Union, without a concomitant change in consciousness or real commitment (especially financial commitment) to these ideals on the part of the state or the general population. I see an analogous situation in Ukraine, where elite state actors have handed "room service disability rights" to a somewhat puzzled populace.

In the United States, disability rights legislation was developed over a half century with the participation of advocacy groups and their lobbying efforts. Between the federal Architectural Barriers Act of 1968, which mandated accessibility, and the much more far-reaching Americans with Disabilities Act (ADA) of 1990, some 50 acts of Congress were passed concerning disability rights. In contrast, in independent Ukraine, the first disability-related legislation, the 1991 Law On the Basis of Social Protection of Invalids of Ukraine, did not emerge out of conversations and debates between different stakeholders in disability affairs; rather, it was authored by a small, elite group of state officials (Sushkevych was among the authors). Unfortunately, the expedient and rather closed manner in which Ukraine's disability legislation was adopted meant that the changed laws were not accompanied by an earnest rethinking of disability issues among the general population, political actors, or many disabled people themselves. None of these groups were exposed to or invited to participate in debates over disability rights in a meaningful way. Again, this contrasts with disability rights history in the United States, where new ways of conceptualizing disability emerged out of disability advocacy communities and were leveraged to enact comprehensive legislation over a period of many years.

Despite considerable challenges, groups committed to change in Ukraine are pursuing promising avenues for turning disability wrongs into disability rights. In addition to the little histories presented above, a few examples include the following: organizing walkathons and competitions where members of the broader community can get to know disabled individuals and their families; organizing lawsuits against builders and companies that fail to comply with accessibility standards; campaigning for members of the disability community running for public office; inviting journalists to write articles on disability-related issues; producing documentary films on aspects of disability experience; developing disability sports; networking with disability rights organizations abroad; and establishing resource and informational centers for disabled people and their allies. However, this work is extremely difficult in the context of a neoliberalizing political and economic sphere, where institutions and representatives of the state are extending less support for "social issues" such as disability, rather than more support as one might expect at this critical juncture.

Here it is illustrative to return to the case of Leonid Chernovets'kyi, the mayor of Kyiv, because his approach to social policy, though somewhat uniquely inflected with evangelical Christian views, is indicative of the state's drawdown of support for vulnerable populations such as the disabled. As the mayor of Ukraine's capital and largest city, Chernovets'kyi's approach to the social contract very well may be a kind of litmus test for the future of social welfare in the country. This profile is a fitting coda to this chapter about organizing empowerment, because it portends a future when community groups may be left completely on their own as state interventions are scaled back and social welfare becomes increasingly privatized.

Chernovets'kyi is a former member of the Verkhovna Rada, and both he and his wife are owners of one of Ukraine's largest banks, Pravex Bank, making Chernovets'kyi "effectively one of the ruling oligarchs of Ukraine" (Wanner 2007:236). Before Chernovets'kyi was elected mayor in 2006 he was already the most visible member of the mega-church Embassy of the Blessed Kingdom of God for All Nations (called the Embassy of God), founded and led by pastor Sunday Adelaja, a Nigerian émigré. As an MP Chernovets'kyi sited his office inside the Embassy of God's main church located in a huge rented sports facility in Kyiv.

As mayor, Chernovets'kyi's approach to social policy is in line with neoliberalizing trends of scaling back the state and leaving support of vulnerable populations to civic groups and individuals. For example, he advocates and participates in charitable support of marginalized populations through faith-based initiatives. Catherine Wanner (2007:237) describes Chernovets'kyi's personal engagement with private and church-based philanthropy:

> Chernovets'kyi fully funds a homeless shelter that has paid staff, including paid medical professionals, and numerous volunteers from the church. The center feeds about a thousand people a day and offers medical treatment, clothing, various hygienic services, and a park for children. Public recognition of his philanthropic efforts is one of the reasons put forward to explain his unexpected victory in the 2006 Kyiv mayoral election in spite of his controversial religious affiliation. Such charitable initiatives, especially directed at the homeless, remain rare

among New Ukrainians [as the very wealthy elite are called in Ukraine].
(Wanner 2007:237)

In the country's neoliberalizing economy, it is likely that, as state-supported welfare entitlements are scaled back, private philanthropists, religious groups, and individuals will be expected to fill in the gaps. This
is a process that may unfold more quickly in Kyiv than in other cities,
under Chernovets'kyi's leadership. Indeed, Chernovets'kyi's entire political program is squarely rooted in free market principles and a privileging
of a "moral" economy or "prosperity theology" (Wanner 2007:236). As
Chernovets'kyi himself explained:

> As a politician and believer, I am deeply convinced that the choice of a
> democratic government and the choice of a market-based economy is
> directly connected with Christian ideology, which is conducive to simple
> people living comfortably and politicians acting morally. . . . [I support
> the creation of] a new political party for Ukraine—a Christian liberal
> party based on Christian values, the principles of economic liberalism
> and Western European democracy. . . . I would build on this model: God
> wants to see all people morally prosperous, and then they will be materi-
> ally prosperous. (Chernets 2004:6–7, cited in Wanner 2007)

Chernovets'kyi did in fact create such a political party and was the
Christian liberal party's unsuccessful candidate for the Ukrainian presi-
dency in 2004. Chernovets'kyi's endorsement of the capitalist ethic is
inflected with prosperity theology, and as a successful businessman and
politician he is able to "equate his staggering wealth with moral purity"
(Wanner 2007:239). The distilled message conveyed by this narrative is
that all blessings shall flow to the morally deserving, and this material
prosperity (and, perhaps, the basic material necessities of life?) comes
from God and His faithful, not from the state. Chernovets'kyi's politics
and the actions he has taken as mayor of Ukraine's largest city telescope
the social reforms that already affect the lives of the hundreds of thousands of disabled persons in Ukraine, and will continue to affect them
as neoliberalizing reforms are introduced into the country's increasingly
"streamlined" economy.

Indeed, since Chernovets'kyi assumed the mayorship of Kyiv in 2006,
informants like Dmitrii have noted with concern his initiatives to with-
draw certain disability benefits such as reduced utilities and rent. Dmitrii
expressed his alarm during a conversation we had via Skype™ in late 2006:

Sarah: What are you up to these days, are you keeping busy?

Dmitrii: "Busy" is not the word for it: I'm fighting for my apartment.

Sarah: What do you mean?

Dmitrii: Our new mayor, Chernovets'kyi, he's made it clear that he's got no time for invalids; he's not a friend of invalids, of disability benefits.

Sarah: Not a friend?

Dmitrii: He's phasing out benefits, and taking things away. Remember I told you I'm way behind on paying my apartment fees, the fees I have to pay for living in my apartment, since it was given to me as a disability entitlement? Well, Chernovets'kyi decided that "delinquent" invalids need to be taught a lesson; he's making an example of us "delinquents." They are going around trying to take away the apartments of all the invalids they can find who are somehow behind in payments, or otherwise in violation or whatever.

During October 2009 I was in Kyiv for several days and Dmitrii invited me to join him at a rally protesting Chernovets'kyi's recent initiatives. As Dmitrii complained to a journalist who interviewed him, Chernovets'kyi, as he saw it, "is selling off all of Kyiv, to the highest bidder." This was contrary to Dmitrii's belief in the common good.

It seems ironic that the wealthy philanthropist mayor Chernovets'kyi wants to phase out benefits for Kyiv's marginalized populations such as the disabled, even though he was voted into the mayorship largely on the basis of Kyivans' admiration for his charitable initiatives. During the election campaign Chernovets'kyi distributed rations of food staples such as rice and buckwheat to elderly retirees for free, prompting some to say that he won "for a kilogram of flour." Voters, especially the elderly, must have interpreted the food distribution as a sign of this politician's commitment to care and attention for the marginalized and vulnerable, not realizing that such care was to be privatized. In any case, those hoping for sustained state support for the disabled and other marginalized citizens in the era of the new "moral economy" may get less than they bargained for.

# 4. Regeneration

## (Re)presenting the "In-Valid"

On August 11, 2006, several dozen new billboards went up in Kyiv. The billboards were concentrated in those city districts considered most impoverished and least developed—districts such as Troeshchyna, a "down-at-the-heels late Soviet moonscape" (Ruble 2003:139) known for its run-down, massive apartment complexes, burgeoning migrant communities, and sprawling outdoor markets. Normally the billboards would not have caused a stir, since by 2006 Ukrainians had grown accustomed to the barrage of advertising now omnipresent all over post-Soviet cityscapes. In the Soviet Union, the lack of consumer choice and the state's control over the market and the press obviated the need for advertising, which was minimal and relatively unobtrusive. In Ukrainian cities today, however, it seems that nearly every square inch of public space is plastered with advertisements. *Big-bordy* (billboards) are part of this advertising frenzy—they line city streets and major roadways to promote all manner of products and services, from cellular phone providers and cars to vodka and cigarettes. Billboards also have become a popular means of promoting candidates for political office; these huge portraits have prompted some to call billboards *big-mordy*, or big mugs (faces).

But the billboard erected on August 11 was different. Unlike the usual colorful and busy ads and "big mugs" that crowd the city, this billboard featured simple white letters and graphics on a somber black background. The sign was divided into two horizontal sections. The top part included just four words: *Mama chomu ia urod,* or "Mama, why am I a freak?" This text was flanked by a white handprint that, as explained by one of the billboard's creators, "did not look quite right."[1] The handprint was six-

FIGURE 4.1. Billboard in Kyiv, 2006. "Mama, why am I a freak? . . . Drug addicts cannot have healthy children." *Reproduced with permission from the Association of Outdoor Advertising of Ukraine.*

fingered, hexadactyly thus signaling the freakishness or monstrosity of the otherwise disembodied child-narrator. Along the bottom section of the billboard ran the message, "Drug addicts cannot have healthy children" (*U narkomaniv ne buvaie zdorovykh ditei*).

What exactly is an *urod*? Urod is a Russian word used to insult and demean; one would likely never call another person urod to his or her face. In Smirnitskyi's *Russian-English Dictionary* (1987:669) urod is translated variously as freak (of nature); monster; monstrosity; ugly person; and fright. Calling a person urod denies a common humanity. What was the word urod doing on a billboard in the middle of Kyiv?

It quickly came to light that an organization called the Association of Outdoor Advertising of Ukraine (Ukr. *Asotsiatsiyi Zovnishn'oyi Reklamy Ukrainy*, AZR) had commissioned the billboard for its Life is Better without Drugs! campaign. (The firm with the winning bid was called Adam Smith Advertising.) AZR initiated the campaign as part of its ongoing efforts to develop a culture of—and a market for—so-called "social advertising" in the country. Public service announcements and social campaigns promoting health, safety, and wholesome lifestyles are rare in Ukraine; there is a culture of resistance to public service messages, which tend to remind many people of Soviet-era propaganda.

AZR's first attempt to stimulate social advertising was in 2005, when it staged a billboard campaign called Let's Make Love! (*Kokhaimosia!*). The Let's Make Love! campaign sought to address Ukraine's demographic crisis; the country has a negative population growth, with population decreasing from around 52 million in 1991 to an estimated 45.7 million. Unlike the stark, forbidding character of the anti–drug abuse campaign, the Let's Make Love! billboards incorporated symbols of national pride— "The country needs more football [soccer] players! Let's Make Love!" They also utilized humor and poked fun at kitschy Soviet propaganda, presumably striving to make modern social advertising more palatable to the postsocialist public ("The country needs more cosmonauts! Let's Make Love!").

The *Mama chomu ia urod* billboard, which many Ukrainians complained was too severe and "cruel," immediately roused a public outcry. Kyivans protested the billboard in newspaper editorials, and journalists debated its merits and flaws. Professionals such as psychologists and addiction specialists weighed in on these debates, and executives from AZR spoke up to defend the tough character and shocking imagery of the billboard (Bidenko 2006, 2008). AZR originally planned to erect 800 of the billboards around the country, but after the uproar in Kyiv, those plans were abandoned. The association issued an apology to those offended by the message, and the billboards in Kyiv were torn down.[2]

The discussions that swirled through Ukrainian newspapers and the internet in reaction to the "Mama, why am I a freak?" billboard are a window onto the nature of public discourse about disability and difference in contemporary Ukraine. In many ways, the Ukrainian public lacks a common language with which to talk about these issues. In articles about the billboard that appeared in some of the most widely read Ukrainian newspapers, news weeklies, and internet newspapers (*Ukrains'ka Pravda, Korrespondent,* 5tv.com.ua, *Segodnia*), there was strikingly little critical analysis of the enfreakment of the billboard (Hevey 1997)—scant mention was made of the violence the billboard's image and text perpetuated toward drug addicts, disabled adults, and disabled children and their mothers.

Although reportedly many of the thousands of complaints received by AZR about the billboard were from parents of disabled children, this fact was not highlighted in most media discussions. For the most part, the voices of those whom the billboard demeaned the most—disabled persons themselves, and their mothers—were silenced in the subsequent media coverage. Of the 222 internet commentaries I reviewed, only one was submitted by the parent of a disabled child. No participant in the two internet forums I analyzed self-identified as a disabled person. This fact supports my observation that ultimately, the disabled are positioned here as objects, as mere vehicles for other discussions (i.e., drug abuse prevention).

One measure of the public reaction to the billboard is the commentaries posted by readers in reaction to newspaper articles on the internet about the controversy.[3] Many of the postings, which often became discussions and arguments between commentators, evaluated the billboard's effectiveness. Internet commentators debated: was the unapologetic, morbid, and "cruel" approach of the billboard in fact the best method to deter people from using narcotics? How would drug users or persons contemplating drug use—and women in these categories in particular—likely react to the billboard? One journalist sought to explore these questions by appealing to the expertise of psychologists, who predicted that the billboard would cause depression in addicts, thus resulting in escalated drug use and possibly even suicide (Litskevich 2006). Overall, however, participants in these discussions showed little sympathy for drug users (the presumed intended audience for the billboards); a common assessment was that addicts are already "beyond help," and the only utility of the billboard might be to deter others—young women in particular—from trying drugs.

Many internet commentators complained that social advertisements should target problems that are "really social" or collective in nature (examples given were campaigns to encourage seatbelt use, and anti-drunk driving campaigns), not supposedly private problems like drug abuse. Critics opined that "normal" people should not have to endure the billboard's negative messages and images, if the intended audience was drug addicts. As one journalist summarized this view, the billboard "puts normal people in a bad mood" (Litskevich 2006). This kind of unquestioned assumption as to who has the right to appear in public reminds one of the so-called ugly laws enacted in cities across the United States beginning in the 1860s, "unsightly beggar ordinances" barring certain persons from public view (Schweik 2009). Chicago's ugly law (City Code 1881) read thus: "Any person who is diseased, maimed, mutilated, or in any way deformed, so as to be an unsightly or disgusting object, or an improper person to be allowed in or on the streets, highways, thoroughfares, or public places in this city, shall not therein or thereon expose himself to public view, under the penalty of a fine of $1 [about $20 today] for each offense"

(Schweik 2009:1–2). In some states the ugly laws were not repealed until the early 1970s.

Most internet commentators who discussed the billboard in a disability context did not question the freakishness of physical disability. Rather, they passionately debated whether or not hexadactyly actually could result from abusing narcotics.[4] These conversations therefore centered on evaluating the accuracy of medical and clinical facts rather than interrogating social representations. The labeling of disabled persons as freaks did not seem to trouble most Kyivans who were interviewed about the billboard in various newspaper profiles or posted reactions on the internet.[5] Of greater concern was the possible effect of the ad on mothers of disabled children. The following comment made by 22-year-old Katerina was typical: "It's terrible! Now all the children who have physical anomalies will think their mothers are drug addicts" (Litskevich 2006). Katerina came close to articulating a critique of one common framing of disability in Ukrainian public discourse—women are often blamed when their child is born disabled. In the popular imagination, congenital disability is often attributed to the sins of the parents, and most often the mother—disability here is the perceived price for the mother's sin or moral failure. In the billboard, the onus for bearing a "defective" child was placed squarely on the woman—the hypothetical child-narrator addressed the mother directly. Besides a few comments stating concern for how the ad might affect mothers of disabled children,[6] the gendered framing of the billboard's message went completely unremarked in public debates.

Few journalists or internet commentators reflected critically on the billboard's use of the extremely negative term urod (freak or monster) to describe disabled persons. Proponents of proper use of the Ukrainian language did complain that urod is "not literary" language, and some internet commentators argued about whether or not the word urod exists in Ukrainian (it clearly exists in Russian), but no media article and few internet commentaries identified urod as an offensive, demeaning term.[7] In fact, when one journalist used the term "children with special needs," terminology now preferred in Ukraine by some disability rights advocacy groups, internet commentators poked fun.[8] One responded, "'Mama! Why are advertisers . . . freaks?':) Or, more politically correct [Rus. *politkorrektno*], 'with special needs.'"[9] Although perhaps intending to critique the billboard, this commentator actually both dismissed the use of inclusive, people-first language as mere political correctness, and reproduced the billboard's semantic linking of the disabled ("special needs") and freaks. Such responses to the billboard did not challenge the use of urod to describe the disabled, but rather reinforced the perception that the disabled are less than human. These commonly held prejudices are part of what relegates disabled persons to a parallel world where they must deal with negative social perceptions in their everyday life.

Rather than question the use of urod to describe disabled children, some journalists instead appropriated the term to formulate their own sensational headlines. In the daily tabloid *Segodnia* (Today), for example, Ol'ga Litskevich's (2006) front-page Russian-language headline read, in bold capital letters: "WHO IS SCARING KYIVANS WITH FREAKS?" [Rus. "KTO PUGAET KIEVLIAN URODAMI?"]. The word FREAKS was printed with red ink. Further section headings in the article read, "'Freaks' Have Entered the Capital," and "Who Ordered the 'Freaks?'"

In a similar vein, internet users commenting on the billboard used inflammatory, offensive language in their very critiques of the "cruel" billboard. The following are just a couple of examples:

> "Finally they are thinking about people [and taking down the billboard]. How did they even come up with such a Down-ish (Rus. *daunskii*) advertising scenario? You get the impression that whoever drew it or designed it wasn't thinking at all."[10]

> "The ad is crippled (Rus. *uboga*). Crippled people thought up this ad, and [crippled people] approved it, too."[11]

This commentator (the same person posted both comments) uses "Down-ish" as an adjective, in a reference to people with Down Syndrome, to describe the billboard as "stupid," or "retarded." And, as described in chapter 2, uboga is a term literally meaning "of God," and contemporary meanings include the following, among others: wretched, squalid, beggarly, and crippled (Smirnitsky 1987:655). The commentator used uboga in its most pejorative sense (which I have translated as "crippled"), even though he or she presumably seeks to criticize the offensive billboard.

Another commentator, a supporter of the billboard, used oppressive language to criticize the billboard's detractors:

> "It was a 100% super advertisement, and as soon as it had begun to work they started taking it down. What's this nonsense—what offense, you'd have to be a cretin (Ukr. *debil*) to be offended by an ad like that. It's got a clear message, and forces those for whom it's not too late, to think."[12]

Two main points should be made here. First, these comments and others like them evidence a complete lack of critical public discourse concerning the use of offensive, discriminatory language to discuss issues of physical and intellectual disability. Second, it could be argued that the flagrant use of a term like urod on the billboard gave members of the Ukrainian public (or, at the very least, readers of newspapers on the internet) permission to include incendiary, insensitive language in their own talk. They reinforced the rhetorical legitimacy of that pejorative language, including the term "freak." No participant in the internet discussions that I perused criticized fellow-commentators' use of pejorative terms like "Down-ish," "crippled," or "cretin."

And what of the billboard's creators and sponsors—how did they justify their representation of disabled children as freaks? The most vocal defender of the billboard was Artem Bidenko, head of the coordinating council of AZR. Bidenko was cited in several newspaper articles about the scandal, and he published his own defense in the online newspaper *Ukrains'ka Pravda* (Ukrainian Truth; Bidenko 2006). Although AZR issued a formal apology to those offended by the billboard, Bidenko was unapologetic in his defense of the billboard's language, imagery, and message. In his article, Bidenko stated, "When you advertise something, there is no time to explain each individual case; an ad must warn [people] about a general situation. Short. Direct. Simple."

Ironically, although citing the merits of a short, direct, and simple approach, he felt obliged to justify the AZR's anti–drug use billboard in a 1,000-word article. Bidenko spent most of the article detailing the history of social advertising in the West, followed by a defense of the Life is Better without Drugs! campaign, and the "Mama, why am I a freak?" billboard in particular. Bidenko defended the billboard's graphics, language, and message in the following terms:

The black-and-white scenes that hang over our streets are strictly intended to, in crude terms, break the stereotypes young people hold about the mafia-hero halo of narcotics. . . . A social advertisement like this one has the interests of society at heart. There are some people who misinterpret the ad, and think it was specially designed to depress them and spoil their lives. That's not so. This is an abstract ad, maximally hyperbolized, the goal of which is to stop the rising drug addiction in Ukraine. . . . Even though the ad is in black and white, it can't be evaluated according to the [binary] Soviet typology of "good or bad." You can't criticize it just because some people's morals are too principled for them to see the word "urod" on the city's streets. . . . No one has died because their moral sensibilities were offended. Untold numbers die from narcotics. Think about that, moralists.

In this way, without referring directly to the ad's controversial portrayal of the disabled as freaks, Bidenko dismissed complaints lodged by "some people" (i.e., parents of disabled children, representatives of advocacy groups, and others) by framing their concerns both as "moralistic" complaints and as products of an alleged simplistic Soviet-era black-and-white, either-or, binary mindset. He had a relatively easy time of it, since the voices of disabled persons and their advocates were largely absent from the debates. One newspaper article did tell of a young woman, Kristina, who was angered by the billboard. Kristina, we learn, was born with hexadactyly; the writer states that, "there were never any drug addicts in Kristina's family," and furthermore, "she never considered herself a freak."[13] The only official complaint receiving wide publicity was that from the All-Ukrainian Association for Harm Reduction, a professional organization of psychologists who expressed concern for the ad's psychological effect on drug users first, and the effects for disabled children second. Paradoxically, it was the All-Ukrainian Association for Harm Reduction that initiated the ad campaign in the first place, through AZR.[14]

I have devoted considerable space to unpacking the *Mama chomu ia urod* billboard and public reaction to it because the incident is illustrative of the common framing of the disabled in Ukraine as monstrous, invisible, and nonhuman. This was underlined in a case that was cause for amusement in the popular press: the positioning of the "freaks" billboard beside another billboard commissioned by the family of blond-haired, blue-eyed Alyosha to congratulate him on the occasion of his birthday. Journalists and others interpreted this happenstance arrangement as a perversely funny but unfortunate juxtaposition, solidifying as it did a clear distinction between normal and freakish, ideal and imperfect. Since commissioning a billboard is not cheap, the contrast also highlighted growing class divisions in the country—privileged, healthy Alyosha beside some anonymous addict's "freak."

The stigma of disability is nothing new; disability has been stigmatized the world over throughout history. What interests me here is how an intentionally macabre reference to physical difference—the white-on-black six-fingered handprint—simultaneously was deployed to repulse and frighten, signify moral weakness, and dehumanize. As a result, the billboard both illustrated and perpetuated the exclusion of disabled persons from full belonging in Ukrainian society. The disabled were rendered noncitizens, without proper or acceptable bodies (only a handprint was left behind), without choices (the powerless child appeals to his or her mother, who is blamed for the child's disability), and without voices (no disabled persons, representatives of advocacy organizations, or others were given space to rebut the billboard). Even in their problematic visibility in the billboard, people living disability in Ukraine are still rendered silent and invisible, relegated to a parallel world in which they live and navigate everyday life.

## Reborn from the Ashes: Popular Genres of Invalidnist'

The "Mama, why am I a freak?" billboard, the messages imbedded in it, and the media response bear some relation to the treatment of disability-related issues in the Ukrainian media more broadly. Since the media is the one place where many people in Ukraine encounter disability and (representations of) the disabled, it is an important site for understanding how the parallel world of the disabled is produced. I have not conducted a formal analysis of media representations of disability in Ukraine, but I can draw some tentative conclusions based on newspaper articles on disability themes I collected between 1998 and 2006. In mainstream newspapers such as the daily tabloid *Fakty i kommentarii* (Facts and Commentary, hereinafter *Fakty*), and the newspaper *Den'* (The Day)—the two papers I consulted most frequently during this period—disability-related articles appeared infrequently, yet four main (at times, overlapping) genres can be identified: the Symbolic, the Sensational, the Critical, and the Personalizing. In some ways these genres are akin to the four visual rhetorics of photographic portrayals of disability in the West identified by Rosemarie Garland-Thomson (2001)—the wondrous, the sentimental, the exotic, and the realistic.

Of course representations of disability in the popular media are part of a larger framework of journalistic practice in postsocialist Ukraine, a vast topic that I cannot cover here. It is important to note that the melodramatic approaches of contemporary Ukrainian journalism described below are by no means unique to portrayals of the disabled; the pity story and heroic character types are common in journalistic writing. Important questions about journalistic responsibility are also especially relevant: Should the press be held responsible for representing social reality fully, with nuance and accuracy, or for advocating for the vulnerable and marginalized? Are these tasks mutually compatible? I cannot address this issue but would like to keep it in mind.

In this schema, the "freak" billboard falls most squarely into the genre of the Symbolic, where a disability—or the disabled person, the invalid—is imbued with or mined for certain deeper meanings and messages. Discussions in the Symbolic vein often revolve around the question, "Why?" or dwell on unraveling some life lessons that disability is presumed to convey. There are frequent references to religious tropes and spiritual notions: disability as a cross to bear, and disability as the result of some past sin in a family, or retribution for a parent's (usually a mother's) moral failure. These references are not always negative; for instance, journalists like to contrast the person's physical imperfections with his or her "big soul" or "kind soul." For example, the title of one newspaper article about the Simonovich family, in which five of the eight children have been diagnosed with congenital hypopituitarism, was "Small people with a big soul" (Malimon 2002). In the Symbolic genre, the phenomenon of disability is often treated as an opportunity to explore philosophical questions: "Are disabled children punishment, or a gift from God?" (Zakharchuk 1999). Formulations such as this one suggest the negation of full personhood for disabled children, who are rendered perpetual children; they also privatize their problems and identify them as primarily the responsibility of parents.

Disability is also used to shed light on social problems. For example, one article examines the plight of women who give birth to disabled children to address the question, "Deserters of the family front: Why are they usually men?" (Kurchina 1998). Indeed, particularly in the late 1990s, when the economic crisis and sense of chaos in the new Ukrainian state was at its peak, and concern over the country's demographic decline was growing, disability (and disabled individuals themselves) were portrayed in the media as representative of a deep-seated social disorder (Hevey 1997:334). Here, disability symbolizes an unequivocal tragedy of the individual, the family, and society, a framing that is common in many world areas.

Typical of this association is the February 5, 1998, cover of the medical newspaper *Health of Ukraine* (Zdorov'e Ukrainy). The cover features a photograph of a lone man in a bright orange wheelchair on the otherwise-deserted grounds of some gray, concrete institution—presumably a hospital or internat. The man's face is turned away from the camera. The photograph—and, in particular, this man and his "unfortunate" fate—is meant to illustrate the following headline and article description: "When there is nowhere else to turn . . . Incredible misfortunes may bring any of us to despair. Only very strong people are able to forge miracles in their fate, to 'be reborn from the ashes.' But what are those to do who do not possess this super-strength?" The article attached to this cover piece focuses on charity and the growing volunteerism movement (Burdyk 1998). Thus, this lonely man in a wheelchair, with both his "misfortune" and his lack of "super-strength" is made a symbol of the deeply troubled Ukrainian society.

In this depiction, the individual becomes an object of pity, another common portrayal of disability in many world contexts, one highly critiqued by disability studies scholars and rights activists. Pity also denies full personhood to the disabled, and "heartbreaking" representations of disabled individuals have tangible influence on public opinion. In one survey of 540 passersby near a Kyiv subway station in 2003, when asked, "How do you relate to invalids?" (Rus. *Vashe otnoshenie k invalidam?*) 47 percent of respondents answered, "I feel sorry for them."[15] This was by far the most frequent response. Like MP Valery Sushkevych, many of my acquaintances who used wheelchairs reported being handed spare change on a regular basis by strangers who assumed they wanted or needed a handout. These stereotypes square with popular perceptions of the disabled in Ukrainian society: nondisabled respondents to a survey in Kharkiv characterized "the typical invalid" as unhappy, nonsexual, dependent, vulnerable, and anxious (Krayzh and Shyngaryova 2002).

Related to the genre of the Symbolic is that of the Sensational. Not surprisingly, portrayals in the Sensational mode appear most often in daily tabloid newspapers such as *Fakty* and *Segodnia*. Sensational stories often focus on the "shocking details" of a person's physical and intellectual anomalies and spell out an individual's or family's hardships and struggles in descriptive, grotesque, and dramatic detail. These are often tales of abuse and rescue, like the case of 37-year-old Nina Gordii, a disabled woman whose parents reportedly confined her in a root cellar and, later, in a pen with chickens, pigs, and dogs, for nearly 20 years. An article in *Fakty* enumerated the abuses Nina suffered in incredible detail and then chronicled her rescue and subsequent "rebirth" in an institution (Malinovskaia 2002).

Also in the Sensational genre are stories of the "miraculous." These accounts resonate with yet are somehow outside of the trope of "overcoming" frequently found in other genres (see the Personalizing genre below), as they claim incredible "recoveries" of disabled individuals. Consider the case of Natasha Nagorna, a woman born with cerebral palsy who reportedly gained strength in her previously "nonfunctioning" arms after giving birth to a baby girl. The headline reads: "Hearing her daughter's cry, Natasha, whose arms had not functioned since childhood, grabbed the

baby from the crib" (Krupina 2002:11).[16] Although such Sensational profiles do present disabled individuals in a positive light to an otherwise
quite indifferent public, any benefit may be undermined by their extrem-
ist claims. Such stories of miraculous recovery also make disabilities seem
willed and create blame-the-victim nuances—if only Natasha had had the
will to use her arms prior to hearing her baby cry, she could have been
healed and saved herself, her family, and the state the agony and expense.
Stories such as these probably sell copy, but they do not for the most part
empower disabled people.

Publications in the Critical genre include articles that focus on the violation of disabled people's rights and often criticize the state's failure to fulfill its responsibilities toward invalids (Romanov and Iaiskaia-Smirnova
2006:232–233). Critical articles may cross into other genres; the Symbolic
or the Sensational, for example, may be deployed to highlight shortcomings in the state's response to the needs of the disabled. One example of the
Critical genre is an article in *Vechernie Vesti* (Evening News) that detailed
the housing woes of disabled individuals who were moved into a new
apartment building after ceding their previous apartments to the state.
Having agreed to the move with the understanding that they could privatize the new apartments, the residents were instead told that the house was
a designated *spetsinternat* (special internat) for the mobility disabled; they
subsequently were left without any apartment ownership at all (Bodnia
2000).

On the one hand, articles of the Critical genre play a watchdog role and
draw attention to legal issues and abuses of power that affect the lives of
the disabled. Here, we see the popular media launching criticisms against
unfair disability policy on the behalf of disabled citizens, a positive development by any measure. On the other hand, such articles may also portray
disabled people not as independent actors, but as recipients of benefits
and charity, a stereotypical representation that disability rights activists
and scholars have long challenged. Interestingly, however, I have noted a
growing positive trend in Critical publications, particularly those in the
more respected (i.e., less tabloid-like) newspapers. Namely, critiques of
Ukrainian social politics vis-à-vis disability increasingly are framed not in
reference to the helplessness of the disabled and their dependence on the
state. Rather, the situation in Ukraine is contrasted unfavorably with that
in the West, especially Western Europe and the United States.

For example, a 1999 article in *Den'* profiled the rehabilitation center
Dzherelo for children with learning difficulties in Kyiv, particularly those
with Down Syndrome (the article used the commonly used Russian term *deti*

*s intellektual'nymi otkloneniiami,* "children with intellectual deviations"), the only such organization in Ukraine at the time. The article is highly critical of the lack of state support for these children and their families; pensions are low, and families receive few services and benefits. The position of the state, according to Dzherelo's founder Raisa Kravchenko, is that such children should be institutionalized; institutionalization in fact represents the bulk of the state's investments in these children. This state of affairs is contrasted with approaches in the West, called "the civilized world" by journalist Sergei Evseev (1999). Examples are given of the "multidisciplinary" approaches to rehabilitation found in Western countries, an approach Kravchenko seeks to replicate and for which she requests state assistance. Playing the international card is a rights strategy that will likely continue to grow, both in and beyond the media.

The fourth and most complex mode of media portrayal of disability in Ukraine is the Personalizing genre. In this genre I include most of the personal profiles of disabled individuals and their families that appear in the Ukrainian press. Overall such profiles of disabled persons are infrequent, but most of my informants had been the subject of at least one such profile, some of them in popular daily newspapers with countrywide distribution. Some of these profiles may include elements of the Symbolic or the Sensational, but overall they serve, through personal interviews and contextualization, to personalize and personify disability for the reading public. In this way, such articles can do the same work as Iryna, Vasyl', and Tanya, who pursued strategies to introduce their fellow citizens to "a real, live invalid." In the case of media portrayals this is not unproblematic, however, since the individuals profiled often are positioned as pitiable and vulnerable, and their dependence on charity is foregrounded. Similarly troubling is the rather opposite tendency to emphasize the individual's heroism and ability to "overcome" his or her disability, a discourse critiqued in the West as the stereotype of the super-crip. In the Personalizing genre the trope of heroism is utilized most frequently when the profile subject is an athlete. One headline for example refers to wheelchair racer Oleksandr Sukhan as a "living legend of Transcarpathia" (P'iatylietov 2000). These contrasting tropes—the disabled as pitiable and heroic—are indicative of the everyday paradoxes that disabled individuals must navigate between the "normal" and parallel worlds.

I have noticed a gender bias in the Personalizing genre. Profiles of disabled women are more likely to dwell on misfortune and to emphasize themes of love lost and love found, motherhood lost and motherhood fulfilled. Also, parental responsibility for disabled children (including blaming women for their children's congenital disabilities) is exclusively assigned to women. These gendered dynamics of blame (and self-blame among mothers of disabled children) is not unique to Ukraine, of course, and women in the United States face similar attitudes (Landsman 2009). In contrast, profiles of disabled men more frequently fall into the heroic, overcoming vein. Women are more likely to be portrayed as victims, or as charity cases, and men as independent actors in control of their own lives. A notable exception to this trend in Ukraine is media portrayals of Svet-lana Trifonova, a well-known paralympic athlete. Early articles on Trifon-ova focused on sports and overcoming challenges (Krasikova 1998). After she married and gave birth to a son, themes of family duty and mother-hood became salient (Aleksandrova 2005).

There are moderate differences between publications intended for a general readership and those intended primarily for disabled persons themselves and other readers specifically interested in disability issues. During the past couple of decades, the main newspapers for a disabled readership have been *Povir u Sebe* (Believe in Yourself) and *Blahovist* (the Ukrainian term for the ringing of church bells), both published in L'viv.[17] Overall these newspapers focus on providing readers with information on disability-related legislation, discussions of disability rights initia-tives, the activities of NGOs and legal structures regulating NGOs' opera-tions, news of recent conferences and events, and various viewpoints on political debates. Personal profiles of disabled individuals appear rather infrequently, with one major exception: during 2002–2003 *Povir u Sebe* featured excerpts of the book *Rick Hansen: Man in Motion* in Ukrainian translation over the course of several issues. Hansen, a Canadian, is an internationally celebrated wheelchair athlete and advocate of spinal cord injury research and sports.

Unfortunately, even when personal profiles of disabled Ukrainians have appeared in these two newspapers, they have not been immune to the essentializing portrayals of the disabled as recipients of charity or as venerable heroes. Disempowering language (descriptions of individuals as "bedridden," "confined to a wheelchair," and others) is found even in these two newspapers, and also in the short-lived journal *Sotsial'ne Part-nerstvo* (Social Partnership), which targeted persons involved in health and disability-related activism.

Given these limitations, it is important to ask, What would a more empowering Personalizing profile in the media look like? In her analy-sis of photographic portrayals of disability, Rosemarie Garland-Thomson argues that photos in the realistic mode, showing disability as typical or ordinary, "can promote practices of equality and inclusion that begin to fulfill the promise of a democratic order" (2001:372). There are a few signs that just such a realistic mode of representation of disability is gaining some ground in post-Soviet states. For instance, Romanov and Iarskaia-Smirnova (2006:230–231) describe a 2002 photo exhibition at the Moscow House of Photography called Pictures That Didn't Suffice, which featured photographs the authors describe as "nontypical, breaking stereotypical portrayals of invalids as sick and marginalized and opening new contemporary horizons for understanding disability and society." In contrast to characteristic popular depictions of disabled persons that highlight difference and freakishness and are designed to elicit sympathy or awe (what Garland-Thomson [2001] would call the exotic and wondrous genres of photographing disability), many of these photographs worked to undo clichés, resisted portraying disabled people as types, and emphasized the individuality of each person. Going further, the well-respected Moscow-based disability rights NGO Perspektiva some years ago held a photo contest for disabled children, who were asked to photograph aspects of their daily lives. These photographs were subsequently exhibited in Moscow.

Profiles of the disabled in Ukrainian media outlets such as the newspapers described above could be similarly empowering if they worked more in this realistic mode. If disability were framed as one facet among many of the individual's life, such realistic profiles could go far to debunk myths of heroism and pathos. Furthermore, a key limitation of current media portrayals of disability in the Ukrainian media is the near total absence of disabled persons as authors writing and speaking for themselves (Kudriashov 2002). Surprisingly, this is the case not only in the widely read daily newspapers such as *Den'*, *Fakty*, and *Segodnia*, but also in the more specialized, disability-focused newspapers and journals.

An occasional exception to this trend was the journal *Liubomyra*, founded and edited by women's and disability rights activist Liubomyra Boichyshyn, with support from the Canada-Ukraine Gender Fund. Disabled persons themselves penned some articles in the journal, especially Liubomyra herself, who has multiple sclerosis. Unfortunately the journal was discontinued. Other of my informants wrote articles from time to time for publication in newspapers and journals—as a lawyer, Oleg Polo-ziuk (2004) was a frequent contributor of short pieces offering legal advice to the disabled. Ihor Rasiuk (2002a, 2002b, 2002c) published a few articles in which he described his life as a resident of several residential institutions and critiqued the state's treatment of disabled "wards of the state," and Denis Petrov (2006) contributes occasionally to news journals such as

*Zerkalo Nedeli* (Weekly Mirror). But in most media discussions of disability, disabled people themselves do not direct the conversation. They are
not necessarily silenced—their voices are elicited by journalists via interviews—but they usually remain passive participants in the conversation.

Given the overwhelming negativity of social attitudes toward disability
and the disabled, it should not be surprising that disabled persons themselves may hold harsh perceptions of "invalids." In a detailed survey of 45
persons in Kharkiv, one-third of whom were mobility disabled, Krayzh and
Shyngaryova (2002) documented generally negative perceptions of the disabled ("invalids"), perceptions shared even by mobility disabled respondents. In fact, disabled informants were reluctant to self-identify as invalids; they described themselves as active but said "the typical invalid" was
relatively inactive. They ranked invalids as being very helpless, but characterized themselves as "not helpless." The disabled respondents characterized invalids as dependent, but described themselves as "only somewhat
dependent." Interestingly, disabled respondents said they were hopeful for
a better future for themselves; they asserted that "the future I" would be
more active, less dependent, and more confident than "the present I."

## Meaningful Encounters

In this context, where the voices of people with physical differences
are quieted, the disabled have for so long been physically hidden from
view, and negative stereotypes are firmly entrenched, what happens when
disabled individuals do appear in public? What are such encounters like,
and what can we learn from them about the (non)status of the mobility
disabled as citizens, as subjects who are seen as belonging, or not? Having been denied a common humanity in the popular imagination, how do
disabled individuals seek to recoup this common humanity in personal
encounters?

The action and interaction of staring is a place to start. Many of my informants described at length the stigma they face as people with a spoiled identity (Goffman 1963) who look different and, as one young woman put it,
thus "spoil the view for other people." I frequently witnessed such encounters during the course of my research. One instance in particular made an
especially strong impression on me. In fall 1998 a friend and I were spending
time in the city center of Kyiv with a man with cerebral palsy named Ihor
who lived on the outskirts of the city in an internat for the disabled and the
elderly. Ihor uses a wheelchair, is spastic, and has difficulty speaking. As we
visited a city park, went into a confectioner's, a pet store, and other shops,

Ihor fell under a collective gaze of Kyivans that can only be described as reproachful. The message was quite clear: "It is unpleasant for us to have to see him; such people do not belong among us."

Rosemarie Garland-Thomson has theorized staring as "an intense form of looking that enacts a relationship of spectator and spectacle between two people. The dynamic of staring registers the perception of difference by the viewer and enforces the acceptance of difference by the viewed. As such, it manifests the power relations between the subject positions of 'disabled' and 'able-bodied'" (2001:346–347). She notes that, "the dominant mode of looking at disability in this [American] culture is staring," and since "it is . . . considered rude in our historical moment to stare," the staring encounter vis-à-vis disability is further dramatized, "making the viewer furtive and the viewed defensive." The end result, she argues, is that "the staring dynamic attenuates the bonds of civil intercourse between equal members of the human community." In other words, the stared at—here, the disabled—are rendered as less, unequal, and noncitizens.

But what happens in a society such as post-Soviet Ukraine where staring in fact is not considered rude? Foreign visitors to the region often become uncomfortable when they find themselves the object of others' unapologetic and seemingly interminable stares. If "a gust of conduct manuals appeared in nineteenth-century America that unanimously affirm . . . that we must not stare at one another" (Garland-Thomson 2009:66), the same did not happen in the Russian Empire. Today there are few social taboos against staring, and parents in contemporary Ukraine and Russia do not tell children to stop staring. Whereas Garland-Thomson argues that the very taboo nature of staring further dramatizes the encounter, it could be the case that the absence of hesitation on the part of the starer also sharpens the stare even further. Thus it becomes even more true that, as Garland-Thomson argues, "staring is the ritual enactment of exclusion from an imagined community of the fully human" (2001:347).

In her analysis of staring as a social relationship, Garland-Thomson unpacks staring as communication, staring as dominance, and staring as stigma assignment. Discussing the latter, she notes that "stigmatization is a social process" that hurtles a body "from the safe shadows of ordinariness into the bull's-eye of judgment" (2009:45). With Ihor that day I became aware that stares have a particular tone, what the online Merriam-Webster's dictionary calls the "accent or inflection expressive of a mood or emotion." No stare is neutral, because the very act of staring is prompted by a perception of difference or distance; when we stare we reveal how we have divided the world into the ordinary and expected, versus the unexpected and extraordinary (Garland-Thomson 2009:33–39). But staring can be more or less purposefully hurtful and alienating, as I learned during my time with Ihor. The stares directed at Ihor seemed consciously wielded to exclude him from the world of the "normal" and, frankly, demolish him. Garland-Thomson has explored the powerful strategies starees can mobilize by staring back, to "take charge of a staring situation, using charm, friendliness, humor, formidability, or perspicacity to reduce inter-personal tension and enact a positive self-representation" (2009:84). This staring back was rather difficult for Ihor, since he cannot always control his movements, including those of his head and face.

As we have seen, this exclusion, this denial of a common humanity, also can be enacted through symbols such as the six-fingered palm print and through language, as in the use of urod and other dehumanizing terms to refer to the disabled. Face-to-face discursive interaction is another site where language mediates difference, often with the result of marginalizing and demeaning the person deemed different. At the same time, personal and public encounters can present opportunities for the excluded and stigmatized to take control of their own self-representation and move others toward knowledge and recognition. These encounters mark the work of mobile citizenship, as disabled persons and their advocates shape a narrative of belonging and forge new, often productive relationships with significant others: support networks, representatives of the state, media voices, and the common person. The following vignettes offer vivid examples of all these dynamics.

### The Inclusive We

On May 9, 2005, several members of Mandry (Wandering or Cruising),[18] a community organization for disabled adolescents in Kyiv, gathered on Independence Square. It was Victory Day, and a parade commemorating the Allied victory in World War II was planned along Khreshchatyk. War veterans had been invited to take part, as well as dignitaries such as President Yushchenko and Prime Minister Tymoshenko. Even though it was raining, thousands of well-wishers lined the street to catch a glimpse of the VIPs and congratulate the veterans, aged yet proud men and women with rows upon rows of medals of service pinned to their jackets.

The members of Mandry at the parade included several young men and one young woman who used wheelchairs, and a few other teenage volunteers who frequently took part in the group's activities. Dmitrii, Mandry's director, said the volunteers were at-risk youth. I accompanied the group

to the parade, having been invited by Dmitrii. We spent over an hour waiting at the curb for the parade to begin, chatting, joking and taking one
another's pictures. Groups of veterans finally began to walk by, and the
young people dutifully ventured out from the curb to congratulate several
of them with a red carnation and a handshake. Having done our part for
the official celebration, the group decided to spend the rest of Victory Day
at a pub down by the Dnipro River. We would have to take cabs, since
public transport had been stopped in the city center, and, in any case, it
was not wheelchair accessible. Dmitrii and the young men headed to an
adjacent street to catch some taxis, while we women—Sveta, a wheelchair
user with multiple sclerosis; two volunteers, Yana and Nastia; and I—went
to find a restroom.

Although the situation is slowly improving, Ukraine has a dismal lack
of public restrooms. Most existing public restrooms are very dirty and
smell terrible; you usually know when a public restroom is close by just
from the stench. In the center of Kyiv there are several public restrooms
located in underground passageways around Independence Square, but
they can be reached only via several long staircases. A few of these staircases have been fitted with wheelchair lifts in the last few years, but I have
never seen them being used. There is a subterranean shopping mall under
Independence Square that has a restroom, but the mall was closed for the
holiday. We decided to head for the All-Ukrainian Labor Union building,
where Yana knew there to be restroom facilities.

Yana and Nastia pulled Sveta up several steps to the building while I got
the door. Once inside the women's restroom, we saw it would not be possible for Sveta to use the toilets. They were of a type common in Ukraine,
squat toilets located on a platform one or two steps up from ground level.
It was decided that Yana would help Sveta use a metal trashcan as a toilet
instead; the trashcan was in a corner of the room but was still in full view of
anyone who might enter the restroom. Nastia and I guarded the door but
could not keep one of the building's workers out—she had seen us enter the
restroom and came to investigate. Nastia tried to stop her, saying, "Excuse
me, but could you please wait to come in, you see there is a girl in a wheelchair here using the restroom and she asked me to tell you to wait . . ."

Seeing Sveta hovering over the trashcan, the woman erupted in surprise: "What do you think you are doing? How dare you?" Yana replied
in a steady voice, "Your facilities are inadequate for our needs so we really
had no choice." I noted Yana's use of the inclusive "we." The woman left
the room only to step back in a few seconds later. Speaking in Sveta's
and Yana's direction, she said, "Just be careful about it, and don't make a

mess. Because, you know . . . *people* use this restroom" (Rus. *Liudi siuda khodiat*).

### Punishment for Slackers

Pasha, who injured his spine in the late 1980s at the age of 19, is an unemployed accountant who lives with his parents in a small village in Eastern Ukraine. During a life history interview in 2005, Pasha told me about his participation, in 1992, in a competition called Knight in a Wheelchair. The participants, 12 male wheelchair users, came from all over the country to a small resort town near Kyiv for the competition, which included categories such as public speaking and self-presentation, talent, and sports. One category that stood out for Pasha was the dance competition.

Contestants were required to dance the tango and the hopak, a traditional Ukrainian dance. As Pasha explained, the men were assigned "healthy" (nondisabled) female dance partners:

They gave us partners from the Institute of Culture, from the choreography department. We were taken to the institute for rehearsals. As they later told us, they said, "You know, guys, they gave you to us as punishment for skipping classes." We just looked at them: "Girls, do you mean to tell us you are slackers? Lazy students?" "Yes!" And they, like, made them dance with us—"here, take these invalids, as punishment."

### "Different" Children

LETTER TO THE EDITOR, OCTOBER 26, 1998
Regarding the *Express* newspaper's publication of the article "Mutant-children" (*Dity-mutanty*), which describes child-invalids in a manner outside the bounds of human decency, the association for the defense of child-invalids with cerebral palsy, Nadiya, issued an unequivocal protest. Journalist L. Iasynchuk has defended her use of words like "monster-children," "mistake of mother nature," "spider children," "children . . . with watermelon heads," and "monster-mutants" as appropriate to describe the children she met in an internat-home she visited. The editor of the *Express* newspaper, deputy of the L'viv city council I. Pochynok, also fully defends the newspaper's approach to child-invalids, declined to engage in a dialogue, did not respond to the association's complaint, and refused a meeting with us. . . . .

The publication of "Mutant-children" has caused a huge uproar among our association's families and our members, who total in the thousands. Parents express their indignation and outrage; they feel defamed and demeaned by the newspaper's article. This does not compromise their feelings of motherly and fatherly love, solidarity, or their desire to defend and always be close to and alongside their "different" ("*inakshymy*") children. But all the same we would like to receive a statement of the official position of the city leaders, of representatives of the state organs of education and social policy, of civic organizations, and especially of outlets of the mass media, a statement that reflects the true public opinion on this question: Who are our children for you? (*Kym ie dlia vas nashi dity?*) Monsters, really? Whose parents are we? What is our worth and that of our children to society? Who are our children for the state? Citizens of what sort? Journalists, who are you writing for? For the ignoramuses thirsty for sensational horror stories, or for normal, cultured, meek, benevolent people? Are you able to admit it when you've made a mistake?

Recognizing a widespread common desire [for L'viv] to become a European city, with a cultured and educated atmosphere, and the center of the spiritual revival of Ukraine, we are hoping for a response to this matter.

—Mykola Swarnyk, co-founder, Nadiya Association of parents
with children with cerebral palsy, L'viv

*Making It Real*

ACT I

In June 2005 I sat with Katia, a woman in her late twenties who was born with mild cerebral palsy, in the office where she was working. A certified schoolteacher, Katia had been hired as an office assistant for a group of young businesspeople who were trying to get a social business off the ground. One goal of the social business was to provide employment to disabled workers, mainly for the tax break. Katia took the job because it paid better than teaching, and was less stressful.

I had met Katia a few days earlier and, eager to practice her English, which she had learned in school and university, she invited me back to the office where she worked for tea and conversation. Knowing of my interest in disability issues, Katia openly discussed her experiences as a disabled young woman—she walks with difficulty and uses wooden arm crutches. Katia told me that if earlier she was extremely self-conscious and hated being in public, now she had learned to "just let it go." She said, in English: "I just don't pay any attention to what somebody says, or does, or asks. . . . It doesn't matter to me." Katia went on to give examples of how "other" (nondisabled) people said things to distance her and emphasize her bodily difference, something she resisted. She continued:

> The problem is not in us [the disabled], but the problem is in the other people. I'm not separated, I don't feel that I am worse, that's nonsense. Other people say that. They ask me, "Is it catching?" It's like in the tenth century! Wild people! "Is it catching? Is it catching?" I don't know if they're serious, but they do [ask that], often. "Is it AIDS?" They are afraid.

Katia and I became friends and saw each other regularly; we had overlapping social networks, and we helped one another with Ukrainian and English translations of various articles and documents. One Saturday I received a call from my friend Dmitrii, who invited me to join him and his organization's members on Khreshchatyk that evening. In summer months, on weekends Khreshchatyk is closed to cars and becomes a bustling pedestrian district full of beer gardens, street performers, and souvenir vendors. Dmitrii said Katia would be there, as would one of his good friends, a man everyone simply called Shaman. Dmitrii was vague when I asked, "What's the occasion?" and simply answered: "We're going to play music." But, as I learned during the course of the evening, Dmitrii and his friends were out to accomplish much more. Their goal, though unstated, was to playfully upend negative public perceptions and harmful stereotypes of disabled people, and the mobility disabled in particular. They accomplished this through a realistic and personalizing public performance of busking—playing drums and passing the hat—on Kyiv's busiest thoroughfare.

ACT II

It was nearly evening when Katia and I met inside the Independence Square subway station and set out to find the others. I complimented Katia on her new outfit—she was wearing a miniskirt and a backless strappy top I had not seen her in before. She smiled and said, "Lately I have gotten braver, and I don't mind showing my body. People tell me I look nice, and I'm inclined to believe them!"

I called Dmitrii's cell phone and learned that he, Shaman, and the others were already setting up. There were eleven people in our group, five of whom used wheelchairs and one of whom used crutches: Dmitrii, Katia, and Oleg Poloziuk; three young people from Dmitrii's youth organization (Mandry)—Sveta, Andrei, and Maxim; three volunteers—Yana, Nastia, and Serhiy; Shaman, and me. We formed a semicircle and Shaman began handing out various percussion instruments he had brought—a large drum, tambourines, and maracas.

Shaman's flamboyant dress drew surprised stares from passersby. He was wearing cut-off cargo pants with moccasins and homemade striped leg warmers (he had cut the feet out of some woolen socks), a rather soiled white tank top, and a black floral vest. On his head was a red and white jester's hat with jingling bells on it; he also wore an unusual headdress involving a meter-long piece of wood that rested across the back of his neck, with a huge bundle of seeds hanging down from the headdress to his chest, like a thick necklace. Shaman had wrapped several long, brightly colored belts and scarves around his waist; he wore numerous amulets around his neck and bracelets were wrapped around his wrists. He had a goatee and his hair was plaited in two long braids. Seeing someone in a get-up such as Shaman's was rare in Kyiv, and people made audible comments about the spectacle as they walked by.

Shaman began to beat out a rhythm on his drum and encouraged the rest of us to join in. Dmitrii had brought a huge, gold-colored trophy, a cup he had won in a sporting event—the cup was to be the kitty into which passersby would toss their change and small bills. In the beginning there was a lot of nervous laughter; we all felt vulnerable—here we were, amateur musicians performing on this busy street with no preparation. I was sitting on the curb beside Katia; both of us were timidly tapping tambourines as we took in the scene, trying to remain inconspicuous. I wondered what was going through people's minds. What did the passersby think about our gang, which included five wheelchair users and a strangely dressed Shaman? At first people stopped to listen in small groups, and then moved on. Were they pausing to listen to the drumming, or to watch this unusual group of people? And what was it like for Dmitrii, Sveta, Oleg, and the other wheelchair users to be "playing for alms," as it were? What was the Shaman's role—was he a musical anchor, or was he positioned to attract attention while deflecting it from the other "freaks" gathered here?

Night fell on Khreshchatyk, and after passing around several bottles of good, dark Obolon beer, everyone began to relax into the performance. Shaman's drumming got increasingly intense and complex, and he began to sing in a guttural, otherworldly voice. Katia and I, emboldened by the beer and the cover of semidarkness, also began to sing, playing off Shaman's monotonous chants with higher-pitched harmonies. We had been playing for a good half hour and by now were drawing larger crowds; at one point I counted nearly 100 people standing around listening to the drumming and singing. Not much money was being placed in the cup, however, so Shaman motioned for me to pick it up and work the crowd. Whenever someone dropped some money in the cup all we performers yelled in unison, "*Spasibo!*" ("Thank you" in Russian).

The mood became increasingly festive. Dmitrii, an accomplished wheelchair sport dancer, invited Yana and me to dance with him, and Dmitrii's virtuosity maneuvering the wheelchair brought even more spectators to our circle. Women from the crowd began to dance with him as well, which drew cheers and applause. Shaman and Dmitrii invited people in the audience to join our drumming circle, and a few brave bystanders started playing drums and tambourines with us.

The evening had begun cautiously and nervously as a group of "invalids" and a few of their friends play-acted a stereotype: the disabled as beggars, and as weirdoes or freaks. Shaman's dress and manner played up this stereotype, too. But the evening of busking was not primarily about making money; it was about subverting negative public discourse. By playing themselves as persons, not stereotypes, Dmitrii and the others personified for the public "real, live disabled people," as Katia later put it. No one reported on the unusual performance in the newspapers, or on television; nor did the group make much money. But the event had transformative effects for the performers and the spectators. By simply gathering as friends to play some drums, have a good time, and interact with the public through music and dance, the group took control of their own image and good-naturedly poked fun at social misperceptions of the disabled as pitiable, impoverished, lonely people. Like one of Rosemarie Garland-Thomson's informants, a disfigured woman who used staring encounters to enact "an assertive outreach toward mutual recognition across difference" (2009:94), Dmitrii and his friends guided their fellow Kyivans toward a self-representation of their own choosing. They creatively inserted themselves into the public eye, and "made it real" to assert a playful, yet powerful, politics of belonging. And for the passersby who stopped to look and listen, and especially for those who picked up a tambourine or partnered with Dmitrii in dance, the encounter might just have been enough to move them from a place of stereotype and assumption toward a place of knowledge and mutual recognition.

## Regeneration

In 2001 the Ukrainian art world witnessed a rather different experiment to challenge popular perceptions of disability. At the Murat Guelman Gallery in Kyiv, artist Yuri Solomko presented a photo exhibition titled Regeneration, which he hoped would compel people to question their assumptions about the disabled or "damaged" body and diverse instantiations of beauty. Depicted in the 11 art photos was Elena Chinka, a double amputee who lost part of both legs at the age of 23, when she fell under a moving train. Chinka, who was an aspiring actress and dancer before the accident, subsequently earned a degree in journalism and worked for a time in television. Today she is a choreographer and teaches dance at two studios in Kyiv. She has developed a unique system of communicating to her students some of the movements she wants them to perform by using her hands and through language (Fesenko 2008).

In the Regeneration series Chinka posed nude and semi-nude, wearing a different mask in each photograph.[19] There is a carnivalesque feel to the photographs, and Solomko cites a trip to Venice, with its "laconic and garish symbols," as the inspiration for the project. As Solomko told one journalist, "Venice, like all European culture, and like the body of my model, does not exist in a state of complete physical perfection, in contrast to before" (Chesnokova 2003). Solomko described Regeneration as forcing viewers to interrogate their own prejudiced aesthetic sensibilities. He said, "In the 'Regeneration' project . . . there's a beautiful body and the only thing preventing us from appreciating it is our own stereotypes. For example, the Venus de Milo is considered the epitome of beauty, but we get disturbed (Rus. *uzhasaemsia*) at the sight of invalids" (Chesnokova 2003). Solomko's point is similar to arguments made by Lennard J. Davis (1997) in his discussion "Nude Venuses, Medusa's Body, and Phantom Limbs." As Solomko described his motivations for creating the Regeneration series, "Elena has great power for life over the disbalance."[20]

Solomko had used disabled models in his work before, in particular in his 2000 series of photographs Live Planet (Rus. *Zhivaia Planeta*). Live Planet featured the bodies (usually closeups of parts of bodies) of subjects, all of whom were physically disabled, onto which maps were projected. Solomko said the impetus for Live Planet was the huge "geopolitical metamorphoses" of the early 1990s, in which "states fell and new ones were formed" (i.e., the Soviet Union and the Soviet successor states; Chesnokova 2003). Solomko wanted to create photographs showing how "social and political depositions" (his gloss for stereotypes) interfere with humans' ability to

FIGURE 4.2. "Baba Yaga." Photograph Yuri Solomko, from the Regeneration series, 2001.

FIGURE 4.3. "Akademia." Photograph Yuri Solomko, from the Regeneration series, 2001.

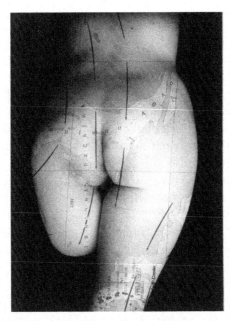

FIGURE 4.4. "In Blue." Photograph Yuri Solomko, from the Live Planet series, 2000.

appreciate the planet as an aesthetic object. He projected world maps onto visibly disfigured bodies to illustrate this disruption—the viewer is unlikely to be able to "get past" the dissonance introduced by the "abnormal" bodies and thus fails to really see and appreciate the projected maps, and vice versa.[21] The Live Planet series is problematic in how it traffics in the grotesque in relation to people's bodies, especially since the perspective is not coming from the subject position of the disabled person being photographed. Davis (1997:64) could have been writing of the Live Planet series when he stated: "The grotesque is defined in this [metaphorical] sense as a disturbance in the normal visual field, not as a set of characteristics through which a fully constituted subject views the world."

Elena Chinka was one of Solomko's models for Live Planet, and he said that after he photographed Chinka, he began to think of her as possessing a "transformed body" and believed that "the entire world could be transformed in the body of this woman" (Chesnokova 2003). He sought inspiration for a project to feature Chinka, and found such inspiration when he traveled to Venice.

The Regeneration series plays on several key ideas (Kovalenko 2005). On the one hand, Solomko wants to emphasize the limitations all humans face—not only are humans, in contrast to some other organisms, incapable of regeneration (of lost limbs, for example); humans also do not possess the capacity to fly like birds or swim like fish. However, we have developed effective means to compensate—airplanes, boats, and prosthetic limbs. At the same time, the artist also wishes to play on the contrast between what is apparent—the façade—and what is hidden—the deep structure, or inner force. Enter the city of Venice with its unique architecture and masquerade culture. Built on the water, "on stilts," as Solomko might say, Venice gives the false impression of being vulnerable and unsteady, when in fact its foundations are strong. The comparison with Chinka, who does not wear prostheses in the photograph, but does use them in her daily life, is clear: the viewer is shown her "incomplete," fragile body but her face is masked. Chinka's prosthetic legs do appear in two of the photographs, but she is not wearing them and they have been transformed into flower vases. This compels the viewer to wonder about the model, to wish to look beyond her exterior and ask, "Who is she, really?"

Chinka's own explanation for using the masks was more ambiguous. She told one journalist that she hid her face so her aged and ailing grandmother, who was never told of Chinka's accident, would not learn that she was a double amputee (Krupina 2003). Chinka explained that she wore her prostheses when visiting her grandmother and took care not to lose her balance. This explanation is not altogether convincing, since Chinka's face is clearly visible and recognizable in one of the Regeneration photographs. One wonders how the viewer's experience of viewing these photographs would change if Chinka had not worn the masks and, especially, if she were "staring back" at the viewer. As Garland-Thomson (2009:84–85) notes, "Portraits can provide their [disabled] subjects with an opportunity to deliberately engage their viewers. . . . Intense eye-to-eye engagement with the viewer can make a subject seem to reach out of the picture to stare down the viewer." Chinka's masks attenuate this possibility.

One of the intended messages of Regeneration is that the body is a mere shell or costume and that "beauty breaks through the horror of tragedy."[22] It is significant that whereas Solomko's Live Planet series centered on deformed and unusual parts of bodies, Regeneration, in contrast, consists of 11 full-body portraits of the artist's subject. Although rooted in the carnivalesque and thus different in mood, and without offering the subject (Chinka) an opportunity to stare back, perhaps the Regeneration portraits nonetheless can do positive work similar to that achieved in the portraits of disabled individuals painted by Doug Auld and Chris Rush (Garland-Thomson 2009:79–96). Using different artistic techniques, Auld and Rush "offer respectful, even beautiful, pictures of people we have not learned to look at in this way," thus, "us[ing] the clout of high art to transform our staring from a breach of etiquette or an offensive intrusion into an act of appreciation" (Garland-Thomson 2009:83–84). Solomko does the same in his Regeneration photographs.

On the one hand, the Regeneration photos draw on a classic form of art, the female nude, which Davis (1997:56) has called "part of the development of a set of idealized conventions about the way the body is supposed to look." At the same time, the photographs upend and poke fun at the nude; Chinka takes on unusual poses that a conventional, non-amputee model would probably be unable to strike. One of the photographs seems backward; Chinka's back is to the camera and she wears a white mask on the back of her head—her face appears to be on the wrong side. Solomko makes use of a round mirror variously positioned on the floor in several of the photographs—Chinka's posterior is reflected in the mirror in one photo, and in several others her "stumps" are reflected. These techniques add visual interest and compel the viewer to think about bodies, body parts, and beauty anew.

Despite how Solomko plays with Chinka's disability, and with the viewer, I would not categorize the Regeneration project as trafficking in the grotesque in the manner of his Live Planet series, or in the manner of Diane Arbus, whose photographs of disabled people some disability studies scholars have critiqued as unequivocally disempowering (Davis 1997:64; Hevey 1997:334–340). There is no doubt that Solomko's work is controversial, and his use of disabled individuals as models in his photographic art has earned him a citation in the critical Wikipedia entry "Attraction to disability."[23] Solomko rejects the label "shock art" to describe his work; he says he does use shock as a method but that the real object of his work is beauty.[24] Solomko has been criticized for exploiting Chinka's disability for his own artistic adventurism, a charge Chinka herself vehemently rejects. Reportedly, Chinka asserted that, "This project [Regeneration] brought me great pleasure. That I was able to communicate a love of life through my very nature (Rus. *estestvom*) is probably the main accomplishment of this work. It was a very interesting game, and I want to continue with similar experiments" (Chesnokova 2003). Chinka indeed appears to revel in this game: "I have a creative nature and I like to discover myself anew, and try something novel" (Kovalenko 2005:55).

The Regeneration photographs of Elena Chinka reject the tropes of pity and sympathy and invite the viewer to consider Chinka's body as an aesthetic object, to contemplate the complex meanings and possible forms of beauty. As stated in the project's gallery description, "People with limited

capabilities are on society's periphery, both because of their physical limitations and due to the psychological barriers formed by regular people,
based on pity and sympathy. But what zones of the human subconscious
produce these barriers? Is it possible to counter these reactions?"[25] Chinka
compared herself to famous fashion model and athlete Aimee Mullins,
also a double-amputee, and said that by posing for Solomko she, like Mullins, "wanted to prove that being without legs is not a catastrophe, and furthermore, is not a career barrier" (Krupina 2003). Chinka said she knew
that the photos of her in Regeneration would cause "shock" and "outcry,"
but she believed the project was effective in challenging and transforming
people's assumptions about "female beauty." Gallery visitors, she noted,
wrote comments such as, "She is beautiful!" "She is strong!" and "She is
divine!" in the guest book (Krupina 2003).

Like Dmitrii and his friends, who asserted a politics of belonging
through their playful street performance, as a woman-model who is not
defined by her bodily imperfections, Chinka, one could say, articulates an
empowering statement by "making it real."

Earlier in this chapter, in the discussion of the "Mama, why am I a
freak?" billboard, I argued that the Ukrainian public lacks a common language with which to discuss issues of disability. The billboard and the discussions that followed in newspapers and online used disability merely as
a vehicle to debate other issues—drug abuse, demographic crisis—and in
the process objectified and silenced the disabled. I find it significant that
in the engagements described subsequently—busking on Khreshchatyk,
and Elena Chinka's modeling, many of the actors—or agents—engage in
embodied performances. These persons seek to effect and shape more
nuanced—yet also more open-ended and relational—discussions about
disability and disability experience not necessarily by launching a campaign of words, of language, but through embodied performances that
invite social interaction and the personalization of experience.

In addition to being firmly rooted in the real (as in Garland-Thomson's
realistic mode), such performances also have a universalizing quality. By
simultaneously acting out stereotypes of the marred invalid (the beggar
in a wheelchair, the grotesque amputee) and subverting them through
physical movement, social interplay, and channeling various instantiations of beauty, Dmitrii, Katia, Elena Chinka, and others argue for a common humanity. They demand to be recognized as persons of worth, in all
their difference and similarity. They do important work to make a space
of meaningful belonging for themselves in the ableist society in which
they live. These individuals reveal the realistic mode to be a potentially

empowering genre of disability performance. Countering popular stereotypes and commonly found literary and artistic portrayals of the disabled as symbolic of a range of states and conditions—lack and disorder, the fantastic, and others—disability rights activists like Dmitrii, cultural actors like Elena Chinka, and increasingly more disabled Ukrainians in general, make the important and subversive move of actually portraying themselves (Smith 2004:4). They thus insert themselves into the citizenry through strategies of personification, asserting themselves as "real, live disabled people," and also as full persons.

# 5. Disability, Gender, and Sexuality in the Era of "Posts"

*Edited field notes*
May 9, 2005. Kyiv, Ukraine. Today was Victory Day, marking the sixtieth anniversary of the victory of the Soviet Union over Nazi Germany in World War II. My friend Dmitrii invited me to watch the Victory Day parade with him and the members of Mandry, his club for disabled adolescents. I saw Dmitrii already waiting for me when I emerged from the subway station into a light drizzling rain, and I walked to meet him at our designated meeting place in front of the Central Post Office. We exchanged the customary and friendly kiss on the cheek upon meeting, and then hid under my umbrella as we chatted and waited for the others. An elderly man using crutches (possibly a WWII veteran) walked up to us, looked at Dmitrii in his wheelchair, then at me, and said, "You are a real woman." He proceeded to wish us health and happiness, and told Dmitrii to value me and keep me close. We both struggled to suppress our giggles—the man clearly assumed Dmitrii and me to be a "family pair," and we were embarrassed (I am married, and Dmitrii has a steady girlfriend).

Although we both took it in stride and started talking about something else after the man walked away, the atmosphere suddenly had changed. I think Dmitrii interpreted the man's words thus: "You are really lucky that you, an invalid, have a woman to take care of you." I also felt that I, as Dmitrii's imagined partner, was being praised for my supposed self-sacrifice in caring for a disabled man. Suddenly Dmitrii, a thirty-eight-year-old athlete and independently living director of an NGO, was thrust into the role of a marginal, dependent invalid. Dmitrii and I never revisited the incident, but it prompted me to take notice of how people's experiences of disability in Ukraine and other postsocialist countries intersect with formations of gender, masculinity, femininity, and sexuality, questions that have been little explored in the post-Soviet context.

## Ethnographic Explorations of Spinal Cord Injury, Gender, and Sexuality

Considerations of the gendering of disability in formerly socialist societies are few and far between, although some research on disability and gender has been conducted in Russia (Iarskaia-Smirnova 2002a, 2002b; Indolev 2001:110–146; Romanov and Iarskaia-Smirnova n.d.), in Lithuania (Šėporaitytė and Tereškinas 2008), and in Slovenia (Zaviršek 2006). In this initial examination of the intersections of disability, gender, and sexuality in Ukraine, I begin by asking general questions similar to those posed by Thomas Gerschick in his influential article "Toward a Theory of Disability and Gender": "How does disability affect the gendering process? How does it affect the experience of gender?" (2000:1263). Also following Gerschick (2000:1267), I consider, "How might the stigmatization and marginalization that [disabled ] women and men . . . face contribute to the creation of alternative gender identities?" Thus I examine how disabled men and women in postsocialist Ukraine both sustain and subvert gendered expectations, both "enact and undo the ordinary terms of both gender and disability" (Smith 2004:4). I consider how the experience of disability can be an avenue for individuals to assert not only alternative gender identities, but also alternative claims to citizenship. This focus allows me to go beyond the common story of the disabled as social exiles and noncitizens to explore creative ways in which disabled people experience and perform citizenship as gendered, embodied subjects.

Although Ukrainian women have been the focus of recent studies of changing gender regimes after socialism, women's roles in the new political economy, and the Ukrainian women's movement (Hrycak 2005, Phillips 2008, Rubchak 1996), little attention has been paid in the scholarly literature to men's changing roles and negotiations of masculinity. By juxtaposing the experiences of spinally injured men and women, we can explore how being disabled affects men's and women's ability to enact gender in contemporary Ukraine, and how disability and gender variously intersect to inform their citizenship struggles. Ethnographic perspectives, which locate theoretical analyses in the day-to-day lives of persons in ways that are very experience near, can contribute valuable insights to the emerging literature on disability and gender.

The most widely known scholarship on gender and citizenship focuses on women and their struggles to assert themselves as citizens in contexts of patriarchy and gender discrimination (Brown 1992; Cornell 1995; Fraser 1989; MacKinnon 1989; and Pateman 1988, 1989). This foundational work often rests on the assumption of the male citizen as the norm, as the unmarked category (cf. Miller 2007). But recent scholarship also has explored how male privilege may be undermined as vectors of ethnicity, sexuality, and others collide with hegemonic constructions of the unmarked, privileged male citizen (Rosenfeld and Faircloth 2006). Disability is another such vector that can erode the male subject's identity and demote him, as it were, to less-than-citizen. How disabled men then jockey for citizenship—how they enact a politics of belonging from a compromised identity as invalid—is thus instructive on two fronts. First, it sheds light on contemporary negotiations of gender in postsocialist contexts, where, as we shall see, disabled men occupy interesting subject positions vis-à-vis gender roles and norms. Second, men's citizenship struggles provide insight into the politics of belonging in Ukraine more generally, as people are compelled to assert themselves as new kinds of citizens in the changing political and economic milieu.

In the first part of the chapter I explore in some detail the life history narratives of two disabled men who live in Kyiv. These men's stories confirm Russell Shuttleworth's (2004) thesis that the experience of disability may enable men to expand the masculine repertoire and shed some of the constraints of hegemonic masculinity. Research on disability, masculinity, and sexuality across cultures increasingly shows that the experience of being disabled might present men with opportunities to subvert traditional and limiting gender expectations and to change their sense of self as men, workers, and sexual subjects in unexpected and empowering ways.[1] This has obvious implications for citizenship, as men may assert a new politics of belonging, a politics that can be instructive for other marginalized groups. This research also reveals, however, that these processes are uneven and may involve a simultaneous reliance on and rejection of hegemonic masculinities in a given context.

My research suggests that the expansion of masculine repertoires is also possible in a post-Soviet society where gender norms and notions about disability still are heavily informed by the strict gender role stereotypes, patriarchal attitudes, rigid body cultures (Brownell 1995), and institutional structures of power of the Soviet regime. By aligning themselves with the standards of hegemonic masculinity in certain situations or in particular aspects of their lives, but undermining such ideals in others, some disabled men in postsocialist Ukraine have been able to refashion, reinterpret, redefine, and reimagine themselves and what it means to be a "real man" (and a citizen) in this rapidly changing society. These negotiations are in many ways tied up with the political and economic transformations that have swept the country during the last decade and a half, making post-Soviet states such as Ukraine especially fruitful sites for investigating how disability experience intersects with larger political and social forces in identity formation. This inquiry thus serves as a case study of social change and disability after state socialism, as persons classified as invalids by the state and by other citizens forge new identities for themselves and carve out a larger and more imaginative space for the disabled in post-Soviet society.

The spinal'nik (spinally injured) community is a particularly apt site for tracking intersections of disability and masculinity, since more men than women in Ukraine become disabled as the result of spinal injuries and war wounds (veterans of the Soviet-Afghan war, for example). Most nationally recognized spinal'niki are men, and in the popular imagination spinal injury, wheelchair use, and the general category of spinal'niki are all associated more with men than with women. Although some women figured prominently in the Soviet-era disability rights initiatives (see Indolev 1998), in post-Soviet Ukraine it appears that women arrived rather later onto the collective action scene. Today, men dominate in leadership positions in NGOs that center on issues of mobility disability. This is especially true for those NGOs that target the adult disabled population and focus on issues of physical rehabilitation and sports. In a sample of 43 NGOs classified as Unions of Invalids, leadership roles were filled almost equally by men and women, but women are more likely to head small-scale organizations serving disabled children, as well as those focusing on care giving, charity, the arts, and spirituality (Sydorenko 2001). Men, on the other hand, tend to lead more powerful organizations (all-Ukrainian unions, as opposed to more small scale regional or city-based organizations) and more prestigious ones such as those centered on rehabilitation, sports, veterans' affairs, human rights, and business.

These dynamics confirm Gerschick's (2000:1265) assertion that "for men with physical disabilities, masculine gender privilege collides with the stigmatized status of having a disability, thereby causing status inconsistency, as having a disability erodes much, but not all, masculine privilege." The life history interviews I conducted revealed that as their masculine privilege is eroded as a result of the stigma of disability, men in Ukraine seek not so much to recoup this privilege as to forge *new* paths to being men in the face of disempowering stereotypes about disabled men. Depending on men's life circumstances, at times this may entail striving to enact hyper-masculine qualities in some areas of life, but just as often it involves a rejection of hegemonic visions of masculinity and includes reimagining one's own possibilities to "be a man."

From this focus on disability, masculinity, and sexuality, I then turn to women's experiences of being disabled. Nationalist narratives in Ukraine associate women with the nation and its reproduction and promote an idealized model of the traditional nuclear family. How do disabled women fit into or outside this ideal? To begin exploring intersections of gender and disability for spinally injured women, I consider women's life narratives to examine how hegemonic neofamilialism—the "focus on the reproductive function of the family . . . [and the privileging of] a traditional division of gender roles" (Zhurzhenko 2004)—and gendered expectations of comportment and lifestyle affect disabled women's enactment of femininity, motherhood, and athletics. I ask how being disabled might shape and constrain women's life strategies in contexts of a disabling built environment and gendered expectations regarding caring, motherhood, and work and career. Like the section on disabled men, this investigation centers on the life stories of two individuals who use wheelchairs after spinal injuries—Viktoria and Nadia.

It is important to note at the outset that we have no concrete data about the structural disadvantages disabled women face in Ukraine in terms of access to education and employment, wage disparities, general economic injustices, and so on, although it is commonly acknowledged within the disability community that such inequalities exist. The same is true in the United States, where disabled women have lower employment and income levels than either disabled men or nondisabled women (Schur 2004:257). In the major state reports on disability in Ukraine, rarely are statistics disaggregated by gender, and the problem of gender inequality is not even mentioned. Documenting and addressing questions of gender and disability—including economic disparities, gender violence, differences in political participation and representation, and others—needs to be a priority for the disability rights movement in Ukraine. However, at present there is a yawning lack of such programs.

One of the most widely known organizations for disabled women, the Liubomyra Women's Informational-Rehabilitation Center, founded by Liubomyra Boichyshyn in 1997, is no longer active. NADU does have a program called Assistance for Creating and Developing the National Disabled Women's Movement. The goals of this program, which began in

2002, are stated as follows: "Activization of the movement of women with disabilities, carrying out educational activities for the leaders and specialists of civic organizations of disabled women, raising the level of qualifications for conducting NGO activities."[2] All of the stated program goals focus on capacity-building for disabled women's NGOs. It is unclear what activities have been pursued in recent years, and the program's website was last updated in 2005. That year nearly all the program activities were related to women and cancer, which may be explained by the fact that the program's coordinator is also the director of a nationwide NGO called Together against Cancer. I do know that KHIOU has sponsored some seminars on issues of gender and disability in the past, but the confederation does not include a specific gender program in its mandate.

This lack of focus on gender disparities is disturbing, especially when disabled women are already less visible than their male counterparts on the disability rights scene. There are many reasons for this, and the narratives of disabled women below touch on some of them: women are burdened with gender role expectations that place them in caregiver roles and assign them the bulk of household chores, and women in Ukraine in general do not view politics as a sphere appropriate to women's interests and talents. But in the case of women with spinal injuries there are physical and psychological factors that can also limit political engagement and participation. Many disabled women are embarrassed to be seen in public, and they also lack confidence in their skills to maneuver a wheelchair. At a meeting of mobility disabled persons I attended during fall 2006, one of the seminars focused on "using the balance" (balancing on the two rear wheels of a wheelchair, a technique often used when going over obstacles such as curb cuts, or going down stairs) and "falling safely in a wheelchair." I noticed that while a few experienced men demonstrated the balance technique and men with "fresh" injuries practiced, most of the women in the group remained to the side, speaking with one another instead of participating in the exercise. I joined in their conversation as the women related to one another their wheelchair-related fears: many were afraid to try using an active, lightweight wheelchair, and were reluctant to practice the balance techniques or other "dangerous" maneuvers. Indeed, whereas most of the men at the meeting used active wheelchairs, the majority of women participants used large, so-called "room" or home wheelchairs, or lever-drive chairs operated by pumping two levers with the hands.

This fear and lack of training in wheelchair techniques is compounded by an inaccessible built environment that especially circumscribes women's independent physical mobility, since as a rule women possess less upper body strength than men and may be unable to go up steps in a wheelchair and get over other barriers. The lack of accessible toilets is also a major challenge for women in particular. All of these factors may contribute to women's reluctance to spend much time outside the home, and thus can contribute to their lack of participation in disability rights activism on a large scale. However, these problems are not often publicly acknowledged, so they remain hidden barriers that perpetuate gender inequality.

### "Stinking, strong, and hairy" versus "One hundred percent woman": Hegemonic masculinity and femininity in Soviet and post-Soviet Ukraine

Most of my informants were born and came of age in the Soviet Union; many of the men served in the Soviet army, and men and women were members of official organizations such as the Young Pioneers and the Komsomol (Communist Youth League). Informants' narrated experiences therefore have been informed by Soviet body cultures and gender ideologies, yet they also evidence resistance to Soviet ideals, as people negotiate alternative visions of gender roles and relations, human rights, the body, and sexuality in postsocialism. In order to contextualize the discussion, it is useful to briefly trace historical and contemporary hegemonic ideas on gender, masculinity, and sexuality in the Soviet Union and Ukraine. There were no large-scale surveys on masculine and feminine ideals in the Soviet Union, Soviet policy on issues of gender and sex-role stereotypes was always inconsistent (Kon 1995:148–157), and questions of gender and especially sex were a closed book throughout much of Soviet history. We do know that there was no singular Soviet masculinity, and existing research shows that in the Soviet Union there was a "striking persistence of alternative forms of manliness despite the 'total' claims of the state" (Friedman and Healey 2002:233). These alternative forms remained largely underground, however, since they ran counter to officially sanctioned ideals of masculinity.

The heady months and years following the Bolshevik Revolution of 1917 were characterized by "socialist dreaming" and bold projects to eradicate sex discrimination, emancipate women, and implement "socialism in one gender." But as Thomas Schrand (2002) has convincingly argued, instead of a gender-neutral socialism, what soon developed was a decidedly masculine one. Representatives of the new Soviet state never seriously questioned traditional gender roles, and initial projects to communalize household chores and child rearing proved dismal failures. Women were encouraged—indeed, required—to engage in paid employment outside the home, yet they retained their traditional domestic responsibilities. In this context, as Schrand (2002:205) notes, in the absence of a critique of the "natural" division between the sexes, women, as workers and participants in the public sphere, were simply moved into masculine roles and men were elevated even further, as "state policies and cultural initiatives restored the balance by bolstering the male side of the equation."

The Communist Party was always a predominantly male institution; although a certain percentage of women in positions of political power were guaranteed through quotas, in the Soviet Union relatively few women advanced in the Communist Party, and those who did were usually given tasks associated with maternal and child welfare, low-prestige issues assumed to be most relevant to their interests. The militarization of Soviet society, as well as the masculine character of programs for industrialization and collectivization, reflected the very male-centered and patriarchal nature of the Soviet regime.

On the other hand, the argument has been made—and this is the perception held by many in post-Soviet Ukraine and Russia—that as a result of this very paternalistic and authoritarian character of the Soviet state, men in the Soviet Union were actually emasculated, and women were masculinized. Suffering from subjection to a totalitarian government, and an inefficient economy characterized by shortages and low wages, many men were unable to become autonomous subjects and display the individual initiative and achievement (i.e., establishing rewarding careers, providing for families, and generally "getting ahead") that was central to hegemonic Soviet notions of masculinity. Indeed, Igor Kharkhordin (1999:164–278) has tracked the individualization drive during Stalin's regime, where the ideal New Soviet Man was described (among other formulations) as a "man-Communist" and "a fighter, full of initiative." The Soviet citizen was exhorted that one must "work on oneself" through strategies of self-planning and hero-identification, pursuits that were couched in male terms (Kharkhordin 1999:246–255).

For later periods, Peggy Watson has examined how the development of state socialism in the USSR within a globalizing (Westward-looking) context meant the creation of aspirations among the populace that the socialist state was unable to meet. This situation left citizens feeling resentful and restless, and fostered "a pattern of fixed coping strategies based on a traditional gender identity which is (within limits) adaptive for women and their families, but ultimately maladaptive for men as men" (Watson 1995:932). Whereas women developed strategies of "learned resourcefulness," argues

Watson, men fell prone to "learned helplessness," a situation to which Watson attributes the strikingly gendered nature of health parameters in the former USSR and Eastern Europe, where life expectancy rates for men have plummeted, and men tend to die more frequently and younger than women. Peter Makara (1994) has analyzed how depressed living standards have collided with men's unfulfilled aspirations to produce anomie and poor health for Eastern European men in the wake of socialism's fall, and writer Oksana Zabuzhko (2002) argues that feelings of failure and emasculation are especially acute for men in Ukraine as a result of the quasi-colonial Russian/Soviet regime that assigned Ukraine a permanent "little brother" or "little Russian" status.

In response to the perceived inability of men in the Soviet Union to be "real men," the "transition" period after state socialism has been characterized by a reassertion of patriarchy at the level of the state and the family, in what some observers perceive to be a crisis of masculinity. Feminist scholars have been alarmed at the re-traditionalization of post-Soviet society in Russia, Ukraine, and other states, where women have been ushered back into hearth and home, while men play the dominant roles in the new market economies and new political structures of postsocialist states (Bridger, Kay, and Pinnick 1996; Einhorn 1993; Gal and Kligman 2000a). This phenomenon has been accompanied by the reassertion of strict gender role expectations for both men and women.

What does it mean to be a "real man" today in post-Soviet states such as Ukraine and Russia? What are the widely accepted criteria for manliness in attitude, deed, and appearance? A few years ago, a male Ukrainian friend (then a high school student) described a "real man" to me in Russian as a "*voniuch, moguch, i volosat*"—someone who is "stinking, strong, and hairy." The image of the voniuch, moguch, i volosat neatly encompasses the ideal or hegemonic masculinity in Ukraine and points to some of the more salient cultural symbols of manhood—physical strength (and being able to protect others, especially one's own family), possessing a certain rawness and burliness of physique (as represented in one's hairiness), but lacking a fixation on one's appearance and not being too obsessed with one's personal hygiene (also denoted by hairiness, and the presence of body odor, the latter simultaneously evidencing one's hard work). The trope of voniuch, moguch, i volosat points to the centrality of the body and a particular body culture to enacting gender in post-Soviet Ukraine, and it underlines especially the importance of the body as a marker of manhood.

Fatherhood, working, and providing in material terms appear to be the most important cultural symbols of hegemonic masculinity in Russia

(Chernova 2002), and the same is also true for Ukraine. In Ukraine a "real man" not only adheres to a particular type of physicality; he is also expected to carry out the appropriate masculine roles in family and society. He should provide for his family; take up domestic activities seen as befitting a man (i.e., help rear and teach one's children, but not regularly undertake housework or cooking); engage in a range of possible activities deemed masculine—military service, mechanics (fixing cars, appliances, electronic devices, and showing a general handiness with tools); and have pastimes such as fishing, playing sports, chess, or cards. Drinking is a decidedly male domain, but there is some ambiguity in how drinking and masculinity intersect: flamboyant social drinking and the ability to hold one's drink are important markers of masculinity, but so is abstinence (which equates to being a good worker, husband, and father) in some contexts.

Economic status is another marker of manhood, but the economic basis of manhood in Ukraine is somewhat different from that described as "American marketplace manhood" by Michael Kimmel (1994). Marketplace manhood is a version of masculinity that emerged in eastern cities of the United States around the 1830s in which a man's identity was derived "entirely from success in the capitalist marketplace, from his accumulated wealth, power, and capital" (Kimmel 1994:13). These criteria were not as operative in the paternalistic Soviet state, where social and economic leveling were stressed and most citizens looked to the state as a provider of basic services and a minimum standard of living. This expectation also informs the experience of disabled men, most of whom receive a disability pension from the state, and being "on disability" is not as stigmatized in the former USSR as it may be in countries with a longer history of capitalism and neoliberal economic policy, including the United States.

But as social welfare in postsocialist Ukraine is revamped, and policies for means testing, targeted assistance, and differentiation of pensions are introduced, being on disability or on welfare in general is becoming increasingly stigmatized (Haney 2002, Phillips 2008). In my research I have found that those disabled men who support their families through entrepreneurial activities, shun state support, and are perceived to do for themselves are generally more respected (and possibly viewed as "better men" in the sense of providing) within and outside the disability community than those who appear more dependent on the state or on the goodwill of others.

Still, reliance on disability pensions, which are very low, and limited access to vocational training and job placement makes disabled men and women much more economically vulnerable than many other citizens in the fragile post-Soviet Ukrainian economy. At the beginning of 2008 the average yearly disability pension for disabled individuals who are considered unable to work (group I "invalids") was 8,880 UAH (740 UAH a month), or around $1,776. This is in stark contrast to the estimated earned income nationwide (PPP $US), which for men was $8,854 in 2007, and $5,249 for women (UNDP 2009:182). According to current legislation some disabled persons may simultaneously draw a pension and engage in paid employment, but legislation is in the pipeline to exclude those with official jobs from drawing disability.[3]

In this situation, there is a strong popular perception that the disabled are and should be poor and destitute, and disabled persons thus are denied both practically and rhetorically the possibility to establish economic independence, one of the major prerequisites for postsocialist citizenship and the postsocialist assertion of masculinity. In Ukraine the disabled frequently frame independent living (IL) more in terms of economic independence than physical independence or general lack of reliance on family and friends. In a survey of 84 mobility disabled persons that I conducted with Ukrainian colleagues, 26 respondents said that, to them, IL means above all financial independence from others and from the state. Only five respondents who gave this answer were women, indicating that disabled men in Ukraine may feel a greater need or more pressure to establish economic independence than do women, even in a political and socioeconomic context that usually prevents them from doing so.

Whereas little research has been done on the rise of masculinism in Eastern Europe after the fall of state socialism (see Watson 1993), the revival of traditional norms of femininity and womanhood in the region has been well documented (Gal and Kligman 2000b, Johnson and Robinson 2007). In Ukraine, Oksana Kis (2007) has argued, gender expectations for women are rooted in two fundamental images—the Berehynia, and Barbie. The Berehynia is a pagan goddess from ancient Slavic mythology, a figure understood to be the guardian of both the family and the nation, and variously conceptualized as a hearth mother, an earth goddess, and a domestic Madonna (see Phillips 2008:50–54; Rubchak 1996, 2005). In the context of the Ukrainian independence movement of the 1980s and early 1990s, and the ongoing negotiation of a Ukrainian national identity, the ancient figure of the Berehynia has been revived as a major symbol of womanhood and motherhood. Kis (2007) notes that the heterogenous Berehynia figure, which combines the core elements of self-sacrificial motherhood, Christianity, and devotion to the nation, "pretends to be an embodiment of a native femininity." She also argues that the Berehynia "has certain matriarchal implications, which encourage a woman to be dominant, competent and decisive but only within her proper domain of competence." The Berehynia as a symbol of Ukrainian womanhood encourages women to engage in the natural and cultural reproduction of the nation, to devote themselves to the maternal role and foster the revival of the traditional Ukrainian family. The Berehynia is the embodiment of the neofamilialism that motivates contemporary nationalist discourse in Ukraine (Zhurzhenko 2004).

Yet in the context of a globalizing market economy and an ever-increasing emphasis placed on consumption as a marker of success and identity, including gender identity, the Berehynia competes with another model for Ukrainian womanhood: Barbie. Kis notes that women are not encouraged to emulate the Barbie doll *per se,* but she argues that Barbie is the embodiment of the kind of lifestyle women in Ukraine are increasingly expected to emulate: "Beautiful, sexy, charming, and correspondingly turned out, a 'Barbie woman' is designed to attain success as a pleasant, attractive toy for a man. For many, Barbie embodies the ideal of heterosexual femininity today" (Kis 2007). The objectification of women's bodies and the emphasis placed on physical appearance as a measure of a woman's worth is obvious in outlets of popular culture, and these trends cause concern for many feminist observers of postsocialist Eastern Europe (Goscilo 1995). Standards of beauty that emphasize outward appearance and perfect bodies are especially problematic for disabled women, whose different physique and limitations in movement place them well outside the range of what is considered beautiful and desirable, or even acceptable. Disabled women thus find themselves engaging in body work for multiple reasons—to maintain personal health by exercising and engaging in sports, and to compensate for a perceived loss of femininity and attractive appearance.

As women in Ukraine have been ushered back into the home and their roles as wives and mothers have been emphasized over that of worker, employment opportunities for women have shrunk and the gender gap in economic security has widened. In 2005 in the total economy a woman's average salary constituted only 59 percent of a man's (UNDP 2009:187). In 2005 just 49.6 percent of females over age 15 in Ukraine were employed, with women's employment at only 79 percent relative to men's employment (i.e., for 100 males employed, only 79 females were employed; UNDP 2007/2008:339). These figures, however, may not reflect men's and women's informal employment, since much work is still carried out in the unofficial or "grey" sector.

For disabled women, gendered expectations regarding employment and economic (in)dependence have mixed effects. On the one hand, as women who are disabled, they are doubly subject to the assumption that work for them is not essential—women who are unemployed generally are not stigmatized, and persons receiving disability pensions are not really expected to work. Thus, a disabled woman's dependence on a state pension, and on significant others (spouses, partners, parents, friends) for economic survival is not as stigmatized as it might be for a disabled man. However, these same gender expectations also mean that disabled women are doubly disadvantaged on the labor market—as disabled persons they face major attitudinal and structural barriers to employment, and they also are subject to gender discrimination. Women in this situation are seeking assistance in securing employment and drawing unemployment benefits; in 2007 just over 42 percent of disabled persons who registered with state employment agencies for retraining and potential job placement were women (MLSP 2008:139). The life stories of two women below illustrate the various strategies disabled women are pursuing for gainful employment and economic success.

### "The Sexual Life of 'Invalids'"

As anywhere, in Ukraine sexuality is also a crucial component of gender identity, but until recently there was little or no open discussion of sex and sexuality. The topic of disability and sexuality has been little explored, even in places like Great Britain with a longer disability rights movement history (see Shakespeare, Gillespie-Sells, and Davies 1996). The topic has received even less attention in the former Soviet Union; as Zoia once said, "People can't seem to utter the word 'invalid' and 'sex' in the same sentence." Cultural myths abound, and in one article sexologist Iurii Prokomenko (2001) succinctly unravels seven "misconceptions about the sexual life of 'invalids' and 'non-invalids.'" (The article itself is problematic in the language used to describe the disabled—Prokomenko refers to "defectives" [Rus. *nepolnotsennye*] and "idiots" [Rus. *debily*].) These misconceptions are the following: 1) the disabled are asexual; 2) the disabled are helpless and therefore needing of protection; 3) the disabled should only marry other disabled individuals; 4) parents of disabled children do not want to educate their children in matters of sexuality; 5) an orgasm is the only path to sexual satisfaction; 6) sexual problems experienced by the disabled are necessarily a result of their disability; 7) a nondisabled person engages in sexual relations with a disabled person only if he has no choice. These stereotypes would be familiar to many disabled persons across the world.

Those few discussions of disability and sexuality that do exist in scholarly and popular discourse in the region are usually dominated by images of men; the sexuality of disabled women is even more silenced. One Russian journal, *Sotsial'naia zashchita* (Social Defense), included a special section for several years titled "Sex for the Elderly and the Disabled." Tellingly, the visual symbol for this section was a photograph of a thin, phallic-looking, prickly cactus in some state of (dis)arousal, a stigmatizing and less than appealing representation of sex. In her sociological analysis of this special journal section, Iarskaia-Smirnova (2002b) concludes that the sexuality of disabled persons receives two primary and contradictory treatments: it is either medicalized and treated as inherently and inevitably problematic, or the sexuality of disabled persons is exoticized (i.e., disabled men are hypersexualized). Heterosexuality is always presumed, and there is no mention of homosexuality or any other alternate sexualities. Although the special section in *Sotsial'naia zashchita* frequently included "sexual biographies" of disabled individuals who told their personal stories, Iarskaia-Smirnova (2002b) notes that these biographies were as a rule written by foreigners (frequently Swedes) and translated into Russian, marking an absence of indigenous literature on the subject of disability and sexuality.

My research has shown that in Ukraine there is a pronounced lack of local discourse—or even a local lexicon—for discussing these important issues. This does not indicate a lack of interest, however. On the contrary, Zoia had some English-language materials on sex translated into Russian and Ukrainian for distribution among the spinal'nik community and found that these booklets quickly became her most popularly requested item. Similarly, one friend noticed that, at a sanatorium for the mobility disabled where he received treatments a few years ago, the chapter on sex (titled "With All My Body and All My Soul") from all of the sanatorium's copies of the book *Zhit' v koliaske* (To Live in a Wheelchair; Indolev 2001) had gone missing—people simply ripped out the treasured chapter and took it home with them for future reference.[4]

Anna Temkina (2002) notes that heterosexuality and sexual potency are the fundamental bases of hegemonic masculinity in contemporary Russia, confirming findings by Zhanna Chernova (2002:537) that in popular discourse a "real man" in Russia is heterosexual, homophobic, and hyperpotent (the opposite of impotent). In a textual analysis of men's journals in Russia from 1990 to 1999, Chernova (2002:542–545) found that men are overwhelmingly positioned as the strong sex and as protectors of women. Women are expected to defer to men in matters of sex; "real men" take the initiative and assume the active position in the sex act. Men are seen as naturally having more sexual potential, due to their supposed capacity for more orgasms, and their perceived overabundance of sperm relative to women's limited number of eggs. Not surprisingly in this light, Russian men's journals position women as objects of men's desire and pleasure, almost solely a means for men to receive sexual satisfaction. As the personal case studies below illustrate, the centrality of the active role, cultural myths about sexual potency, and the emphasis on exclusive heterosexuality in constructions of hegemonic masculinity in postsocialist countries like Ukraine are problematic in the context of disabled men's lives, given their lived realities and the stereotypes that surround disability and sexuality in the region. Women's sexuality is never directly mentioned in media coverage of disability issues; rather, any allusion to disabled women's sexual lives is channeled into considerations of childbearing and motherhood. Even so, disabled women still must struggle to be seen as appropriate and desirable (re)producers of the nation by pursuing strategies to make up for their "lack."

### Men's Personal Narratives of Disability, Masculinity, and Sexuality

I have known Dmitrii since 2002, and I met Anton for the first time during 2005. I have conducted approximately 20 hours of taped interviews with Dmitrii, and I spent many more hours with him in one-on-one conversations and in group talk and activities. During 2005 I conducted a four-hour-long taped life history interview with Anton, interviewed him over the telephone for several more hours, and also enjoyed lengthy, informal face-to-face discussions. Follow-up research was conducted with both men during fall 2006.

The focus of my interviews and conversations with these men was not specifically issues of negotiating masculinity and disability, but these questions did sometimes emerge in the course of our conversations. Dmitrii and Anton knew that I was interested in a broad range of issues relating to disability—including gender, masculinity, and sexuality—but I did not press the subject unless they initiated it themselves or seemed open to such a discussion. The cultural taboos surrounding sex and discussions of it in the former Soviet Union affirm the importance of long-term ethnographic research and the establishment of trust in researcher-informant relationships in order to adequately investigate certain topics. Among my informants Anton was exceptional in the openness with which he discussed questions of sexuality in both abstract and personal terms. By contrast, I had known Dmitrii for several years before we were able to have in-depth discussions about sexuality.

It is important to note that both Anton and Dmitrii were injured in their twenties, after they already had become adults, begun careers, and established gender identities. Also, they received traumatic spinal cord injuries right around the time of the fall of the Soviet Union amid immense political, societal, and economic upheavals. Their stories therefore are illustrative of the intersection of a range of factors on identity formation, including disability, masculinity, and sexuality, but also ethnicity, age, and political, social, and economic change. Although I certainly would not claim these two ethnographic cases as representative of men's experiences of disability in Ukraine as a whole, I do believe that Dmitrii's and Anton's stories touch on many important aspects of how men currently are negotiating disability, masculinity, and sexuality in their lives, and the broader implications for a politics of belonging. In analyzing their narratives I am also drawing on my familiarity with broader dynamics of gender negotiations and disability processes in Ukraine, as well as my knowledge of the narrated experiences of other disabled men and women.

### Dmitrii

In 1989, Dmitrii was in his early twenties when he was injured in an industrial accident. He received a blow to the back resulting in an incomplete compression fracture in the lumbar region (L1–L5). When describing how becoming disabled affected his sense of self, Dmitrii once said, "As a teenager, when I was still healthy, I was afraid of invalids. I didn't know who they were, or what had happened to them. Myself, I felt like Duncan McCloud [the Highlander]—immortal." For a year after his injury Dmitrii underwent intensive but primarily self-styled rehabilitation therapy with the assistance of a network of friends who lived with Dmitrii and his aging mother on a rotating basis.

Before his injury Dmitrii was employed as a tank driver and sniper in the Soviet army, and later as a metalworker and a welder. After his injury he was employed for a time in a private rehabilitation clinic, but otherwise Dmitrii has not held official and steady employment, despite his self-description and self-perception as a blue-collar worker. Other than payments for some temporary and unofficial jobs, his primary source of income has been a disability pension. Dmitrii has become increasingly involved in community organizing in support of disability rights: a few years ago he became the director of an NGO, a position that sometimes substitutes for paid employment and has opened up a range of quasi-business opportunities for him; he also holds a position in one of the more visible coalitions of disability advocacy NGOs.

As is common in Ukraine, where, as one friend put it, "If doctors say you won't walk again they think they are giving you a death sentence," for years Dmitrii thought of his wheelchair use as a temporary setback. In addition to rigorous physical training, he also endured more than 20 surgeries, which finally resulted in the partial amputation of one leg. This is just one example of the medicalization of disability in postsocialist states like Ukraine and many other places; in the case of Dmitrii we see a certain type of medicalized masculinity (Rosenfeld and Faircloth 2006) in which mobility ("walking again") is made central to manhood and "overcoming" traumatic injury and disability.

In this context, most of my informants mentioned Valentin Dikul, the famous Russian strongman who recovered completely from a spinal cord injury and later opened an expensive rehabilitation clinic in Moscow, promising to put the spinally injured "back on their feet." Many of my acquaintances had found inspiration in Dikul's story, but only one was treated in his clinic for a short period of time. Other informants told lengthy stories about different courses of rehabilitation they had undergone in Kyiv and other locales, confirming Iarskaia-Smirnova's (2002a) observation that rehabilitation experiences and mobilizing events are frequently central themes in the life history narratives of disabled men in the former USSR. As Matthew Kohrman (2005:124) has similarly noted for China, in Ukraine the perceived importance of mobility and mobilizing events is quite gendered. Going out in public (being mobile) is seen as an important aspect of masculinity, but women seem more worried by their visible imperfections and are given more leeway to stay at home in their "traditional" setting.

Similarly gendered differences characterize the stigma attached to spinal injury. In the culture of stigma that surrounds bodily difference, the disabled often are blamed for their own bodily state, particularly in the case of the spinally injured, many of whom are injured in accidents. However, I have heard from members of the spinally injured community in Ukraine that men after spinal cord injury are not as stigmatized or self-critical as women. Since men are expected to "live dangerously," and it is a common view that "scars complement a man," and "boys will be boys," men come in for less harsh judgment than women after traumatic injury.

Nevertheless, stigmatizing processes are still operative, with the result that disabled men—particularly those mobility disabled men who may use wheelchairs, crutches, or wheeled platforms—are stereotyped as beggars, degenerates, alcoholics, and drug addicts, when in fact an exceedingly small proportion of disabled persons publicly ask for alms. Interestingly,

many disabled men who do beg on the streets (and most such panhan-
dlers are men) don camouflage outfits, whether or not they are really veterans. Thus, militarized and heroic masculinity is harnessed to engender
sympathy and validation.

Although there is a major push among disability rights groups in
Ukraine for universal design and accessibility, architectural barriers continue to place limits on the physical movement of those who have trouble getting around. In this extremely barrier-ridden context, mobilizing
events and an overall emphasis on individual mobility take on a particular importance. Since public transportation is inaccessible to wheelchair
users, Dmitrii, for example, travels almost everywhere he needs to go in
his push wheelchair, using the busy city streets. On an average day he covers 15 to 20 miles, which can take as long as 2.5 hours. Like most buildings
in Ukraine, the apartment complex where Dmitrii lives is not wheelchair
accessible, so to reach his apartment he must navigate a flight of stairs in
his wheelchair.

Dmitrii's stories about his attempts to use public transportation—an
endeavor that sometimes compelled him to elicit help from bystanders—
often included reflections on masculinity as he juxtaposed himself with
other men. Dmitrii complained that men always seem reticent to help lift
him and his wheelchair into a bus or tram, or up steep stairs, while women
and "little homeless kids" are always ready to assist. During one interview
he offered:

> Once a group of nuns carried me into a church. There weren't any men
> around, only meatheads (Rus. *mudaki*), excuse me for the expression.
> . . . Sometimes I come up to the tram or the bus and ask a bloke (Rus.
> *muzhik*), "Can you help?" Suddenly he develops 48 illnesses on the
> spot—"Oh, my finger hurts, my back is out. . . ." Most often it's women
> who help. As they lift me into the tram I look around and say loudly,
> "Well, looks like there are no men left. They must have all fallen in the
> Kulikov battle [between Russians and Tatars in 1380]; we're left with
> only meatheads."

Here Dmitrii contrasts his own robust physical condition (he has likely
traveled miles in his wheelchair to reach the bus) with that of the (non)-
men who refuse to assist him, and he criticizes these men for their lack of
strength, goodwill, and chivalry as women struggle to lift him into the bus.

In this regard Dmitrii's vision of masculinity and being a "real man"
maps onto the image of the voniuch, moguch, i volosat, someone who

is "stinking, strong, and hairy." In Dmitrii's reflections on "real men," he overtly underscores the importance of physicality and physical strength to manliness. Indeed, in Russia, Iarskaia-Smirnova (2002a:124) notes that physicality seems to be more important in identity formation for disabled men than for other men. My research confirms her findings; I also found that in Ukraine, maintaining optimum mobility and a developed physique is an important part of the sense of self and sense of manhood for many mobility disabled men.

In the former USSR sports were an avenue to promote "cultured masculinity," and sports play an especially important role in the identities of disabled men in Ukraine today. Julie Gilmour and Barbara Evans Clements (2002:210) note that in the postwar Soviet Union, sportsmen became purveyors of "the essentials of masculinity," which included "such 'healthy' behavior as hard work, physical exercise, service to profession and nation, and devotion to family," all of which were preferred characteristics of the New Soviet Man. These qualities were the antithesis of "uncultured masculinity," which involved smoking, drinking, sexual adventures, and "aggressive physical self-assertion both in relation to other men and to women" (Gilmour and Clements 2002:210). In this context, it is not surprising that some of the first state-sanctioned disability awareness events in the former USSR revolved around athletics and extreme displays of physical fitness, such as the super-marathons undertaken by wheelchair users beginning in 1991 and 1992. And as discussed in chapter 3, sports is a major focus of the disability rights movement in Ukraine today, and the paralympic movement has made dramatic progress in recent years.

Sports play a crucial role in Dmitrii's life, even though he was not very interested in sports before his injury. During the last 15 years Dmitrii has participated in a vast array of wheelchair sports, from track and field to billiards and basketball. During my initial visit to Dmitrii's apartment in 2002 for our first official interview, he immediately began to talk about sports, and he showed me all the medals he had won in various competitions.

The conventional view is that sports serve as an avenue for disabled men to recover lost masculinity by tackling physical challenges and developing the physique. But writing of Russia, Iarskaia-Smirnova (2002a:121) reflects on the more complex role that athletics may occupy in the lives of many disabled persons, especially men:

> Public activity, and the feeling of belonging to a team or a collective, allows an individual to reevaluate personal identity: to be less disabled

and more courageous. However, courage in disability in this context does not exactly align with the dominant canon of masculinity. Here, rather, we find articulate not the domination of invulnerable strength, but *difference* [as one disabled athlete said]: "*I am an inconvenient* [Rus. *neudobnyi] person . . .*" [emphasis in original]. Here, the personal becomes political.

Indeed, in Ukrainian disability sports there is often an element of awareness-raising and political protest, as represented by the annual Treat Me As Equal demonstration in Kyiv, where wheelchair users educate the general public about wheelchair sports and issues of accessibility. On the other hand, as personal interviews with men such as Dmitrii have shown, it is true that sports may hold intensely personal meanings for individuals, as well as having the capacity to help men gain self-confidence after traumatic injury, come to terms with their new identities, and explore new visions of masculinity for their own lives as disabled men.

For Dmitrii, wheelchair sport dance has been a way to deal with the feelings of inadequacy "as a man" that plagued him after he was injured and began using a wheelchair. Early in our acquaintance, Dmitrii did not seem comfortable talking about his sexual experiences directly. Instead, he offered clues to the challenges that disability posed to his identity as a sexual being by telling me funny stories. For example, at the end of the first life history interview I conducted with Dmitrii in 2002, he told me of an encounter he had with a young woman, Lara, whose reaction to him he described as "typical" in its denial of manhood to disabled men in Ukraine. During a weekend at a friend's dacha in the countryside, Dmitrii spent the night with Lara, who appeared sullen and very quiet the next morning. That afternoon the group of about ten young people was sitting around the table, eating and talking, when Dmitrii finally asked her, "Lara, what's wrong with you? Why are you so quiet?" Dmitrii told me what happened next: "She said, 'You know, Dmitrii, I didn't know you were a man.' It grew silent as the grave around the table, and I remember one poor guy just standing there with his shish kebab, and his mouth hanging open . . . ."

During another interview Dmitrii reflected with humor on the pervasive societal—and even medical—ignorance that surrounds disability and sexuality. To illustrate, he told of a recent encounter he had with a woman pharmacist in Kyiv, when he wanted to buy a condom catheter, a condom-like device that is placed over the penis and attached to a drainage tube, allowing one's urine to pass into a urinary storage bag. The pharmacist had no idea what Dmitrii was talking about, and when he described the item as "a condom, for invalids, with a little 'pip' on the end," she asked what the little "pip" was for. Dmitrii could not resist joking with her: "It gives us a better chance of impregnating a woman." "Really?" the pharmacist asked wide-eyed, "How?" Dmitrii continued his ruse: "It directs all the sperm into one powerful jet." After relating this story he reflected back on the incident: "She's a pharmacist; it's her job to know these things. If that's her level of knowledge, what can we expect from the general public?" This story is all the more powerful when one considers that in Ukraine pharmacists perform some of what would be considered physicians' roles in the United States—they offer extensive medical advice and dispense a range of products and pharmaceuticals without prescriptions (sharps, antibiotics, and many others).

Although Dmitrii often made joking sexual references in casual talk, it was not until I had known him for three years that he began to tell me openly about what he called his "sexual fears" after his injury. Once at a café after I told Dmitrii about my struggles to overcome shyness around new acquaintances, he also began to discuss his personal "complexes": "I'm a normal guy, I love women, I like to have fun, but I find it almost impossible to take the next step with a woman. To be honest, I began dancing in order to overcome this terror (Rus. *strakh*) in front of women."

Dmitrii said that dancing has given him "some kind of emotion, some kind of passion that goes beyond the mechanics of the dance itself." He described dancing as a means to interact with a range of people, including the nondisabled, and especially women, and as a way to be physical and "put myself on stage" in a way that is affirming and, at times, erotic. He hopes that, having gained confidence in himself as a performer, and by cultivating new bodily experiences brought to him through the physicality and emotion of dance, he will feel more comfortable initiating intimacy with women. Thus although Dmitrii does at times draw on and seek to embody hegemonic notions of masculinity, with emphasis on strength, chivalry, and other qualities seen as manly, through dance he also seeks to broaden the masculine repertoire to include emotion, passion, and a kind of alternate life rhythm that he sees himself as uniquely situated to enjoy as a disabled man who uses a wheelchair.

As has been described for other places (Bruun 1995), disabled individuals, and disabled men in particular, are sometimes thrust into the role of moral hero, inspiring models of moral fortitude. Indeed, the disabled are lauded in the popular media when they are perceived to exhibit traits such as determination, courage, and strength, those qualities seen as appropriate to an "ideal man" who has fallen into harsh conditions (Iar-skaia-Smirnova 2002a:123). A discourse of overcoming has become prevalent in discussions of disability—one weekly half-hour show dedicated to issues of disability and social rehabilitation that ran on Ukrainian television in the late 1990s was called *Podolannia,* or Overcoming. A similar program was titled *Vykhid* (Exit), which in the Ukrainian context of inaccessibility, stigmatization, and public silence on disability issues implies similar processes of "overcoming," or "going for it."

Dmitrii is sometimes posited as just such a hero. He cuts a striking figure when dancing, and exudes confidence, playfulness, and feeling; this has led other people and organizations to appropriate his image for their own purposes. Dmitrii's story has been recounted in many venues, including newspapers and inspirational documentary videos. However, at times he becomes a depersonalized hero, since his photograph is frequently found in the pages of newspapers and journals without any explanation or story about Dmitrii. In such appropriations Dmitrii is sometimes assigned a sort of hypersexual identity. One acquaintance insisted that "only Dmitrii would do" as the star in a how-to video on sex for the disabled she was planning, a project Dmitrii rejected and jokingly dismissed as "porn for invalids." He mused, "I already have a sort of wild reputation—what would people say about me if I bared my butt in that video?"

One of Dmitrii's major regrets is that he is unlikely to become a father; as he said, "The doctors say it isn't going to happen." Dmitrii was married for a short time to a woman (also a wheelchair user) who left him for a "healthy" man with whom she subsequently had a child. The failed marriage was not so much a blow to Dmitrii as the fact that he could not have children with his wife. Adoption is not an option, since laws in Ukraine prohibit disabled persons from adopting children. Similar barriers to adoption exist in Russia, and Lev Indolev (2001:130) posits the state's reasoning thus: "The state . . . assumes that [the disabled] cannot raise a child or—even worse, supposes that they will begin to exploit the child." Zoia often pointed out the contradiction that, although many people with spinal injuries were injured as adults and already had children, "no one sees disabled adults as parents." She contrasted this negative reaction with the situation described to her for Sweden, where, she was told, semen is collected from men immediately after spinal injury, in case their reproductive capacity is compromised and they still want to parent children.

Disabled men such as Dmitrii thus are often unable to fulfill one of the popularly perceived prerequisites for appropriate manhood—fathering children. This social expectation is vividly displayed in the 1982 film by B. Durov "I Can't Say Goodbye!" The hero, Sergei, who became disabled on the job, partially regains his lost masculinity by returning to work and also by impregnating his wife. At the end of the film he comes even closer to completely recouping his manhood, as he begins to stand up from his wheelchair (Romanov and Iarskaia-Smirnova n.d.). Here, working and reproducing are not enough; a real man must be "healed." Lacking the opportunity to become a biological or adoptive parent, Dmitrii acts as a sort of surrogate father for the youth in the NGO he directs. In the past he was also a popular first contact person, an individual designated to visit persons in the hospital with new spinal cord injuries to talk positively about life after traumatic injury.

Dmitrii is currently not married but is in a long-term relationship with a woman with a history of bisexuality. A few other men with spinal injuries that I interviewed also noted that their sexual partners and girlfriends tend to be women who are open to bisexual relationships, "threesomes," "creative positions," and innovative ways of receiving and giving sexual pleasure, all of which go against the grain of the hegemonic heterosexuality that characterizes Ukrainian society. Anton's story below will further illustrate how constructions of hegemonic masculinity—which emphasize men's sexual (hyper)potency and their responsibility to take the active role in sex, and assume exclusive heterosexuality—become subverted in the context of the lives of disabled men.

Although Dmitrii does draw on elements of hegemonic masculinity in his understanding of what it means to be a "real man," he also has sought avenues to cultivate a new kind of masculine identity for himself, for example through dance and mentoring. For him this is not a seamless process, and he is not entirely comfortable discussing issues of masculinity and sexuality, at least not with this foreign female researcher. He often deflects serious conversation by making jokes, and he frequently refers to the "absurdity and paradoxes of life" as a way to veer the conversation toward topics more comfortable for him.

Dmitrii's story also is reflective of the multiple and contradictory ways in which disabled men are positioned in popular discourse (asexual, heroes, hypersexual) and the range of possible responses enacted by individuals in particular contexts. In Dmitrii's case, such responses have included simultaneously pursuing strategies to recapture "lost" masculinity by adhering to a certain body culture (intense physical conditioning, sports, striving to "walk again") but also exploring alternate physicalities and visions of masculinity through nontraditional (for Ukraine) sports such as wheelchair sport dance. Overall, Dmitrii's personal ethos could be characterized as one of creativity and nonconformity. He does not submit readily to the authority of others, and his actions can be rather unpredictable. Indeed, I was often advised by others who knew Dmitrii to "expect the unexpected" from him. He sees himself as going against the grain, and frequently articulates his commitment to "live by no one's rules but my own."

These negotiations are important for understanding how Dmitrii sees himself belonging, as a citizen, in contemporary Ukrainian society. On the one hand he is highly individualistic, placing great value on the ability and the right to make his own decisions. At the same time, Dmitrii is chronically strapped economically and depends on his many friends for support, especially when he has health crises, approximately once or twice a year. Indeed, he has a wide circle of friends, including people from all walks of life; his intimate circle of friends includes an out-of-work hippie-musician (Shaman), a gangster, and a computer geek, among others. These friends are important to Dmitrii's "devil may care" persona; he refers to his friendship with unconventional persons as evidence of his own nonconformity.

Yet Dmitrii's individualistic attitude is counterbalanced by his commitment to assisting others, particularly those who are disabled, in his position as the director of an NGO for disabled youth. Dmitrii's NGO does not organize large-scale events, and the group is not visible on the national or even the Kyiv level. Rather, Dmitrii bases most of his advocacy initiatives on helping the young people in his organization form relationships with one another and, crucially, with nondisabled youth. He does this by involving volunteers—many of them at-risk youth—in the NGO's activities, and providing opportunities for "his kids," as he calls them, to broaden their circle of acquaintances.

Busking is a good example. By organizing a drumming circle for himself and other wheelchair users in the middle of Kyiv's busiest pedestrian thoroughfare and staging a performance to ask for donations, Dmitrii was winking at the public. He and his fellow spinal'niki were saying, "We know what you think of us; you think we are pitiful, that we are beggars. We'll play along, but only to show you how wrong you are." They staged the performance, however, not to push the public further away, but to invite people into the drumming circle, so they could meet and get to know "real, live invalids." This scenario encapsulates, I think, the playful terms in which Dmitrii asserts himself as a citizen, terms that are informed by his experiences of disability and a perceived compromised masculinity: "I do belong, but not in the way you think I do."

## Anton

Anton's story is indicative of ways that gender, ethnicity, and political identity intersect with and inform an individual's experience of becoming disabled. Anton's case is also rich for thinking about the diverse claims to citizenship that disabled men may assert. This is because on the one hand, Anton takes an affirmation approach (Swain and French 2000) to disability—he believes being injured and becoming mobility disabled has improved his life. Paradoxically, however, he eschews any kind of specifically disability-related identity, political or otherwise, and interprets disability communities in quite a negative light. Therefore, although Anton values his personal experience of disability as a positive and dynamic aspect of his "self" or "I," by rejecting a collective disability identity he ends up mobilizing a rather individualized politics of _non-belonging_.

Like Dmitrii, Anton was injured in 1989. Anton was twenty-nine years old when he was shot through the stomach and back in a rather valiant scenario—on the dark streets of Kyiv he was trying to protect his best friend from men he thought were armed criminals. (They turned out to be intoxicated police officers.) Anton's official diagnosis is a "gunshot wound to the nerve endings," and he walks (and runs) with forearm crutches. Anton says that when people find out he was shot "they assume I'm a veteran from the [Soviet–]Afghan war, a policeman, or a bandit." As a young man Anton served in the Soviet military before attending university and becoming an engineer. Now Anton does not hold a paying job, but he receives a disability pension and rents out a second apartment that he inherited from his parents; income from the latter allows him to live comfortably as a single person.

Anton's family had German roots, and as Germans his grandparents suffered in the waves of repression during the period of Stalin's rule, especially during World War II. Anton's ethnicity (he identifies as Russian-German) and family history play an important role in his self-identity. He never supported the Soviet regime and he continues to associate disability politics and a disability identity with the (to him) suspicious realm of the official. He avoids structures of power as much as possible and also distances himself from the disability community. Anton once told me how he greets one friend over the telephone who works with international development organizations on issues of disability rights: "_Kak tam_ 'disabled people?'" (Rus. "How are those 'disabled people?'"). Anton's use of the English phrase "disabled people" (he does not otherwise speak English) indicates a certain self-detachment from this "group," and also evidences

*[margin note: sounds abt right.]*

his recognition that "disabled people" is a reified category that may or may not exist in reality but is frequently targeted by various interventions and appropriated for various purposes.

Anton was one of the few people I interviewed in Ukraine who espoused a fairly clear-cut affirmation narrative of disability. More than once he referred to his injury as "the best thing that ever happened to me," and he said that he would not go back and change the course of events if given the chance. During interviews and casual conversations Anton often contrasted the lifestyle he led before his injury with the one he now cultivates, and concluded that he is much "healthier" now than he would have been had he not been injured. In fact, he believes that in many ways the experience of becoming disabled "saved" him. Before his injury, according to Anton, he drank and smoked, was a womanizer, and "was obsessed with one thing—sex." His injury and subsequent disability, he said, forced him to rearrange his priorities, and Anton believes he is "a better man" as a result.

Today, Anton practices a rigorous personal program of mental and physical training, and he has developed a focused life philosophy based on the writings of the famous Soviet athlete Iurii Vlasov (1990). Gilmour and Clements (2002:212–215) note that Vlasov was one of the key figures through which the Soviet regime promoted development of a "cultured masculinity" for Soviet citizens through sports during the 1950s and 1960s. In his 1990 article titled "The Confluence of Difficult Circumstances," which was originally written in the 1970s, Vlasov details his own rise to fame in Soviet sports and his subsequent decade-long illness and fall from grace (see also Brokhin 1977:193–223), and he presents a program for developing and maintaining health and youthfulness through mind-body training. Anton rereads this twenty-page article often, and refers to it as "my Bible." Some of the mind-body practices promoted by Vlasov, all of which make up what Vlasov calls the "healing power of overcoming," include positive thinking and belief in oneself, controlling one's thoughts and emotions, dream work, constant physical activity, and ever-increasing and more challenging physical training.

Anton's Vlasov-based personalized routine includes an early-to-bed, early-to-rise sleep regime; a daily exercise program consisting of meditation, stretching, weight training, and running up to seven kilometers a day; as well as abstinence from alcohol and smoking. (It is difficult to abstain from alcohol in Ukraine's heavy drinking culture, and I noted that Anton does in fact drink on occasion.) This regime is sometimes interrupted by chronic pain in Anton's legs, a problem that keeps him awake at night and sometimes consumes his thoughts. He tries to rely on mind-body practices to control the pain, but he also began using painkillers two years ago. Despite his struggles with chronic pain, in interviews and conversations Anton gives the impression of being fully in control, and he exudes the self-discipline that he says is necessary for staying in top physical shape.

Anton realizes that living alone and having few material needs are luxuries that permit him to rigorously pursue his life philosophy and physical training. Other men I spoke with noted that one must be a "judicious egoist" (Rus. *razumnyi egoist*) to undertake such total programs of mental and physical training, but responsibilities to family and work often prevent other disabled persons from leading the type of lifestyle Anton pursues. Anton noted that, because he exercises so much and takes great care with his health, other men after spinal injury call him a "scared invalid"; they think he is in denial. Anton counters that he has to keep up this strict regime to "maintain his physical function" and retain the level of mobility he has achieved, and especially to avoid "sitting" in a wheelchair.

Anton does not so much stigmatize *koliasochniki* (Rus. wheelchair users) as much as he argues that, in a barrier-ridden environment such as that found in Ukraine, he is much more mobile using crutches than he ever could be using a wheelchair. On the other hand, Anton is critical of those who do not "work on themselves" as rigorously as he does, and he named for me several men who he thinks could have worked harder not to "sit down" in a wheelchair after spinal cord injury. His life history narratives sometimes approximated what Smith and Sparkes (2004:621) call the "quest narrative," through which spinally injured men "meet suffering head on; they accept impairment and disability and seek to *use* it." However, unlike Smith and Sparkes's informants in the U.K., Anton did not use "journey" metaphors in his quest narrative; neither did he talk in terms of "progress" or moving toward a particular destination or goal (such as "recovery"). Perhaps it is because I first interviewed Anton a full 16 years after his traumatic injury that he seems very content with his life and "where he is," aside from his struggles with chronic pain. He jokingly noted that becoming an "invalid" at the age of 29 allowed him "to retire early, as I always dreamed to," and pursue his "real passion in life," yachting.

A self-diagnosed *yakhtoman* (an invented Russian word, a play on the word *narkoman,* or drug addict), Anton spends all of his free time in spring, summer, and early fall on his yacht at the Kyiv Reservoir. Significantly, yachting is one way in which Anton is separated (and separates himself) from the disability community in Kyiv—yachting is seen as a luxurious sport for anyone, and especially for the disabled, who are stereotyped, sometimes justifiably, as financially needy. Even though Anton has tried to promote yachting among the disabled, he says others have shown little interest in the sport.

Anton admits that, unlike Dmitrii, he consciously separates himself from other disabled persons; he says he has more in common with the nondisabled. This detachment from a disability identity appears to be part of Anton's philosophy of independence; he sees many other disabled persons as dependent on the state and on the rations they get from advocacy NGOs. He also dislikes the culture of the disability community, which he characterizes (wrongly, in my experience) as "drinking and complaining." Although he does receive a disability pension, Anton usually forfeits other benefits such as free medical care and health trips to sanatoriums. Although Anton could receive medical care at no cost in his local clinic, he usually prefers to seek out trusted specialists, for whose services he is willing and able to pay.

In explaining these preferences Anton stresses that he is an independent, self-providing person in need of help from no one. He thus pursues the ideals of individualism, initiative, and independence that are increasingly valued as criteria for being a "real man" in contemporary Ukraine, especially in the current transition to a market economy and neoliberal governance. As Iarskaia-Smirnova (2002a:125) found for some of her male interviewees in Russia, Anton constructs his masculinity around "resisting the power of circumstances and institutions, and delivering [himself] from dependence." When another disabled man he had invited to join him for a yachting outing did not show up, Anton phoned him and found the man was still asleep at midday. When he hung up he turned to me and blurted, "Invalids, man!" (Rus. *Invalidy, blin!*). He was frustrated with the man's lack of accountability and self-control—Anton surmised that he was "sleeping it off" after a night of drinking. These were traits Anton associated with the Ukrainian disability community in general, traits he rejected for himself.

Clearly, a philosophy of independence and overcoming are central to Anton's strategies for enacting masculinity after disability; in his copy of Vlasov's article he wrote, "The healing power of overcoming!" across the top of one page in large letters. The discourse of overcoming, one that Anton finds personally meaningful, sits uneasily with some worldwide disability rights perspectives. These rights perspectives emphasize the traps that tropes such as "overcoming" set—disability and disabled persons are automatically positioned in negative, vulnerable terms, and disability is framed as a barrier rather than a meaningful component of identity, a potentially positive attribute, and so on.

But before brushing it aside as an outdated and naïve construction, it is important to consider the social and political contexts in which overcoming has become a salient narrative in Ukraine. Overcoming, which emphasizes individual initiative and personal striving, seems a natural product of the transition to a market-based economy and the dismantling of the socialist state and welfare system. In this context, a historic emphasis on social solidarity and citizens' reliance on the state are rapidly being replaced by the ideals of individualism, personalization, privatization, and independence. Overcoming is appealing to people like Anton because it references the individual and his or her potential for action in a society where the disabled have been denied agency, independence, and even personhood.

Adherence to a particular body culture is another key component of how Anton cultivates his own masculinity. Anton is proud of the developed physique of his upper body, and in newspaper photos and television programs about him he is usually shown working out on his exercise equipment at home, often bared to the waist. At the same time, Anton does not seem at all embarrassed or troubled by his atrophied legs. For his computer desktop Anton chose a photo of himself taken by a reporter that shows him sitting on his yacht in shorts and no shirt. Although Anton's face and tanned and "ripped" chest and arms take precedence in the photo, he is sitting with one leg prominently in the foreground, and with his crutch propped up beside him. One gets the impression that Anton is refusing to let his "better half" be objectified by hiding other parts of his body. The photo, I think, shows how Anton seems eminently at ease with his bodily difference and disability. So although Anton does adhere to some of the body standards of hegemonic masculinity in Ukraine—strength and an athletic build—he talks of his physical training more in the personal terms of maintaining health and mobility than living up to society's standards of "being a real man."

But there was a time immediately post-trauma when Anton was not so comfortable with his new body, especially when negotiating intimacy with women. He referred to sex as "the biggest sore spot for any spinal'nik," and said, "It is devastating for a man to lose his potential, and with any spinal'nik that is the first thing to go" (Rus. *vyletat'*). During several casual conversations, and over the telephone, Anton described to me at length how he reestablished himself as a sexual being over the course of several years.

The initial part of this history was tied up with his former wife, Zina. Anton was twice divorced at the time of his injury, and he had broken up with his long-time girlfriend Zina a few months before the accident. He woke up in the hospital to find Zina by his side, and Anton often described how she loved "the role of nurse, savior, and mother" as he became the willing object of her "womanly duty" after his injury. Although Anton and Zina married soon after he was injured, they divorced a couple of years later, probably, Anton suspects, because he no longer "needed" her as he had immediately post-trauma. However, he also said that their pre-injury relationship was based on "little besides sex and orgasms, an inadequate basis for any marriage."

Over the course of several conversations Anton related to me his own explorations of sexuality after spinal injury. In the early period after his trauma, said Anton, he was not able to satisfy Zina sexually. After he realized that, even though he cannot feel his penis, he could in fact have an erection, he began (with Zina, "who already knew me inside out," as he put it) to develop ways to arouse himself with a partner. These involved taking certain positions, using mirrors, and giving sex a more emotional basis than he had previously: "Now I have to see someone's eyes to become aroused." Today, even though Anton focuses much of his energy elsewhere, sexuality continues to play a central role in his everyday life and in his enactment of masculinity. He has frequent sexual liaisons, and he iterated that, "More experienced and knowledgeable women actually are attracted when they know a man has a problem in this area. Let's not forget that sex is about more than having an erection or not."

Sometimes Anton gives himself injections (papaverina and fentolamin) to achieve an erection with women who "do not suspect I have any problems," but more often he has sought to explore a more meaningful and creative sexuality than he previously enjoyed, and to cultivate what he calls "the emotional and more adventurous aspects of sex." For Anton this has meant a subversion of the hegemonic ideal of men as sexual brutes who must take the active position; on the contrary, he notes that many of the women who are attracted to him are "exhibitionists" (his term) looking for a more unusual, empowering, and creative sexual experience. Like Dmitrii, Anton indicated that he has had frequent sexual interactions with women with some history of bisexuality, and who thus overstep the dominant sexual norms in Ukraine. So although for Anton sexuality is an important part of his identity as a man, he has cultivated a type of sexuality based not so much on the standards of virility and potency, but more on sensitivity to his partners and a certain letting go or breaching of conventional sexual norms.

There are other ways that Anton goes against the grain of hegemonic masculinity, and these transgressions have caused certain dilemmas for him. In many ways, as a single man and especially as a disabled man, Anton occupies an ambiguous gender position—in some contexts he rather unwillingly becomes a social female. Several years ago he nursed his dying mother—a caring role that would normally be assigned to a woman—and he lives alone, keeps house for himself, and cooks his own meals. Anton once told me, "Women don't take me seriously. They see me as a supplement (Rus. *dopolnénie*) to the men they already have in their lives. . . . They tell me all kinds of private details that they wouldn't even tell their best girlfriends. . . . I don't really mind, I actually find it interesting, but sometimes of course it makes me angry." When positioned as a social female, Anton is assigned more empathy and a greater level of complete trust and intimacy than are most men (Kaufman 1994:150).

But Anton's status as a man—one very interested in sexual relationships—complicates the role he is assigned by women as a social female. He described how in relationships with women he "plays different roles," as a (sexual) male and a (social) female. Anton noted that many of his serious relationships have been with married women who are seeking from him what they feel deprived of by their husbands—sometimes it is interesting sex, and sometimes it is a sympathetic listening ear. On the one hand, Anton says he is more or less satisfied with the roles women expect him to play, but he also wishes women could see him as a "real man" instead of "just a supplement."

Anton also admits that the "pity factor" has prevented him from occupying equal footing with his intimate partners. In Ukraine, pity and infantilization are common aspects of popular perceptions of disability. Disabled men in particular are stereotyped as helpless and psychologically vulnerable, and are presumed to have a powerful need to be taken care of by self-sacrificing women. In reflecting back on his marriage to Zina and the way she cared for and protected him after his injury, Anton noted that, "pity (Rus. *zhalost'*) figured prominently in our relationship." Further, he added, "In fact, since my injury all my relationships have been based on pity. . . . Every woman who shows interest in me expects me to be grateful, stick out my tongue, and pant." Anton said the women in his life think they are doing him a favor, "presumably because I am helpless and I don't deserve them." He said he will never get used to this treatment, and he is very reluctant to accept this role as grateful dependent or the object of charity.

In this situation, Anton, like several other men with spinal cord injuries I interviewed, has not been able to have the sort of family life he would like. Like Dmitrii, Anton would like to become a father, and says his medical tests "show it is possible," but he doubts it will happen since he has not been successful in maintaining long-term relationships with women. According to Anton, he has grown accustomed to having intense yet temporary relationships with women, and he has learned not to plan a future with his girlfriends.

Overall, Anton's negotiations of manhood and masculinity after spinal injury have hinged on the important issue of independence. In insisting on his independence—especially physical and financial independence—from others and from the state, Anton both asserts his masculinity in line with hegemonic constructions, and makes a political statement by rejecting the structures of power that govern disability in post-Soviet Ukraine. However, the strong assumption by others—especially those women with whom he has intimate ties—that he is to be pitied, and should be "grateful for their attention," partially subverts his identity as an independent "real man." Anton is left to pursue his interests such as yachting and exercise on his own, and watch women come and go in his life through what he refers to as "my revolving door."

Anton's case is also interesting for the contradictory way in which the body figures into the politics of belonging (i.e., citizenship) vis-à-vis disability and masculinity. On the one hand, Anton's strict adherence to a self-styled and self-enforced bodily regime of exercise, diet, and sleep—seems to lend support to Foucauldian perspectives on ways in which regimes of power come to control bodies through varied means, including through the individual's self-surveillance. Anton's bodily regime benefits the state, since he only rarely seeks state-provided medical care or support. At the same time, his reluctance to take advantage of or submit to this care also makes him more immune from surveillance, thus depriving the state of a measure of power over his life. Also, Anton's stated reasons for performing his bodily regime are to retain maximal functionality and mobility and thus to preserve his independence, both from other people and from institutions of the state.

It could be argued that, in striving to stay fit and mobile, declining to associate with other disabled people, and rejecting a disability identity, Anton in a sense mobilizes a politics of *non-belonging*. In other words, he strives (perhaps unsuccessfully, given attitudinal and institutional constraints) to base his claims to citizenship wholly or partially outside discussions of disability by stressing those things he is not: dependent, impoverished, disillusioned, alcoholic, immobile. This does not necessarily mean that Anton is a "scared invalid," as others have called him. To

the contrary, he is trying to shift the terms of the debate from what disabled people need, demand, or deserve, to what they can contribute. But
because Anton rejects a disability identity *per se* and has distanced himself
from disability communities, it is unlikely that his personal philosophy of
belonging will translate into a more politically oriented assertion for collective action. Also, his politics of non-belonging ends up assigning negative characteristics to disabled people and their communities, the very
thing that disability rights activists are working against.

## Women's Personal Narratives of Disability, Femininity, Motherhood, and Work

I first met Viktoria and Nadia in 2003 in Kyiv, where both women were
invited participants in a consciousness-raising event for wheelchair users
called Treat Me As Equal. At that time Viktoria was 33 years old and Nadia
16. I videotaped the event and afterward was invited to visit the rehabilitation center where many of the out-of-town participants—including
Nadia, who lives in a small town in Western Ukraine—were staying over-
night. I spoke further with Nadia there, and tape-recorded a short personal interview with her. I met Viktoria again several weeks later, when
she agreed to a life history interview that we conducted at an outdoor café
near her apartment in Kyiv. Between my 2003 and 2005 research trips to
Ukraine, I kept in touch with Nadia via electronic mail and surface post,
but I was not in contact with Viktoria. In 2005 I interviewed both women
once more—Nadia was again visiting Kyiv for the Treat Me As Equal campaign, and I interviewed Viktoria in her home.

Each time I met them, both Viktoria and Nadia were beautifully made
up and fashionably dressed; they obviously took great care with their
appearance and presented themselves as modern, stylish women. When I
interviewed Nadia in 2005 at the Kyiv train station, she had just returned
from a shopping trip in the city center, an excursion she said was the highlight of her visit to the city. The women's focus on the trappings of outer
appearances contrasted strongly with my male informants' self-presenta-
tions. Another difference was that Viktoria and Nadia did not talk as much
as the men did about the shame of having to ask for help from passersby
to overcome architectural barriers. To be sure, the women did complain
about the lack of an accessible environment, but depending on others did
not seem to bother them as much, a reaction in line with conventional gender expectations that assign women a measure of dependency in certain
situations. And in general, women in Ukraine are less mobile than men in

the sense of automobility, or "autonomous, self-directed movement" facilitated by automobiles (Featherstone 2004:1) because of cultural stereotypes positioning women as unfit and incapable drivers. Together, these cultural expectations—that women are "naturally" less mobile, and it is not shameful for a woman to ask for physical assistance—may explain the women's less negative reaction to asking for assistance from strangers.

I felt a special connection with each of these women, but for different reasons. I had heard a lot about Viktoria before I ever met her—she was a member of Zoia's organization for the spinally injured, and Viktoria's name and story frequently came up in my conversations with spinal'niki. She was held up as a positive example of disabled motherhood in Ukraine, where popular opinion questions the ability and very right of disabled persons to parent children. When we met in 2003 I was a new mother, having given birth to my first child in 2001, and Viktoria and I enjoyed sharing stories of childbirth and motherhood. Viktoria gave me valuable parenting advice, and I marveled at her two well-behaved daughters. It occurred to me that a disabled woman who decides to become a mother when cultural stereotypes position them as unfit and incapable of motherhood must work doubly hard to be what in the United States is known as the "supermom." I expect this is as true in many other countries as it is in Ukraine (Wates and Jade 1999).

Nadia on the other hand was the youngest informant in my study— she is full of energy and enters any conversation or setting like a breath of fresh air. She has an endearing sense of humor and asked me challenging questions about American culture, constantly reminding me that ethnography is not about extracting information from informants but is a process of mutual inquiry and dialogue. Nadia was interested in my research and always wanted to know details about my publications—what I had published and what reaction the material received from readers. She was eager to converse in English, and I was only too happy to oblige—this ability to relax linguistically probably also contributed to the special connection I felt with Nadia.

All the same, I did not come to know these two women as well as I did Dmitrii and Anton, and we did not develop the kind of rapport necessary to broach certain topics. The subject of sex did not come up in our conversations, for example, and the women did not go into personal details of body care and hygiene, in contrast to the two men. The interview settings also undoubtedly played a role: none of the interviews with Viktoria and Nadia were truly private—I interviewed Viktoria at the café and at her apartment; her two daughters were present both times, and her partner took part in the second interview. I interviewed Nadia at a rehabilitation center and at the Kyiv train station. Speaking with Nadia primarily in English did lend a measure of privacy, of course, but some people around us did understand English.

As a disabled mother and athlete Viktoria is well known in various circles in Ukraine, and her story has appeared in several newspaper articles. In 1998 she was also the featured guest on a television talk show called *"Zhinka na vse 100,"* or "100 Percent Woman." I noted that Viktoria related many of the same story lines in these various interviews, and she repeated them in her taped life history interview with me. This shows that Viktoria has fashioned a personal narrative around her experience of injury and disability, a narrative that is highly gendered. I recognized this for other individuals in my study, both men and women.

In recounting Viktoria's story I follow much the same pattern as with Dmitrii and Anton, presenting details of her life and her narratives and analyzing these in terms of gendered expectations and intersections of gender and disability. Viktoria's experiences are illustrative of several key moments in the gendered experience of disability after socialism, including constructions of family, parenting, and motherhood; body knowledge and personal agency; gender, disability, and sports; and women's economic empowerment. Nadia's story reflects these same themes, but my approach for Nadia is different. I introduce Nadia primarily through our written correspondence, and through translated interview excerpts. Following on the heels of Viktoria's story much of this material speaks for itself, and the approach allows the reader to become acquainted with Nadia more on her own terms.

### Viktoria

Viktoria received her spinal cord injury in 1986 when she was 16 years old. The very circumstance of her injury underscores the problem of gender violence in Ukraine: Viktoria was attacked in her own apartment by an acquaintance who intended to rape her. To escape the attack she broke the apartment window and jumped from the second story. The fall was not that high but Viktoria landed on her head, resulting in an injury to her spinal cord. She considers herself lucky since she has full use of her arms, and as she said, "By all accounts my injury should have left me a *sheinitsa,"* or tetraplegic (Rus.).

Viktoria describes the injury as "losing my body, losing my appearance (Rus. *vneshnost'*) . . . my atrophied legs looked so awful." For a long time she was embarrassed to go outside, and she hid inside the apartment where she lived with her mother. Viktoria said she was afraid to look "healthy" people in the eyes, she was ashamed of her wheelchair, and she especially did not want her former boyfriends to see her, "to see what I'd become." Viktoria frames her initial experience of becoming disabled as one of total loss. She recounts the trauma of "being healthy and suddenly losing everything, being ripped away from everything, all at once." Viktoria says she had a wide circle of friends before she was injured—she was studying sewing at a technical college and was involved in dance and music ensembles—but they all completely abandoned her after her accident. Former schoolmates would see Viktoria on the street and pretend not to recognize her. She said, "Today all my friends are people I met after my accident; none of them knew me before." Becoming disabled meant that Viktoria was unmade as a citizen—she became invisible and lost her social ties. She was made immobile not only by her compromised physical state and the disabling built environment, but by social attitudes and the withdrawal of relationships that stripped her of agency.

Both men and women I interviewed after spinal injury experienced this initial period of intense shame over their bodily "loss," and for some the shame was long-lasting. But I agree with my informants who asserted that women are seen as—and feel themselves to be—especially "out of place" when they become disabled. Although embedded in contemporary cultural norms about beauty and the body, such attitudes also have an important historical-cultural component. It is still true that many people have never had personal contact with a visibly disabled person; much of what they know about the disabled comes from popular culture. And public representations of the disabled have for so long been dominated by disabled men that disabled women simply do not occupy that discursive space. For instance, disabled characters in Soviet films were always men. Women were assigned roles as nurses—caregivers of these men, whose gender identity was temporarily questioned. The disabled man's loss of masculinity was illustrated by his position relative to the caregiving woman's; he usually lay prostrate while she either bent over him or stood up nearby (Romanov and Iarskaia-Smirnova n.d.) These pervasive gendered representations make disabled women feel doubly stigmatized.

Viktoria says that after her injury she convinced herself that "nothing would come of my life, I would never be with a man, never get married." Her views changed, however, when she first visited a sanatorium in Saki. There Viktoria saw people in wheelchairs kissing one another, a sight she says "kept me awake all night." Indeed, the sanatoriums for the spinally injured where many mobility disabled persons are provided "health trips" once every few years (and sometimes more often) are important sites where social relations of friendship and courtship are cultivated. Socializing with others who had experienced similar injuries was empowering for Viktoria on a number of levels. She learned that "people can really live like this, in a wheelchair," and she gained more self-assurance and confidence in her own future. In Saki Viktoria met Boris, a man several years her senior who was also spinally injured. The two fell madly in love and were married soon after, despite the objections of Viktoria's mother, who said her fiancé was too old. Viktoria and Boris lived in two different cities, which also complicated matters. Viktoria says that meeting Boris helped her take the focus off her own misfortunes and stop worrying so much about her changed bodily appearance—"all my attention was on him; I didn't even think about myself."

When Viktoria became pregnant in 1994, the idea of a disabled woman in a wheelchair deciding to become a parent was objectionable to many of her compatriots. In Ukraine as in many areas of the world, "cultural stereotypes imagine disabled women as asexual, unfit to reproduce, overly dependent, unattractive . . . generally removed from the sphere of true womanhood and feminine beauty" (Garland-Thomson 2004:89). Not surprisingly in this context, my informants who had become parents after spinal injury reported negative reactions from representatives of the structures of power such as social services and the housing authority. Valentyna, for example, was injured as a young girl when she fell out of a tree. She gave birth at age 34, and her husband also has a spinal injury. Families in which both parents are disabled—as is true in Valentyna's case and Viktoria's—often are thought especially unlikely and unfit parents. Once when she phoned her social worker's supervisor to complain about the quality of service, Valentyna's complaints were dismissed by an official who told her: "You should have thought about that when you were having kids." When Valentyna and her husband applied for a larger apartment to accommodate both them and their growing son, they were likewise scolded for their decision to have a child. As previously mentioned, disabled persons in Ukraine and Russia officially are not allowed to adopt, a discriminatory restriction that positions the disabled as inherently incompetent and perhaps as perpetual children themselves.

As a woman who decided to have children after becoming disabled, and who has told her story to the Ukrainian public on television talk shows and in the pages of widely read newspapers, Viktoria is in many ways a trailblazer. During the 1990s and early 2000s, the media latched on to the then-sensational story of spinally injured, wheelchair-using women giving birth; newspaper features and other media accounts profiling Valentyna, Viktoria, and other of my informants appeared. Paralympic champion Svetlana Trifonova's transition to motherhood was a major item in this genre. In a sense, then, disabled motherhood in Ukraine is a subversive act. Today however, disabled motherhood is no longer so much cause for media attention, because it has become more commonplace and somewhat more accepted. It could be argued that what many disabled women who become mothers seek is precisely the opportunity to be a "normal" woman, to articulate a "regular" identity as a mother (Finger 1990:140; Mintz 2007:140). In this, rather than challenging gender stereotypes, they seek to more closely conform to gender expectations about women as mothers.

Indeed, gendered expectations concerning disability and parenthood are still very much operative, and parenting is seen as more natural and feasible for disabled women than for disabled men. In 2005 a single father lost custody of his daughter after he received a spinal injury, a situation that ignited protests by a Ukrainian NGO organized to defend the rights of single fathers, including disabled fathers. At one protest in Kyiv, to prove their parenting capabilities, disabled fathers staged competitions in braiding girls' hair, singing lullabies, and playing darts (Vitvits'ka and Azarenko 2005). Of course, these tasks do not seem particularly central to good parenting, and the group might have made a stronger statement by emphasizing that successful child rearing involves instilling values and life lessons and setting a positive example, and is not primarily rooted in the mundane physical tasks that disabled persons may or may not be able to perform.

When Viktoria became pregnant in the mid-1990s, social stigma still ran quite high. In many world contexts disabled women who embark on motherhood are faced with a double stigma, since "both women and the disabled have been imagined as medically abnormal—as the quintessential sick ones" (Garland-Thomson 2004:81). If pregnancy is often framed by the medical establishment as a "condition," as an illness to be medically managed, this is doubly true for the disabled pregnant woman, who is already labeled as "sick" before becoming pregnant (Finger 1990). This was the case for my informants in Ukraine, and spinally injured women who became pregnant turned to one another for advice and support, "like a chain," as Valentyna described it. When Viktoria recounts her decision to have children, and the preparations she made to do so, she frames her actions as painstakingly planned and well thought out. Her narrative is carefully constructed to show that she did not undertake motherhood on a whim or by mistake; rather she followed a responsible, informed approach. Viktoria emphasizes that she became pregnant against her mother's wishes and against the advice of some medical personnel. Here Viktoria underscores above all her own agency, an agency that seems rooted primarily in her body. She does not deny the complications her spinal injury and compromised physical state posed for her pregnancy and birthing, but here Viktoria's body is not broken and disabled. Rather, her body is productive. Furthermore, the only entity that possesses full knowledge of her body is Viktoria herself.

Viktoria says she astutely prepared herself for childbirth by reading a stack of books on midwifery and doing all kinds of prenatal exercises. There is an assumption in Ukraine that women with spinal injuries must deliver via cesarean section, a practice that is not necessarily supported by obstetrical protocol in other world contexts. According to Viktoria, she was the first spinally injured woman in Ukraine to give birth vaginally. She attributes this feat to her "stubborn nature," but also gives credit to a very supportive obstetrician at the hospital where she gave birth, in her native city in Central Ukraine. He told her, "You are strong, you are healthy, let's give it a try, we can always cut [perform a C-section] if we need to." Viktoria emphasizes that she did not embark on a vaginal birth from a position of selfishness: "I told them they could cut me up and down and sideways, as long as they didn't touch the baby." Viktoria says she received excellent support from the physicians, midwives, and nurses who delivered her prenatal care in her hometown; women in Kyiv, she said, get less personal attention and encouragement as disabled mothers-to-be.

In some sense Viktoria's birth stories are reminiscent of those of American women in the natural childbirth movement who have sought to flee the medical gaze and the high-tech, medicalized birthing procedures of modern American medicine. Like these women, Viktoria privileged her own knowledge of her body, refusing to cede authoritative knowledge of childbirth and the childbirth experience to medical experts (Davis-Floyd and Sargent 1997). When describing her first pregnancy in 1995, Viktoria highlights how she exercised agency and took control of her own pregnancy, even as a first-time mother. Her obstetrician became very concerned when Viktoria's blood pressure became erratic and protein developed in her urine. He wanted to put her in the hospital on bed rest. Viktoria resisted, however, and convinced the medical personnel that such problems were "normal" for people with spinal injuries. She says she listened to her body, and used her existing knowledge of her own biology to understand the physical changes she was experiencing, to resist the diagnoses and recommendations of her physicians.

Viktoria's physician had her check into the birthing ward a week before her due date, a near universal practice in Ukraine and Russia. As an extra precaution Viktoria's mother was asked to stay with her in the hospital. Viktoria's contractions began during the night, but to avoid awaking her mother ("She panics") she endured them until morning in silence, at which point she alerted the nurse that she was ready to deliver. Since no stretcher could be found to wheel her into the birthing room, Viktoria used her own wheelchair. She stresses wheeling herself to the delivery room, and her ability to silently endure contractions while other women screamed in pain, to emphasize her self-control and agency. The second time Viktoria gave birth—about three years later—she resisted medical interventions even further. She declined to check in to the birthing ward early, and labored at home as long as she could. Thirty minutes after Viktoria called an ambulance she delivered the baby at the birthing hospital. Few nondisabled women in Ukraine would pursue this strategy (nor would the medical establishment allow it), which only underscores Viktoria's sense of confidence in her body and her dedication to mediating her own labor and delivery. When describing her decision Viktoria set herself apart from the other laboring women, whose screams and loud yelling she said she wanted to avoid. She thus narrated herself as being more in control than "normal" birthing women.

In her deep knowledge of her body Viktoria thus mirrors Dmitrii and Anton, both of whom emphasized their physical body as a major component of their self-image and self-knowledge. Like Anton, Viktoria follows a rigorous physical exercise regime. She developed for herself a strict schedule of exercises for different body areas on different days, taking only Sunday off as "family day." Viktoria notes that she combines this exercise regime with many other daily physical tasks such as cleaning, cooking, laundering, and playing with her children. Thus her commitment to keeping fit through exercise exists on top of her "regular" physical tasks, namely those domestic chores assigned primarily to women.

Failure to continue carrying out one's gendered household tasks can weigh heavily on women who become disabled; as one journalist wrote of another spinally injured woman, "What bothered Iryna the most was that she could no longer keep the apartment spotlessly clean" (Volkova 2006). As a woman subject to certain gender role expectations, Viktoria, like most disabled women (and some disabled men), does not have the privilege of being what my friend Pasha called a "judicious egoist," someone like Anton with ample time and opportunities to pursue physical fitness and rehabilitation. Viktoria and other disabled women are also subject to gender ideals that assign a caring role to women. Although Viktoria did not comment directly on this tension, it is reasonable to assert that disabled women find themselves expected to care for others even as they may require care themselves, particularly in places like Ukraine where social services are inadequate, technical aids are few, and physical rehabilitation is spotty. In many areas in-home assistance is only provided through state social services to disabled persons who are single. This places additional burdens on disabled and nondisabled women alike, since the assumption is that women in the household will deliver care where it is needed. Viktoria has already begun to train her daughters in "female" domestic chores—in 2003 when the eldest was just nine years old, she described how they already helped her with the laundry, washing everything by hand and hanging it out to dry. The girls frequently fought over who would get to use the small lightweight iron Viktoria had bought for them to share.

Despite the time Viktoria devotes to her family and to domestic chores, for her as for Dmitrii, Anton, and many others, athletics is a major avenue for self-fulfillment, personal achievement, and physical fitness. Before having children Viktoria participated in the long-distance wheelchair-racing scene. She stopped racing after she got pregnant, however, and Viktoria reported that her male teammates criticized her decision to have children and said she was throwing away her sports career. She took up competitive fencing for a time beginning in 2003 but says she never really enjoyed fencing as a sport: "I was only successful in fencing because I have a lot of endurance, and I'm strong. I never did master the technical aspects." Furthermore, fencing began to affect her health negatively, so Viktoria abandoned it to pursue dance, her real passion. Unlike Dmitrii, who did not become interested in dance until after his injury, Viktoria was an accomplished dancer before her accident. Since the early 2000s she has pursued wheelchair sport dance seriously, and she is a member of a dance club in Kyiv. Viktoria won the Ukrainian championship in Latin dance and also took first place at the 2005 European championship.

Viktoria was not the only woman wheelchair user I met who had practiced a sport normally associated with combat and self-defense, and more masculine endeavors. In 2005 martial arts emerged on the disability sports scene in Ukraine, in particular aikido and jujutsu. Both are considered grappling arts; they involve somewhat "soft" movements requiring little physical energy, and practitioners are taught to use their attacker's energy against him or her instead of opposing it directly. In Ukraine, among spinally injured athletes mainly women pursue these martial arts. The first formal courses in aikido and jujutsu for wheelchair users were developed at a rehabilitation center called *Shans* (Chance) in Bila Tserkva, a small city near Kyiv. The trainer, Viktor Kraievskii, emphasizes the health benefits of these practices, which he says aid in the development of the shoulder muscles, contribute to overall well-being and muscle development, and help alleviate depression (Nikonova 2006). In an article published about the center's initiative in a major Ukrainian newspaper, Kraievskii and his trainees, both women, also noted that it is important for disabled persons to have effective means for protecting themselves from attack. The examples all focused on robberies; one of the women described how she has repeatedly been robbed when visiting a sanatorium in the Crimea:

> As soon as you leave the gates of the sanatorium, problems start. . . .
> A simple stroll around the park or on the beach can end up costing a
> wheelchair-user a lot. Thieves surround us and literally strip us. They
> take our money, jewelry, clothing, shoes. . . . [B]ut the material insult
> is not the worst: imagine how helpless one feels when you are dumped
> from the wheelchair and they riffle through your pockets! The local
> police don't even try to find the thieves, so we have only ourselves to
> depend on. We have to be ready for confrontations with hooligans and
> be able to rebuff them (Rus. *umet' dat' im otpor*). (Nikonova 2006)

I found it curious that although the article noted that disabled women were at risk for being robbed, rape was not mentioned. I met one of the women athletes from Bila Tserkva, Tetiana, during fall 2006 and had the chance to talk further with her about her motivations and experiences for taking up jujutsu and aikido. Again she stressed the problem of being robbed on the street, noting that thieves see visibly disabled persons—and those who use wheelchairs in particular—as "easy targets." However, Tetiana also talked more generally about disabled women needing to defend themselves against "aggression" and "attacks," and I believe she meant sexual aggression and rape. She said that, for her, practicing martial arts had given her more self-confidence and self-esteem, knowing she was prepared to defend herself if necessary. Plus, she enjoyed aikido and jujutsu as physical activities she said seemed to "fit" women. The problem of violence against women is one that is often discussed in informal conversations among people in the "parallel world" of the disabled, but there is little acknowledgement of it in the popular media or in official discourse.

The pressure to conform to certain standards of physical beauty (what Kis [2007] calls the Barbie model) is amplified for disabled women like Viktoria, who by definition do not live up to locally valued standards of physical perfection. Social stereotypes are already skewed against the disabled, whose physical difference often is highly stigmatized. Thus disabled women feel compelled to maintain and enhance their physical image in the ways that are possible—through strict body maintenance involving exercise and sports, for example, and also by utilizing cosmetics and other beauty enhancers. Volkova's (2006) description of a spinally injured woman named Iryna could be applied to many of my female informants as well: "She never allows herself to go out in public without a manicure and a nice hairdo." Viktoria clearly takes great care with her appearance— she is always nicely dressed with smart hair styling and modest, attractive makeup. She mentioned several times during our conversations that she does not want her daughters to be embarrassed because their mother is disabled. She spends a lot of time with her daughters out-of-doors, and it is important to her that they do not feel uncomfortable or left out as the children of a visibly disabled mother. She is likewise conscientious about looking nice when she visits their school.

When I interviewed Viktoria in 2003, she seemed quite content with her life. We sat outside at a street café near the apartment where she lived with her husband and their two daughters. The girls skated nearby on their new roller blades as we talked. Viktoria spoke of being well integrated into the neighborhood; the girls and she finally had been able to relocate there to join Boris in the apartment he owned. The only complaint she had about her living environment was that the apartment was located on the seventh floor of a building whose elevators frequently broke down, sometimes leaving her stranded at home for days at a time. Viktoria said she enjoyed visiting the produce market nearby, where she had become acquainted with some of the sellers, women who "know the main points of my story" and with whom she enjoyed conversing on a daily basis. Her daughters had many friends around the neighborhood; there was a nice park nearby where she frequently went with the girls and she had come to know other mothers that way. The girls' school was very good—much of the instruction was in English and Viktoria had a good relationship with the teachers and other parents.

Viktoria did talk about the challenge of raising a family on two disability pensions. Her pension was especially small, since she had been injured at age 16 and had never worked. Of this situation Viktoria said, "I want to work. I never planned on depending on the state. When I got married I knew I could support my children, and my family." She said she knows she is at a disadvantage on the labor market, "when even healthy people can't find a job." Although she did say that Boris's pension was considerably higher since he was a "labor invalid" (Rus. *invalid truda*), having been injured on the job, she did not say much else about Boris, whom I had never met.

Viktoria's living situation was quite different when I saw her again in 2005. Actually I had arranged to interview a spinally injured man named Sergei, and when I arrived at his apartment I was rather surprised to find Viktoria and her daughters living there too. I ended up conversing with Sergei and Viktoria together, but they did not comment directly on how they had come to be partners. Later several of my friends from the disability community filled me in on the general details: Boris reportedly had become less and less committed to Viktoria and the girls, finding himself too old to be a father. Viktoria and Sergei got to know one another at various events, eventually he invited her and the girls to move in to his apartment, and Viktoria agreed. This must have been a serious decision for Viktoria, especially since the transition was not an easy one for her daughters. As Viktoria and Sergei described, now the girls were in a new school where much of the instruction was not in English, as they were used to, but in German, a language they had never studied. They felt disoriented in this region of the city, where it took them a while to make new friends. Both girls had been very involved in dance classes, but since there were no lessons offered in their new neighborhood they had had to abandon their favorite pastime, at least for the time being.

The new living arrangement offered several environmental advantages for Viktoria—Sergei's apartment was on the first floor, and the building had a wheelchair accessible ramp at the entrance. Also, several new wheelchair accessible trolleybuses had appeared in Kyiv, and one of them serviced the region of the city where Viktoria and Sergei now lived. I never had the opportunity to ask Viktoria more about her decision to move in with Sergei. Had she fallen in love? Did she need a change of pace? Were her motivations also practical (i.e., economic)? I never found out.

Viktoria told me about one positive development: her newfound success as a senior manager for Oriflame, a direct marketing cosmetics company founded in Sweden in the 1960s that now operates in 61 countries with over three million distributors.[5] (Oriflame is similar to the American company Avon.) Oriflame products appeared in Ukrainian stores beginning in 1992, and the Swedish cosmetics have been sold in Ukraine via direct marketing since 1997.[6] The company's growth corresponds with a huge increase in consumption of cosmetics and perfumery by women in Eastern Europe since the fall of state socialism (Ghodsee 2007). During our 2003 interview Viktoria had mentioned her activities with Oriflame—she was invited to join the company by her neighbor, who acted as Viktoria's "sponsor." That year Viktoria had been recognized for her sales success at a large meeting of Oriflame distributors. She described the event in the following way: "Over a thousand people stood up and applauded me. . . . Some of them approached me and asked me questions like, 'How do you work, where do you search for clients, how do you present the products?' I told them how an invalid differs from a healthy person. I said, 'So you have a much better chance to succeed, to reach the heights you aim for . . . .'"

During our conversation in 2005 and in an interview with Viktoria that was published in an Oriflame journal, she stressed that being disabled presents her with challenges that other distributors do not face. For example, she manages most of her orders by telephone, since she cannot easily get around to visit her regular clients and recruit new ones. When she started with Oriflame Viktoria learned most of what she needed to know through printed materials and audiotapes of seminars and lectures, all provided by her sponsor. Viktoria frames her success with the company as an inspiration to other Oriflame representatives, and this validation seems very meaningful to her.

Working as a direct marketer and rising through the ranks as a senior manager presumably has brought important economic benefits to Viktoria. I do not know how much she earns, but she did say that she approached the work as "a chance for my family's economic survival" (Rus. *vozmozhnost' vyzhit' moei sem'e*). So to some extent she has been able to achieve a measure of economic empowerment in a context where many women remain economically disadvantaged and face much gender and wage discrimination on the labor market. Also, Viktoria frequently mentioned the social benefits of working as an Oriflame distributor; in fact, she named "socializing" (Rus. *obshchenie*) as the aspect of the work she most values: "It [socializing] allows me to continuously develop. You mustn't stop, you have to keep going forward." Viktoria valued her Oriflame-based social networks and friendships and relished the opportunity to become a leader and organize her own master classes for other up-and-coming distributors. Significantly, the business meetings, trainings, and master classes offered opportunities for dissolving or at least softening the boundaries of the "parallel worlds," albeit temporarily and on a very small scale.

As a cosmetics distributor and now manager for a direct marketing company, Viktoria has been able to take advantage of some of the economic shifts in postsocialist Ukraine. Oriflame and similar companies

(Avon, Amway, and Mary Kay, all of which have traveled to the post-Soviet world) embody many of the hallmark characteristics of the neoliberal economy: personal drive, the personalization of consumption through client-seller relationships, and a can-do philosophy of personal and group motivation. The Oriflame company's core values are:

> Togetherness: People who work together and share the same goals achieve greater results. They motivate each other and know that pulling together is more rewarding than going it alone.
> Spirit: People with a can-do spirit have a winning attitude and never give up. They are committed to do what it takes to succeed.
> Passion: Passionate people have the power to change the world. They love what they do, they believe in it. They know deep down that they can make a difference.[7]

In her personal narratives Viktoria also espouses these values, and this articulation is reinforced by changing media representations of Viktoria over the years. In the late 1990s and early 2000s Viktoria and her family were featured in at least three newspaper articles, and on the talk show "100 Percent Woman." All these outlets praised Viktoria for her courage and achievements, especially her accomplishments as a mother. However, the family's impoverished state was always emphasized, and one newspaper article focused entirely on the debts Viktoria and Boris had incurred for electricity and telephone service, both of which the utility companies threatened to shut off. Viktoria was positioned as dependent on the beneficence of state functionaries and social agencies; she was a "doer" but also very much a "user" of services, benefits, and charity.

In contrast, by 2005 Viktoria's achievements as a doer were emphasized, at least by Oriflame Ukraine in its monthly journal, and by Viktoria herself. It is important to note that the company's philosophy of "togetherness" and "pulling together" is similar to the notion of interdependence promoted by some disability rights activists and scholars as an alternative to the common liberal trope of independence as an empowering life goal for the disabled. Feminists such as Barbara Hillyer (1993) have critiqued this liberal tendency within the disability rights rhetoric, arguing that privileging independence obscures the fact that "disability itself demands that human interdependence and the universal need for assistance be figured into our dialogues about rights and subjectivity" (Garland-Thomson 2004:88). That Oriflame's focus on cooperation and mutual support resonates so strongly among women in Eastern Europe is itself fascinating: it

echoes the familiar socialist rhetoric on the importance of the work collective, but it is packaged together with the direct marketing model, perhaps the quintessential example of the capitalist entrepreneurial spirit.

The direct marketing business offered Viktoria a viable avenue for
making a living, no small matter given the difficulties the disabled face
in Ukraine's labor market. But how long will her "history of success" (as
it was called in the Oriflame journal feature) last, especially in light of
the worldwide economic crisis that began in 2008? In the absence of a
real restructuring of labor laws and true improvements in job training
and placement services for the disabled, how many women will be able
to follow in Viktoria's footsteps to forge viable individual solutions to the
collective, widespread problem of poverty and unemployment among the
disabled, especially disabled women? Viktoria's story suggests that leveraging the rhetoric of interdependence might be a way to start a productive
dialogue about women, gender, and disability in postsocialist Ukraine.
Interdependence is a notion with which the populace is already familiar,
and if carefully presented it may be a powerful way to launch a gender
critique—of inequalities between disabled men and women in terms of
economic empowerment and opportunities for education and work, of
gender expectations that doubly penalize disabled women, and of gender
inequalities within the disability rights movement itself.

### Nadia

Nadia received a spinal injury at the age of nine when she was hit by a car
while walking along a rural road. She began attending regional and nationwide disability awareness events when she was thirteen and thus came of age
as a *spinal'nitsa* (the word for spinally injured woman) in well-established
activist circles. Like most of the younger people I met, however, Nadia did
not pursue any organized political activism in support of disability rights.
She did have some excellent mentors in activist communities, fellow wheelchair users who Nadia said saw themselves as her protectors. When I interviewed her for the second time in 2005 Nadia, who is quite beautiful, said
that she had begun getting lots of attention at recent meetings—people
made comments on how she was "growing up," and they drew attention to
the fact that she had started wearing makeup. Nadia said she did not really
mind: "It's nice to know that people see me, that I'm not a gray mouse."

Nadia, who studied English in high school and at university, wrote all
her letters to me in English. During our face-to-face conversations we
also spoke mostly in English. When reproducing the letters and interview

transcripts I have edited them lightly but they still convey the unique texture of Nadia's English writing and speech. Nadia gave me written permission to use her letters. Unfortunately I did not make copies of the letters I sent Nadia by surface post, so they are not included here.

JULY 16, 2003
Letter received via electronic mail

Dear Sarah,

Now I have an opportunity to write you a letter, because I am in Caritas.[8] Maybe I told you that sometimes I visit it and write letters to my friends. I think, you remember me, we were at the [Treat Me As Equal] meeting in Kyiv. First of all I'd like to congratulate you with your birthday. Happy birthday to you! I wish you joy, happiness, health, love. Let all your dreams become true. Good luck to you in everything!

After the meeting I went to Dnipropetrovs'k. There were basketball competitions between seven regions of Ukraine. There were seven teams and we took sixth place because we were not well prepared. But I am very glad that I was present at these competitions and I have a lot of impressions. It was my first time in this city and I liked it very much.

You told me that you were going to move to another place to live. Write me your new address.

Have you written your article about Ukrainian meetings already? You said that you would send me photos from the meeting. Send them, please, if you can. I think that we'll meet in the future, maybe in Kyiv or somewhere else. Write me about how you are and everything about your work. I'll be waiting for your letter.

Best wishes from Nadia.
P. S. As you see I write you in English, because I am not sure you can read Ukrainian well and it is good practice for me.

DECEMBER 20, 2003
Letter received via international surface post

Dear Sarah,

I got your letter a long time ago, thank you very much for it and especially for the pictures. They are very nice. I beg your pardon for not writing for so long but I haven't been to Caritas since I sent you e-mail last summer.

It'll be Christmas holidays and New Year soon. And I decided to send you this post-card with congratulations . . . After all the winter holidays, on the 20th of January I'll have my birthday. I'll be seventeen. I'm waiting for this day very much. I think we'll have a lot of guests (our relatives and my friends of course).

This year is my last year in the school. Next year I have to enter some educational establishment. I want to enter L'viv Polytechnic University, it's my dream . . . It's very important for me to have a higher education . . .

Will you come to Kyiv in May again? When you'll be in Ukraine, we'd be very glad to see you in our place. If you want you also can telephone us . . . I'll be waiting for your letter. Merry Christmas and Happy New Year!
XXX
Love
Nadia

---

FEBRUARY 10, 2004
Letter received via international surface post

Dear Sarah,

I was very glad to receive your letter and picture. Sarah, you have a very handsome son, and husband, too . . . I send you my picture too.

Our family had a nice New Year and Christmas . . . Now all the holidays are in the past, the new studying semester began and I have to study again . . . Almost all the time I spend at home and I have enough time to think about my plans for the future. I'm going to enter the Sociology Department of the L'viv Polytechnic University (I have to take several entrance exams). I also want to continue my English study there, because English is one of the main subjects.

I have a friend (with disability), who is a fourth-year student at the University. He studies directly [on site], it's easier for him, because he lives in L'viv near this University. I'd like to study *zaochno* [distance learning] during three years; it costs $450 a year. We need to pay for the study, because there is no free of charge zaochno department, [instruction is free] only [if you study] direct. . . . In this university it [zaochno] means that I have to take four examination periods (*sesiia*) a year. I need to go to the University to take all exams. But I have a big problem. I live too far from L'viv and Polytechnic University. From my place to L'viv takes two and a half hours by train (we have no car and we must go by train). I need to live in L'viv, and buy (or take in credit) or rent an apartment near University. As for *hurtozhitok* (dormitory), I'll not be able to live there, because there are a lot of stairs there and, as a rule, it has four or five floors without an elevator. I think you understand what I mean, that's why I need to live in the apartment. The University won't provide me with hurtozhitok or flat. I have to pay for it myself, but it's too expensive for me . . .

There is a foundation (stock reserve) in L'viv, which can pay for studying of people with disabilities. We phoned them and they said to phone them next week, because there isn't money in the fund now and they could not say anything. Maybe this fund will pay for my studying . . . but they don't say exactly. . . . I think I'll be able to pay for books and other supplies (I have a pension, 85 UAH, it's $15 a month). Here are all my thoughts.

I also want to continue to play basketball, but at home I can't do it, there isn't any place for this game, no balls, etc. I can play tennis [ping-pong] (on the table, of course) a little. Maybe, when we'll meet in future, we'll be able to play [table] tennis together. These games need training, I'll be training when I'll live in L'viv.

Sarah, I'm waiting for your letter . . . Write me soon. Tell "Hello" to your family.

Best regards.
Nadia

---

OCTOBER 12, 2004
Letter received via international surface post

Dear Sarah,
I'm sorry for not writing so long. A month ago I came back from the sanatorium in Donets'k region (it's near Russia). In this sanatorium I had a very nice rest with my sister Masha. I don't remember maybe I have written about it in my previous letter, that there are only two specialized sanatoriums for people with disabilities in Ukraine. One of them is in Donets'k region and the other one is in Saki, Crimea. Though this sanatorium is far from my place (it takes us 26 hours to get there by train) I like this place very much. I've met there a lot of my old friends and got acquainted with new ones.

At the beginning of July I entered my favorite L'viv University. Yes, I'm a student now! I'm very glad. I passed three exams. Ukrainian, mathematics and English. These exams weren't easy, but I did it.

I'm still living at home. But I want to live in L'viv and I really need it, because I'll have to take my examination period soon. It will be too expensive for me to go from [my town] to L'viv almost every day. I think that if we can't buy or rent the flat in L'viv, I will be glad to live in a dormitory. It's very interesting to live there. Every weekend Masha comes back home from L'viv with lots of impressions of "dormitory life." She has so many friends there. The only problem is the stairs.

Our L'viv organization wrote a letter to this University asking them to do a renovation in one of the dormitories and make it accessible for people with disabilities (maybe only the first floor). This repair must be done before the beginning of December. I'm waiting for it because I don't want to stay at home all the time, it's boring. . . .

At the end of May I was in Kyiv. I wish you were there too. I would be very glad to see you . . . Tell our big hello to your family.

Best wishes.
Nadia


EDITED EXCERPT FROM INTERVIEW WITH NADIA, JUNE 12, 2005
Location: Kyiv train station, as Nadia was preparing to return home after a disability awareness event in Kyiv. (Interview took place in English.)

Sarah: Tell me about your studies. Because we were writing letters back and forth and you were telling me that you wanted to start your studies in L'viv, the faculty of social work, and you were hoping to live in L'viv in an apartment or a dormitory. So what happened?

Nadia: Nothing happened with the dormitory and this is the problem, because I think there is no money for the repair, for the building, that is one problem. Because of course I need a ramp, you understand. . . . And another thing [I need] is a nice toilet which is comfortable for me, and other things. Our dormitories, they are a room, and to the toilet it's a long way to go; there may only be one toilet for the whole floor. And it's difficult—I can live there, but I will not be able to live there alone—I cannot go outside, I can't go to the toilet. And it's difficult. As for an apartment, I have no money, because I'm not working. I can work, I want to work, but I have no experience working because I'm a first year student. I don't even know people who could hire me, because students without a baccalaureate [can't get jobs]. . . . But I still want to, I still want to do something in my life.

S: Maybe in the next few years, you'll be able to live in L'viv and study directly?

N: I want to study directly, it is a good idea, but it's not a good idea with the stairs. . . . There are about seven buildings where we study, and all the time at breaks we have to go from one to the other, and when it's summer, it's okay. But when it's winter, it's difficult for walking people to go, but for me . . . Yes, I know I have friends and there will be people who can help me. But [they are] not with me all the time. Because as a student I have my problems to go make a xerox, [or] to get a book from the library, and . . . I will have to go alone. . . . I know what this is because I dealt with it studying in school and there were stairs, there was a library and all these problems. . . . And I know it and I don't want to study directly. It's difficult for the psyche.

. . . I don't have a friend from my group because I am "externat" [external student], but I have friends from home, they are studying . . . at Polytechnic, but not in my specialty, not sociology. My sister Masha studies English and my friend Oksana will be an economist. But they will not be able to be with me because they have their [own] problems, their [own] lessons. That's all.

S: Why did you decide to specialize in sociology, and social work?

N: Because it's work for people, it's work on the computer, it's work with people from other countries, I hope. Yes, I like to help people, to listen to what they want, to help to solve their problems. When I read the books, it's about how to behave with old people, what they think, what they want, how to help them, what problems they can have. I think I'll be able to do that, but in [my little town], I don't think I will open myself. . . . I mean . . . I want to be in a large, bigger town, maybe a city . . . [where] there will be more possibilities to find work that I'll like. I'd like it, I think, because . . . it's a bigger area for work.

. . . Maybe I want a lot, but I want [it]. Maybe I want a lot to live in the city, but I want [it]. It's good that I want something. Mama said, "Nadia, maybe you want a lot. Maybe many children of your age haven't been to Kyiv, and you were here many times." Maybe it's not a lot, but for our village it is.

S: How many people are in your village?

N: My village, I don't know. It has maybe ten streets, little ones, one park, one church, one club, with a lot of mud outside (laughs). . . . I don't like it because of the bridge. I like it because it's a river, but it's with stones and a lot of stairs. Very bad stairs, they are not comfortable at all, even for walking people. It's difficult. It's long and when I go through these stones it makes me angry. Because someone is walking fast, and I [have to say], "Wait a minute, wait for me." I don't like it at all.

S: So how do you practice your sports?

N: My sport? What do you mean? Which sport . . . ?

S: Like yesterday you won the competition at the event so you must have some training, right?

N: No [laughs]. . . . I had practice maybe when I was going to school everyday. Yes, there are little stairs, curbs, and stones, and I have to use the balance [to pick up the front wheels of my wheelchair]. It's practice for these kinds of sports—to go fast. Because I always want to sleep more and then its half past—let's go! Every morning. And we have to go fast not to be punished by the teacher. It was my "sport" every morning. It was my training . . . .

S: You went all the time to regular public school, right? You didn't have the teacher come to your house?

N: I had the teacher come to me when there was snow outside; I phoned them and asked, "Would you be so kind as to come to my place?" I don't like it because it's only me and only my teacher in the room, and I can't write from the book, I can't look at the book when I'm talking. When there are a lot of people you can do something to get a nicer mark (laughs). . . . But I like it, my school, but not the stairs. I hated the subjects physics and chemistry because they were on the second floor. "Boys, come here, boys where are you?" every time. Sometimes girls [helped] when [I couldn't find] the boys.

S: That's hard.

N: It's hard, but only the stairs. I hate them. That's the problem of my life: stairs, I hate them everywhere, everywhere. Okay, the stones on the bridge, okay. But not stairs. The dormitory stairs, the university stairs, here you go outside, and stairs. "Hello, stairs," every time.

---

OCTOBER 12, 2005

Letter received via international surface post

Hello, my dear Sarah!

Thank you for your letter and the photo. Sorry for my silence.

The day before yesterday my sister Masha and I came back from Evpatoria. There was a camp of active rehabilitation for disabled people from Dnipropetrovs'k region. You think what did I do there, a girl from far [away little town]? I was there as an instructor of aerobica (like gymnastics, with the music). During these camps (it's ten days) "new" disabled (most of them are just after hospital) are taught how to use the wheelchair, to dress, take a bath and other important things by themselves. At these camps there are also such trainings as table tennis, long bow, workout and other moving games.

My sister Masha was there in a service group (walking young people, who help on the trainings and during the camp). We lived in that paralympic sport center, Mirnyi [building], I think. You saw it, didn't you? You must have such camps of active rehabilitation in your country, too. Do you know it? I have been to these camps several times. My first camp was in 1999, thanks to Hrybalskyy.

This year I took two exam periods. There are two more to take this year. My dormitory situation is a "hurting topic" for me. I don't know if a thing like that is realistic in Ukraine. It's difficult to try to go out to a city and begin a real independent life, [it is taking] so long . . .

I have no e-mail, I wish I had it. I guess it's easier to communicate by e-mail?

This term I'll have such courses as public relations, interpersonal communication, community-based work, social work with families, domestic violence, and others. . . . I'll be waiting for your letter, Sarah. Bye-bye. How were your trips to Ottawa and Washington? Tell my hello to your guys!

Nadia

---

JANUARY 25, 2007
Letter received via electronic mail

Hello Sarah and your family,
It is Nadia from Ukraine writing to you. Today we got connected to the Internet, and we have a new e-mail address :-)

I have a great news for you, on the eleventh of November I got married. Here are photos from our wedding-party. My husband's name is [Andriy], he is 20 now. He is from [a city in] the center of Ukraine. Now we live in my house. And I changed my surname :-) Do you change your surnames after you get married? How are you? Write me at this e-mail address.

Bye, with the best regards,
Nadia and our family

---

FEBRUARY 13, 2008
Letter received via electronic mail

Dear Sarah and your family,
Thank you very much for the beautiful post-cards you have sent us!

I'm very glad that there are four of you in your family now. I congratulate you with the son Micah!!! He is so nice, like his mother. I think he looks like you, Sarah.

As for me, I have a new baby too:-) her name is Marianka, almost nine months [old]. . . .

Sarah, please, write me, if you'll have time. Now when I have the e-mail, it's so difficult to write letters:-) Write about your son (the weight, what he eats, etc. As a young mother, like you, I'm interested in everything about babies).

How are you?

With the best wishes,
Nadia

---

FEBRUARY 13, 2008
Letter sent via electronic mail

Dear, dear Nadia!!
I am so happy to hear from you. Congratulations on your baby girl! That's so wonderful! You have got to write and tell me everything about Marianka. And what a sweet name you have chosen. She's nine months already, so she's bigger than my Micah, who turns seven months old tomorrow. Tell me, are you enjoying your baby? I am so happy about Micah. He is very relaxed and happy.

How about Marianka? What is her personality like? Are you nursing her? Micah just started sitting up, and he isn't crawling yet. He is very big—already he is wearing clothes for a one-year-old!

So, are you living at home in [your town], and what is your day like? Are you home with the baby? I was keeping Micah all day until about a month ago. Now in the mornings he goes to a babysitter for five hours, and I work at home. I miss him when he's gone but it is nice to do some work, too.

What was your birth experience like? Did you have a cesarean section? I had one with Roman but not with Micah. Did you get advice from other women with spinal injuries? Do you have help with your baby from your mom, sister, husband, etc., and is your husband happy with the baby? Will you continue your studies, or are you already finished? You can see I have many questions! Send pictures, okay? I am attaching a photo for you. Write soon Nadia, and best of luck!!

FEBRUARY 14, 2008
Edited letter received via electronic mail

Hello Sarah!!!

I'm so glad to get this message from you! I wrote you several times, but every time there was no answer. I wrote you from a different address, I use it all the time, but as I guess, you didn't get that message. At first I thought that you are busy with the baby, then that I have wrong address. But nevertheless I'm happy that we can keep in touch at this address.

Micah is so nice on the photo! Thank you! I send you [a photo of] Marianka. I think that she is like your Roman when he was a baby. When she wants to sleep she must to do a concert, she wants to be everywhere, and at once! But I'm very, very happy about her!!!! She is my little baby girl and I love her so much, although last two months she still doesn't want to sleep and I have to help her to go to sleep.

Marianka can sit, but she can't sit still; every time she wants to go somewhere, she lays on the stomach, she wants to crawl but doesn't know how to do it, and she gets nervous. Then I take her in my arms and she begins to laugh. Some days ago Mari began to speak "baba," our baba [granny] was very happy, and then the baby said "abba" and "bababa" and our baba understand that Marianka didn't call her yet. She just says those funny words of babies. She also can say "mama," but not really calling me. She has six teeth already. And what about Micah's teeth?

Yes, I have a cesarean section. Mari was a very little, 2300 g, and what was Micah's weight? How much does he weigh now? Marianka, I don't know exactly, but about 9 kg. When it was warm, we went to our village clinic and weighed her. Now its winter, we don't go outside, it's too cold.

My husband and I live at my home, my mama and husband helps me with the baby. My father is working in Russia. Where does Sasha [your husband] work? My husband works in coal mine. Dangerous, but he wants to. He is 21, like me now. I have the bachelor's degree now. I passed the last bachelor exams with Marianka, she was 1.5 months then in June. But I had to go with her, because I nursed her every 2–3 hours. We rented the car and the mama of Andriy (my husband), Marianka, and I went to the University. Next year I hope to get a magistr [master's degree].

Write me, and tell my big hello to your family.

With love
Nadia

Nadia's life, it seems, has developed rather differently from how she'd planned it. Nadia had hoped to study as an on-campus student, finish her social work degree, and find a job, preferably in a city. As it turned out, Nadia is a young mother, living with her husband and her mother in the house where she grew up, in the village. In marrying and giving birth in her early twenties Nadia follows a common pattern in Ukraine, where women tend to marry quite young. Her husband is employed in a difficult, risky job (mining), and Nadia is not working. She is delighted with her daughter and hopes to pursue a master's degree in the future. It may be tempting to wonder if Nadia has "given in and given up" to the established gender stereotypes that privilege motherhood over a woman's career, and subject women to economic dependence on men. Yet, it is important to remember that Nadia's accomplishments—earning a bachelor's degree at a prestigious national university, acting as a coach at an AR camp, and marrying and giving birth, would have been thought of as quite remarkable for a young disabled woman just a decade ago. That she has achieved all this and more at age 21 is certainly proof that as Nadia herself said, "Maybe I want a lot, but I want it."

At the same time Nadia's story sheds light on the human costs of the injustices that limit the opportunities for disabled persons in many places around the world: lack of accessible built environments, inadequate support services, confusing and contradictory legislation (e.g., that governing education benefits), barriers to education (here higher education in particular), and limited employment opportunities, even for those who possess a university degree. I often wondered how Nadia's life would have been different had she been offered housing in a (thus far, nonexistent) wheelchair accessible dormitory in L'viv as a direct, on-campus student. Could she then have participated more fully in campus life, and what impact would her presence have had for her fellow students, the university community, and for Nadia herself? She told me she had no friends in her cohort at the university. What social networks might Nadia have mobilized as an on-campus student, and would they have improved her chances for finding employment? It was never clear to me whether Nadia ended up paying for her education or not, and I wondered what economic benefits living and studying on campus could have yielded.

In many ways Nadia and her husband face challenges common to all young adults in the country: entering university and financing a higher education, finding a job, and making ends meet while starting a family. In this one might say that Nadia has been "mainstreamed," that the trope of the parallel world no longer applies to her. But we should not discount the structural violence that limits life possibilities for Nadia and other disabled Ukrainians, who still by no means enjoy a level playing field with their nondisabled compatriots. But since no data has been collected on gender disparities in education, employment, and income level, it is difficult to fully situate Nadia's experiences within a broader context of gender, disability, and economic inequality.

## Living Disability, Living Gender

The life stories of disabled men and women in Ukraine reveal a complicated picture of how "disability . . . work[s] its way along the axis of gender" (Smith 2004:4) to shape life expectations, possibilities, and strategies. My informants' experiences reveal masculinity, femininity, sexuality, and citizenship in disability contexts to be complex phenomena that are negotiated and renegotiated, day-to-day, in diverse social, political, and interpersonal contexts. Their stories also provide a window onto the variety of experiences among men and women after spinal injury, and the range of possible responses to changing political, economic, and social climates.

An important issue these stories bring to light is the question of role fulfillment—how disability affects men's and women's ability to conform to accepted norms of feminine or masculine behavior, and the strategies they develop to do so. Alternatively, to what extent do disabled men and women reject stereotypical gender expectations, and what alternative gender identities might they establish?

As disabled men in a society that associates disability with lack and loss of capacity, Dmitrii and Anton are to some extent denied their own masculinity (Gershick and Miller 1997:457). How do they then establish themselves as gendered subjects? On the one hand, aspects of Dmitrii's and Anton's enactments of masculinity do include the cultivation of a type of hyper-masculinity based on the attitudes and practices of hegemonic masculinity. In Gerschick and Miller's (1997) terms, they enact strategies of reliance on norms of hegemonic masculinity. In the Ukrainian popular imagination, these pursuits (i.e., sports, rigorous physical training, or a "fixation" on a specific pastime) are often understood in terms of compensation—making up for one's perceived lack by seeking to excel in a particular arena.

Yet ethnographic interviews with these men reveal that strategies of reformulation of personal criteria of masculinity are also important, a concept developed by Gerschick and Miller (1997). As they note, "the gender practices of some men exemplify alternative visions of masculinity that are obscured but available to men in [a given] culture" (p. 457). It must not be overlooked that men such as Dmitrii and Anton are broadening masculine repertoires not only for themselves, but for others in Ukrainian society (Shuttleworth 2004). In a context where societal norms governing the body, gender, and sexuality have historically been top-down, patriarchal, and very conservative—at least at the level of the official—these men's negotiations with and occasional resistance to hegemonic masculinities provide those around them with examples of the potentially empowering effects of subverting or overstepping hegemonic norms of gender, masculinity, femininity, and sexuality.

In my conversations and correspondence with Viktoria, Nadia, and other disabled women in Ukraine I did not get the impression that they experienced a sense of "rolelessness," a concept suggested by Fine and Asch (1985) to argue that disabled women often are viewed as incapable of fulfilling traditional adult social roles, and that their attempts to identify with traditional female gender roles end up reinforcing the stereotype of the disabled person as dependent and passive. To the contrary, the disabled women I came to know appear to have devoted themselves headlong to their roles as mothers and homemakers, even while pursuing activities outside the home and the family such as dance, sports, study, and work.

In terms of negotiating the dominant models of Ukrainian femininity—Berehynia and Barbie—Viktoria and Nadia seem to have positioned themselves somewhere in the middle. As disabled women they will likely never be identified as the ideal "reproducer of the nation"; nor will they be heralded as the very embodiment of physical beauty. But they do want to express themselves as women in ways that are socially acceptable. They strive to hold together a version of the traditional nuclear family so promoted in the official discourse of neofamilialism (Zhurzhenko 2004), and here they face challenges common for nondisabled women—economic woes, gender role stereotypes that produce a double burden for women, and strained domestic relationships. Women like Viktoria and Nadia pursue these goals with very little help from the state.

None of this is easy, and these women and other disabled mothers I met in Ukraine have to work hard to establish their right to motherhood in the public eye. At the same time, they seem relatively comfortable accepting assistance from others. Viktoria and Nadia both relied heavily on the support of their own mothers. Another friend of mine who already was a single mother of four when she became a tetraplegic has received much help from members of a nearby church and from Zoia's and Sasha's NGO. But this does not mean that these disabled mothers see themselves as users; to the contrary, they stress the contributions they make to society, the ways they seek to support themselves and their families, and the fact that they are raising their children to be conscientious, contributing citizens. This is why I find the concept of interdependence promising for thinking about intersections of disability and gender, and how all disabled people (men and women) might be empowered by leveraging this notion.

Likewise, Dmitrii's and Anton's stories provide examples of how claims to citizenship are being reformulated among disabled persons in contemporary Ukraine. Though in different ways, both men are challenging the existing criteria through which the disabled are offered membership in Ukrainian society. These men reformulate the rules of the game through various acts of subversion—upsetting popular stereotypes, rejecting identity labels, refusing to conform to various societal norms, and so on. Most important, these men's stories reveal the creative ways in which disabled men in the post-Soviet world are broadening masculine repertoires and visions of citizenship.

Although both men emphasize discrimination and highlight the difficulties of being labeled invalidy and treated as such in post-Soviet Ukrainian society, their stories also include elements of an affirmation model of disability. This is very significant in the post-Soviet context, where public perceptions concerning disability are still very negative, and disability as a subject for scholarly inquiry is entirely new. I also think the disabled mothers I interviewed (and presumably disabled fathers, though I have not examined disabled men's parenting experiences here) are doing important work in inculcating respectful and nuanced attitudes toward disability and the disabled in their children. Viktoria beamed when she related this scene to me: "Once my daughter was playing on the playground with another girl, and I was eavesdropping on their conversation. The other girl was bragging about her mother, naming certain things she could do. My daughter's reply was simple: 'My mother is an invalid. She can do anything!'"

# Conclusion

Summer 1998. Pasha was 19 years old and preparing to enter the Polytechnical Institute to study electrical engineering. While helping a relative move some items from a hayloft, Pasha lost his footing and fell to the ground. The fall was not that high, but he happened to land hard on his back, on a piece of broken brick, resulting in an incomplete compression fracture to the fifth thoracic vertebra. Luckily, Pasha was operated on two hours after his fall by an experienced surgeon. After recuperating in the hospital for several months, Pasha learned that his parents, who had been living and working in Russia, had bought a small house back in their native Ukrainian village. Pasha, who now used a wheelchair, would live with them. Having seen all his plans for college and an engineering career go up in smoke, Pasha says he spent the next two years "driving himself crazy," mad at the world and at himself.

Pasha calls the day he was broken his "second birthday," the day his life started over. An avid athlete, he had trained in gymnastics since early childhood and had traveled with a hiking club all over the mountains of the Caucasus. He had lived in Central Asia and Siberia and traveled throughout the former Soviet Union camping and fishing. Pasha studied hard in school and earned excellent grades; subsequently he was released from compulsory military service and was offered automatic admission to the institute of his choice. This was not the future he had envisioned for himself: living with his aging parents, lonely, stuck inside a house in a tiny village. Pasha's father did what he could to modify the home—he knocked down a wall in the small kitchen to make an indoor toilet, and he widened all the doors. But Pasha needed help to get around outside, and his parents were at work all day. The unpaved village roads were muddy ruts in the spring and sheets of ice in the winter, making it nearly impossible for

Pasha to get any exercise outside. Rarely did anyone come to call—Pasha says people in his village were embarrassed to visit his house: "Everyone has all these stereotypes and fears. They think invalids must be crazy (Rus. *ubogi*), and that if they visit me they will encounter a smoke-filled room, unpleasant medicinal smells, and my forlorn, pale face. They feel pity but don't know what to do about it: Should they give me money? Or something else? So they just don't come."

Few services were made available to Pasha in his rural environs, but he was entitled to health trips to sanatoriums for the spinally injured. Pasha says that meeting other people with spinal injuries gave him the jolt he needed to reassess his life. He began corresponding with these new friends via long and frequent telephone conversations, an option made economically feasible thanks to entitlements providing free or discounted phone service to the disabled. Pasha also became a ham radio operator and was able to communicate with other enthusiasts throughout the world. He got involved in wheelchair marathons, an endeavor that allowed him to keep himself in good physical shape, further expand his social networks, and travel.

Pasha knew that as a spinal'nik he had little to no chance of pursuing the engineering career he had dreamed of. And anyway, his own experiences living disabled in a rural setting steered him in a different direction. Pasha recognized a pressing need to improve social and rehabilitation services, especially for those disabled persons living in the "periphery," outside the major urban centers. He took his idea to representatives of the local SoBez, or department of social protection, but was told, "We cannot help you because you do not have a higher education." Not to be deterred, Pasha began to seek out opportunities to enroll in university in the town nearest his village. After much negotiating with the university administration, in the late 1990s Pasha finally was admitted to study economics, a profession he says he consciously chose as one that was "feasible" in light of his "current status—an invalid in a wheelchair."

Even harder than enrolling as a university student was finding housing in the town. In fact, Pasha could not find a single landlord willing to rent him a room. As he described, "They are befuddled by the wheelchair. Even though I assure them that I'm healthy and can take care of all my physical needs on my own, they are afraid I'll cause them problems—extra trouble—and they'd rather not bother. It's just easier to find a healthy boarder than to take a risk on someone like me." Like Nadia, with no place to live in the town Pasha was compelled to complete his studies "indirectly," going in several times to take his exams and pick up lecture materials, but studying mostly on his own and living with his parents at home in the village. He did become friendly with several classmates, especially Denis, an age mate who visited Pasha from time to time. Pasha and Denis had much in common: both were born to Russian or Ukrainian parents living in the Caucasus, where they spent their own childhoods; thus they considered themselves "products of the Soviet friendship of the peoples." Both were interested in art, philosophy, and spirituality. Pasha told me once that he and Denis got on so well because they complemented one another's weaknesses with their own strengths: "I have talents that he lacks, and vice versa, so we help one another out."

When Pasha graduated in 2003, he learned that the university administration and faculty had seen him as a "test case." Pasha explained: "They told me they had been very worried when they admitted me. They were afraid I would fail and would shame them. At the graduation ceremony they thanked me for my perseverance, and said, 'Thank God you didn't disappoint us.'" According to Pasha, one of his instructors said the following: "You are the first invalid in a wheelchair who has successfully completed a degree in the entire history of our university. . . . We watched you closely to see if people like you could process the amount and level of information that we teach." Pasha responded, "Smells like discrimination to me" (Rus. *diskriminatsiei popakhivaet*).

"perpetual children"

Armed with his university diploma, Pasha again approached the SoBez office with his plans for improving services for the disabled. But, he said, "They were still unwilling to support me. I realized that all the talk about a higher education had just been a ruse to get rid of me (Rus. *otmazka*); they had no intention of giving me a job or listening to my ideas." After this disappointment Pasha continued to search for a job. Economists are usually highly sought after specialists, but Pasha faces blatant discrimination as a disabled person. Office managers, bank administrators, and other potential employers tell Pasha bluntly their reasons for not hiring him: they would have to make workplace accommodations for him, which they are unwilling to do. Pasha concedes that yes, in the case of inaccessible entrances perhaps a ramp would need to be installed, or a few boards could be laid down. But, he quipped, "What other accommodations do they think I need? I've got a good head on my shoulders, and I'm well trained. Hey, I even come with my own chair!" In 2005 Pasha told me he visited the unemployment office in the nearby town once a week. He said, "I know they get sick of seeing me, but I feel like I have to pressure them a little and constantly remind them that I exist and that I'm looking for work." In the meantime, Pasha lived on his disability pension and tutored school children and university students in how to use computers. Ironically, in light of the university's previous suspicion of his intellectual abilities, at times he even got paid to write papers and final theses for university students who then submitted the work as their own, a practice not uncommon in Ukraine.

To make matters worse, while a university student Pasha developed health problems that eventually became life threatening. Although he was experiencing acute abdominal pain, he insisted on being driven to take a required exam, fearful that there would be no making it up. As he sat in the terribly cold auditorium waiting to be called, Pasha's bladder ruptured. He underwent emergency surgery and seemed to be recovering well when a month later he again doubled over with pain in his abdomen. The doctors he consulted, who Pasha admits had no idea how to treat spinally injured persons, did X-rays and diagnosed a stomach ulcer. A subsequent surgical procedure revealed Pasha's stomach to be in perfect shape, but suddenly his bladder again ruptured, right along the scar from the first surgery. Pasha was told that the initial bladder surgery had been botched; the incision was poorly closed. Doctors assured Pasha that his bladder should not give him further problems. But a few months later, again a ruptured bladder. Says Pasha: "I said to heck with this rural medicine—I'm going to Kyiv."

Pasha appealed to Zoia and Sasha, and also to our mutual friend, Lidia, a retired woman who has been involved in disability advocacy since the late 1990s. Pasha showed up in Kyiv with a high fever and extremely low hemoglobin counts. Lidia lived near a hospital with reputable specialists who had experience treating spinally injured persons with all manner of health crises. However, as a non-Kyivan, Pasha was not eligible for treatment there. Through her contacts and bureaucratic finesse, Lidia managed to get Pasha admitted for surgery by pretending that she was his cousin. Somehow, this gave Pasha a temporary honorary status as a local, and finally he received proper care. In addition to taking care of these complicated negotiations, Lidia also secured monetary donations from sponsors to cover Pasha's medical costs, which were especially high since he was not a registered resident of the city. Lidia's support of Pasha was widely acknowledged and praised in the disability community; once a friend who did not know Pasha or Lidia personally said, "Oh right, he's that guy whose life was saved by a woman here in Kyiv, some distant relative of his."

I marveled at the way several of Pasha's friends and acquaintances, including Lidia, rallied around him. After recovering in the hospital he lived for a time with Lidia in her tiny apartment where he continued to recuperate. Pasha and Denis spent a lot of time together, as Denis now lived in Kyiv where he worked several part-time jobs to support himself. Pasha eventually went back home to the village, but he visited Kyiv frequently, staying at Lidia's and continuing to look for work in the capital city. During our conversations Pasha often said he did not want to be a burden to his parents, who were aging and both ready to retire, or to his sister, who had her own family to care for. Once Pasha told me about how a man had seen him on the street and asked him to come talk to his daughter, a young woman who had fallen into despair after a spinal injury. Pasha said, "She was just lying there and her parents were doing everything for her. I told her that we have to do our best to be independent and not burden our parents. Parents need independence, too; they have their own lives and can't be all wrapped up in ours."

Zoia and Sasha checked in with Pasha from time to time; they inquired about his job-seeking efforts and whether his health was okay. Yet I noted that even though Pasha was well known in the spinal'nik community, he was rather marginalized. I was not able to work out the source of this exclusion—Pasha did say he had some personal conflicts with a few prominent athletes and activists, and his status as a person from the "periphery" may also have played a role.

When I first met Pasha in 2003 he had traveled to Kyiv from the village to visit Denis and observe a disability rights awareness event in which he had not been invited to participate. He still enjoyed seeing his fellow spinal'niki, but he stayed with Lidia rather than with the other wheelchair users, who were housed at a private rehabilitation facility in the city. I kept in touch with Pasha via electronic mail and learned that he was still in the village, unsuccessfully looking for work, helping his parents, and biding his time.

In 2005 I again met Pasha in Kyiv; he had come to observe the same event, again without an invitation to participate. Lidia, Denis, Pasha, and I took an excursion to one of the city's riverfront beaches afterward. On our way back we took a trolleybus, and with no good place to situate himself Pasha had to straddle the aisle with his chair while holding onto two metal poles for dear life. The bus driver, who doubled as a conductor selling tickets to passengers, made it clear that she did not appreciate having to navigate around Pasha and his chair: every time she passed by she demonstratively stepped over the front wheels and said, "Good God!" (Rus. *Gospodi!*) in an exasperated voice for all to hear. It occurred to me that this is how Pasha must have felt earlier at the disability awareness event from which he was formally excluded, and in many other contexts as well— superfluous, an "inconvenient person" (Iarskaia-Smirnova 2002a:121).

I was in Kyiv again in 2006 and soon after my arrival I visited Lidia to have lunch and get caught up on recent happenings in the parallel world. She forewarned me that Pasha was "being made to be more independent," more self-sufficient. Lidia continued, "If you notice a change in his relationships, that's why. Denis, Zoia, and I—we've all agreed that it's for the best." Lidia had begun to feel that Pasha was using her, not least because of his frequent stays in Kyiv where he always stayed in her tiny apartment. According to Lidia, Pasha was on board and accepted the change. I learned that Pasha's parents had decided to sell their house and retire to a village in eastern Ukraine, near the city of Kharkiv. Still unemployed, Pasha was living there, too. Lidia and Pasha's other friends disapproved—"There's nothing there for him"—but they were not throwing him a life raft. That fall I spent some time with Pasha in Kharkiv—I was doing research there and he had been invited to help out for a couple of weeks with a camp for wheelchair users as a paid instructor. He was lodging temporarily with the camp's organizers in their home, but not wanting to inconvenience them, Pasha did his best to meander around town during the day and just show up to their apartment at bedtime. He continued to look for a job but encountered the same discrimination as before: potential employers insisted they would be unable to provide him with a "specialized workplace," but when asked what such accommodations would entail other than a makeshift ramp, they were unable to come up with a response.

I was surprised to learn that Pasha and Denis were no longer close. I had spent considerable time with the two of them and their friendship seemed strong. But, said Pasha, when he visited Kyiv now Denis never had time for him, and told him so directly. Pasha explained, "Last time I called him up and said, 'Come on, surely you've got time to sit and have a cup of coffee or a beer, and a chat.' He replied, 'Actually, no I don't,' said he had to go, and just hung up. It hurts my feelings of course, and I don't understand it, but what else can I do?" I did not hear Denis's side of the story but surmised that keeping his distance was part of the pact to help Pasha be "made to be more independent." Pasha had no other close friends; he knew practically no one in the village where he now lived, and he could count his acquaintances in Kharkiv on one hand.

That fall Pasha and I traveled together by train to an event in a small town near Kharkiv; the town's first community organization for the disabled was opening, and we were both invited to the gala banquet. The champagne was flowing and the guests danced to loud pop music and sang karaoke. Pasha looked to be having a good time and I noticed that one woman in particular was taking an interest in him. On the train back

*[handwritten note:] neoliberal individualism in an inherently communal context.*

to Kharkiv Pasha was despondent. He got visibly angry as he expressed his frustration about what had happened at the party; he said it was a common scenario: "At events like that, women fall all over me for a good time, I've no shortage of attention when it's all for fun. But when it comes to getting serious, no one is interested." There was desperation in Pasha's voice: "Sarah, tell me, what's wrong with me, why am I still alone?" It was painful to witness Pasha's recognition of his social estrangement, which seemed to have gotten worse during the three years I had known him. I worried about Pasha because it was clear that he was successively losing his "close ones" and the important social ties so crucial to survival in postsocialist states, particularly for those already living in or near society's margins (Höjdestrand 2009:112–134).

Pasha's story—and the stories of many other disabled people in the region—reveals some of the dehumanizing effects of "democratization" in Ukraine and other postsocialist countries. Along with neoliberal economic reforms have been ushered in corresponding social reforms and the promotion of key neoliberal values. These include the privileging of various techniques of the self that are seen as necessary for success in the market economy—independence, self-reliance, self-esteem, self-possession, and others. Social policy reform works in tandem with a transforming public sentiment: as populations such as the disabled are detached from certain institutions through pension reform and revamped social services, so too are they detached from certain relationships as friends, family, and further significant others enact strategies to "make them be more independent." Individuals like Pasha who previously were offered a leg up now are being told to "change yourself" as a first and crucial step to changing society (Rivkin-Fish 2004). Pasha has been encouraged to enact an internal self-politics that effectively depoliticizes his predicament of discrimination and exclusion and threatens to estrange him from important potential mechanisms of empowerment such as civic organizations, political institutions, and support groups. Such self-centered strategies for life improvement are not necessarily apolitical, but they do reduce politics to the level of the individual (Matza 2009:512–513).

The either overt or implied promotion of such self-centered techniques for managing life are predicated on the assumption that the state can offer only limited help for those in need, and in today's Ukraine that may indeed be the case. The reassessment of citizens' disability group status, pension reform, and the recent emphasis on job training and employment all point to the state's rolling back of disability benefits and support. And even in spaces where the state appears to be strong—for example the supposed robust role MSEK plays in assigning an individualized rehabilitation program, or the role of MLSP and local employment offices in job placement for disabled workers—when one scratches the surface a rather empty state space is revealed, a "patchy and variegated space of regulation" (Dunn 2008:255) at best. Given all the structural constraints he faced, it was not fair to untie Pasha from his intimate relationships while placing the burden of success on him alone. Instead of emphasizing—as he had in 2003—the "stamp" or social stereotypes that structured treatment of the disabled and often colored official policy, in 2006 Pasha was left wondering, "What's wrong with me?" *forest for trees*

Pasha's impasse—one with which many marginalized citizens in postsocialist states can identify—generates insights into how states can be made more accountable, and what roles diverse groups of citizens may play in calling governments and fellow citizens to account. And despite the florescence of new neoliberal logics in structuring institutions, relationships, and self-identity, the story of living disability also shows how projects for revitalization and rehabilitation in states such as Ukraine may involve engaging with both the residual and the new, often in unexpected ways. As Karolina Szmagalska-Follis (2008) shows in her study of the repossession of an abandoned army base in Western Ukraine as a rehabilitation facility for persons released from prison, victims of human trafficking, and returned asylum seekers, varied and seemingly incompatible models for life can coexist and commingle in the parallel worlds inhabited by those dispossessed by the massive transformations of the last two decades. Viktor G., a "self-described anarchist with a social worker's calling" (2008:332), appropriated these post-Soviet ruins in a project of redemption that thoroughly rejected Western donor aid and civil society discourses. Viktor G. is also a staunch individualist; however, the source of his individualism lies not in Western neoliberal logics, but in a specifically Ukrainian model of anarchism, that of Nestor Makhno (1888–1934). Although Viktor G. has no deep nostalgia for the Soviet period, his refuge and rehabilitation facility nonetheless "reproduces precisely that which has been lost in the process of the 'unmaking of Soviet life' (Humphrey 2002), that is the all-embracing domain of collective work and life" (Szmagalska-Follis 2008:341). Such hybrid forms show how the individualizing techniques of neoliberalism are not the only ones available for managing life in postsocialist states.

Seen in this light, it becomes obvious that the disabled and their advocates in Ukraine are dipping into the experience of the socialist past to strategize survival and empowerment, even as they invest themselves in the changing atmosphere of market reforms and the individualizing techniques that accompany them. Furthermore, they are piecing together examples and models taken from other countries and international contexts, including North American physical therapy, Swedish active rehabilitation, and Western models of inclusive education and early intervention. The melding of various historically and situationally informed approaches to improving how disability is lived in Ukraine is crucial to the success of the disability rights movement. Those working for empowerment need the flexibility such hybrid strategies can contribute for navigating the enormous gaps that exist between state rhetoric and state practices, between popular narratives and realities, regarding disability.

One vivid example includes the empty space left behind by the state's discursive shift from a social protection approach to a rights approach in disability policy (MLSP 2008, see chapter 2). It is impossible to have social protection without rights, and vice versa, and in reality many of the disabled in Ukraine today are left with neither. There is also a basic tension between the growing prevalence of empowerment narratives that promote individual independence and self-sufficiency, and a lack of adequate state and community support to facilitate such self-possession. In the absence of such state- and community-based supports, many disabled persons and their friends and family members find it difficult or impossible to fully cope with the burden of care, a tragedy that has been documented for other neoliberalizing states such as Brazil (Biehl 2005). Although concepts of independent living (IL) have been influential for some in the Ukrainian disability community, without the kinds of support services provided by IL centers in the United States and Canada, prospects for enacting independent living in Ukraine today are highly circumscribed. In this context, interventions with a focus limited primarily to the individual's capacity to independently carry out the tasks of daily living hold little promise for significantly improving disabled people's lives on the whole.

What is needed are innovative strategies for enabling mobile citizenship through the opening of opportunities for the disabled and other marginalized populations to engage various institutions and political and social actors to build networks, enact interdependence, and become more economically and socially mobile. Based on a decade and a half of research in Ukraine on questions of health, healing, gender, community organizing, and disability, I believe one very promising tactic to positively transform the landscape of living disability after socialism is to reimagine and rewrite kinship. Inscribing disability into kinship imaginaries and practices, and disseminating new and compelling narratives of kinship concerning disability, can lead to a reenvisioning of citizenship that is more interdependent, tolerant, and inclusive.

## Kinship and Mobile Citizens     *you read her!*

In proposing kinship terrain as an important location for reimagining and re-presenting disability as politics, practice, and experience, I am inspired by Rayna Rapp and Faye Ginsburg's (2001) work on disability, kinship, and citizenship in the contemporary United States. By examining disability narratives that occur in "public storytelling" in the media and other public outlets, Rapp and Ginsburg document the efforts of families to "rewrite" kinship. Such rewritings, they assert, "are crucial to creating a new cultural terrain in which disability is not just begrudgingly accommodated under the mandates of expanded post-1970s civil rights legislation, but is positively incorporated into the social body" (2001:535). Indeed, Rapp and Ginsburg argue that it is precisely experience-based disability narratives, as authored by the disabled themselves and/or their family members, that have helped disseminate "intimate insights [of disability] among a broader public . . . to mobilize an extraordinary and rapid transformation since the 1970s in the way such notions as rights, entitlement, and citizenship are conceived" (2001:537–538).

Rapp and Ginsburg present wide-ranging examples of these disability narratives, many of which expand the notion of kinship and family beyond the normative gendered nuclear family structure and extend notions of relatedness, mutual responsibility, and the locus of care beyond the insular family and home: Japanese novelist Kenzaburo Oe's book *A Healing Family* (1995); television shows such as *Life Goes On,* starring Chris Burke, a man with Down Syndrome; advocacy internet sites; and other interventions that expand the domains of public intimacy in relation to disability. Key to the work performed by these disability narratives is a refusal to individualize disability experience or propose individualizing solutions to what are in fact "cultural and social dilemmas" (Rapp and Ginsburg 2001:534, fn. 1). Rapp and Ginsburg argue that

> [t]he complexities of mobilizing the necessary medical, therapeutic, and social support [to care for a disabled person] reveal the limits of kinship within a gendered nuclear family structure. It is through this revelation, we suggest, that some begin to reimagine the boundaries and capacities of kinship and to recognize the necessity of broader support for caretaking. On occasion, they are motivated to rewrite kinship in ways that

circulate within larger discursive fields of representation and activism. (Rapp and Ginsburg 2001:540–541)

To describe the potential of such expansive notions of kinship and responsibility for changing the nature of discussions of disability and advancing disability rights, Rapp and Ginsburg write:

> The proliferation of publicly circulating representations of disability as a form of diversity we all eventually share—through our own bodies or attachments to others—offers potential sites of identification and even kinship that extend beyond the biological family. . . . It is our argument that such public storytelling—whether in family narratives, memoirs, television talk shows and sitcoms, movies, or, most recently, through Web sites and internet discussion groups—is crucial to expanding what we call the social fund of knowledge about disability. In opening up the experiential epistemology of disability, as shaped by and shaping the intimate world of nonnormative family life, such forms of public culture widen the space of possibility in which relationships can be imagined and resources claimed. . . . We suggest that such representations . . . are foundational to the integration of disability into everyday life in the United States, a process that is in turn essential to the more capacious notions of citizenship championed by the disability rights movement. (Rapp and Ginsburg 2001:534–538)

Rapp and Ginsburg thus trace a crucial link between expanded ideas and practices of kinship and care, the mobilizing of support networks and rights activism, and the extension of citizenship claims:

> We suggest that these mediated spaces of public intimacy—talk shows, on-line disability support groups, Web sites, and so on—are crucial for building a social fund of knowledge more inclusive of the fact of disability. These media practices provide a counterdiscourse to the naturalized stratification of family membership that for so long has marginalized, in particular, those disabled from birth. It is not only the acceptance of difference within families, but also the embrace of relatedness that such models of inclusion present to the body politic that makes these spaces potentially radical in their implications. (Rapp and Ginsburg 2001:551)

I have quoted these scholars at length because the insights they offer related to changing narratives of disability, kinship, and citizenship in the United States that hold great potential for energizing disability rights efforts and jump-starting mobile citizenship in other world areas. Given the region's recent experience of state socialism, rewriting kinship as an advocacy tactic may resonate especially strongly in Eastern European states such as Ukraine. There are several historical trends and recent developments that lead me to this conclusion.

First, although trends of individualization and privatization shape post-socialist worlds in important ways, a strong ethos of collective responsibility, shared experience, and mutual assistance continues to shape social life. The proliferation of mutual aid societies and support groups in the region is evidence of this. Such groups often are not perceived as progressive or innovative since frequently they insist on vulnerable groups' entitlement to support and resources from the state, thus seeking to recoup the Soviet-era social safety net. But these associations do important work to support fellow citizens marginalized from the new markets, and they foster a sense of relatedness between members, and between different organizations and their constituents. For example, a mutual aid association I studied in the late 1990s, a group for large families, readily invited single mothers, social orphans, battered wives, and other persons in need into their fold. They also donated food and clothing to orphanages. The director said, "We don't differentiate; everyone needs help in their own way, and that's what we're here for." Another organization, a support group for retired women, cooperated with other seemingly "unrelated" mutual aid associations, including a group for veterans of the Soviet–Afghan war. The organizations included one another in their activities because, as the director of the women's group told me, "Our work can benefit their members, and vice versa, so why not cooperate?" And although the experience of state socialism has led some to reject wholesale the officially imposed discourse of the collective good, for many in the region the basic idea of a socially shared responsibility toward fellow citizens continues to ring true.

One fundamental premise underlying the kind of public rewriting of kinship that Rapp and Ginsburg explore is the notion of disability as a potentially universal experience—if we live long enough, we will all become disabled. This truism, sometimes called a universal model of disability, already has found some traction in Ukraine, and some of my informants iterated this idea. One activist who had participated in a Dutch-sponsored project said, "One of my goals is to make disability less exceptional, and more normal for people. You never know—you may become disabled, either temporarily or permanently, or one of your loved ones might. So any improvements we are asking for—accessibility of buildings and transport, for example—are really improvements for everyone." In the United States the leveraging of this kind of argument sometimes is criticized as potentially watering down the disability rights agenda, since it may encourage the nondisabled to engage with demands for restructuring only if such changes are perceived as directly beneficial to themselves. But in Ukraine, where being disabled still is so highly stigmatized, it is an important and meaningful intervention.

Further, families—and parents in particular—have been a major force in the Ukrainian disability rights movement. Parents of disabled children have spearheaded early intervention programs, calls for the deinstitutionalization of disabled children, and projects for inclusive education. At the same time, the movement has not been limited to families, but includes friends and acquaintances of disabled persons and their families as well. For example, perhaps the most widely known advocate of early intervention for disabled children in Ukraine, Anna Kukuruza in Kharkiv, became invested in disability issues when her best friend had a disabled child. The parents' movement provides a strong, well-developed base from which to expand narratives of family, kinship, responsibility, and citizenship (Swarnyk 2005).

A potential challenge to the kind of reimagining of kinship described by Rapp and Ginsburg is the neofamilialism that permeates postsocialist Ukraine, where the traditional nuclear family often is idealized as the bastion of moral culture and a refuge from the encroachment of the state, which is quite happy to retreat from its previous paternal obligations. As explained by Lynne Haney and Lisa Pollard (2003:12), oftentimes in postsocialist Eastern Europe "the state draws on familial models and metaphors to abdicate its social responsibilities." However, it is also the case that the language of family is a malleable narrative, and can be variously leveraged by political actors and social groups for a range of purposes. Haney (2003), for example, has shown how the politics of familialism in postsocialist Hungary and the Czech Republic have been espoused for quite different ends—to rationalize welfare retrenchment in Hungary, and to justify welfare expansion in the Czech Republic. So although interventions perceived as subversive of the idealized, insular, hierarchical family structure could face resistance and become counterproductive, carefully couching rights claims and other disability advocacy narratives in a familiar language of family and kinship—while expanding the frame of kinship domains beyond the insular nuclear family unit by drawing on equally familiar ideas of social responsibility, relatedness, and mutual help—is a powerful starting point for changing social attitudes toward disability and the disabled in postsocialist locales such as Ukraine. Let me be clear: I am *not* advocating that responsibility for supporting disabled persons and securing equal rights for disabled individuals be assigned to discrete families, or that the traditional nuclear family is a site best suited for addressing disability-related concerns. Rather, I am arguing quite the opposite: exploding notions of relatedness, mutual responsibility, and interdependence beyond the bounds of "the naturalized stratification of family membership" (Rapp and Ginsburg 2001:551) will help the disabled enact a more mobile citizenship.

Crucially, "reimagin[ing] the boundaries and capacities of kinship and . . . recogniz[ing] the necessity of broader support for caretaking" (Rapp and Ginsburg 2001:540) would open space for critiques related not only to disability issues, but to other social problematics, too. As in the United States and many other places, in Ukraine the burden of care for disabled family members is overwhelmingly assigned to women as the traditional caregivers. Rewriting kinship and expanding notions of responsibility of care beyond the nuclear, heteronormative family thus becomes a critique of gender inequality and discrimination in and beyond the family. The recognition of families' struggles to cope without adequate state support is fundamental to kinship-expanding disability narratives, which then become a strong critique of state withdrawal and abandonment. Such an expanded notion of family, relatedness, and responsibility would also force a recognition of the varied forms of families that actually exist in Ukraine and all over the world—single-parent households, blended families, extended families, domestic partnerships, and many others.

But how best to build "a social fund of knowledge more inclusive of the fact of disability" while simultaneously developing "a counterdiscourse to the naturalized stratification of family membership" (Rapp and Ginsburg 2001:551)? Rapp and Ginsburg elaborate the potential of media (television, print, the internet) to enrich this social fund of knowledge. The material I examined in chapter 4 offers several promising strategies for inserting meaningful and transformative disability narratives into the media and other venues of public storytelling in Ukraine. In my discussion of media portrayals of disability and the disabled, I noted that rarely are disability narratives recounted in the first person. Disability narratives most frequently are filtered through a journalist's perspective, and the phenomenon of disability is hitched to a few pervasive tropes—the heroic, the sensational, the symbolic, and so on. In contrast, through everyday encounters disabled persons and their advocates may take advantage of opportunities for developing a realistic mode of living and understanding disability, whether by staging a playful street performance by disabled musicians, or taking care to use the inclusive "we" in public speech and thus emphasizing social and moral ties of relatedness between nondisabled and disabled individuals. Such realistic performances are a powerful means for expanding disability narratives, especially when they are initiated by disabled persons themselves. Therefore, concerted efforts need to be made to ensure that disabled persons and collectives may enter the public eye on and in their own terms, not as symbolic representations of human fortitude or as vehicles for sociopolitical critique (e.g., impoverished, pitiful "invalids" as evidence of society's moral decay), but as real-life human beings in relationships and possessing dynamic personal histories.

Such interventions are important for making disability familiar—making it real—as a common social phenomenon, as an aspect of life that touches a significant portion of the population at any given time. Sociologists Polina Alpatova and Tetiana Zub (2006) make a convincing argument that when state-based services are adequate and social stigma is dispelled, being disabled becomes just another aspect of a person's identity, not a limiting factor preventing the person from taking advantage of various opportunities. In such conditions "invalid" is no longer a social status that supersedes all other characteristics of the person; being disabled is rather a fact of life that needs to be addressed, but that does not severely limit one's life possibilities. Media-based personal portraits are important for engendering this view of disability as a familiar fact of life.

It is important that these media-based interventions be initiated and designed by the disabled and their advocates themselves. Denis Petrov, a journalist who is blind, is exemplary in this regard. Petrov has published several articles in the nationally distributed newspaper *Zerkalo Nedeli* (Weekly Mirror) on disability-related themes; his articles make living disability real for readers through Petrov's direct, candid, and witty style. In one article, titled "Superman-2," which presents strong arguments for inclusive education of blind children in regular schools, Petrov invites the reader to "[i]magine yourself in the place of such a [blind] person. Your day starts just like anyone else's. You leave the house and everything is going along fine . . . ." (Petrov 2006). Petrov goes on to describe a typical day in the life of a person with limited sight, not to elicit pity but to point out all the ways that disabled people are excluded—how they are disabled—by a society unwilling to accept them as full members. The way Petrov addresses readers using the formal "you" in Russian (*vy*) serves to personalize the experience; it is an inclusive move. To judge by the commentaries posted by internet readers of Petrov's articles in *Zerkalo Nedeli*, his pieces are making positive impacts. Commentators write, "The author elicits deep, DEEP respect," "Great article," and "Well written!" A lengthier commentary reads, "Denis, many thanks for the article. We have needed this material for a long time. Thanks to *ZN* for publishing it. I hope it will have some resonance. . . . You can count on my support and help."

NGOs and other community-based groups can play an important role by initiating information and image campaigns. The Soviet-era history of social exclusion of the disabled has produced profound ignorance about the disabled, and among the general public disability rights and policy reform are seen as back-burner issues at best. In this context, NGOs need to direct more efforts toward informing the public about disability issues and improving popular perceptions of disability and the disabled. Several television programs on disability issues, such as the now defunct series called *Podolannia* (Overcoming), seem to have made positive impacts; NGOs could raise consciousness through similar programs and develop innovative public service announcements. Ukraine's paralympic athletes, who have done exceedingly well in the last several Paralympic Games, have been almost completely detached from disability rights activism. Their success and positive public image could be harnessed to forward disability rights.

As part of this effort, activists and NGOs could initiate various kinds of research on disability, since there is a dearth of even basic statistical data on housing, education, and employment characteristics of the disabled. Such data would contribute on many levels to advancing a rights agenda and formulating improved services. Research that stimulates and disseminates public storytelling is also crucial to facilitating the reimagining of kinship and building more inclusive social worlds. Work being done by some Kharkiv-based scholars is a promising start in this direction (Alpatova and Zub 2006).

Digital communications technology offers further opportunities for collaboratively crafting and disseminating disability narratives while simultaneously reframing notions of kinship and relatedness. The internet is an important tool for establishing and maintaining social networks; many of my informants in Ukraine are avid users of the internet and World Wide Web who use electronic mail and Skype™ to communicate with friends and acquaintances across town and across the world. People like Sasha Pavlov have established identities in virtual worlds where they socialize and share information. I have not found any statistics regarding access to and use of the internet among the disabled in Ukraine, but

among the population as a whole in 2005, 97 of 1,000 persons were internet users (UNDP 2007/2008:274). In Kyiv, the telecommunications company Voliacable provides free internet connections to certain categories
of the disabled. According to a 2007 Presidential decree, the State Information Committee is working with other government entities on a project called "Internet Access for People with Limited Physical Capabilities";
such access would be financed by city governments (MLSP 2008:177).[1]

We can assume that use of internet technologies will continue to grow
among the disabled and in the population as a whole. In a context where
"larger and larger segments of the global population find that the life-
scapes they construct for themselves are irrevocably composed of both
physical and virtual realities" (Jordan 2009:182), digital communications
offers opportunities to "work the borders" (Reeves 2008) that separate the
disabled and nondisabled. The "blurrings" produced by new communication technologies, described by Brigitte Jordan (2009:182) as, "the processes by which cultural practices, lifestyles, and underlying ideologies are
reshaped in relation to one another," seem ripe for introducing narratives
of relatedness, interdependence, and kinship to reshape public discourse
around disability. Perhaps these technologies possess the potential to fundamentally change the terms of the debate and reimagine the boundaries and borders of the parallel world. As Bach and Stark (2005:38) write,
"new technologies . . . present opportunities to communicate in entirely
new ways and to perform radically new functions. Especially because
these technologies are interactive, their adoption becomes an occasion for
innovation that restructures interdependencies, reshapes interfaces, and
transforms relations." Creative innovations and collaborations could be
consciously introduced in weblogs, digital publications, and many other
internet-mediated communications to expand and reshape how disability
is perceived, discussed, narrated, and lived.

Other avenues also need to be accessed to shift public thinking about
disability away from negative stereotyping, fear, and pity, and to expand
notions of relatedness and kinship. Like Iryna, who organized the job fair
in her town, rights activists and others committed to helping improve
social attitudes need to pursue opportunities to facilitate interaction
between disabled and nondisabled persons and to promote a discourse
of inclusion and interdependence. Placing more emphasis on inclusive
education for disabled children would have a long-term positive impact
on the next generation's attitudes toward disability and the disabled. And
as the educational system is reformed, there is a vital need for disabled
people themselves to play a key transformative role. This is one of the

reasons the curriculum reform programs regarding physical therapy and social work have been successful in L'viv—disabled persons and their family members and friends are directly invested in reforms as activists and educators. As part of their pedagogy Mykola Swarnyk and his colleagues at L'viv Polytechnic encourage diverse members of the disability community to visit their courses to present guest lectures, interact with students, and lead hands-on, experiential activities. Student cohorts often include several students who are themselves disabled, which positively impacts the learning process. In their study of students of occupational therapy and nursing management in Volgograd, Russia, Packer et al. (2000) found that inviting members of the All-Russian Organization of Invalids (VOI) to design and teach a course titled Introduction to the Problems of People with Disabilities in Russia had a positive effect on students' attitudes toward disability and the disabled. Further, students at the same institution who were not enrolled in the course also showed improved attitudes, so the pedagogical strategy had extended beneficial effects. Reforms in the region to further expand the educational opportunities available to the disabled are important for training a diverse professional workforce of educators, social workers, and rehabilitation specialists. Classroom-based interactions between disabled and nondisabled students can facilitate the "embrace of relatedness that such models of inclusion present to the body politic" (Rapp and Ginsburg 2001:551), a praxis that is then expanded further into people's work and social lives.

Public storytelling animates all these areas of life—outlets of mass media, the internet, the classroom, and many others—and the voices of the disabled need to be heard in these stories. At this historical juncture in postsocialist, marketizing states, it is crucial that personalizing disability narratives be circulated not to privatize disability experiences and let the state off the hook, but rather to reiterate the importance of shared social support and to expand notions of kinship, relatedness, and mutual responsibility beyond the bounds of the traditional family group. Paul K. Longmore (1995) elegantly described a shift in values that, if broadly adopted, can transform society. This shift entails the privileging of "not self-sufficiency but self-determination, not independence but interdependence, not functional separateness but personal connection, not physical autonomy but human community." It is my fervent hope that just such an orientation will characterize the next chapter of living disability after socialism.

## In Other Words . . .

The word used most often in Ukraine, Russia, and other former Soviet countries to describe persons with a range of physical, mental, and intellectual challenges is "invalid." In one sense, invalid is an official designation, an identity conferred upon one by the state apparatus and its various health and social welfare institutions. When one refers to another—or to oneself—as an invalid, oftentimes it is in reference not only to the person's physical or mental characteristics, but also to his or her membership in an official category of citizens with a particular relationship to the state, which affords them access to a range of benefits and entitlements. "Invalid" carries with it also the assumption that the referent—the invalid—does not (and cannot) work. This identification is rooted in the Soviet system of classification and support of invalids as a category of citizens who by definition did not possess labor capacity, or whose ability to work had been partially compromised.

Thus there is a tangible sense in which the term invalid connotes loss and lack, whether of physical movement, intellectual acuity and so on, or of the ability to fulfill expected social roles (as worker, for example). Although designation as an invalid confers upon one certain material benefits, it is still a negative identity marker that emphasizes difference and deficiency. So although the term is still widely used in legal documents, in the press, in public discourse, and by people considered invalids themselves—including many of those active in rights initiatives—today some people resist identification as invalids and the negative connotations the term carries.

As one might expect, among those who reject the term invalid there is not widespread agreement on what acceptable alternative terminology should be used. Disability scholars and activists from Canada and the United States have introduced the terms "persons with special needs" (*liudy z osoblyvymy potrebamy*) and "persons with limited possibilities" (*liudy z obmezhenymy mozhlyvostiamy*), and such terms are gradually making their way into legislation, official discussions of disability, and popular media accounts. Some activists have adopted these phrases to replace "invalid" in their daily speech, but this is rather rare. Many find these terms too wordy and cumbersome; as one man said, "'People with special needs,' I don't like that expression. Just say 'invalids.' It is short, precise, and accurate. I personally see nothing offensive about the term."

Some reject phrasings such as "persons with special needs" on a different basis; Vasyl', an activist and entrepreneur from near L'viv, for example, thought talk of "special needs" placed the onus on the individual, thus diminishing the important social aspects of disability. Vasyl' explained, "I don't consider myself an invalid. I'm a normal person—I just don't walk with my own legs. . . . [I don't like the term] 'people with special needs.' I have the same needs as other people; I just can't satisfy them in our society." Vasyl' preferred the use of *nepovnospravnyi,* a word that apparently is new to the Ukrainian language and whose literal English translation would be, roughly, "not fully functioning." Nepovnospravnyi does not appear in any of my Ukrainian-English or English-Ukrainian dictionaries, and most native speakers with whom I have consulted aver that it is probably a loan word from Polish.

Nepovnospravnyi is a relational term—arguably, the degree of "function" (or lack of function) is not necessarily rooted in the individual person but may be externally imposed or generated. This sense—that one is limited not by his or her physical condition *per se,* but by constraints imposed by a society that fails to take into account the diversity of its members—means that nepovnospravnyi closely approximates how "disabled" is often used in activist and scholarly discussions in the West.

It is with these nuances in mind that I have made choices to privilege certain terminologies over others in this book. In my choice of terminology I am, on the one hand, taking a cue from informants such as Vasyl', who want to highlight the social origins and aspects of disability and disability experiences, and, on the other hand, I am gesturing toward the rich disability studies literature that examines disability as "a socially driven relation to the body" (Davis 1995:3), as simultaneously rooted in biology yet always and everywhere socially mediated. As such, I choose to privilege the use of "disabled" as an adjective, rather than "disability"

as a noun. Although I am aware of arguments for the "people-first" terminology preferred by many U.S. disability rights activists and some disability studies scholars, I am not entirely comfortable with how this usage
could be interpreted as implying that disability is an objective, organically
rooted state that resides in the individual, rather than something socially
and environmentally produced. Following Gail Landsman (2009), who
examines women's diverse experiences of mothering disabled children,
I write of disabled persons, not "people with disabilities." As Landsman
(2009:12, citing Overboe 1999:24) notes, identifying people adjectivally as
disabled—which is preferred by many British disability studies scholars—
acknowledges that people are "primarily disabled by society rather than by
a quality intrinsic to . . . [them] . . . and that disability may not only inform
one's life but be a positive factor in it." I try to use the word "invalid" only
to reference local understandings or usage or in translating direct quotes
from interviewees, and at times I consciously bracket off the word with
quotation marks.

I choose not to frame my discussions in terms of the distinction between
disability and impairment, the latter problematically characterized by
international bodies such as the World Health Organization (WHO) as,
in the words of Matthew Kohrman, "a deviation from universal norms
of biomedical status, a form of acultural, apolitical, ahistorical facticity"
(2005:28). The assumption that biological difference and physical "devi-
ance" can be measured against an objective standard, in a scientifically
neutral way, runs counter to the rich research in anthropology and related
disciplines documenting the complicated cultural and political influences
that shape biomedicine variously in different places and times (Lock 2002,
Rapp 1999). Additionally, reliance on the impairment–disability dyad,
where impairment is concretely rooted in the physical body and disability
is defined as "the disadvantage or restriction of activity caused by a contemporary social organization which takes no or little account of people
who have physical impairments . . . " (Union of the Physically Impaired
Against Segregation 1976:3–4) has, until recently, precluded critical analysis of corporeal experience and the cultural, political, and historical forces
that shape understandings and treatments of bodies across time and space
(but see Corker and Shakespeare 2002, Frank 2000, Linton 2006, Shakespeare 2006, Thomas 2007). Indeed, Devva Kasnitz (2008:29) has identified "developing a more nuanced theory of impairment–disability" as one
project at "the cutting edge of disability studies."

My avoidance of the terminology of impairment is not to deny the
physical challenges my informants face; indeed, bodily injury, surgeries

NOTES ON TERMINOLOGY AND METHODS

and other medical-technical procedures, various health concerns, and the daily routines of personal hygiene were constant topics of conversation during my research, and they come up frequently in these pages. But I also want to approach bodily phenomena as socially parsed, as emerging from particular body cultures (Brownell 1995) and as differentially experienced, a viewpoint that constructions of impairment/disability may not fully capture.

## Doing Research In and Of the Parallel World

For the project that unfolds in these pages, in contrast to my previous major research in Ukraine, I did not have the luxury of conducting field research for long, uninterrupted stretches of time. These constraints necessitated a certain creativity in research methodology, as I made short regular trips to the field and sustained contact with informants via telephone, electronic mail, Skype™, and surface post. In summer 2002 I formally launched this research by spending a month in Kyiv. With Zoia, Sasha, Oleg, and Dmitrii as my key contacts and key informants, I scheduled interviews with a range of persons, including representatives of disability-related NGOs, particularly those representing the interests of spinal'niki (spinally injured persons) and other mobility disabled persons, as well as social workers, rehabilitation therapists, and state officials. I also met and interviewed disabled persons who were not directly connected to activist circles. I speak Russian and Ukrainian, both of which are used in Ukraine, and interviews were conducted according to the interviewees' preferences. A few interviews were conducted in English, but the vast majority took place in either Russian or Ukrainian, or in a mixture of both languages.

I also undertook participant observation with several NGO leaders and their organizations, getting to know them, their concerns, and their strategies through informal interaction and conversation. I attended their meetings and special events, participated in daily activities, and carried out formal and informal interviews. I attended an array of events, including formal "actions" (aktskii)—events structured to draw attention to particular disability rights issues, especially lack of accessibility of public spaces—parades, exhibitions (such as the Inva-Expo, which highlighted new technological and social means for rehabilitation), and more casual gatherings of people in the disability community. During this early period of the research I was based in Kyiv, the capital city of around 2.6 million persons and the political heart of the country, but I became acquainted with informants from other cities and towns during their travels to Kyiv. Since 1999 when I first met Zoia and Sasha I have examined the work of 26 disability rights NGOs from all over Ukraine. I have followed several of these groups for just a few years, but others, such as Lotus, I have tracked for ten years.

Since this study focuses on a historically oppressed population and has significant policy relevance, I have sought to include members of the Ukrainian disability community in each stage of the project, including research design, the carrying out of surveys and interviews, and presentations of findings. To this end, during summer 2002 I collaborated on an in-depth survey with Oleg and Dmitrii; we each compiled questions based on our own motivations and interests and surveyed 51 disability rights activists who traveled to Kyiv for a disability rights event. Through the surveys we collected socioeconomic data, and asked a range of open-ended questions concerning respondents' definitions and perceptions of disability, social services, "independent living," and rehabilitation. We also explored respondents' subjective experiences of various governmental and nongovernmental services, and we elicited information about their social networks. We have since extended this survey and administered it to a range of NGO leaders and their constituents (84 respondents in total) throughout the country. The sample includes respondents from many cities and smaller towns, including Kyiv, L'viv, Ternopil', Donets'k, Kherson, Uman', Kremenchuh, Svitlovods'k, Poltava, Kryvyi Rih, Dnipropetrovs'k, and others.

Based on data compiled from the initial survey, I then (also in 2002) conducted a roundtable meeting with disability rights activists, social workers, rehabilitation professionals, policymakers, and volunteers. These discussions centered on the tensions between official definitions of and interventions concerning disability, social protection, and rehabilitation, and the subjective experiences of disabled persons. In summer 2003 I spent a month in Kyiv carrying out life history interviews with key figures in the disability rights movement to home in on the most crucial issues for further research.

During four months in spring and summer 2005 and six weeks in fall 2006, I returned to Ukraine to expand the research via further participant observation, taped personal interviews, and video ethnography. In total, I have conducted structured and semi-structured interviews—including 15 life history interviews—in Ukrainian, Russian, and English with approximately 90 people including activists, scholars, policymakers, educators, lawyers, medical professionals, volunteers, and others. Of these, I consider

27 to be key informants. These are people whom I have interviewed repeatedly, or who have provided information of a specific or general nature that one way or another has informed this study in significant ways. Key informants have included mostly mobility-disabled persons with a range of backgrounds (class, region, gender, ethnicity, and age), including some who participate in disability rights advocacy efforts and some who do not. The 15 life histories serve as case studies of the variety of experiences of disability over a lifetime (Frank 2000, Kasnitz 2001), and they are indicative of pivotal facets of disability experience such as medicine and rehabilitation; social services; disability rights activism; education and employment; access to assistive and information technology; issues of family, gender, and sexuality; sports and the arts; and urban and rural disparities. The life history interviews also reveal how disability intersects with class, ethnicity, gender, sexuality, and other identity vectors to produce particular subject positions.

Since 2002, with the assistance of colleagues in Ukraine, I have compiled a large collection of Ukrainian- and Russian-language disability-related literature (government reports, newspaper articles, academic works, popular books) and video material, and have carried out my own photo and video documentation. The internet, electronic mail, and Skype™ have allowed me to keep up with current events in the so-called parallel world of disability in postsocialist Ukraine and to stay in touch with my informants and friends, which has facilitated a good deal of ongoing follow-up research.

This is a multi-site project that includes the perspectives of mobility-disabled persons and their advocates from all over Ukraine, an important consideration in a country characterized by significant regional differences in local economies, available medical and rehabilitation services, the existence or absence of disability rights NGOs, and the attitudes of representatives of local governments. Although the bulk of the initial research was focused on Kyiv, in 2005 and 2006 I expanded the geographical focus considerably by working in cities such as L'viv, Novyi Rozdil, Ternopil', Rivne (all in western Ukraine), Donets'k (in eastern Ukraine) and Evpatoria (in southern Ukraine). Interviews were conducted with informants from other towns and cities, including Mykolayiv, Kryvyi Rih, Uman', Kam'ianets'-Podil's'kyi, Obukhiv, Berdychiv, Svitlovods'k, and Mariupol', among others. During 2006 I traveled to Moscow, Russia, to interview several disability rights activists, including Denise Roza of the NGO Perspektiva and journalist Lev Indolev, and for two weeks in fall 2009 I collected follow-up data in Kyiv and Kharkiv.

In this text I usually use the Library of Congress system of transliteration for Ukrainian and Russian. For purposes of simplification, I transcribe the Ukrainian letter "є" as "ie" and "ї" as "yi" (except in the case of *Ukraina*), and the Russian letter "ё" as "e." In the text and bibliography I refer to published Ukrainian and Russian authors, and public personages and their organizations, according to how they write their names in English. Direct quotes and words or phrases used by informants during interviews and casual speech are transliterated and translated according to the language used by the informant. All translations are my own, except where otherwise noted.

Unless otherwise indicated, photographs are courtesy of the author.

INTRODUCTION

1. To protect their identity, I have assigned most informants pseudonyms. Exceptions include Oleg Poloziuk, a friend and research collaborator, and other informants who are public figures and whose identity would be nearly impossible to conceal. These include Yaroslav Hrybalskyy, Lev Indolev, Oksana Kunanec-Swarnyk, Valery Sushkevych, and Mykola Swarnyk. Similarly, I have assigned pseudonyms to some nongovernmental organizations I describe (e.g., Lotus) but refer to some key organizations and institutions by their real names: Rekryteringsgruppen for Active Rehabilitation (RG) and the National Assembly for Disabled of Ukraine (NADU).

2. For details on changing disability-related terminology in Ukraine, as well as a description of my research methods, see "Notes on Terminology and Methods." For this project I conducted interviews in Russian, Ukrainian, and sometimes English. In the text when a Russian word or phrase is transliterated, I indicate this by the abbreviation "Rus." If no indication is given (as here with invalidnist') the transliterated word or phrase is Ukrainian. When both Ukrainian and Russian variants are given, they are distinguished by the abbreviations "Ukr." and "Rus." For convenience, throughout the text I use the Russian transliteration spinal'nik(i) (spinally injured person[s]), since this term is most often used by Russian speakers.

3. To best capture the texture of the manifesto as a living document, I have sought to render the translation as close as possible to the original. Thus I have included elements such as words that were stricken through and parenthetical questions concerning word choice and other details.

1. A PARALLEL WORLD

1. This is according to the available statistical analyses provided by neurosurgical departments of medical institutions in Ukraine from 1994 to 2001 (Poloziuk 2005b).

2. Oleg Poloziuk, personal communication, 2005.

3. From the National Spinal Cord Injury Statistical Center, http://www.spinal cord.uab.edu/show.asp?durki=119513&site=4716&return=19775 (accessed December 15, 2009).

4. From Sci-Info-Pages, "Spinal Cord Injury Facts & Statistics," http://www .sci-info-pages.com/facts.html (accessed December 15, 2009).

5. In the mid-2000s under the direction of Andrew Hall, the New Zealand Spinal Trust generously granted permission for activists in Ukraine and Russia to translate a handbook produced by the Trust, *Back on Track: A Basic Introduction for Those Learning to Live with a Spinal Cord Injury* (Verkaaik 2004), for a Ukrainian and Russian readership. Lev Indolev (2007) translated the Russian edition, and the Ukrainian edition is in press (Alekseeva, Phillips, and Syedin, 2010). The Russian book is being distributed free of charge to the spinally injured in Russia thanks to the All-Russian Organization of Invalids (VOI). The June Phillips Memorial Mission to Ukraine, an organization I started in 1998, is supporting the costs associated with publishing and distributing the Ukrainian-language edition.

6. In the United States causes of death among persons with spinal injuries increasingly approximate those among their noninjured cohorts of the same age: cancer and cardiovascular disease (Sci-Info-Pages, "Spinal Cord Injury Facts & Statistics"). Whereas previously renal failure was the cause of death that appeared to have the greatest impact on reduced life expectancy for this population, today such causes of death are pneumonia, pulmonary emboli, and septicemia. From the National Spinal Cord Injury Statistical Center website.

7. At the time, 15,000 rubles (the Soviet currency) were roughly equivalent to $15,000. However, due to price fixing the ruble had more real value and thus more purchasing power than the U.S. dollar.

8. In the United States, median hospital and rehabilitation stays for spinal-injured persons have decreased significantly since the 1970s. Between 1973 and 1979 those who entered a Model System immediately following injury were hospitalized in the acute care unit for a median of 24 days. From 2005 to 2008, the median stay in acute care units was 12 days. Median days in rehab units decreased from 98 to 37 days. Average hospital charges for the first year after injury vary widely, from $236,109 for those with incomplete motor function at any level, to $801,101 for those with high cervical injuries (C1–C4). Average subsequent yearly costs are approximated at $16,547 and $143,507 for these two groups, respectively. From the National Spinal Cord Injury Statistical Center website.

9. UNDP (2009:172). This data is from 2007. The GDP per capita in the United States in 2007 was $45,592. "PPP (purchasing power parity) [is] a rate of exchange that accounts for price differences across countries, allowing international comparisons of real output and incomes. At the PPP US$ rate (as used in

this Report), PPP US$1 has the same purchasing power in the domestic economy as US$1 has in the United States" (UNDP 2009:171).

10. UNDP (2009:200). For comparison, I list public expenditures on health as a percentage of total government expenditure in other countries: Germany (17.6 percent), France (16.7 percent), United States (19.1 percent), U.K. (16.5 percent) Canada (17.9 percent) and the Russian Federation (10.8 percent) (UNDP 2009:200–201).

11. UNDP (2009:182). The gender gap in income decreased slightly between 2005 and 2007; men's average salary fell, while women's rose (see UNDP 2007/2008:327). For comparison, in the United States women's income relative to men's in 2007 was 62 percent, in the U.K. it was 67 percent, and in Norway 77 percent (UNDP 2009:186–187).

12. Ukaz Prezydenta Ukrainy (Decree of the President of Ukraine) 900/2005, http://naiu.org.ua/index.php?option=com_content&task=view&id=99&Itemid =87 (accessed December 16, 2009).

13. The Provision on the IPRI and the Method of Formulating the IPRI were adopted in 1992 (Ruling of the Cabinet of Ministers of Ukraine No. 83, February 22, 1992; and No. 16.01/47 January 20, 1992).

14. This information came from Zoia, and this is my translation of her Russian phrase.

15. According to the U.S. Bureau of Labor Statistics, in August 2009 the unemployment rate among the civilian, noninstitutional disabled population in the United States was 16.9 percent. See "Labor Force Statistics from the Current Population Survey," http://www.bls.gov/cps/cpsdisability.htm (accessed December 16, 2009).

16. Extracted from *Vidomosti Verkhovnoi Rady* (News of the Verkhovna Rada) 45:237 (2001), http://naiu.org.ua/index.php?option=com_content&task= view&id=57&Itemid=75 (accessed December 16, 2009).

17. These grant applications were submitted to several international granting agencies, including Counterpart Alliance for Partnership (a civil society program designed to cultivate social partnerships between NGOs and local governments; see Phillips 2008:81–91), the International Renaissance Foundation (part of the Soros Foundations Network), the European Commission, and others.

18. Individuals working for various international development granting agencies in Ukraine never confirmed this culture of kickbacks to me. It seemed to be common knowledge, though, among the NGO activists and scholars I knew who had been through the granting process.

19. According to Oleg Poloziuk, wheelchair users may receive two new chairs every two years if they can "prove that they live an active way of life," but few people know of this possibility. He counsels his fellow spinal'niki to couch such requests in terms of their plans to attend university and seek employment.

20. See www.activeworlds.com (accessed December 16, 2009).

2. OUT OF HISTORY

1. The English translation is Cassandra Hartblay's (2006:22).

2. Article 18 of the Law of the USSR On State Pensions, July 14, 1956.

3. For a similarly insightful analysis of disability in German cultural history, with a particular focus on wartime, see Carol Poore's (2007) remarkable book *Disability in Twentieth-Century German Culture.*

4. Differentiation between invalids in the early Soviet era was also class-based. As noted by Shek (2005:381), in the 1930s disabled "class enemies" (White Army veterans, kulaks [former landowners], former factory owners, tsarist officers, and others) were excluded from programs to educate and provide employment for invalids.

5. Bernice Madison provides case studies of several internaty based on her research in the RSFSR and the Uzbek Republic in the early 1960s (1968:243–250). Although I write about internaty in the past tense here, it must be stressed that the system of internaty for the elderly and disabled is still intact in postsocialist countries. To varying degrees in different countries, strategies for deinstitutionalizing the disabled are being pursued. Such efforts are accelerated somewhat in the new European Union countries such as Bulgaria, Romania, Croatia, and Former Yugoslav Republic of Macedonia, but progress is very slow. For ethnographic studies of present-day internaty in Russia, see Iarskaia-Smirnova and Romanov, eds. (2002).

6. See also Grigorenko (1998), Korkunov et al. (1998), Malofeev (1998), and Thomson (2002).

7. Ruben David Gonzalez Gallego has a fascinating personal history. As he learned only as a teenager, he is the maternal grandson of Ignacio Gallego, the secretary general of the Spanish Communist Party in the 1960s, whose daughter Aurora (Ruben's mother) was sent by her father to Moscow for "re-education." In Moscow, Aurora married a Venezuelan student and gave birth to twins. The other baby died, and Ruben was placed in an internat at his grandfather's request; apparently Aurora was told that both sons had died. Ruben Gallego's reunion with his mother is chronicled in two documentaries, the Italian film "Siluro rosso: La straordinara storia di Rubén Gallego" (Red Torpedo), and the Russian film, "Pis'mo materi" (Letter to Mother).

8. From the biography of Henry Enns on the CCDS website at http://www.disabilitystudies.ca/htm%20files/Henry%20Enns/henrybio.htm (accessed December 16, 2009).

9. See the CCDS home page at http://www.disabilitystudies.ca/ (accessed August 17, 2009).

10. See the Washington Declaration, from the Global Perspectives on Independent Living for the Next Millennium Summit held in Washington, D.C., in September 1999, a document that outlines strategies for promoting the independent living movement in a global context: http://www.ilru.org/html/projects/international/1-declaration.htm (accessed December 16, 2009).

11. *Vidomosti Verkhovnoi Rady* (News of the Verkhovna Rada) 21:253 (1991), http://naiu.org.ua/index.php?option=com_content&task=view&id=21&Itemid =75 (accessed December 16, 2009).

12. See "Mykhailo Papiiev [former Minister of Labor and Social Policy]: Dopomoha povynna buty adresnoiu (Assistance must be targeted)," http://www .mlsp.gov.ua/control/uk/publish/article?art_id=66534&cat_id=34928 (accessed December 16, 2009).

13. See the project description at Canadian Centre on Disability Studies, http://www.education-inclusive.com/en/index.php (accessed December 16, 2009).

14. See Resolution N. 1686 of the Cabinet of Ministers of Ukraine (December 8, 2006), http://naiu.org.ua/content/view/545/85/ (accessed December 16, 2009).

## 3. DISABILITY RIGHTS AND DISABILITY WRONGS

1. For more detailed accounts of civil society building in Ukraine and Eastern Europe since the early 1990s, see Phillips (2008), especially chapter 2, "Ukrainian NGO-graphy," (pp. 63–106). See also Mendelson and Glenn (2002) and Henderson (2003).

2. This information is from a profile of Yaroslav on RG's website, http://www .rekryteringsgruppen.se/ (accessed December 16, 2009).

3. Contrary to these guarantees, the state continues to offer wheelchair users either outdated models like the KIS or wheelchairs of poor quality made in China. Most persons who desire active wheelchairs buy them out-of-pocket. Used foreign-made active wheelchairs cost between $1,000 and $2,500.

4. From a report prepared by sociologists at the V. N. Karazin Kharkiv National University, Analiz potrebnostei zhitelei goroda Khar'kova v sotsial'nykh uslugakh (Analysis of the social service needs of the residents of Khar'kov) (2006:81–82).

5. See http://www.rekryteringsgruppen.se/php/english.php (accessed March 9, 2007).

6. See Ukaz Prezydenta Ukrainy (Decree of the President of Ukraine) 900/2005, http://naiu.org.ua/index.php?option=com_content&task=view&id= 99&Itemid=87 (accessed December 1, 2008).

7. Descriptions of NADU's international activities are found at http://naiu .org.ua/index.php?option=content&task=view&id=244 (accessed August 21, 2009).

## 4. REGENERATION

1. At http://5.ua/newsline/198/40/29840 (accessed September 28, 2009).

2. Another billboard erected as part of the Life is Better without Drugs! campaign was similar in style to the "Mama, why am I a freak?" effort, with text

reading "Mama, why did I die?" The billboard featured a childish sketch of a gravestone. Here I focus on the "Mama, why am I a freak?" billboard, since it is more relevant to my focus on disability. Also, the "freak" billboard produced more social commentary than its "why did I die?" companion.

3. I have examined articles and readers' commentaries on the following two sites: "Apolohiia reklamy," http://pravda.com.ua/news/2006/8/21/46334.htm (*Ukrains'ka Pravda*) and "Sotsial'nuiu reklamu protiv narkomanii demontiruiut," http://korrespondent.net/kyiv/163450 (*Korrespondent*) (accessed December 15, 2009). In the following notes, commentaries from *Ukrains'ka Pravda* are labeled "UP," and those from *Korrespondent* are labeled "K." I numbered the commentaries on both sites from top to bottom—as of December 10, 2008, there were 161 commentaries on UP (therefore, UP1–UP161), and 61 on K (K1–K61). When referring to specific comments in the analysis I give the commentary number and the commentator's handle (nickname).

4. UP44 (UHRA), K35 (1), and K57 (vydra).

5. Exceptions include UP2 (Yamato), UP119 (Vozmushchennaia), and UP150 (wip).

6. K33 (SUN), UP16 and UP75 (nau1), UP113 (olexas), UP119 (Vozmushchennaia), and UP125 (Nana).

7. The grammatical and other mistakes in the billboard generated abundant commentary on the internet sites: UP6 (Honduras_Petrovich), UP146 (Vid'verto), and UP148 (wip). UP154 (artist) noted that although the billboard only included four words, it also included four mistakes.

8. See http://korrespondent.net/kyiv/163450 (accessed September 9, 2009). The journalist used the inclusive terminology in reference to comments made by an NGO leader who protested the billboard.

9. K1 (beaner).

10. K61 (www).

11. K18 (www).

12. K42 (NELS).

13. See http://5.ua/newsline/198/40/29840 (accessed September 28, 2009).

14. See http://www.kommersant.ua/doc.html?docId=703465 (accessed September 9, 2009).

15. Friends in Kyiv shared this unpublished research report with me.

16. According to the journalist Krupina (2002:11), doctors explained this unexpected development thus: "The birth of the baby mobilized the inner resources of her organism, which heretofore were in a 'deep sleep.'" Natasha herself believed that "God returned her health as a reward for protecting the life of [her daughter] Svetlanka" (i.e., she refused the abortion her doctors and caregivers had advocated).

17. *Blahovist* is published jointly by the SOIU and the L'viv Oblast' Association of Invalids, and does not appear to be affiliated officially with any church or religious group. However, religious subjects are frequently covered in the paper,

and the official logo contains the phrase "Be charitable, as your Father is charitable." *Povir u Sebe* ceased operations in 2006 with the death of its charismatic editor-in-chief, Borys Mashtaliarchuk.

18. Mandry is a pseudonym. The word comes from the Ukrainian verb *mandruvaty*, to travel or to voyage, and Mandry is also the name of a popular Ukrainian band. The colloquial nature of the expression, and its loose meaning "to get around" or "to wander about," fit Dmitrii's NGO well.

19. Solomko's Regeneration series may be viewed at http://www.guelman .kiev.ua/rus/people/solomko/3e26d864511c5/ (accessed September 9, 2009).

20. Electronic mail, in English, received from Yuri Solomko, October 1, 2009.

21. Solomko's Live Planet photographs may be viewed at http://www.guelman .kiev.ua/rus/people/solomko/3e26e9fd92d39/ (accessed September 9, 2009).

22. See the description of the Regeneration project on the Guelman Gallery website: http://www.guelman.kiev.ua/rus/gallery/galleryprojects/regeneration/ (accessed September 9, 2009).

23. See http://en.wikipedia.org/wiki/Attraction_to_disability (accessed September 9, 2009).

24. See http://www.guelman.kiev.ua/rus/gallery/galleryprojects/regeneration/ (accessed September 9, 2009).

25. See http://www.guelman.kiev.ua/rus/gallery/galleryprojects/regeneration/ (accessed September 9, 2009).

## 5. DISABILITY, GENDER, AND SEXUALITY IN THE ERA OF "POSTS"

1. See Shuttleworth (2004) on men with cerebral palsy in the United States; Sparkes and Smith (1999, 2002) and Smith and Sparkes (2004) on men who experienced spinal injuries playing rugby in the U.K.; and Iarskaia-Smirnova (2001, 2002a, 2002b) for discussions of the experiences of disabled men in Russia.

2. See the program's website at http://naiu.org.ua/index.php?option=content &task=view&id=235 (accessed December 15, 2009).

3. From an interview with V'iacheslav Kyrylenko, Ukraine's former Minister of Labor and Social Policy, published in "Novi vidpovidi na stari pytannia" (New answers to old questions), *Sotsial'ne Partnerstvo* 3(4):5.

4. Indolev's chapter includes the most comprehensive explanation of love, family, and sex after spinal cord injury I have found in the region. Written for persons with spinal injuries themselves, the book approaches issues of sexuality (for men and women) from many different angles. Indolev includes passages from letters he has received from wheelchair users all over the former USSR, including Ukraine, and he offers valuable advice on subjects ranging from erogenous zones and types of erections and orgasms to personal hygiene, planning pregnancies, and fighting legal battles for adoption or keeping one's children.

My informants especially appreciated the frankness and sense of humor with which Indolev (himself spinally injured) presents the issues. Indolev's book *Zhit' v koliaske* is available online at http://indolev.enabled.ru/index.php?id=book (accessed December 15, 2009).

5. Information from the Oriflame website, http://www.oriflame.com/About _Oriflame/About-Oriflame/ (accessed December 15, 2009).

6. From the Oriflame Ukraine website, http://www.oriflame.ua (accessed December 15, 2009).

7. From http://www.oriflame.com/About_Oriflame/Our-Vision-and-Core -Values/ (accessed December 15, 2009).

8. Caritas Internationalis is an international umbrella charitable organization rooted in the Catholic Church.

CONCLUSION

1. Decree No. 1228, December 18, 2007, On Additional Immediate Measures for the Creation of Favorable Living Conditions for Persons with Limited Physical Capabilities. Available at http://naiu.org.ua/content/view/1343/87/ (accessed December 15, 2009).

Aleksandrova, Alina. 2005. Naidorozhcha nahoroda—Syn (The most precious honor—a son). *Sotsial'ne partnerstvo* 1–2(2–3):50–52.

Alekseeva, Olga, Sarah D. Phillips, and Myhailo Syedin, eds. 2010. *Znovu v dorohu* (Back on track: A handbook for those learning to live with a spinal cord injury). Kyiv: Ros'.

Alpatova, Polina, and Tetiana Zub. 2006. Liudyna z obmezhenymy fizychnymy mozhlyvostiamy v mis'komu seredovyshchi (A person with limited physical capabilities in the city setting). *Ukrayins'kyi sotsium* 1(12):7–16.

Alter, Sutia Kim. 2002. Case Studies in Social Enterprise: Counterpart International's Experience. Washington, D.C.: Counterpart International, Inc. http://www.virtueventures.com/files/cicases.pdf (accessed December 24, 2004).

*Analiz potrebnostei zhitelei goroda Khar'kova v sotsial'nykh uslugakh* (Analysis of the social service needs of the residents of Khar'kov). 2006. V. N. Karazin Kharkiv National University, Kharkiv, Ukraine.

Arzinger and Partners Ukraine. 2008. Newsletter No. 12, February 7, 2008. http://www.chamber.ua/files/documents/updoc/tax_legal/57/newsletter_january_eng_20080208.pdf (accessed April 3, 2009).

Bach, Jonathan, and David Stark. 2005. Recombinant Technology and New Geographies of Association. In *Digital Formations: IT and New Architectures in the Global Realm,* ed. Robert Latham and Saskia Sassen, 37–53. Princeton, N.J.: Princeton University Press.

Baranova-Mokhort, Serhiy. 2005. I znova pro nabolile—pratsevlashtuvannia invalidiv (Again about the most painful issue—protection of invalids' rights). *Svoia Hazeta* 03(019):6.

Barnes, Colin. 1991. *Disabled People in Britain and Discrimination: A Case for Anti-Discrimination Legislation.* London: Hurst and Co.

Bidenko, Artem. 2006. Apolohiia reklamy (Eulogy for an advertisement). *Ukrayins'ka Pravda* (online), August 21, 2006. http://pravda.com.ua/news/2006/8/21/46334.htm (accessed September 9, 2009).

———. 2008. Sotsial'na reklama poza zonoiu dosiahnennia (Social advertisement beyond reach). *Ukrayins'ka Pravda* (online), August 4, 2008. http://life.pravda .com.ua/problem/4896f9f8d35b2/ (accessed September 9, 2009).

Biehl, João. 2005. *Vita: Life in a Zone of Social Abandonment.* Berkeley: University of California Press.

Blitt, Robert C. 2008. Babushka Said Two Things: It Will Either Rain or Snow; It Either Will or Will Not: An Analysis of the Provisions and Human Rights Implications of Russia's New Law on Nongovernmental Organizations as Told Through Eleven Russian Proverbs. *George Washington International Law Review* 40(1):1–86.

Bodnia, Tat'iana. 2000. Nazvali dom spetsinternatom i zapretili invalidam privatizi-rovat' kvartivy (They called the building a spetsinternat and forbade invalids to privatize apartments). *Vechernie Vesti* 022(307):6.

Boellstorff, Tom. 2008. *Coming of Age in Second Life: An Anthropologist Explores the Virtually Human.* Princeton, N.J.: Princeton University Press.

Bondarenko, Halyna. 2005. Personal communication. Information received via electronic mail September 1, 2005.

Bridger, Sue, Rebecca Kay, and Kathryn Pinnick. 1996. *No More Heroines? Russia, Women and the Market.* London: Routledge.

Brokhin, Yuri. 1977. *The Big Red Machine: The Rise and Fall of Soviet Olympic Champions.* Trans. Glenn Garelik and Yuri Brokhin. New York: Random House.

Brown, Julie V. 1989. Societal Responses to Mental Disorders in Prerevolutionary Russia. In *People with Disabilities in the Soviet Union,* ed. William O. McCagg and Lewis Siegelbaum, 13–37. Pittsburgh, Pa.: University of Pittsburgh Press.

Brown, Wendy. 1992. Finding the Man in the State. *Feminist Studies* 8(1):7–34.

Brownell, Susan. 1995. *Training the Body for China: Sports in the Moral Order of the People's Republic.* Chicago: University of Chicago Press.

Bruun, Frank Jarle. 1995. Hero, Beggar, or Sports Star: Negotiating the Identity of the Disabled Persons in Nicaragua. In *Disability and Culture,* ed. Benedicte Ingstad and Susan Reynolds Whyte, 196–209. Berkeley: University of California Press.

Burch, Susan. 2000. Transcending Revolutions: The Tsars, the Soviets, and Deaf Culture. *Journal of Social History* 34(2):393–401.

Burdyk, Ekaterina. 1998. Kogda idti bol'she nekuda . . . Problemy obezdolennykh: Nashi ili chuzhie? (When there is nowhere else to go . . . The problem of the unfortunate: Ours or someone else's?) *Zdorov'e Ukrainy* 2:27.

Charlton, James I. 1998. *Nothing About Us Without Us: Disability Oppression and Empowerment.* Berkeley: University of California Press.

Chernets, Vadim. 2004. L. M. Chernovets'kyi: Blagodaria Bogy . . . (L. M. Cher-novets'kyi: Thanks to God . . .) *Posol* 1:6–7.

Chernova, Zhanna. 2002. Normativnaia muzhskaia seksual'nost': (Re)presentatsii v mediadiskurse (Normative male sexuality: (Re)presentation in media dis-course). In *V poiskakh seksual'nosti,* ed. Zdravomyslova and Temkina, 527–545.

Chesnokova, Ol'ga. 2003. Transformatsiia tela bez nog (Transformation of a body without legs). *Kievskie vedomosti* 18(2823), January 29, 2003.

Clements, Barbara Evans, Rebecca Friedman, and Dan Healey, eds. 2002. *Russian Masculinities in History and Culture.* Houndmills, U.K..: Palgrave.

Corker, Mairian, and Tom Shakespeare, eds. 2002. *Disability/Postmodernity: Embodying Disability Theory.* London and New York: Continuum.

Cornell, Drucilla. 1995. *The Imaginary Domain: Abortion, Pornography, and Sexual Harassment.* New York and London: Routledge.

Davis, Lennard J. 1995. *Enforcing Normalcy: Disability, Deafness and the Body.* London: Verso.

———. 1997. Nude Venuses, Medusa's Body, and Phantom Limbs: Disability and Visuality. In *The Body and Physical Difference: Discourses of Disability,* ed. David T. Mitchell and Sharon L. Snyder, 51–70. Ann Arbor: University of Michigan Press.

Davis-Floyd, Robbie, and Carolyn Sargent, eds. 1997. *Childbirth and Authoritative Knowledge: Cross-Cultural Perspectives.* Berkeley: University of California Press.

DeJong, Gerben. 1979. Independent Living: From Social Movement to Analytic Paradigm. *Archives of Physical and Medical Rehabilitation* 60:435–446.

Derzhavna Dopovid (State Report). 2002. *Pro stanovyshche invalidiv v Ukraini ta osnovy derzhavnoi polityky shchodo vyrishennia problem hromadian z osoblyvymy potrebamy.* (On the situation of invalids in Ukraine and the basis of state politics for addressing the problems of citizens with special needs.) Kyiv: Sotsinform.

Dunham, Vera S. 1989. Images of the Disabled, Especially the War Wounded, in Soviet Literature. In *People with Disabilities in the Soviet Union,* ed. William O. McCagg and Lewis Siegelbaum, 151–164. Pittsburgh, Pa.: University of Pittsburgh Press.

Dunn, Elizabeth C. 2004. *Privatizing Poland: Baby Food, Big Business, and the Remaking of Labor.* Ithaca, N.Y.: Cornell University Press.

———. 2005. Standards and Person-Making in East Central Europe. In *Global Assemblages: Technology, Politics, and Ethics as Anthropological Problems,* ed. Aihwa Ong and Stephen J. Collier, 173–193. Malden, Mass.: Blackwell.

———. 2008. Postsocialist Spores: Disease, Bodies and the State in the Republic of Georgia. *American Ethnologist* 35(2):243–258.

Dunn, Ethel. 2000. The Disabled in Russia in the 1990s. In *Russia's Torn Safety Nets: Health and Social Welfare during the Transition,* ed. Mark G. Field and Judyth L. Twigg, 153–171. New York: St. Martin's Press.

Dunn, Stephen P., and Ethel Dunn. 1989. Everyday Life of People with Disabilities in the USSR. In *People with Disabilities in the Soviet Union,* ed. William O. McCagg and Lewis Siegelbaum, 199–234. Pittsburgh, Pa.: University of Pittsburgh Press.

Edele, Mark. 2008. *Soviet Veterans of the Second World War: A Popular Movement in an Authoritarian Society 1941–1991.* Oxford: Oxford University Press.

Einhorn, Barbara. 1993. *Cinderella Goes to Market: Citizenship, Gender and Women's Movements in East Central Europe*. London: Verso.

Escobar, Arturo. 1994. *Encountering Development: The Making and Unmaking of the Third World*. Princeton, N.J.: Princeton University Press.

Evseev, Sergei. 1999. Chinovnikov nuzhno lechit' ot dushevnoi nedostatochnosti (Bureaucrats should be treated for shortcomings of the soul). *Den'* 30(567):8.

Farrell, Janet. 1999. *Ukraine! "What on Earth am I Doing Here?" A Canadian Consultant's Adventure in Ukraine*. Burlington, Ontario: Janet M. Farrell & Associates.

Featherstone, Mike. 2004. Automobilities: An Introduction. *Theory, Culture and Society* 21 (4/5):1–24.

Fefelov, Valerii. 1986. *V SSSR invalidov net!* (There are no invalids in the USSR!) London: Overseas Publications Interchange Ltd.

Ferguson, James. 1994. *The Anti-Politics Machine: "Development," Depoliticization, and Bureaucratic Power in Lesotho*. Minneapolis: University of Minnesota Press.

Fesenko, Liliana. 2008. Lishivshis' nog, kievlianka prepodaet tantsy v sobstvennoi baletnoi shkole (Having lost her legs, a Kyiv woman teaches dance in her own ballet school). *Komsomol'skaia Pravda v Ukraine* (online), February 19, 2008. http://kp.ua/daily/190208/35116/ (accessed September 9, 2009).

Fieseler, Beate. 2005. "Nishchie pobediteli": Invalidy Velikoi Otechestvennoi Voiny v Sovetskom Soiuze ("Suffering Victors": Invalids of the Great Patriotic War in the Soviet Union). *Neprikosnovennyi zapas* 40–41(2–3). http://magazines.russ.ru/nz/2005/2/fi33.html (accessed September 9, 2009).

———. 2006. The Bitter Legacy of the "Great Patriotic War": Red Army Disabled Soldiers under Late Stalinism. In *Late Stalinist Russia: Society between Reconstruction and Reinvention*, ed. Juliane Furst, 46–61. London and New York: Routledge.

Fine, Michelle, and Adrienne Asch. 1985. Disabled Women: Sexism without the Pedestal. In *Women and Disability: The Double Handicap*, ed. Mary Jo Deegan and Nancy Brooks. New Brunswick, N.J.: Transaction Books.

Finger, Anne. 1990. *Past Due: A Story of Disability, Pregnancy, and Birth*. Seattle: Seal Press.

Foucault, Michel. 1963. *Madness and Civilization: A History of Insanity in the Age of Reason*. New York: Random House.

———. 1977. *Discipline and Punish: The Birth of the Prison*. New York: Vintage Books.

———. 2008. *The Birth of Biopolitics: Lectures at the College de France 1978–1979*. Houndmills, U.K.: Palgrave Macmillan.

Frank, Gelya. 2000. *Venus on Wheels: Two Decades of Dialogue on Disability, Biography, and Being Female in America*. Berkeley: University of California Press.

Fraser, Nancy. 1989. *Unruly Practices: Power, Discourse, and Gender in Contemporary Social Theory*. Minneapolis: University of Minnesota Press.

———. 1997. *Justice Interruptus: Critical Reflections on the "Postsocialist" Condition*. New York and London: Routledge.

Friedman, Rebecca, and Dan Healey. 2002. Conclusions. In *Russian Masculinities,* ed. Barbara Evans Clements, Rebecca Friedman, and Dan Healey, 223–235. Houndmills, U.K.: Palgrave.

Gal, Susan, and Gail Kligman. 2000a. *The Politics of Gender after Socialism.* Princeton, N.J.: Princeton University Press.

———, eds. 2000b. *Reproducing Gender: Politics, Publics, and Everyday Life after Socialism.* Princeton, N.J.: Princeton University Press.

Gallego, Ruben. 2006. *White on Black.* Trans. Marian Schwartz. Orlando, Fla.: Harcourt.

Gardner, Katy, and David Lewis. 1996. *Anthropology, Development and the Postmodern Challenge.* London and Sterling, Va.: Pluto Press.

Garland-Thomson, Rosemarie. 2001. Seeing the Disabled: Visual Rhetorics of Disability in Popular Photography. In *The New Disability History,* ed. Paul K. Longmore and Lauri Umansky, 335–374.

———. 2004. Integrating Disability, Transforming Feminist Theory. In *Gendering Disability,* ed. Bonnie G. Smith and Beth Hutchinson, 73–103.

———. 2009. *Staring: How We Look.* Oxford: Oxford University Press.

Gerschick, Thomas J. 2000. Toward a Theory of Disability and Gender. *Signs* 25(4):1263–1268.

Gerschick, Thomas J., and Adam Stephen Miller. 1997. Gender Identities at the Crossroads of Masculinity and Physical Disability. In *Toward a New Psychology of Gender: A Reader,* ed. Mary M. Gergen and Sara N. Davis, 455–475. New York and London: Routledge.

Ghodsee, Kristen. 2007. Potions, Lotions and Lipstick: The Gendered Consumption of Cosmetics and Perfumery in Socialist and Post-Socialist Urban Bulgaria. *Women's Studies International Forum* 30(1):26–39.

Gilmour, Julie, and Barbara Evans Clements. 2002. "If You Want to Be Like Me, Train!": The Contradictions of Soviet Masculinity. In *Russian Masculinities,* ed. Barbara Evans Clements, Rebecca Friedman, and Dan Healey, 210–222. Houndmills, U.K.: Palgrave.

Girman, Alla. 2006. Osoblyvosti politychnoi uchasti osib z funktsional'nymy obmezhenniamy u suchasnomu politychnomu protsesi v Ukraini (Characteristics of the political participation of persons with functional limitations in the contemporary political process in Ukraine. [Summary of dissertation submitted for candidate's degree in political science at Dnipropetrovs'k National University.])

Goffman, Erving. 1963. *Stigma: Notes on the Management of Spoiled Identity.* New York: Simon and Schuster.

Goscilo, Helena. 1995. New Members and Organs: The Politics of Porn. In *Postcommunism and the Body Politic,* ed. Ellen E. Berry, 164–194. New York: New York University Press.

Grigorenko, Elena L. 1998. Russian "Defectology": Anticipating *Perestroika* in the Field. *Journal of Learning Disabilities* 31(2):193–207.

Gudkov, Lev. 2005. The Fetters of Victory: How the War Provides Russia with Its Identity. *Neprikosnovennyi zapas* 40–41(2–3). http://www.eurozine.com/ pdf/2005-05-03-gudkov-en.pdf (accessed September 9, 2009).

Haney, Lynne. 2002. *Inventing the Needy: Gender and the Politics of Welfare in Hungary.* Berkeley: University of California Press.

———. 2003. Welfare Reform with a Familial Face: Reconstituting State and Domestic Relations in Post-Socialist Eastern Europe. In *Families of a New World: Gender, Politics, and State Development in a Global Context,* ed. Lynne Haney and Lisa Pollard, 159–178. New York: Routledge.

Haney, Lynne, and Lisa Pollard. 2003. Introduction: In a Family Way: Theorizing State and Familial Relations. In *Families of a New World,* ed. Lynne Haney and Lisa Pollard, 1–14.

Hartblay, Cassandra. 2006. An Absolutely Different Life: Locating Disability, Motherhood, and Local Power in Rural Siberia. Honors Thesis, Macalester College. http://digitalcommons.macalester.edu/cgi/viewcontent.cgi?article =1000&context=anth_honors (accessed September 9, 2009).

Henderson, Sarah L. 2003. *Building Democracy in Contemporary Russia: Western Support for Grassroots Organizations.* Ithaca, N.Y.: Cornell University Press.

Herzfeld, Michael. 1992. *The Social Production of Indifference: Exploring the Symbolic Roots of Western Bureaucracy.* New York: Berg.

Hevey, David. 1997. The Enfreakment of Photography. In *The Disability Studies Reader,* ed. Lennard J. Davis, 332–347. New York and London: Routledge.

Hillyer, Barbara. 1993. *Feminism and Disability.* Norman: University of Oklahoma Press.

Höjdestrand, Tova. 2009. *Needed by Nobody: Homelessness and Humanness in Post-Socialist Russia.* Ithaca, N.Y.: Cornell University Press.

Hrycak, Alexandra. 2005. Coping with Chaos: Gender and Politics in a Fragmented State. *Problems of Post-Communism* 52(5):69–81.

———. 2006. Foundation Feminism and the Articulation of Hybrid Feminisms in Post-Socialist Ukraine. *East European Politics and Societies* 20(1):69–100.

Humphrey, Caroline. 2002. *The Unmaking of Soviet Life: Everyday Economies after Socialism.* Ithaca, N.Y.: Cornell University Press.

Iangulova, Liia. 2001. Iurodivye i umalishennye: genealogiia inkartseratsii v Rossii (Holy fools and lunatics: A genealogy of incarceration in Russia). In *Mishel' Fuko i Rossiia: Sbornik statei* (Michel Foucault and Russia: A collection of articles), ed. Oleg Kharkhordin, 192–211. St. Petersburg: European University in St. Petersburg; Letnyi Sad.

Iarskaia-Smirnova, Elena. 2001. Social Change and Self-Empowerment: Stories of Disabled People in Russia. In *Disability and the Life Course,* ed. Mark Priestley, 101–112.

———. 2002a. Muzhestvo invalidnosti (Disabled masculinity). In *O muzhe(n)stvennosti,* ed. Serge Alex Oushakine, 106–125.

———. 2002b. Stigma "invalidnoi" seksual'nosti (The stigma of "disabled" sexuality). In *V poiskakh seksual'nosti*, ed. Elena Zdravomyslova and Anna Temkina, 223–244.

Iarskaia-Smirnova, Elena, and Pavel Romanov. 2007. Perspectives of inclusive education in Russia. *European Journal of Social Work* 10(1):89–105.

———. 2009. Geroi i tuneiadtsy: ikonografiia invalidnosti v sovetskom vizual'nom diskurse (Heroes and spongers: Iconography of disability in Soviet visual discourse). In *Vizual'naia antropologia: rezhimy vidimosti pri sotsializme* (Visual anthropology: regimes of recognition under socialism), ed. Elena Iarskaia-Smirnova and Pavel Romanov, 289–331. Moscow: Variant, TsSPGI.

———, eds. 2002. *Sotsial'naia politika i sotsial'naia rabota v izmeniaiushcheisia Rossii* (Social politics and social work in a changing Russia). Moscow: INION RAN.

Indolev, Lev. 1998. *Kak eto bylo: Ocherki istorii invalidnogo dvizheniia v Rossii i sozdaniia VOI* (How it was: Notes from the history of the invalids' movement in Russia and the founding of the All-Russian Organization of Invalids.) Moscow: VOI.

———. 2001. *Zhit' v koliaske* (To live in a wheelchair.) Moscow: Soprichasnost'. Available online at http://indolev.enabled.ru/index.php?id=book (accessed October 4, 2009).

———, ed. and trans. 2007. *Snova v dorogu: Samye pervye svedeniia dlia tekh, kto uchitsia zhit' posle travmy spinnogo mozga* (On the road again: Critical information for those learning to live with a spinal cord injury). Moscow: VOI.

Ingstad, Benedicte, and Susan Reynolds Whyte. 2007. Introduction: Disability Connections. In *Disability in Local and Global Worlds,* ed. Benedicte Ingstad and Susan Reynolds Whyte, 1–32. Berkeley: University of California Press.

Ipatov, A. V., O. V. Serhiieni, T. H. Voitchak, O. A. Dniprova, and T. V. Anan'ieva. 2005. Poriadok vstanovlenniia invalidnosti v Ukraini (Procedures for establishing disability in Ukraine). *Sotsial'ne partnerstvo* 4(5):18–21.

Johnson, Janet, and Jean Robinson, eds. 2007. *Living Gender after Communism.* Bloomington: Indiana University Press.

Jordan, Brigitte. 2009. Blurring Boundaries: The "Real" and the "Virtual" in Hybrid Spaces. *Human Organization* 68(2):181–193.

Kaganovsky, Lilya. 2008. *How the Soviet Man Was Unmade: Cultural Fantasy and Male Subjectivity under Stalin.* Pittsburgh: University of Pittsburgh Press.

Kasnitz, Devva. 2001. Life Event Histories and the US Independent Living Movement. In *Disability and the Life Course,* ed. Mark Priestley, 67–78.

———. 2008. Commentary: Collaborations from Anthropology, Occupational Therapy and Disability Studies. *Practicing Anthropology* 30(3):28–31.

Kaufman, Michael. 1994. Men, Feminism, and Men's Contradictory Experiences of Power. In *Theorizing Masculinities,* ed. Harry Brod and Michael Kaufman, 142–163. Thousand Oaks, Calif.: Sage.

Kharkhordin, Igor. 1999. *The Collective and the Individual in Russia.* Berkeley: University of California Press.

Khomenko, Iryna. 2003. Disability Community Capacity Increases through the

Reforming Social Services Canada-Ukraine Project. *Canadian Centre on Disability Studies (CCDS) Bulletin* 7(4):2–3.

Kikkas, Kaido. 2001. Lifting the Iron Curtain. In *Disability and the Life Course*, ed. Mark Priestley, 113–122.

Kimmel, Michael S. 1994. Consuming Manhood: The Feminization of American Culture and the Recreation of the Male Body, 1832–1920. In *The Male Body: Features, Destinies, Exposures*, ed. Laurence Goldstein, 13–41. Ann Arbor: University of Michigan Press.

Kis, Oksana. 2007. "Beauty Will Save the World!" Feminine Strategies in Ukrainian Politics and the Case of Yulia Tymoshenko. http://www.yorku.ca/soi/_Vol_7_2/_HTML/Kis.html (accessed September 9, 2009).

Koch, Erin. 2007. Recrafting Georgian Medicine: The Politics of Standardization and Tuberculosis Control in Postsocialist Georgia. In *Caucasus Paradigms: Anthropologies, Histories and the Making of a World Area*, ed. Bruce Grant and Lale Yalçin-Heckmann, 247–271. Berlin: LIT Verlag.

Kohrman, Matthew. 2005. *Bodies of Difference: Experiences of Disability and Institutional Advocacy in the Making of Modern China*. Berkeley: University of California Press.

Kon, Igor S. 1995. *The Sexual Revolution in Russia*. Trans. James Riordan. New York: Free Press.

Konovalov, Alexander, Vladimir V. Yartsev, and Leonid B. Likhterman. 1997. The Burdenko Neurosurgery Institute: Past, Present, Future. *Neurosurgery* 40(1):178–185.

Korkunov, Vladimir V., Alexander S. Nigayev, Lynne E. Reynolds, and Janet W. Lerner. 1998. Special Education in Russia: History, Reality, and Prospects. *Journal of Learning Disabilities* 31(2):186–192.

Kovalenko, Halyna. 2005. Divchyna, iaka tantsiuie uvi sni (The girl who dances in her sleep). *Sotsial'ne partnerstvo* 1–2(2–3):54–55.

Koval'skaia, Anna. 2004. The Price of Choice. www.temnik.com.ua (accessed December 26, 2004). Internet site no longer operative. Article reproduced on the Ukraine List, Vol. 327, December 27, 2004.

Krasikova, Elena. 1998. Nosiat na rukakh. Tak ved' est' za shto! (They carry her. She deserves it!) *Segodnia* No. 215, November 4, 1998.

Krayzh, Irina, and Elena Shyngaryova. 2002. Psychological Analysis of Social Stereotype of "Invalid." *Vestnik khar'kovskogo universiteta* 550:149–154.

Krupina, Larisa. 2002. Uslyshav krik dochki, Natasha, u kotoroi s detstva ne deistvovali ruki, vykhvatila malyshku iz krovatki (Hearing her daughter's cry, Natasha, whose arms had not functioned since childhood, grabbed the baby from the crib). *Fakty i kommentarii* 119(1181):11, 30.

———. 2003. Prochitav v gazete o Lene Chinke, lishivsheisia obeikh nog, no prodolzhavshei tantsevat', moskovskii biznesmen tselyi den' gnal mashinu iz Moskvy v Kiev, shtoby potselovat' devushke ruku (Having read in the newspaper about Lena Chinka, who lost her legs but continues to dance, a Moscow businessman drove all day from Moscow to Kyiv to kiss her hand). *Fakty i komentarii* 2512, December 25, 2003. http://www.facts.kiev.ua/Dec2003/2512/05 .htm (accessed September 24, 2009).

Krylova, Anna. 2001. "Healers of Wounded Souls": The Crisis of Private Life in Soviet Literature, 1944–1946. *The Journal of Modern History* 73:307–331.

Kudriashov, Leonid. 2002. Zhurnalisty-invalidy: Ostannia z menshyn chi povnopravni uchasnyky informatsiinogo protsesu? (Disabled journalists: The last of the minorities or full participants in the information process?) *Povir u sebe* 21–22(189–190):2.

Kunanec-Swarnyk, Oksana. 2005. Sotsial'ni i politychni aspekty nepovnospravnosti v Ukraini (Social and political aspects of disability in Ukraine). Paper presented at the Sixth Congress of the International Association of Ukrainian Studies, Donets'k, Ukraine, June 29–July 1, 2005.

Kurchina, Ol'ga. 1998. Dezertiry semeinogo fronta: Pochemu chashche vsego imi stanoviatsia muzhchiny? (Deserters of the family front: Why are they usually men?) *Fakty i kommentarii* 98(0178):8.

Lampland, Martha, and Susan Leigh Star, eds. 2009. *Standards and Their Stories: How Quantifying, Classifying, and Formalizing Practices Shape Everyday Life.* Ithaca, N.Y.: Cornell University Press.

Landsman, Gail Heidi. 2009. *Reconstructing Motherhood and Disability in the Age of "Perfect" Babies.* New York and London: Routledge.

Ledeneva, Alena V. 1998. *Russia's Economy of Favours:* Blat, *Networking and Informal Exchange.* Cambridge: Cambridge University Press.

Lewis, David, and Tina Wallace, eds. 2000. *New Roles and Relevance: Development NGOs and the Challenge of Change.* Bloomfield, Conn.: Kumarian Press.

Lindenmeyr, Adele. 1996. *Poverty is Not a Vice: Charity, Society, and the State in Imperial Russia.* Princeton, N.J.: Princeton University Press.

Linton, Simi. 2006. *My Body Politic: A Memoir.* Ann Arbor: University of Michigan Press.

Litskevich, Ol'ga. 2006. Kto pugaet Kievlian urodami? (Who is scaring Kyivans with freaks?) *Segodnia* 182(2423):1–2. http://archive.segodnya.ua/pdf/0806/060815 _SEG_KIE_01.pdf (p. 1) and http://archive.segodnya.ua/pdf/0806/060815_SEG _KIE_02.pdf (p. 2) (accessed September 9, 2009).

Lock, Margaret. 2002. *Twice Dead: Organ Transplants and the Reinvention of Death.* Berkeley: University of California Press.

Longmore, Paul K. 1995. The Second Phase: From Disability Rights to Disability Culture. *Disability Rag and Resource Sept./Oct. 1995.* http://www.independent living.org/docs3/longm95.html (accessed September 5, 2009).

Longmore, Paul K., and Lauri Umansky, eds. 2001. *The New Disability History: American Perspectives.* New York: New York University Press.

Lur'e, L. Ia. 1996. Zhizn' i sochineniia Ivana Pryzhova (The life and work of Ivan Pryzhov). In Pryzhov, *26 Moskovskikh prorokov,* 3–10.

MacKinnon, Catharine A. 1989. *Toward a Feminist Theory of the State.* Cambridge, Mass.: Harvard University Press.

Madison, Bernice Q. 1968. *Social Welfare in the Soviet Union*. Stanford, Calif.: Stanford University Press.

———. 1989. Programs for People with Disabilities in the USSR. In *People with Disabilities in the Soviet Union*, ed.William O. McCagg and Lewis Siegelbaum, 167–198. Pittsburgh, Pa.: University of Pittsburgh Press.

Makara, Peter. 1994. Policy Implications of Differential Health Status in Eastern and Western Europe: The Case of Hungary. *Social Science and Medicine* 39(9):1295–1301.

Malimon, Natal'ia. 2002. Malen'kie liudi s bol'shoi dushoi (Little people with a big soul). *Den'* 123(1384):22.

Malinovskaia, Tamara. 2002. Geroinia publikatsii "Faktov" 37-letniaia Nina Gordii, kotoruiu roditeli 20 let derzhali v khlevu vmeste s kurami, svin'iami i sobakami, uzhe polgoda zhivet v dome-internate, gde nashla sebe podrugu (The heroine of an article in "Facts," 37-year-old Nina Gordii, whose parents kept her for 20 years in a pen with chickens, pigs, and dogs, has lived in a home-internat for the past half a year, where she found herself a friend). *Fakty i kommentarii* 124(1186):24.

Malofeev, Nikolai N. 1998. Special Education in Russia: Historical Aspects. *Journal of Learning Disabilities* 31(2):181–185.

Marunych, V., A. Ipatov, O. Serhiieni, and T. Voitchak. 2004. Pliusy ta minusy indyvidual'nykh prohram reabilitatsiyi invalidiv (Pluses and minuses of individual programs of rehabilitation of invalids). *Sotsial'ne partnerstvo* 1(1):22–23.

Matza, Tomas. 2009. Moscow's Echo: Technologies of the Self, Publics, and Politics on the Russian Talk Show. *Cultural Anthropology* 24(3):489–522.

McCagg, William O. 1989. The Origins of Defectology. In *People with Disabilities in the Soviet Union*, ed. William O. McCagg and Lewis Siegelbaum, 39–61. Pittsburgh, Pa.: University of Pittsburgh Press.

McCagg, William O., and Lewis Siegelbaum, eds. 1989. *People with Disabilities in the Soviet Union: Past and Present, Theory and Practice*. Pittsburgh, Pa.: University of Pittsburgh Press.

Mendelson, Sarah, and John Glenn, eds. 2002. *The Power and Limits of NGOs: A Critical Look at Building Democracy in Eastern Europe and Eurasia*. New York: Columbia University Press.

Miller, Ruth A. 2007. *The Limits of Bodily Integrity: Abortion, Adultery and Rape Legislation in Comparative Perspective*. Aldershot, U.K.: Ashgate.

Ministry of Labor and Social Policy of Ukraine (MLSP). 2008. *Pro stanovyshche invalidiv v Ukrayini: Natsional'na dopovid'* (On the situation of invalids in Ukraine: National report). Kyiv: Ministry of Labor and Social Policy of Ukraine.

Mintz, Susannah B. 2007. *Unruly Bodies: Life Writing of Women with Disabilities*. Chapel Hill: University of North Carolina Press.

Miroiu, Mihaela. 2004. State Men, Market Women: The Effects of Left Conservatism on Gender Politics in Romanian Transition. Address at Indiana University, Bloomington, January 23, 2004.

Myloserdia. 2003. Television program produced for the National Television

Company of Ukraine by Magnolia-TV. Author: Iryna Voronina, Executive Producer: Ievheniia Tkachenko.

Naulko, V. I. 1993. *Kul'tura i pobut naselennia ukrayiny* (Culture and traditions of the peoples of Ukraine). Kyiv: Lybid'.

Nikonova, Larisa. 2006. Koliasochniki zashchishchaiut sebia sami (Wheelchair users defend themselves). *Argumenty i fakty: Zdorov'e* 29(621):11.

Novi vidpovidi na stari pytannia (New answers to old questions). 2005. *Sotsial'ne partnerstvo* 3(4):4–5.

Oe, Kenzaburo. 1995. *A Healing Family*, ed. S. Shaw and trans. Stephen Snyder. Tokyo: Kodansha International.

Ong, Aihwa. 2006. Mutations in Citizenship. *Theory, Culture and Society* 23(2–3):499–531.

Oushakine, Serguei, ed. 2002. *O muzhe(n)stvennosti* (On (fe)maleness). Moscow: Novoe literaturnoe obozrenie.

Packer, T. L., C. Iwasiw, J. Theben, P. Sheveleva, and N. Metrofanova. 2000. Attitudes to Disability of Russian Occupational Therapy and Nursing Students. *International Journal of Rehabilitation Research* 23(1):39–47.

Pateman, Carole. 1988. *The Sexual Contract*. Stanford, Calif.: Stanford University Press.

———. 1989. *The Disorder of Women: Democracy, Feminism and Political Theory*. Stanford, Calif.: Stanford University Press.

Petrov, Denis. 2006. Chelovek mogushchii-2 (Superman-2). *Zerkalo Nedeli* 10(589), March 18–24, 2006. http://www.zn.ua/3000/3050/52878/ (accessed September 24, 2009).

Petryna, Adriana. 2002. Life Exposed: Biological Citizens after Chernobyl. Princeton, N.J.: Princeton University Press.

Phillips, Sarah D. 2005. Will the Market Set Them Free? Women, NGOs, and Social Enterprise in Ukraine. *Human Organization* 64(3):251–264.

———. 2008. *Women's Social Activism in the New Ukraine: Development and the Politics of Differentiation*. Bloomington: Indiana University Press.

P'iatylietov, Kostiantyn. 2000. Oleksandr Sukhan: Zhiva lehenda Zakarpattia (Oleksandr Sukhan: Living legend of Transcarpathia). *Blahovist* 50–51:4.

P'iatylietov, Kostiantyn, and Yaroslav Hrybalskyy. 1996. Aktyvnyi invalidnyi vizok: chy potribnyi vin dlia nas? (Active wheelchair: do we need it?) *Blahovist*, October 1996.

Plath, David W. 1980. *Long Engagements: Maturity in Modern Japan*. Stanford, Calif.: Stanford University Press.

Polevoi, Boris. 1946. *Povest' o nastoiashchem cheloveke* (The tale of a real man). Moscow: State Publisher of Children's Literature of the Ministry of Culture.

Poloziuk, Oleg M. 2002. Problemy sotsial'noyi roboty z liud'my z osoblyvymy potrebamy (Problems of social work with people with special needs). Paper in possession of the author.

———. 2004. Iurydychna Konsul'tatsiia (Legal Consultation). *Sotsial'ne partnerstvo* 1(1):21.

———. 2005a. Disability in Ukraine: Prospects for Promoting Social Rehabilitation. Paper in possession of the author.

———. 2005b. Problems of Socio-Legal Protection of Disabled Persons with Spinal Cord Injuries in Ukraine. Paper presented at the Sixth Congress of the International Association of Ukrainian Studies, Donetsk, Ukraine, June 29–July 1, 2005.

Ponomar'ova, Maryna, and Kostiantyn Melekhin. 2006. Invalidy aktyvno doluchaiut'sia do vyborchoho protsesu (Invalids are actively involved in the election process). http://5.ua/newsline/207/0/23179/ (accessed September 19, 2009).

Poore, Carol. 2007. *Disability in Twentieth-Century German Culture*. Ann Arbor: University of Michigan Press.

Popov, Ye. F., and M. I. Balla. 2005. *Comprehensive Ukrainian-English Dictionary*. 3rd rev. ed. Kyiv: Chumatskiy Shliakh.

Priestley, Mark, ed. 2001. *Disability and the Life Course: Global Perspectives*. Cambridge: Cambridge University Press.

Prokomenko, Iurii P. 2001. Seks i invalidnost': Predrassudki v otnoshenii seksual'noi zhizni invalidov i neinvalidov (Sex and disability: Notes on the relations of sexual life of invalids and non-invalids). *Seksolog*. http://www.doktor.ru/articles/article.html?id=56460 (accessed September 19, 2009).

Pryzhov, Ivan. 1996. 26 *Moskovskikh prorokov, iurodivykh, dur i durakov, i drugie trudy po russkoi istorii i etnografii* (26 Moscow prophets, God's fools, and fools, and other works on Russian history and ethnography), ed. L. Ia. Lur'e and V. I. Shubinskii. Saint Petersburg: EZRO; Moscow: INTRADA.

Rapp, Rayna. 1999. *Testing Women, Testing the Fetus: The Social Impact of Amniocentesis in America*. New York and London: Routledge.

Rapp, Rayna, and Faye Ginsburg. 2001. Enabling Disability: Rewriting Kinship, Reimagining Citizenship. *Public Culture* 13(3):533–556.

Rasiuk, Ihor. 2002a. Fenomen Tsiurupyns'koho dytiachoho budynku (The phenomenon of the Tsiurupyns'kyi children's home). *Liubomyra* 2:24–26.

———. 2002b. Iz tsyklu "Tsiurupyns'ki opovidannia" (From the cycle "Tsiurupyns'kyi stories"). *Liubomyra* 4:22–28.

———. 2002c. Zalyshytysia liudynoiu (Remaining human). *Liubomyra* 3:25–26.

Raver, Sharon A. 2006. The Debate Over Integration of Students with Disabilities in Ukraine. *Journal of Global Awareness* 7(4):47–56.

———. 2007. The Emergence of Inclusion for Students with Disabilities in Ukraine. *International Journal of Special Education* 22(1):32–38.

Raver, Sharon A., and Kateryna Kolchenko. 2007. Inclusion of School-Aged Children with Disabilities in Ukraine. *Childhood Education* 83(6):370–373.

Raymond, Paul D. 1989. Disability as Dissidence: The Action Group to Defend the Rights of People with Disabilities in the USSR. In *People with Disabilities in the Soviet Union*, ed. William O. McCagg and Lewis Siegelbaum, 235–252. Pittsburgh, Pa.: University of Pittsburgh Press.

Reeves, Madeleine. 2008. Materializing Borders. *Anthropology News* 49(5):12–13.

Rekryteringsgruppen. 2002. *See the Potential, Not the Limitations.* Stockholm: Rekryteringsgruppen.

Riordan, Jim. 1977. *Sport in Soviet Society: Development of Sport and Physical Education in Russia and the USSR.* Cambridge and New York: Cambridge University Press.

———. 1980. *Soviet Sport Background to the Olympics.* New York: Washington Mews Books.

———. 1990. Disabled "Afgantsy": Fighters for a Better Deal. In *Social Change and Social Issues in the Former USSR: Selected Papers from the Fourth World Congress for Soviet and East European Studies,* ed. Walter Joyce, 136–157. New York: St. Martin's Press.

———, ed. 1988. *Soviet Education: The Gifted and the Handicapped.* London and New York: Routledge.

Rivkin-Fish, Michele. 2003. Review of Life Exposed: Biological Citizenship after Chernobyl (Adriana Petryna). *Medical Anthropology Quarterly* 17(4):503–504.

———. 2004. "Change Yourself and the Whole World Will Become Kinder": Russian Activists for Reproductive Health and the Limits of Claims Making for Women. *Medical Anthropology Quarterly* 18(3):281–304.

———. 2005. *Women's Health in Post-Soviet Russia: The Politics of Intervention.* Bloomington: Indiana University Press.

Romanov, Pavel, and Elena Iarskaia-Smirnova, eds. 2005. *Nuzhda i poriadok: Istoriia sotsial'noi raboty v Rossii, XX v.* (Need and Order: History of Social Work in Russia, 20th Century). Saratov: Center for Social Policy and Gender Studies; Nauchnaia kniga.

———. 2006. *Politika invalidnosti: Sotsial'noie grazhdanstvo invalidov v sovremennoi Rossii* (Disability politics: Social citizenship of people with disabilities in contemporary Russia). Saratov: Nauchnaia kniga.

———. Forthcoming. Telo i diskrimi-natsiia: Invalidnost', gender i grazhdanstvo v postsovetskom kino (Body and discrimi-nation: Disability, gender and citizenship in post-Soviet film). In *On Gender, Nation, and Class after Socialism,* ed. Elena Gapova. Vilnius: European Humanities University.

Rose, Nicholas. 2006. *The Politics of Life Itself: Biomedicine, Power, and Subjectivity in the Twenty-First Century.* Princeton, N.J.: Princeton University Press.

Rosenfeld, Dana, and Christopher A. Faircloth, eds. 2006. *Medicalized Masculinities.* Philadelphia, Pa.: Temple University Press.

Rubchak, Marian J. 1996. Christian Virgin or Pagan Goddess: Feminism versus the Eternally Feminine in Ukraine. In *Women in Russia and Ukraine,* ed. Rosalind Marsh, 315–330. New York: Cambridge University Press.

———. 2005. Yulia Tymoshenko: Goddess of the Orange Revolution. http://eng .maidanua.org/node/111 (accessed September 24, 2009).

Ruble, Blair A. 2003. Kyiv's Troeshchyna: An Emerging International Migrant Neighborhood. *Nationalities Papers* 31(2):139–155.

Sassen, Saskia. 2000. Spatialities and Temporalities of the Global: Elements for a Theorization. *Public Culture* 12(1):215–232.

———. 2007. Introduction: Deciphering the Global. In *Deciphering the Global: Its Scales, Spaces and Subjects*, ed. S. Sassen, 1–20. New York: Routledge.

Schrand, Thomas G. 2002. Socialism in One Gender: Masculine Values in the Stalin Revolution. In *Russian Masculinities*, ed. Barbara Evans Clements, Rebecca Friedman, and Dan Healey, 194–209. Houndmills, U.K.: Palgrave.

Schur, Lisa. 2004. Is There Still a "Double Handicap?" Economic, Social, and Political Disparities Experienced by Women with Disabilities. In *Gendering Disability*, ed.Bonnie G. Smith and Beth Hutchinson, 253–271.

Schweik, Susan M. 2009. *The Ugly Laws: Disability in Public*. New York: New York University Press.

Šėporaitytė, Deimantė, and Arturas Tereškinas. 2008. Physically Disabled Men in Lithuania: Between the Disability Disguise and Oppositional Masculinity. In *Gender Matters in the Baltics*, ed. Irina Novikova, 383–402. Riga: LU Akademiskais apgads.

Shakespeare, Tom. 2006. *Disability Rights and Wrongs*. London and New York: Routledge.

Shakespeare, Tom, Kath Gillespie-Sells, and Dominic Davies. 1996. *The Sexual Politics of Disability: Untold Desires*. London: Cassell.

Shek, Ol'ga. 2005. Sotsial'noe iskliuchenie invalidov v SSSR (Social exclusion of the disabled in the USSR). In *Nuzhda i poriadok*, ed. Pavel Romanov and Elena Iarskaia-Smirnova, 375–396. Saratov: Center for Social Policy and Gender Studies; Nauchnaia kniga.

Shilova, Ol'ga. 2005. Razvitie gosudarstvennoi seti statsionarnykh uchrezhdenii po obsluzhivaniiu invalidov i pozhilykh grazhdan v Samarskom krae (The development of public network of institutions for the disabled and elderly citizens in Samara region). In *Nuzhda i poriadok*, ed. Pavel Romanov and Elena Iarskaia-Smirnova, 102–127. Saratov: Center for Social Policy and Gender Studies; Nauchnaia kniga.

Shuttleworth, Russell P. 2004. Disabled Masculinity: Expanding the Masculine Repertoire. In *Gendering Disability*, ed. Bonnie G. Smith and Beth Hutchinson, 166–178. New Brunswick, N.J.: Rutgers University Press.

Smirnitsky, A. I., ed. 1987. *Russian-English Dictionary*. Moscow: Russky Yazyk Publishers.

Smith, Bonnie G. 2004. Introduction. In *Gendering Disability*, ed. Bonnie G. Smith and Beth Hutchinson,1–6. New Brunswick, N.J.: Rutgers University Press.

Smith, Bonnie G., and Beth Hutchinson, eds. 2004. *Gendering Disability*. New Brunswick, N.J.: Rutgers University Press.

Smith, Brett, and Andrew C. Sparkes. 2004. Men, Sport, and Spinal Cord Injury: An Analysis of Metaphors and Narrative Types. *Disability and Society* 19(6):613–626.

Solzhenitsyn, Alexander. 1985. *The Gulag Archipelago 1918–1956: An Experiment in Literary Investigation*. Trans. Thomas P. Whitney and Harry Willetts; abridged by Edward E. Erickson. New York: Harper and Row.

Sparkes, Andrew C., and Brett Smith. 1999. Disrupted Selves and Narrative Recon-
structions. In *Talking Bodies: Narratives of the Body and Sport,* ed. Andrew
C. Sparkes and Martti Silvennoinen, 76–92. Jyvaskyla: SoPhi, University of
Jyvaskyla.

———. 2002. Sport, Spinal Cord Injury, Embodied Masculinities, and the Dilemmas
of Narrative Identity. *Men and Masculinities* 4(4):258–285.

Starks, Tricia. 2009. *The Body Soviet: Propaganda, Hygiene, and the Revolutionary
State.* Madison: University of Wisconsin Press.

Strathern, Marilyn. 1996. For the Motion (The Concept of Society is Theoretically
Obsolete). In *Key Debates in Anthropology,* ed. Tim Ingold, 60–66. London:
Routledge.

Sushkevych, Valery. 2005. Personal communication, interview conducted May 29,
2005.

Sutton, Andrew. 1988. Special Education for Handicapped Pupils. In *Soviet Education: The Gifted and the Handicapped,* ed. Jim Riordan, 70–94. London and New
York: Routledge.

Swain, John, and Sally French. 2000. Towards an Affirmation Model of Disability.
*Disability and Society* 15(4):569–582.

Swarnyk, Mykola. 2005. Rol' bat'kiv ditei z osoblyvymy potrebamy v rusi za prava
nepovnospravnykh v Ukraini (The role of parents of children with special
needs in the movement for disability rights in Ukraine). Paper presented at the
Sixth Congress of the International Association of Ukrainian Studies, Donetsk,
Ukraine, June 29–July 1, 2005.

Sydorenko, Oleksandr. 2001. *Kyiv: Hromads'ki orhanizatsii ta blahodiini fondy:
Dovidnyk* (Kyiv: Civic organizations and charitable foundations: A guide). Kyiv:
Innovation and Development Centre.

Szmagalska-Follis, Karolina. 2008. Repossession: Notes on Restoration and
Redemption in Ukraine's Western Borderland. *Cultural Anthropology*
23(2):329–360.

Tchueva, Ekaterina. 2008. "Mir posle voiny": Zhaloby kak instrument reguliro-
vaniia otnoshenii mezhdu gosudarstvom i invalidami Velikoi Otechestvennoi
Voiny ("World after the War": Complaints as an instrument of regulating the
relationships between the state and the disabled in the Great Patriotic War). In
*Sovetskaia sotsial'naia politika: Tseny i deistvuiushchie litsa, 1940–1985* (Soviet
social policy in 1940–1985: Scenes and actors), ed. Elena Iarskaia-Smirnova and
Pavel Romanov, 96–120. Moscow: Variant; Center for Social Policy and Gender
Studies.

Temkina, Anna. 2002. Stsenarii seksual'nosti i gendernye razlichiia (Scenarios of
sexuality and gender difference). In *V poiskakh seksual'nosti,* ed. Elena Zdravomyslova and Anna Temkina, 247–286. St. Petersburg, Russia: Dmitrii Bulanin.

Thayer, Millie. 2001. Transnational Feminism: Reading Joan Scott in the Brazilian
Sertão. *Ethnography* 2(2): 243–272.

Thomas, Carol. 2007. *Sociologies of Disability and Illness: Contested Ideas in*

*Disability Studies and Medical Sociology.* Houndmills and New York: Palgrave Macmillan.

Thomas, Carol, and Mairian Corker. 2002. A Journal around the Social Model. In *Disability/Postmodernity,* ed. Mairian Corker and Tom Shakespeare, 18–31. London and New York: Continuum.

Thomson, Kate. 2002. Differentiating Integration: Special Education in the Russian Federation. *European Journal of Special Needs Education* 17(1):43–47.

Tøssebro, Jan. 2004. Understanding Disability. *Scandinavian Journal of Disability Research* 6(1):3–7.

Tremain, Shelley. 2002. On the Subject of Impairment. In *Disability/Postmodernity,* ed. Mairian Corker and Tom Shakespeare, 32–47. London and New York: Continuum.

Union of the Physically Impaired Against Segregation (UPIAS). 1976. *Fundamental Principles of Disability.* London: UPIAS.

United Nations Development Program (UNDP). 2007/2008. Human Development Report 2007/2008. http://hdr.undp.org/en/media/HDR_20072008_EN_Complete.pdf (accessed September 9, 2009).

———. 2009. Human Development Report 2009. http://hdr.undp.org/en/media/HDR_2009_EN_Complete.pdf (accessed October 5, 2009).

Verkaaik, Julian, ed. 2004. *Back on Track: A Basic Introduction for Those Learning to Live with a Spinal Cord Injury.* Christchurch, NZ: The New Zealand Spinal Trust, as part of the Burwood Academy of Independent Living.

Virtanen, Riku. 2008. *The Survey on the Ratification Processes of the Convention on the Rights of Persons with Disabilities in Seven States.* Vaasa: Oy Arkmedia Ab; Center for the Human Rights of People with Disabilities (VIKI).

Vitvits'ka, Solomiia, and Serhii Azarenko. 2005. Samotni tatusi-invalidi vymahaiut' rivnykh iz zhinkamy prav stosovno dohliadu za dytynoiu (Single disabled fathers fight for equal rights with women to care for children). http://5.ua/newsline/184/0/14950/ (accessed September 19, 2009).

Vlasov, Iurii. 1990. Stechenie slozhnykh obstoiatel'stv (The confluence of difficult circumstances). In *Iskusstvo byt' zdorovym, chast' 3* (The art of being healthy, part 3), ed. S. B. Shenkman, 2–21. Moscow: Fiskul'tura i sport.

Volkova, Anna. 2006. "Kogda ot menia ushel muzh, zatem umerla mama i tiazhelo zaboleli syn i sestrichka, ia poniala—nado zhit'!" ("When my husband left me, and my mother died and my son and my sister became very ill, I realized—you have to live!") *Fakty i kommentarii,* February 8, 2006. http://www.facts.kiev.ua/archive/2006-02-08/9978/index.html (accessed September 6, 2009).

Voropai, Oleksa. 1993. *Zvychayi nashoho narodu* (Traditions of our people). Kyiv: Oberih.

Vovk, Khvedir. 1995. *Studiyi z ukrayins'koyi etnohrafiyi ta antropolohiyi* (Studies in Ukrainian ethnography and anthropology). Kyiv: Mistetstvo.

Wanner, Catherine. 2007. *Communities of the Converted: Ukrainians and Global Evangelism.* Ithaca, N.Y.: Cornell University Press.

Wates, Michele, and Rowan Jade, eds. 1999. *Bigger Than the Sky: Disabled Women on Parenting*. London: Women's Press.

Watson, Peggy. 1993. The Rise of Masculinism in Eastern Europe. *New Left Review* I/198:71–82.

———. 1995. Explaining Rising Mortality Among Men in Eastern Europe. *Social Science and Medicine* 41(7):923–934.

Wedel, Janine. 1998. *Collision and Collusion: The Strange Case of Western Aid to Eastern Europe 1989–1998*. New York: St. Martin's Press.

White, Anne. 1999. *Democratization in Russia under Gorbachev, 1985–91: The Birth of a Voluntary Sector*. New York: St. Martin's Press.

Zabuzhko, Oksana. 2002. Gendernaia struktura ukrainskogo kolonial'nogo soznaniia: k postanovke voprosa (Gender structure of the Ukrainian colonial consciousness: framing the question). In *O Muzhe(n)stvennosti*, ed. Sergei Alex Oushakine, 378–394.

Zakharchuk, Marina. 1999. Nedetskaia mudrost': Segodnia v Ukraine zhivet svyshe 152 tysiach detei-invalidov (Un-childlike wisdom: Today in Ukraine there are more than 152,000 child-invalids). *Den'* 158(695):1, 6.

Zaviršek, Darja. 2006. Disabled Women's Everyday Citizenship Rights in East Europe: Examples from Slovenia. In *Women and Citizenship in Central and Eastern Europe*, ed. Jasmina Lukic, Joanna Regulska, and Darja Zaviršek, 185–204. Aldershot, U.K.: Ashgate.

Zdravomyslova, Elena, and Anna Temkina, eds. 2002. *V poiskakh seksual'nosti* (In search of sexuality). St. Petersburg, Russia: Dmitrii Bulanin.

Zhurzhenko, Tatiana. 2004. Strong Women, Weak State: Family Politics and Nation Building in Post-Soviet Ukraine. In *Post-Soviet Women Encountering Transition: Nation-Building, Economic Survival, and Civic Activism*, ed. Kathleen Kuehnast and Carol Nechemias, 23–43. Washington, D.C.: Woodrow Wilson Press.

Note: Page numbers in *italics* refer to illustrations.

academic discipline of disability studies, 78

accessibility issues: and active wheelchairs, 98; and ambulocentrism, 18; architectural barriers, 24, 27, 41, 98, 187, 218–21, 222, 223, 226; assessments of, *78, 79;* and assistance from strangers, 24, 187, 202; and construction of new buildings, 132–33; enforcement of accessibility laws, 133; and lawsuits, 135; and local representation, 132–34; and National Ukraina Center, 114; and public transportation, 24, 133, 187; and reluctance to leave homes, 24; in Soviet era, 18, 24; and voting facilities, 99–100

accountability of states, 238

Action Group to Defend the Rights of the Disabled in the USSR, 72

active rehabilitation (AR), 110–20; about, 26–27; benefits of, 41; costs of, 111, 113; day camp for wheelchair users, 115–17; and exemplary models, 34, 117–18; financing for, 111; first-hand account of, 222–23; and "group of eight" friends, 3–4; and

independent living initiatives, 80; innovation in, 109, 115–17; instructors for, 27, 110–11, 116; introduction of, to Ukraine, 98; local implementation of global programs of, 107–108; local promotion of, 107–108, 109–10, 110–20; and Lotus, 38–39; and National Ukraina Center, *113,* 113–15; and paralympic games, 115; participants, 111; standardization of, 109–18; state's role in, 113–15, 119. *See also* rehabilitation

Active Worlds, 37–38, 41

Adam Smith Advertising, 140

adaptive technology, 18

Adelaja, Sunday, 136

adoption of children, 191, 206

advertisements featuring "freak" term, 139–47, *140*

advocacy initiatives, 102–103

aikido, 210–11

Alekseeva, Olha, *75*

Alisa Society for the Disabled, 128

All-Russian Association of the Blind (VOS), 69, 121

All-Russian Organization of Invalids (VOI), 75, 77, 248

All-Russian Organization of the Deaf (VOG), 69, 121

All-Russian Production-Consumption
Union of Invalids (VIKO; Promkooperatsiia), 69–70, 76
All-Ukrainian Association for Harm
Reduction, 146
All-Union Invalids' Society, 71
Alpatova, Polina, 94, 245
ambulocentrism, 17–18
Americans with Disabilities Act (1990),
135
amputees, 2
Andrei, 161
Anton: daily routine, 195; and disabled
community, 194–95, 197; identity of,
194, 201; independence of, 197, 201;
individualism of, 197–98; and masculinity, 184, 194–202, 227, 229; and
overcoming-of-disability narrative,
197–98; pension, 194, 197; physical conditioning, 195, 196, 198, 201;
and politics of non-belonging, 194,
201–202; relationships with women,
198–99, 200–201; yachting, 196–97
Arbus, Diane, 167
architectural barriers, 24, 27, 41, 98, 187.
See also accessibility issues
Architectural Barriers Act (1968), 135
artels, 69–70, 127
Artem factory, 35–36
Asch, Adrienne, 228
the Assembly (NADU). See National
Assembly of Disabled of Ukraine
(NADU)
Assistance for Creating and Developing the National Disabled Women's
Movement, 174
assistance from strangers, soliciting, 24,
187, 202
Association of Outdoor Advertising of
Ukraine (AZR), 140–41, 145
asylums, 45–46
athletics: development of, 135; and dis-
ability rights movement, 97; fenc-
ing, 210; marathons, 28, 74, 188; and

masculinity, 188–89; paralympic
games, 23, 101, 114, 188, 246; and rehabilitation, 28; in Soviet era, 28, 73–74,
188–89, 195; wheelchair sport dance,
117, 162, 189, 190, 192–93, 210
Auld, Doug, 166–67
autonomy, 177

Bach, Jonathan, 247
Barbie image, 181, 212, 228
bathrooms, public, 157, 176
battlefield medicine, 16
beauty standards, 181, 186, 202, 212
bedsores, 19
begging: and internat system, 62; of
iurodivye, 44, 47, 49; and masculinity,
186–87; and stereotypes of disabled
persons, 186–87
Belarus, 3, 26, 110
Berehynia image, 180–81, 228
Berkeley, California, 80
Bidenko, Artem, 145–46
billboards featuring "freak" term, 139–47,
*140*
biobureaucracy, 84, 85
biological citizenship, 7, 11, 89, 130–31
bisexuality, 192, 199
bladder infections, 19
*Blahovist,* 152
blame for disability, 151–52, 186
Blazhennyi, St. Vasilii, 48
blind citizens: and education, 64, 245;
and employment, 69, 126–27; in Tsarist Russia, 46, 49
Blue Danube gathering points, 61
Boichyshyn, Liubomyra, 80, 153, 174
Bolshevik Revolution, 50, 51
Brazil, 239
"breaking" events (*zlamatysia*), 14
Brezhnev, Leonid, 72
British social model (BSM), 81–83
Brown, Julie, 46
building construction, 132–33. See also
accessibility issues

Burdenko Neurosurgery Institute in Moscow, 16
bureaucracy in disability services, 36, 84, 85
Burke, Chris, 240
busking, 160, 168, 193

Cabinet of Ministers, 75
Canada, 80, 91, 98
Canada-Ukraine Gender Fund, 153
Canadian Centre on Disability Studies (CCDS): about, 79–80; and disability studies course, 78; educational initiative, 93; and Independent Living Resource Center, 81, 83; influence of, 79, 91; and support for accessibility projects, 133
Canadian International Development Agency (CIDA), 78
caregivers: employment of, 21; families as, 45, 46; and kinship model, 240–41; pensions for, 20, 29; in Tsarist Russia, 45; as women's responsibility, 210, 244
categorization of disabilities, 2
Catherine II, Empress of Russia, 45
catheters, 189–90
CCDS-CIDA Reforming Social Services Canada-Ukraine Project, 80
Champaign-Urbana, Illinois, 80
charitable giving, 105
Chernobyl nuclear catastrophe, 86
Chernova, Zhanna, 183
Chernovets'kyi, Leonid, 105, 136–38
children: adoption of, 191, 206; attitudes about disability, 229; congenitally disabled children, 59–60; and education, 63–64; and entitlements, 59–60; families of, 63, 64, 65; infantilization of disabled persons, 148, 200; and institutionalization, 62, 63, 65–66, 92, 151; and local activism, 81; and parents' movement, 121; in Soviet era, 20, 59–60
Chinka, Elena, 163–69, *164, 165*

Christianity, 136–37
church-based philanthropy, 136–37
churches, 45, 46
citizenship: biological citizenship, 7, 11, 89, 130–31; and employment, 59; and masculinity, 172; mobile citizenship, 8, 90–92, 156, 244; and neoliberalism, 42, 90; and personification, 130–31; social utility of citizens, 50, 59, 76, 84; in Soviet era, 58; and stares of strangers, 155; and *urod* ("freak") billboard, 147
civic and charitable organizations. *See* NGOs
classifications of disability, 51, 59
Clements, Barbara Evans, 188, 195
coalition building, 120–25
Coalition for Defense of the Rights of Invalids and Persons with Intellectual Disabilities, 121–22
Codex Alimentarius, the World Trade Organization's (WTO), 112
coexistence, 238
cognitive disabilities, 64
collective consciousness, potential for, 61
collective farms (*kolkhoz*), 58, 59
collective responsibility, 242, 244
communications technology, 246–47
Communist Party, 55, 58, 107, 177
community awareness of disability issues, 135
competition between disability organizations, 42, 105, 111, 115, 124–25
condom catheters, 189–90
Confederation of Civic Organizations of Invalids of Ukraine (KHOIU), 124
"The Confluence of Difficult Circumstances" (Vlasov), 195
construction, 132–33. *See also* accessibility issues
contagious disease and public perceptions of disability, 160
context, importance of, 108–109
corticosteroids, 16

Counterpart International, Inc., 104, 124
critical media representations of disability, 147, 150–51
culture of disability, 67–68
Czech Republic, 243

Dal, Vladimir, 49–50
Davis, Lennard J., 163, 165, 167
dead souls employment practices, 31, 96
deaf citizens, 46, 64, 69, 126–27
defectology, 64
definition of disability in Ukraine, 85
DeJong, Gerben, 80
democratization, 237
demographic decline, 148
*Den'* (The Day), 147, 150–51, 153
Departments of Public Welfare, 45–46
dependents of disabled persons, 52
deportation of disabled citizens, 59
differentiation of disabled persons, 59–61, 89
Dikul, Valentin, 186
Directly Observed Treatment, Short-Course (DOTS), 112
*Disability in Local and Global Worlds* (Ingstad and Whyte), 108
Disability Issues in Social Work course, 78–79
disability rights movement, 97–138; and accessibility issues, 24; and employment, 87; generation gap in, 42; and internat system, 92–93; international/transnational organizational interaction, 91; lobbying by organizations, 93; media coverage of, 152; and mobile citizenship, 91; and NADU reports, 87–89; and overcoming-of-disability narrative, 197–98; and paralympic athletes, 246; and political marginalization, 99–103; and public storytelling, 241; in Soviet era, 10, 67–68, 71–77, *73;* and universal model of disability, 243; voting rights, 99–100; women's participation in, 176

Disabled Peoples' International (DPI), 79
disabled veterans, 50, 52–59, 60–61, 76
diversity, 1, 10
diving accidents, 13–14
Dmitrii: and busking session, 160–62; economic status, 185, 193; employment, 4, 185; and "group of eight" friends, 1–2, 5; heroic image of, 191; individualism of, 193; and Mandry organization, 156–57, 160–62, 192, 263n18; and manifesto of the group of eight, 5; and masculinity, 184, 185–93, 227, 229; and parenthood, 191–92; and political participation, 100; and sexuality, 189–90, 191; at Victory Day celebration, 170; wheelchair sport dance, 189, 190, 192–93
documentaries, 135
*doma-internaty* ("home-internaty"), 61–62, 65–68, 70–71, 92
Donets'k Regional Hospital for Restorative Treatment, 19
Dostoyevsky, Fyodor, 47
Down Syndrome, 144, 150–51, 240
drinking, 179
drug addiction media, 139–47, *140*
Dunn, Elizabeth, 111, 115
Dunn, Ethel, 63
Dunn, Stephen, 63
*duraki* ("fools" or "idiots"), 45
Durov, B., 192
Dzherelo (Wellspring) rehabilitation center, 121

early intervention programs, 243
economy, 6, 86
Edele, Mark, 53, 58
education: academic discipline of disability studies, 78–79; barriers to, 2, 7, 28, 40, 41, 66, 68–69, 218–21, 222, 223, 226; inclusive education, 28, 93, 243, 245, 248; internat system, 65–68, 93; L'viv Polytechnic University, 78,

218, 221, 248; post-Soviet reforms, 3;
in Soviet era, 3, 61–69, 76–77; special
education, 63–64
elections and voting, 99–100
employment: barriers to, 2, 7, 40, 41,
125–26; and citizenship, 59; and classifications of disability, 51; of disabled
veterans, 53; and discrimination,
236; exploitation of disabled persons,
127–28; fake work arrangements, 31,
40, 128; and gender, 21, 174, 181–82,
259n11; improving opportunities
for, 96; individual pursuit of, 42;
and individual rehabilitation plans
(IPRIs), 94–95, 96, 126; and "invalids" term, 50; and job fair, 128–29;
legislation on, 30–31; and neoliberalism, 237; and pensions, 87; post-Soviet reforms, 3; quotas for hiring disabled persons, 30–31, 69, 77, 96; and
rehabilitation, 69–71, 76, 94–95; and
rights of disabled persons, 87; segregation of disabled persons, 69–70;
and social utility of citizens, 50, 59,
76, 84; in Soviet era, 19, 50–52, 53–59,
69–71, 76–77, 88; and state benefits, 2;
statistics on, 30; vocational training,
25, 53, 54, 55, 77, 96, 127, 237; work
collectives, 69, 77
empowerment of disabled individuals:
and active rehabilitation, 118–19; and
inadequate state support, 239; and
influence on policy making, 4; integrated approach to, 80; and media
coverage of disability, 153; and Rekryteringsgruppen philosophy, 34
Enns, Henry, 79
entrepreneurial spirit, 7
Eurasia Foundation, 104
Evseev, Sergei, 151
exclusion of disabled individuals, 53, 155
exemplary institutions, 51
exemplary models (role models), 34,
117–18

Exit television program, 191
Express newspaper, 158–59

"faking" disability, 86
Fakty i kommentarii (Facts and Commentary), 147, 149, 153
familiarity of disability, 101, 129, 245
families: as caregivers, 21, 45, 46, 58; and
disability rights movement, 243; and
disabled children, 63, 64, 65; and gender roles, 178–79, 180–81; and institutionalization, 63; and kinship model,
239–40, 241, 242, 243–44; neofamilialism, 174, 181, 228, 243; in Soviet era,
58; varied forms of, 244
fatality rates, 18–19, 258n6
fear of disabled persons, 247
Fedorovna, Maria, 46
Fefelov, Valerii, 72–73
feminism, 134–35
fencing, 210
Fieseler, Beate, 53, 54, 55, 58, 59
Fine, Michelle, 228
Foucault, Michel, 89
Foundation for the Rehabilitation of
Invalids (FRI), 107
"freak" billboard, 139–47, 140, 148, 168
free market economy. See market
economy
Fund for the Social Protection of Invalids, 31
funding sources for organizations,
104–105

Gallego, Ruben, 67, 260n7
Garland-Thomson, Rosemarie: on
engagement of viewers, 166; and portrayals of disability, 147, 152–53; on
staring, 155, 156, 162
gender: and caregiving role, 21; and
domestic responsibilities, 209–10, 228;
gender violence, 204; and inequality, 21, 174, 259n11; male privilege, 172,
173–74; and media representation of

disability, 151–52; and public representations of the disabled, 205; scholarship on, 171–72; in Soviet era, 176–78;
and spinal injuries, 205. *See also*
men and masculinity; women and
femininity
generation gap, 42, 105–106
Gerschick, Thomas, 171, 173, 227
Gilmour, Julie, 188, 195
Ginsburg, Faye, 240, 242, 243, 244
*glasnost'* (openness), 76
globalization, 6
"God's fools" (*iurodivye*), 44–45, 47,
48–49
Gorbachev, Mikhail: and disability
rights movement, 97, 107; reform policies of, 75, 76, 107
Gordii, Nina, 149
Great Britain, 182
Griboedov, A. S., 63
"group of eight" friends, 1–2, 3–6, 10
Gudkov, Lev, 52–53
Gus'kov, Gennadii, 71, 75

Haney, Lynne, 243
*A Healing Family* (Oe), 240
health care in Ukraine: costs of, 20–21;
facilities, 17, 25; and institutionalization, 63; and pressure sores, 19; in
Soviet era, 55; and spinal injuries,
14–15, 16, 19, 40; surgical emphasis, 16;
and Ukrainian independence, 16
*Health of Ukraine*, 148–49
heroism media trope, 152, 190–91
hexadactyly, 139–40, 143, 146
Hillyer, Barbara, 215
"holy fools" (*iurodivye*), 44–45, 47, 48–49
"home-internaty" (*doma-internaty*),
61–62, 65–68, 70–71, 92
homosexuality, 183
housing, 24
*How the Soviet Man Was Unmade*
(Kaganovsky), 56–57

*How the Steel Was Tempered*
(Ostrovskii), 56
Hrybalskyy, Yaroslav: and accessibility
issues, *78;* and active rehabilitation,
26, 110, 118–19, 119–20; activism of,
106–108; on disability rights movement, 72, 97; and Independent Living Resource Center, 78, 81; and L'viv
Independent Living Resource Centre,
80
Hrycak, Alexandra, 125
humanitarian aid, 104
humanity of disabled individuals,
139–47, 148
Hungary, 243
hygiene, 203
"hysterics" (*klikushi*), 47

*I Can't Say Goodbye!* (1982), 192
Iakovlevich, Ivan, 49
Iangulova, Liia, 45
Iarskaia-Smirnova, Elena: on masculinity, 188, 197; on portrayal of disability,
153; on rehabilitation, 186; on sexuality of disabled persons, 183; on Soviet
era, 57; on special education, 63; on
sports, 188–89
Iasynchuk, L., 158
identity: intersectionality in, 7–8; and
physicality, 188; and rejection of
labels, 229; and stigmatization of disabled, 90
Ihor, 154–56
immutable mobiles, 111
impairment/disability distinction, 82,
251–52
inclusion of disabled persons, 2, 40
Inclusive Education for Children with
Disabilities in Ukraine, 93
income sources, 31–32, 33–34, 38, 40. *See
also* employment
independence: and active rehabilitation,
27; Anton's emphasis on, 197, 198, 201;

economic independence, 180; and inadequate state support, 239; and interdependence, 215, 248; as neoliberal value, 237; and Pasha, 235, 236
independent living (IL), 80–81, 107, 180, 239
Independent Living Centres (ILC), 79
"Independent Living: From Social Movement to Analytic Paradigm" (DeJong), 80
Independent Living Resource Center, 78
Individual Program of Rehabilitation and Adaptation of the Invalid (IPRI): and active rehabilitation, 114; assignment of, 238; and employment, 94–95, 96, 126; and physical rehabilitation specialists, 96; purpose of, 25–26, 94
individualization of social problems, 6, 119, 130, 240
Indolev, Lev: on active rehabilitation, 98; on adoption of children, 191; on ambulocentrism, 18; on hierarchical ranking of disabled persons, 60; on Soviet-era rights movement, 71; translation of spinal cord injury handbook, 258n5
infantilization of disabled persons, 148, 200
infectious disease and public perceptions of disability, 160
Ingstad, Benedicte, 108
institutions and institutionalization: calls for deinstitutionalization, 243; for disabled children, 62, 63, 65–66, 92, 151; internat system, 61–62, 65–68, 70–71, 92; in modern Ukraine, 92; in Soviet era, 51, 54, 61, 76; in Tsarist Russia, 45
insurance offered by Soviet government, 20
interdependence: and communication technologies, 247; and independence, 215, 248; and intersections of

disability and gender, 216, 229; and kinship model, 239–40; and mobile citizenship, 244; promotion of, 83, 134; transformative power of, 248
internat system, 61–62, 65–68, 70–71, 92, 127
international organizations and standards: and accessibility projects, 133; benefits from, 103; influence of, 91; and standardization of practices, 110–18; waning support from, 104. *See also* Rekryteringsgruppen for Active Rehabilitation (RG)
internet: communication via, 246–47; and mobile citizenship, 91; soliciting medical advice through, 19
"Internet Access for People with Limited Physical Capabilities," 247
intersectionality, 7–8
Introduction to the Problems of People with Disabilities in Russia (university course), 248
*invalidnist'* (invalid-ness), 2
"The Invalids' Manifesto," 4–5, 6, 10, 90
"invalids" term, 49–50, 249–52
Invasport (National Committee for Sports of Invalids of Ukraine), 74, 113–14
Iryna, 125, 128–29, 130, 247
isolation of disabled persons, 23, 53, 66
*iurodivye* ("God's fools" or "holy fools"), 44–45, 47, 48–49

Jordan, Brigitte, 247
journalists, 135
jujutsu, 210–11

Kaganovsky, Lilya, 56–57
Kashchenko, V. P., 63
Kasnitz, Devva, 82, 251
Katia, 159–62
Kharkhordin, Igor, 177
Khrushchev, Nikita, 61

*khrushchovki* housing, 24
kidney infections, 19
Kimmel, Michael, 179
kinship, 239–44, 246–48
Kis, Oksana, 180, 212
KIS model wheelchair, 24
Kiselev, Iurii, 72, 75
*klikushi* ("hysterics"), 47
Knight in a Wheelchair competition, 158
Kohrman, Matthew, 186, 251
*kolkhoz* (collective farms), 58, 59
Kolomenskyi, Danilushka, 47–48
Korchaginets, 74
Kraievskii, Viktor, 211
Kravchenko, Raisa, 121, 151
Krayzh, Irina, 154
Krylova, Anna, 55, 58
Kukuruza, Anna, 93, 243
Kunanec-Swarnyk, Oksana, 81, 84, 95, 121

labour-medical boards (VTEK), 54
Landsman, Gail, 251
language with which to discuss disability, 141, 168, 183
languages of Ukraine, 1–2
Law on the Basis of Social Protection of Invalids of Ukraine (1991), 30–31, 85, 135
lawsuits, 135
legislation, disability related: accessibility issues, 133; and grassroots activism, 75; media coverage of, 152; on reassessment of the status of disabled persons, 86; scope of reform, 85
Let's Make Love! campaign, 141
letter to the editor of the *Express,* 158–59
Lidia, 234–35, 236
*Life Goes On* television series, 240
Life is Better without Drugs! campaign, 140, 145
Lithuania, 26, 171
Litskevich, Ol'ga, 144
*Liubomyra,* 153

Liubomyra Women's Informational-Rehabilitation Center, 174
Live Planet exhibition, 163, 165, 167
local implementation of global programs: of active rehabilitation (AR), 107–108, 109–10, 110–20; and importance of context, 108–109; innovation in, 112, 115–17
Longmore, Paul K., 248
Lotus, 32, 33–35, 38–39, 41
L'viv Independent Living Resource Centre (LILRC), 80
L'viv Oblast' Section of the Foundation for the Rehabilitation of Invalids (FRI), 107
L'viv Polytechnic University, 78, 218, 221, 248

madhouses, 45–46
Makara, Peter, 178
Makarevna, Mother Matrena, 48
Makhno, Nestor, 238
Maliarevskii, I. V., 63
*Mama chomu ia urod* billboard, 139–47, *140,* 148, 168
Mandry organization, 156, 160–62, 192, 263n18
manifesto of the group of eight, 4–5, 6, 10, 90
marathons, 28, 74, 188
Mares'ev, Aleksei, 56
marginalization, 6, 156, 235
Maria, 1, 4, 5
market economy: and gender roles, 178; negative effects of, 6–7; and personification, 131; reaction to reforms, 101–102; values associated with, 7, 237. *See also* neoliberalism
marriage: of Anton, 199, 200; of Dmitrii, 191; misconceptions regarding, 182; of Nadia, 223, 226; in Tsarist Russia, 45; of Viktoria, 206, 212–13
martial arts, 210–11
Maxim, 161

media, disability in, 147–54, 190–91, 244–45

medical care. *See* health care in Ukraine

medical model of disability, 88, 186

Medical-Labor Expert Commission (VTEK), 84–85

Medical-Social Expert Commission (MSEK), 85, 94, 238

men and masculinity, 184–202; and assistance from strangers, 187; cultural symbols of, 178–79, 187–88; and economic status, 179–80; emasculation of, 177–78; male privilege, 172, 173–74; and mobility, 186; and pensions, 179–80; personal accounts of, 185–93, 194–202, 227; public representations of, 205; scholarship on, 171; and sexuality, 183–84, 189–90, 191, 198–99; in Soviet era, 57, 176–78, 195; and spinal injuries, 173; and sports, 188–89; and stigmatization of disabled, 186

mental disabilities, 45–49

*metsenatstvo* (patronage), 46

military medicine, 16

Miller, Ruth A., 227

Ministry of Education, 66

Ministry of Justice, 120

Ministry of Labor and Social Policy (MLSP), 35, 36, 127, 238

Ministry of Social Services, 69

minstrels, 49

miracles as represented in the media, 149–50

Miroiu, Mihaela, 134–35

Mishchenko, Svitlana, 128

mobile citizenship, 8, 90–92, 156, 244

mobility of disabled: defined, 4; and identity formation, 188; and masculinity, 186; and perspectives of disabled, 4; of women, 202–203. *See also* accessibility issues; active rehabilitation (AR)

monasteries, 45, 46

moral failures, 143, 148

mothers of disabled children: blame for disability placed on, 151–52; and "freak" billboard, 142, 143, 147; media representations of, 148

Mullins, Aimee, 168

Murzkina school, 46

mutual aid societies, 242

Nadia, 216–27; and active rehabilitation camp, 222–23; and cultural models of femininity, 228–29; education, 218–21, 222, 223, 225, 226; employment, 220; interviews with, 202–204; marriage, 223; motherhood, 224–25, 226, 228; and sports, 222; and urban vs. rural environments, 221

Nadiya (Hope) NGO, 81, 121, 158–59

Nagorna, Natasha, 149–50

Narodnaia Rasprava (People's Reprisal), 47

Nastia, 157, 161

National Assembly of Disabled of Ukraine (NADU): about, 102; criticisms of, 123; and disabled women, 174–75; founding of, 122; and Invasport, 114; lobbying and legislative reform efforts of, 124, 125; reports on status of disabled population, 87; and Sushkevych, 102, 114, 122, 123

National Committee for Sports of Invalids of Ukraine (Invasport), 113–14

National Ukraina Center, *113*, 113–15

neo-Decembrists, 52, 53

neofamilialism, 174, 181, 228, 243

neoliberalism: and active rehabilitation, 119; alternatives to, 238; and citizenship, 42, 90; and disability rights movement, 135–36; effect on marginalized populations, 6–7; and personification, 130–32; and self-perceptions of postsocialist Ukrainians, 42; and social safety nets, 6–7, 86; values associated with, 237. *See also* market economy

*nepovnospravnyi* ("not fully functioning"), 250
Netherlands, 91, 133
networking groups, 74–75, 135
neurosurgery, 16
Neurosurgical Institute, 25, 27
New Economic Policy (NEP), 69
NGOs (nongovernmental organizations): barriers to, 104–106; boom
period, 102–103; challenges faced by,
41–42; competition between, 42, 105,
111, 115, 124–25; and consciousness
raising, 246; and empowerment, 106;
financial challenges of, 104–105; and
gender, 173; generation gap, 105–106;
leadership of, 105–106, 173; media
coverage of, 152; number of disability-
related organizations, 103; and political candidates, 134; societal perceptions of, 105–106; state financing of,
104–105
non-belonging, politics of, 194, 201–202

Oe, Kenzaburo, 240
Oleg: education, 3, 28–29, 68; employment, 3; on government bureaucracy,
36, 84; and "group of eight" friends,
1–2; on health care in Ukraine, 16;
and manifesto of the group of eight, 5;
wheelchairs, 24
Oleksandr, 5
Olympic games (1980), 23
Omelchenko, Oleksandr, 105
On Immediate Measures for Creating
Favorable Conditions of Living for
Persons with Limited Physical Capa-
bilities (Decree No. 900), 24, 133
On the Basis of Social Protection of
Invalids of Ukraine (1991), 30–31, 85,
135
"100 Percent Woman" television talk
show, 204, 215
Orange Revolution, 99, 100
Oriflame, 213–16

Orthodox Church, 44, 46, 47
Ortsport (Orthosport), 74
Ostrovskii, Nikolai, 56
Our Ukraine party, 100
*Overcoming* television program, 191
overcoming-of-disability narrative: and
disability rights movement, 197–98;
and masculinity, 186; in media coverage of disability, 149, 151–52; prevalence of, 190–91; in Soviet era, 56–57

Packer, T. L., 248
parallel world, disability as: about,
40–41; and mainstreaming, 226; and
media representation of disability,
147; and political life, 100; and stigmatization of disabled, 89–90; and
violence against women, 211–12
paralympic games, 23, 101, 114, 188, 246
parents and parenthood: and assistance
from others, 228–29; blame for disability placed on, 151–52; and disability rights movement, 243; disabled
persons as parents, 191–92, 200–201,
206–209; and "freak" billboard, 142,
143, 147; media representations of,
148; parents' movement, 121; in Soviet
era, 176–77; Viktoria's motherhood,
203, 228
parliamentary elections in 2006, 99
Party for Rehabilitation of the Chronically Ill of Ukraine, 100
Pasha, 116, 158, 231–38
patronage, 46
Pavlov, Ivan: family life, 21; financial
issues, 29; home environment, 22;
income sources, 38; and Lotus, 34;
ramps for Sasha, 22; and Sasha's accident, 21
Pavlov, Sasha, 13–42; accessibility issues,
22; and active rehabilitation, 26,
29, 110; activism of, 35–36, 40; baptism ceremony, 17; and competition
between disability organizations, 115;

daily routine, 25, 27, 37–38; diving accident, 13–14, 15, 16–17; education, 25, 28; on effects of standardization, 118; employment, 29–30, 31–32, 38; family life, 21; financial issues, 29, 33–34; financing medical care, 20; home environment, 22; hospital experience of, 17–18, 19–20; income sources, 38; injury, 37; and Lotus, 33–35, 38–39, 41; marathons, 28; and Pasha, 234; pension, 20, 29, 34, 38; rehabilitation, 25–26; reluctance to go outside, 24, 25; and Vanya, 17–18; virtual world of, 37, 41, 246; visitors, 22–23; wheelchairs, 22, 24, 27, 33

Pavlova, Zoia: and active rehabilitation, 26, 110; activism of, 35–37, 38–39, 40; baptism ceremony, 17; career of, 21, 29; caregiving role of, 19–20, 21; and competition between disability organizations, 115; diving accident of Sasha, 13, 14, 15, 16–17; on effects of standardization, 118; family life, 21; financial issues, 20, 29, 33–34, 38; home environment, 22; in-hospital care for Sasha, 19–20; injury, 37; and Lotus, 33–35, 38–39, 41; on parenthood of disabled persons, 191; and Pasha, 234; pension, 20, 29, 34; premium placed on actions, 32–33; on sex lives of disabled persons, 182; social network of, 7

penal camps, 59

pensions: for caregivers, 20, 29, 34; criticisms of, 86; for disabled citizens, 20, 29, 34, 40, 86; and economy of Ukraine, 86, 125; and employment, 87; inadequacy of, 86, 179–80; and neoliberalism, 86–87; in Soviet era, 52, 55, 84, 88; and stigmatization of disabled, 179, 182

perceptions of disabled persons, 23, 154, 180

*perestroika* (restructuring), 76

personalizing media representation of disability, 147, 151–52

personhood of disabled persons, 149, 169

personification, 129–32

Perspektiva, 153

Peter I, Emperor of Russia, 45, 46

Petro, 5

Petrov, Denis, 153, 245–46

philanthropy, 46, 136–37

Phillip Morris, 104

photographic portrayals of disability, 152–53

physical therapy, 19, 95–96, 120, 248

Pictures That Didn't Suffice exhibition, 153

pity, disabled persons as objects of, 149, 152, 167, 200, 201, 247

Pochynok, I., 158

*Podolannia* television show, 191, 246

Pogodin, Nikolai, 56

*pokazukha* ("window-dressing") culture, 76

Poland, 3, 6

Polevoi, Boris, 56

policy, disability, 84–92; and government bureaucracy, 84; and neoliberalism, 86–87; political candidates, 135; and reforms, 81, 84–86, 88–90; role of disabled in, 81

political participation of disabled population, 99, 101

political parties, 100

Pollard, Lisa, 243

Poloziuk, Oleg: and active rehabilitation, 110; and busking session, 161; on definition of disability, 85; as journal contributor, 153; wheelchairs, 9, 259n19

*The Possessed* (Dostoyevsky), 47

*Povir u Sebe* (Believe in Yourself), 152

Pravex Bank, 136

presidential elections of 2004, 99

pressure sores (bedsores), 19

privatization of responsibilities, 6, 119, 130

privatized medicine, 16
Prokomenko, Iurii, 182
Prometheus, 74
Promkooperatsiia (All-Russian Production-Consumption Union of Invalids; VIKO), 69–70, 76
property rights, 45
*proroki* ("prophets"), 44–45, 47
prosperity theology, 137
protests, potential for, 61
Pryzhov, Ivan, 47–48
psychological aspects of disability, 23, 27, 55–56
public restrooms, 157, 176
public service announcements, 139–47
public storytelling, 240–41, 244, 246, 248
public transportation, 24, 133, 187
punishment, disabled persons intended as, 158

quest narratives, 196

RabFaks ("work faculties"), 69
rape, 211
Rapp, Rayna, 240, 242, 243, 244
Rasiuk, Ihor, 65–66, 67, 153
Rasputin, 45
Reforming Social Services Canada-Ukraine Project, 78
Regeneration exhibition, 163–69, *164, 165*
rehabilitation: and employment, 69–71, 76, 94–95; Individual Program of Rehabilitation and Adaptation of the Invalid (IPRI), 25–26, 94, 96; integrated rehabilitation, 95; lack of available services, 19; and masculinity, 186; physical rehabilitation programs, 95–96; psychological rehabilitation, 27; resources for, 25–26; in Soviet era, 69–71; and sports, 28; standardization of practices in, 111–18; vocational rehabilitation, 25. *See also* active rehabilitation (AR)
Rekryteringsgruppen for Active

Rehabilitation (RG): and disability rights movement, 97; exemplary models (role models), 34, 117–18; and "group of eight" friends, 3–4; influence of, 91; introduction of AR camps, 110; local implementation of programs, 110–18; methodology of, 108; mission, 118; and standardization of practices, 111, 112–13, 115–16, 117–18; and wheelchairs, 98. *See also* active rehabilitation (AR)
relatedness, 240–48
religious institutions, 45
religious tropes, 148
renal failure, 19, 258n6
resource and informational centers, 135
restrooms, public, 157, 176
*Rick Hansen: Man in Motion* (Hansen and Taylor), 152
rolelessness, 228
Romanov, Pavel, 57, 63, 153
"room service feminism," 134–35
Rossolimo, G. I., 63
Rush, Chris, 166–67
Ruslan, 5
Russia: accessibility issues in, 18; active rehabilitation camps in, 110; Civil War veterans, 50, 52, 59; disability policy, 43; disability rights movement, 10; and gender, 171, 178–79; history of disability in, 44–49; and Lotus, 38; and neoliberalism, 6; and parenthood, 191; and sexuality, 183; sports in, 188–89

Sakharov, Andrei, 72
samovars, 52
sanatoriums, 205–206, 219
Sasha. *See* Pavlov, Sasha
Schrand, Thomas, 176, 177
*Segodnia,* 144, 149, 153
self-esteem, 237
self-sufficiency, 237, 239. *See also* independence

Seniukov, Dmitrii, 98
sensational media representation of disability, 147, 149–50
Sergei, 5, 213
Serhiy, 161
sexuality: cultural myths surrounding, 182; and gender roles, 183–84; homosexuality, 183; hypersexual identities, 191; and masculinity, 183–84, 198–99; medicalized vs. exoticized treatment of, 183; and men and masculinity, 183–84, 189–90, 191, 198–99; open discussions on, 182–83; and sexual partners, 192, 199; social attitudes toward, 189–90; of women, 183–84, 203
Shakespeare, Tom, 82
Shaman, 161–62, 193
*Shans* (Chance) rehabilitation center, 211
Shchybryk, Maria, 121
Shek, Ol'ga, 62
Shilova, Ol'ga, 50
Shkola Zhyttia (School of Life), 121
Shuttleworth, Russell, 172
Shyngaryova, Elena, 154
Simonovich family, 148
sin, 143, 148
size of disabled population, 3
Skype™, 246–47
Slovenia, 171
Smith, Brett, 196
SoBez ("social protection" office), 127, 232, 233
social advertising, 139–47
social model of disability, 77–84, 88
"social parasites," 58–59
social safety nets, 6–7, 86
social work, 78–79, 248
soldiers, 49, 50
Solomko, Yuri, 163–69, *164, 165*
Soros Foundation, 124
*Sotsial'naia zashchita* (Social Defense) journal, 183
Soviet Union, 49–77; accessibility issues in, 18, 24; and advertising, 139;

differentiation of disabled persons, 59–61; disability agencies and organizations of, 84–85, 121; disability policy of, 43, 72, 76–77, 88, 89; and disability policy of modern era, 44, 77; disability rights movement, 10, 67–68, 71–77, *73*; and education, 3, 61–69, 76–77; and employment, 19, 50–52, 53–59, 69–71, 76–77, 88; gender roles in, 176–78; health care under, 15–16; insurance offered to schoolchildren, 20; internat system, 61–62, 65–68, 70–71; and "invalids" term, 49–50; isolation of disabled persons, 2, 53, 66; masculinity in, 57, 176–78, 195; and "overcoming" cultural narrative, 56–57; and pensions, 52, 55, 84, 88; rehabilitation resources, 25; and "social parasites," 58–59; and social utility of citizens, 50, 59, 76, 84; sports in, 28, 73–74, 188–89, 195; state benefits, 52, 53, 55, 84; stigmatization of disabled, 23, 53; and wheelchair sports, 28. *See also* Russia
Sparkes, Andrew C., 196
Spasskaia labor colony, 59
spinal injuries: and ambulocentrism, 17–18; and blame for disability, 186; categorization of disabilities, 3; culture of denial surrounding, 25, 40; gendered differences in, 186; of "group of eight" friends, 2; and health care in Ukraine, 14–15, 16, 19, 40; and masculinity, 173; one-year survival rate, 18–19; and pensions, 86; prevalence of, 14; and rehabilitation, 25–28, 110; and self-care, 19; shame surrounding, 205; and standards of beauty, 212
*spinal'niki* (persons with spinal injuries or diseases), 2
"spoiling the view," 154
sports. *See* athletics
Stalin, Joseph, 52, 57–58
Standard State Program of Rehabilitation, 94

standards of living, 4

standards of practice, 108, 109, 110–18

stares of strangers, 24, 154–56

Stark, David, 247

Starks, Tricia, 73

state benefits: and Chernovets'kyi, 137–38; and differentiation of disabled persons, 59–61; for "group of eight" friends, 2; inadequacy of, 86; Individual Program of Rehabilitation and Adaptation of the Invalid (IPRI), 25–26; and neoliberalism, 237–38; piecemeal delivery of, 3; requests for, 7; in Soviet era, 52, 53, 55, 84; unemployment benefits, 126; wheelchairs, 9, 34, 36–37, 113, 259n19

State Budget for Civic Organizations of Invalids, 104

State Building Committee, 132–33

State Information Committee, 247

statistical data on disability, 246

Statute on Social Protection of Workers, 50

stereotypes of disabled persons: as beggars, 186; shifting public thinking on, 247; as social parasites, 58–59; subverting popular stereotypes, 160, 162, 229; survey on, 149

stigmatization of disabled: gendered differences in, 186; and invalid parents, 207; and parallel world of the disabled, 41; and pensions, 179, 182; and relationship with the state, 90; in Soviet era, 23, 53; and stares of strangers, 154–56; and universal model of disability, 243; and *urod* ("freak") billboard, 146

*A Story about A Real Man* (Polevoi), 56

subversion, 229

Sukhan, Oleksandr, 74, 75, 152

"Superman-2" (Petrov), 245–46

super-marathons, 74, 188

support groups, 242

Sushkevych, Valery: and legislation, 135; and NADU, 102, 114, 122, 123; and National Ukraina Center, 113–15; political career of, 101, 102, 122–23, 124; spare-change incident, 102, 149; and spinal'nik community, 7; on voting barriers, 99–100

Sutton, Andrew, 64

Sveta, 157, 161

Swarnyk, Mykola: and accessibility issues, 78, 79, 133; on Coalition, 121–22; and day center for disabled children, 81; on internat system, 65, 92; letter to the editor of the *Express,* 158–59; and parents' movement, 121; and participation of disabled in education, 248; on social context of disability, 83

Sweden, 91, 191

symbolic media representation of disability, 147, 148

Szmagalska-Follis, Karolina, 238

Tanya, 131–32

Tchueva, Ekaterina, 54–55, 61

television programs on disability issues, 191, 204, 215, 240, 246

Temkina, Anna, 183

territorial centers (TerCenters), 93–94

Thomson, Kate, 64

*To Live in a Wheelchair* (Indolev), 183

Together against Cancer, 175

toilets, public, 157, 176

Tolstoi, Aleksei, 56

"Toward a Theory of Disability and Gender" (Gerschick), 171

transportation, public, 24, 133

Treat Me As Equal demonstration, 189, 202

Trifonova, Svetlana, 74, 152, 207

Trok, Katarzyna, 26, 110

Tsiurupyns'kyi school-internat, 65–66, 67

Turbota (Care) program, 105

Tymoshenko, Yulia, 101

*ubogi* ("of God"), 45

ugly laws, 62, 142–43

Ukrainian Association of Specialists of Physical Rehabilitation, 95

Ukrainian Association of the Blind (UTOS), 121, 126

Ukrainian Association of the Deaf (UTOG), 121, 126

Ukrainian Center for Professional Rehabilitation of Invalids, 127

Ukrainian Foundation for the Rehabilitation of Invalids (FRI), 80

Ukrainian Party for Justice–Union of Veterans, Invalids, Chernobyl Victims, and Veterans of the Soviet-Afghan War (UPS-SVIChA), 100

*Ukrains'ka Pravda,* 145

UN Convention on the Rights of Persons with Disabilities (2006), 88, 89

unemployment benefits, 126

Union of Organizations of Invalids (SOIU), 121, 122

United Kingdom, 80

United States: civic organizing in, 42; disability policy of, 91; disability rights struggles in, 134, 135, 243; and gender inequalities, 174; independent living in, 80; spinal injuries in, 14, 258n6; "ugly laws" of, 62; and universal model of disability, 243

universal model of disability, 242–43

University of Manitoba Faculty of Social Work, 78

University of Physical Culture in L'viv, 95

*urod* ("freak"), 139–40, 143–44

Valentyna, 206, 207

Vanya, 17–18, 20

Vasyl', 98–99, 129–32

*Vechernie Vesti,* 150

Verkhovna Rada (National Parliament), 102, 123, 136

veterans, 50, 52–59, 60–61, 76

Victory Day celebration, 170

Viktoria, 204–16; appearance emphasis of, 204–205, 212; and cultural models of femininity, 228–29; employment, 212–16; financial status, 212–13, 215; interviews with, 202–204; motherhood, 203, 228; pension, 212–13; physical conditioning, 209; pregnancy and childbirth, 206-207, 208–209; relationships with men, 205–206, 212–13; self-knowledge of, 208–209; and sports, 204, 210

violence against women, 204, 211–12

*vizochnyky* (wheelchair users), 2. *See also* wheelchairs and wheelchair users (*vizochnyky*)

Vlasov, Iurii, 195

Volkova, Anna, 212

volunteerism, 58

voting rights, 99–100

Vsevolod, 5

Vygotsky, L. S., 64

*Vykhid* television program, 191

walkathons, 135

wanderers, 44, 49

Wanner, Catherine, 136

Wasilewskaia, Wanda, 56

Watson, Peggy, 177–78

"we" and use of inclusive language, 156–58, 245

wheelchairs and wheelchair users (*vizochnyky*): active wheelchairs, 27, 33, 34, 36–37, 98, 110, 113, 261n3; camps for (*see* active rehabilitation); and gender, 173, 175–76; and independence, 27; KIS model wheelchair, 24, 261n3; and pensions, 86; and political participation, 99, 100; of Sasha, 22; and sports, 28, 117, 162, 188, 189, 190, 192–93, 210–11; state benefits, 9, 34, 36–37, 113, 259n19; *vizochnyky* term, 2

White, Anne, 62, 69–71

*White on Black* (Gallego), 67

Whyte, Susan Reynolds, 108
women and femininity, 202–27; and
    assistance from strangers, 187, 202;
    and beauty standards, 181, 186, 202;
    as caregivers, 21, 58, 210, 244; cul-
    tural models, 180–81, 228; domestic
    responsibilities of, 176–77, 209–10;
    and economic status, 181–82; and
    employment, 181–82; and gender
    expectations, 180–81, 228; and gen-
    der inequalities, 21, 174; lack of con-
    fidence, 175; mobility of, 202–203;
    and pensions, 179–80, 182; personal
    accounts of, 204–16, 216–27, 228;
    reluctance to leave homes, 175, 186;
    reproductive role of, 184; and rest-
    room facilities, 157, 176; and roleless-
    ness, 228; and sexuality, 183–84, 203;
    in Soviet era, 58, 176–77, 177–78; and
    stigmatization of disabled, 186; vio-
    lence against women, 204, 211–12; and
    wheelchair skills, 175–76
work collectives, 69, 77

workbook employment arrangements,
    31
World Confederation for Physical Ther-
    apy (WCPT), 95
World Health Organization (WHO),
    112, 251
World War I veterans, 50, 52
World War II veterans, 2, 52–59, 60–61,
    76

Yana, 157, 161–62
Yushchenko, Viktor, 24, 100, 133

Zabuzhko, Oksana, 178
Zaitseva, Ol'ga, 72
"Zalyshytysia liudynoiu" (Rasiuk), 66
*Zerkalo Nedeli* (Weekly Mirror), 154,
    245–46
*"Zhinka na vse 100,"* 204, 215
*Zhit' v koliaske* (Indolev), 183
Zhuravko, Oleksii, 124
Zoia. *See* Pavlova, Zoia
Zub, Tetiana, 94, 245

**SARAH D. PHILLIPS** is Associate Professor of Anthropology at Indiana University Bloomington. She is author of *Women's Social Activism in the New Ukraine* (Indiana University Press, 2008).

CPSIA information can be obtained
at www.ICGtesting.com
Printed in the USA
LVOW13s1358270817

546567LV00022B/176/P

9 780253 222473